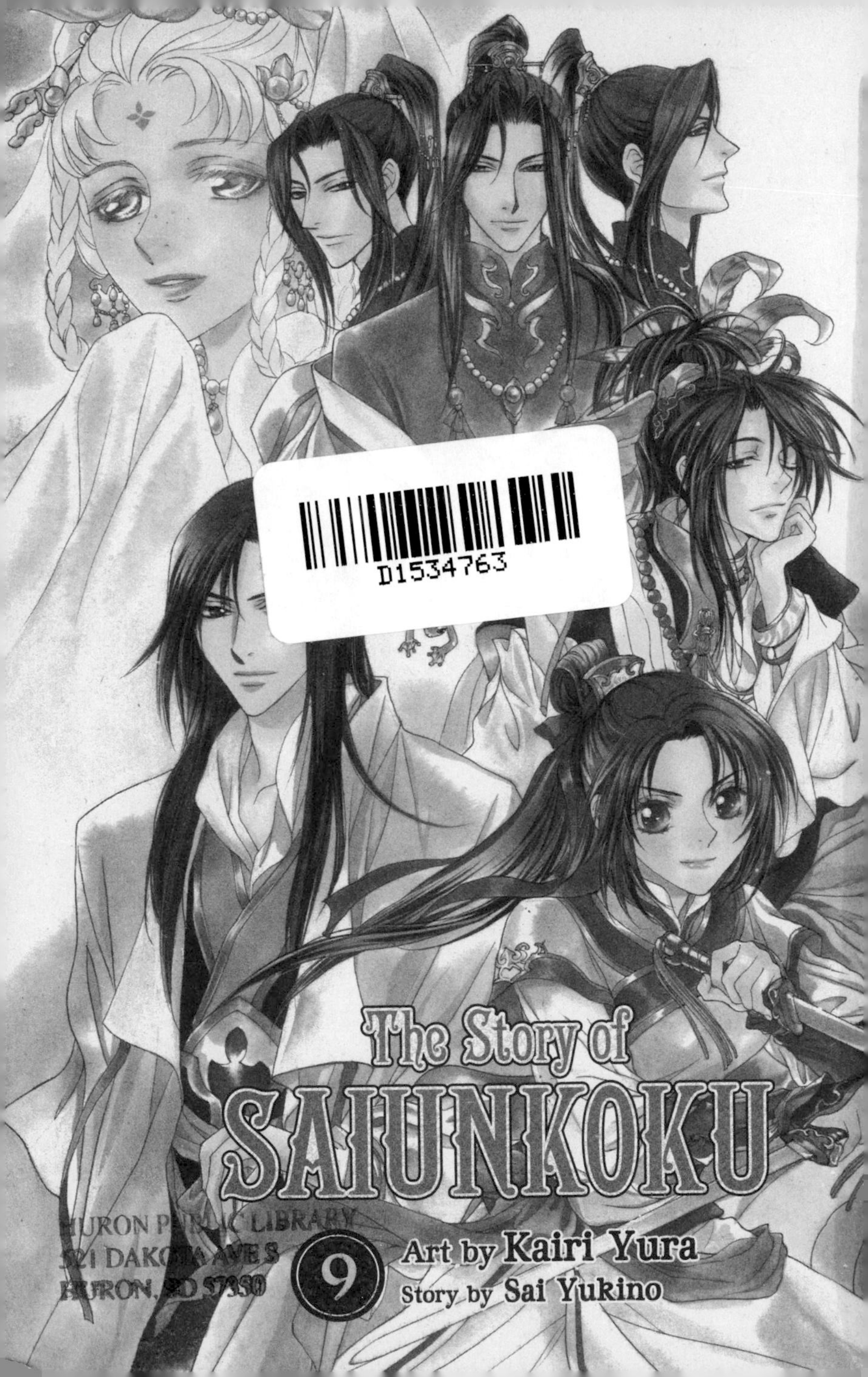

The Story of SAIUNKOKU

9

Art by Kairi Yura

Story by Sai Yukino

Volume 9
Contents

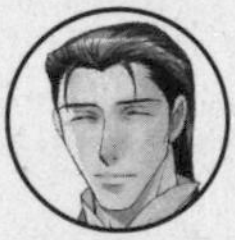

Shoka Hong
The eldest son of the Hong Clan and Shurei's father. He holds a leisurely post as the Imperial Archivist, but there is a darker side to this ex-assassin as well.

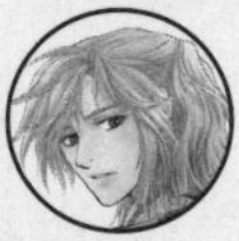

Seiran Shi
After being taken in by Shurei's father, Shoka, Seiran has served the Hong household as its faithful retainer ever since. He is actually Ryuki's older brother.

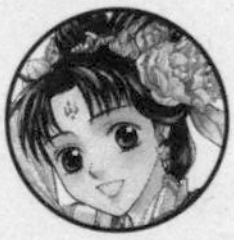

Shurei Hong
A young noblewoman of the prestigious but impoverished Hong Clan. Having passed the Imperial Civil Exam, she is now the country's first female civil servant.

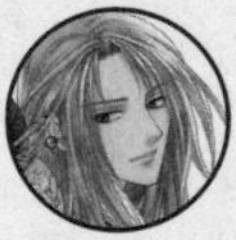

Ryuki Shi
The young emperor of Saiunkoku. He has been pining ceaselessly for Shurei since her departure from the Inner Court.

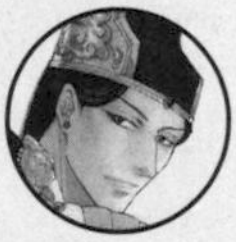

Reishin Hong
The second son of the Hong Clan. He loves Shoka and Shurei dearly but seems unable to admit to Shurei that he is her uncle.

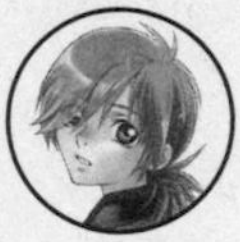

Eigetsu Toh
At 13 years old, he is the youngest person to pass the Imperial Civil Exam with the top score. He has a quiet, low-key personality.

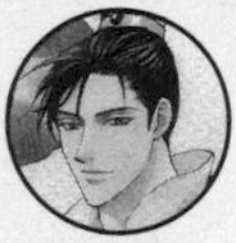

Shuei Ran
A military officer. He is a general of the Yulin Guard, a squad of soldiers charged with protecting the emperor. He is inseparable from Koyu (much to his friend's ire).

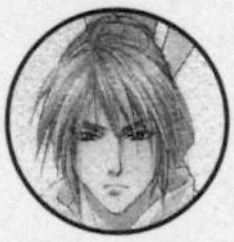

Koyu Ri
A civil servant renowned throughout the court as a genius, currently stuck in a frivolous position (perhaps?) serving Ryuki. He has a hopelessly bad sense of direction.

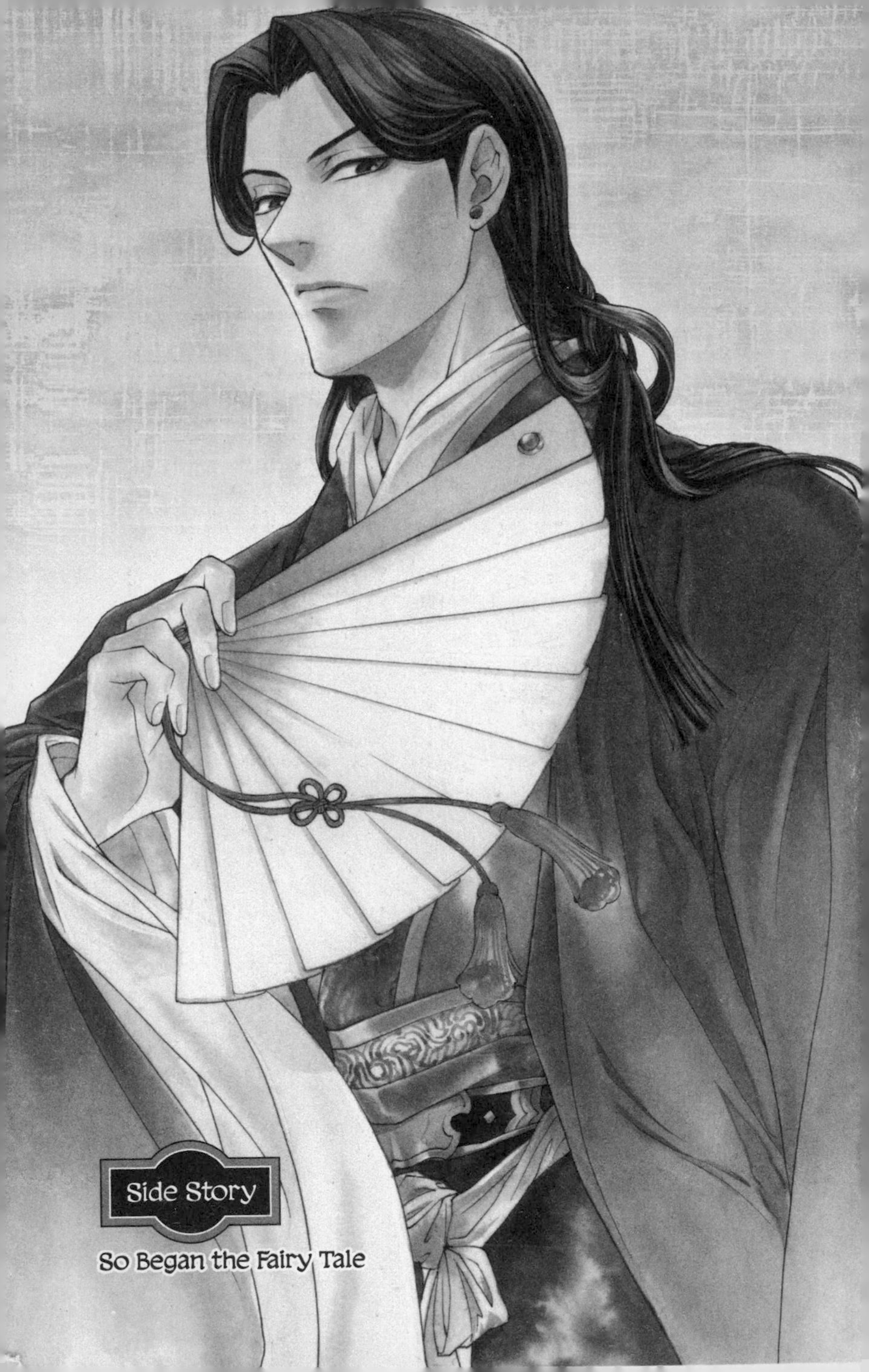
Side Story
So Began the Fairy Tale

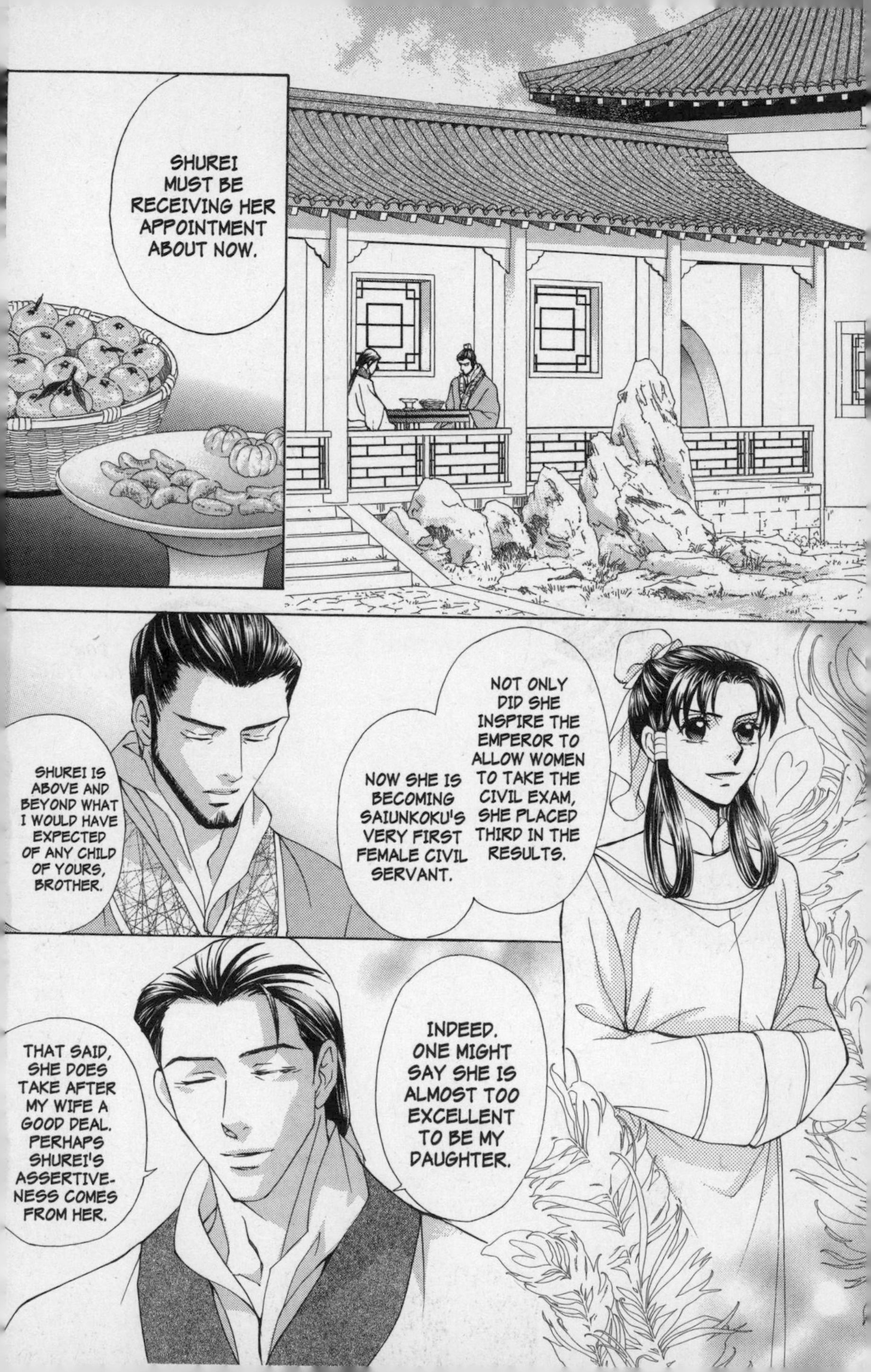
SHUREI MUST BE RECEIVING HER APPOINTMENT ABOUT NOW.
NOT ONLY DID SHE INSPIRE THE EMPEROR TO ALLOW WOMEN TO TAKE THE CIVIL EXAM, SHE PLACED THIRD IN THE RESULTS.
NOW SHE IS BECOMING SAIUNKOKU'S VERY FIRST FEMALE CIVIL SERVANT.
SHUREI IS ABOVE AND BEYOND WHAT I WOULD HAVE EXPECTED OF ANY CHILD OF YOURS, BROTHER.
INDEED. ONE MIGHT SAY SHE IS ALMOST TOO EXCELLENT TO BE MY DAUGHTER.
THAT SAID, SHE DOES TAKE AFTER MY WIFE A GOOD DEAL. PERHAPS SHUREI'S ASSERTIVE-NESS COMES FROM HER.

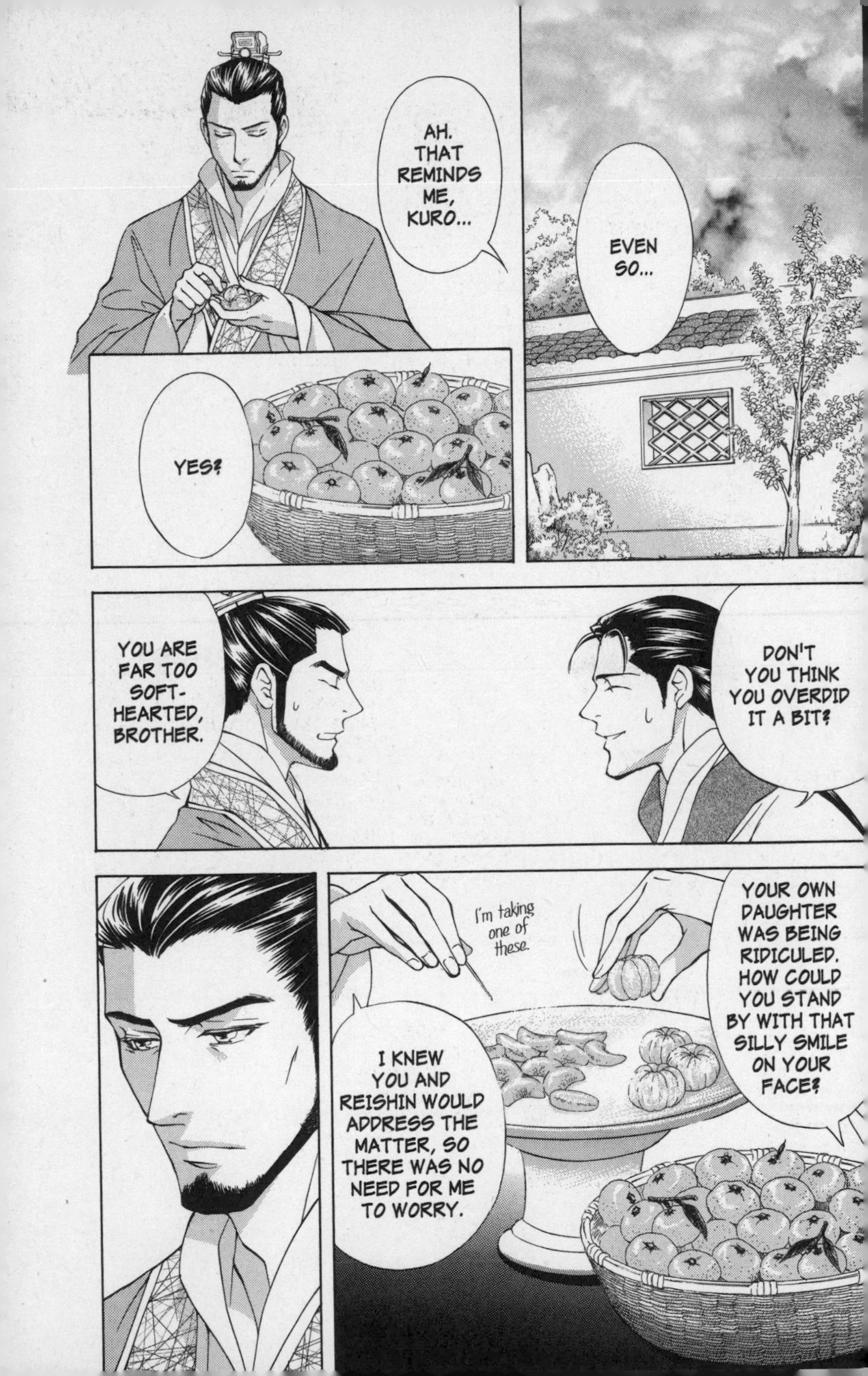
EVEN SO...
AH. THAT REMINDS ME, KURO...
YES?
DON'T YOU THINK YOU OVERDID IT A BIT?
YOU ARE FAR TOO SOFT-HEARTED, BROTHER.
YOUR OWN DAUGHTER WAS BEING RIDICULED. HOW COULD YOU STAND BY WITH THAT SILLY SMILE ON YOUR FACE?
I'm taking one of these.
I KNEW YOU AND REISHIN WOULD ADDRESS THE MATTER, SO THERE WAS NO NEED FOR ME TO WORRY.

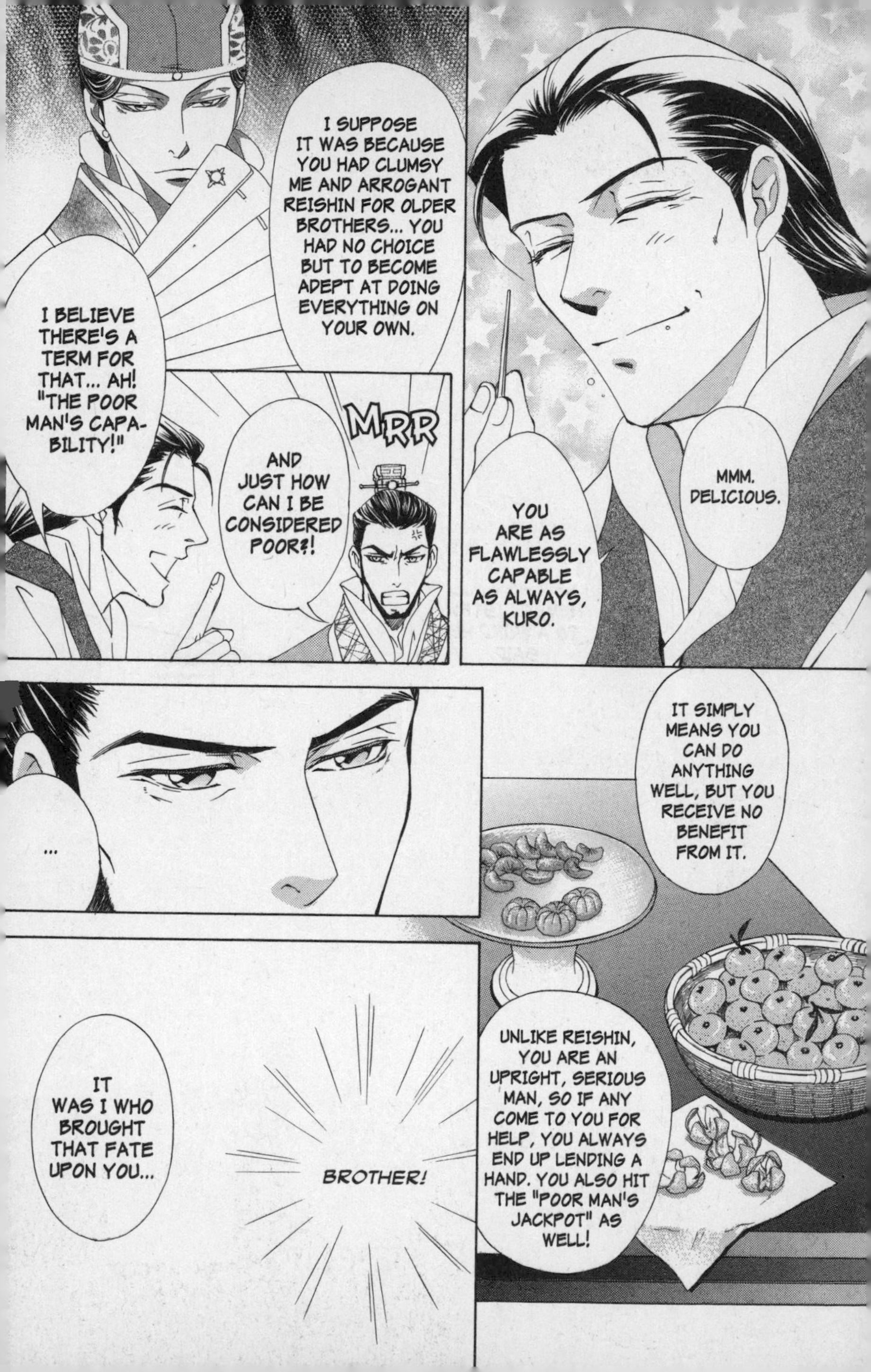
MMM. DELICIOUS.
YOU ARE AS FLAWLESSLY CAPABLE AS ALWAYS, KURO.
I SUPPOSE IT WAS BECAUSE YOU HAD CLUMSY ME AND ARROGANT REISHIN FOR OLDER BROTHERS... YOU HAD NO CHOICE BUT TO BECOME ADEPT AT DOING EVERYTHING ON YOUR OWN.
I BELIEVE THERE'S A TERM FOR THAT... AH! "THE POOR MAN'S CAPA-BILITY!"
MRR
AND JUST HOW CAN I BE CONSIDERED POOR?!
IT SIMPLY MEANS YOU CAN DO ANYTHING WELL, BUT YOU RECEIVE NO BENEFIT FROM IT.
UNLIKE REISHIN, YOU ARE AN UPRIGHT, SERIOUS MAN, SO IF ANY COME TO YOU FOR HELP, YOU ALWAYS END UP LENDING A HAND. YOU ALSO HIT THE "POOR MAN'S JACKPOT" AS WELL!
...
IT WAS I WHO BROUGHT THAT FATE UPON YOU...
BROTHER!

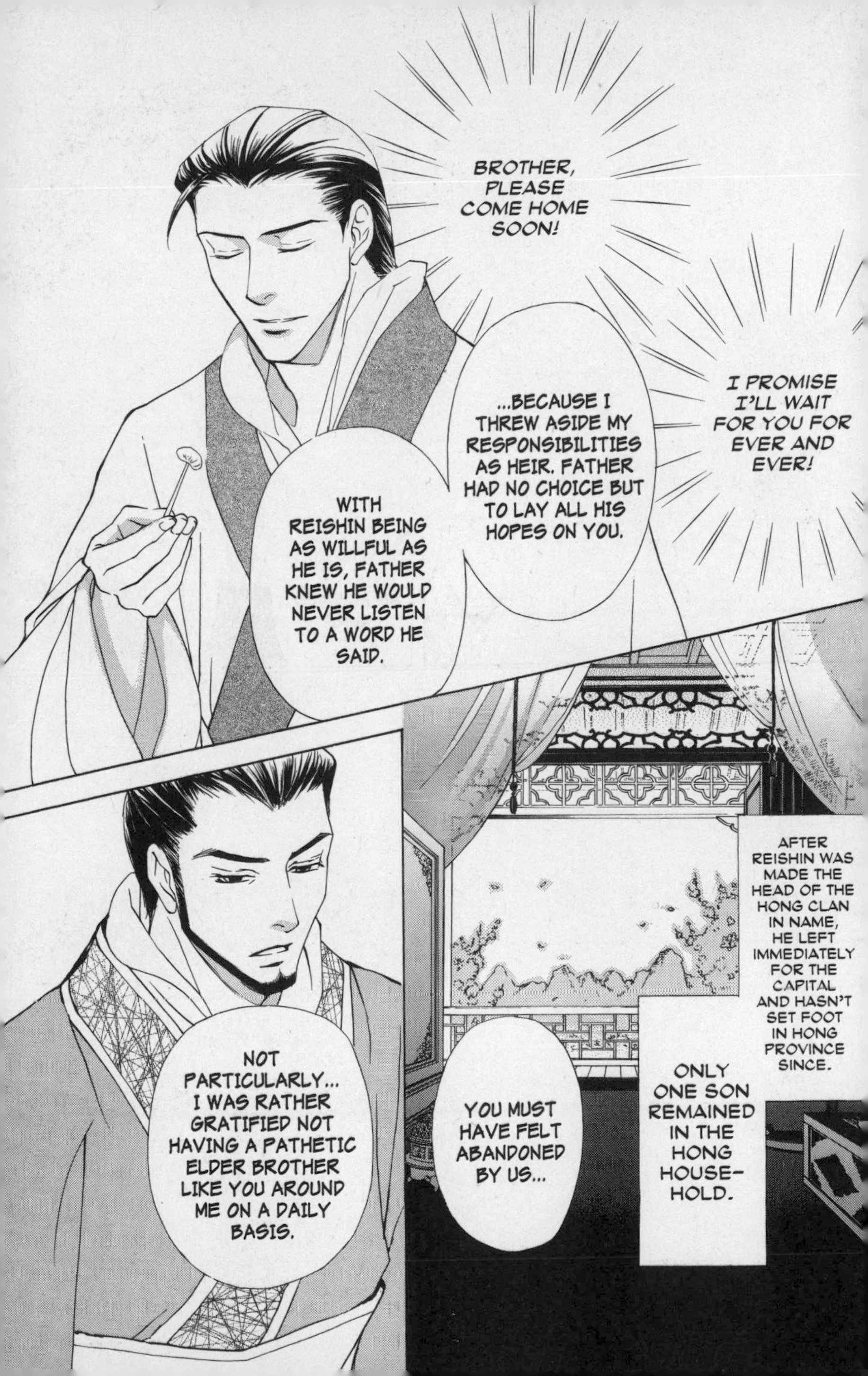
BROTHER, PLEASE COME HOME SOON!
I PROMISE I'LL WAIT FOR YOU FOR EVER AND EVER!
...BECAUSE I THREW ASIDE MY RESPONSIBILITIES AS HEIR. FATHER HAD NO CHOICE BUT TO LAY ALL HIS HOPES ON YOU.
WITH REISHIN BEING AS WILLFUL AS HE IS, FATHER KNEW HE WOULD NEVER LISTEN TO A WORD HE SAID.
AFTER REISHIN WAS MADE THE HEAD OF THE HONG CLAN IN NAME, HE LEFT IMMEDIATELY FOR THE CAPITAL AND HASN'T SET FOOT IN HONG PROVINCE SINCE.
ONLY ONE SON REMAINED IN THE HONG HOUSE-HOLD.
YOU MUST HAVE FELT ABANDONED BY US...
NOT PARTICULARLY... I WAS RATHER GRATIFIED NOT HAVING A PATHETIC ELDER BROTHER LIKE YOU AROUND ME ON A DAILY BASIS.

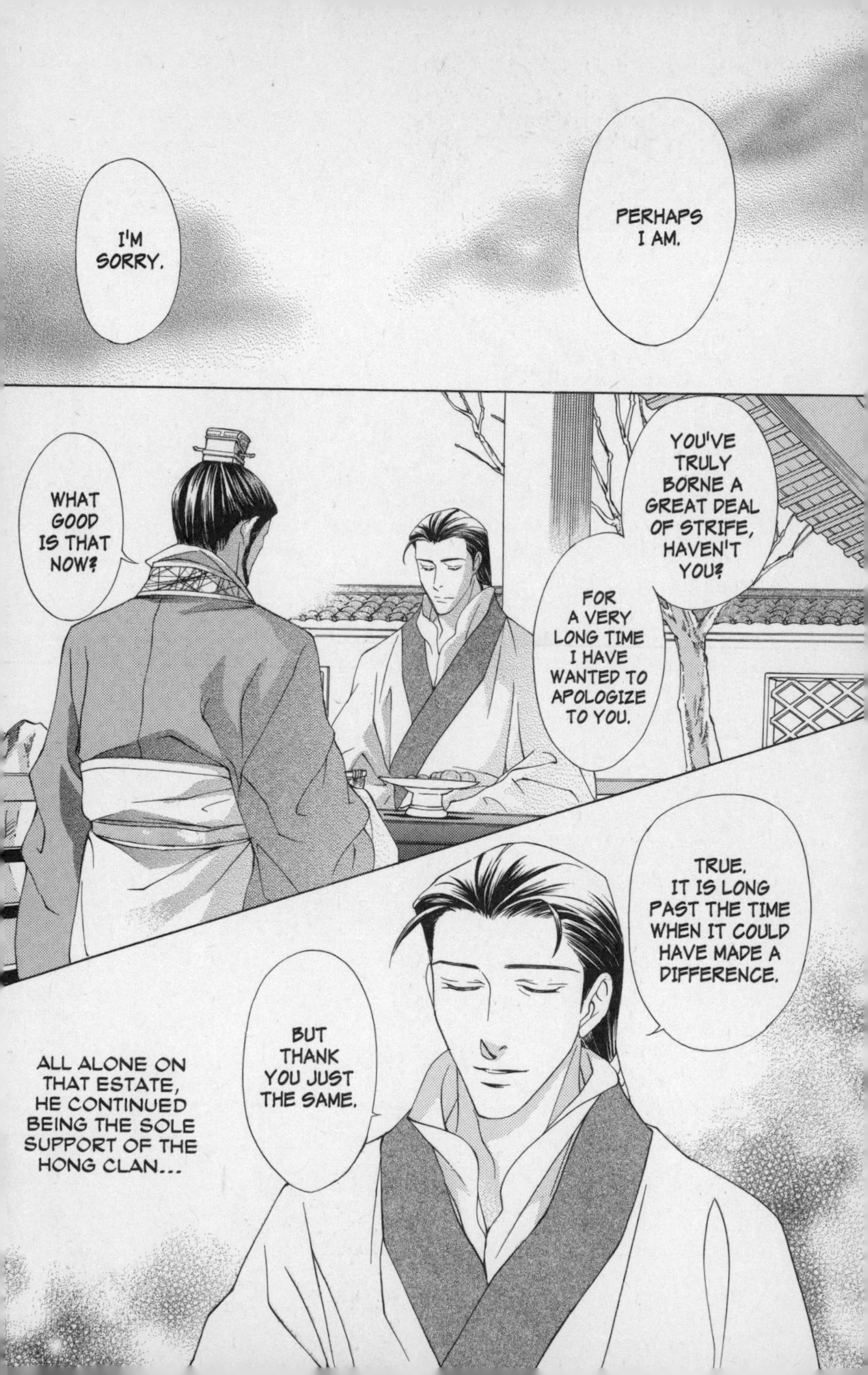
PERHAPS I AM.
I'M SORRY.
YOU'VE TRULY BORNE A GREAT DEAL OF STRIFE, HAVEN'T YOU?
FOR A VERY LONG TIME I HAVE WANTED TO APOLOGIZE TO YOU.
WHAT GOOD IS THAT NOW?
TRUE. IT IS LONG PAST THE TIME WHEN IT COULD HAVE MADE A DIFFERENCE.
BUT THANK YOU JUST THE SAME.
ALL ALONE ON THAT ESTATE, HE CONTINUED BEING THE SOLE SUPPORT OF THE HONG CLAN...

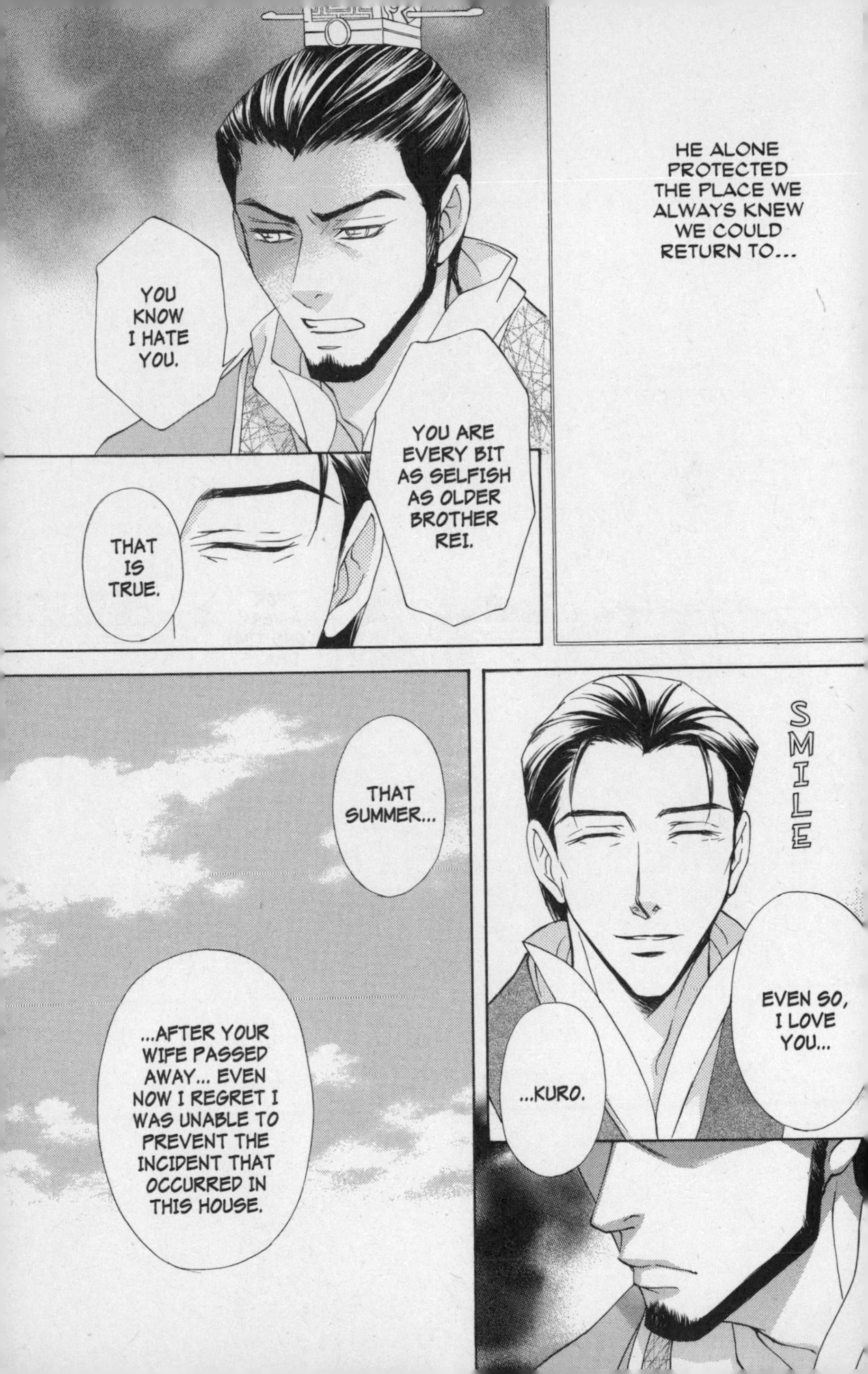
HE ALONE PROTECTED THE PLACE WE ALWAYS KNEW WE COULD RETURN TO...
YOU KNOW I HATE YOU.
YOU ARE EVERY BIT AS SELFISH AS OLDER BROTHER REI.
THAT IS TRUE.
SMILE
EVEN SO, I LOVE YOU...
...KURO.
THAT SUMMER...
...AFTER YOUR WIFE PASSED AWAY... EVEN NOW I REGRET I WAS UNABLE TO PREVENT THE INCIDENT THAT OCCURRED IN THIS HOUSE.

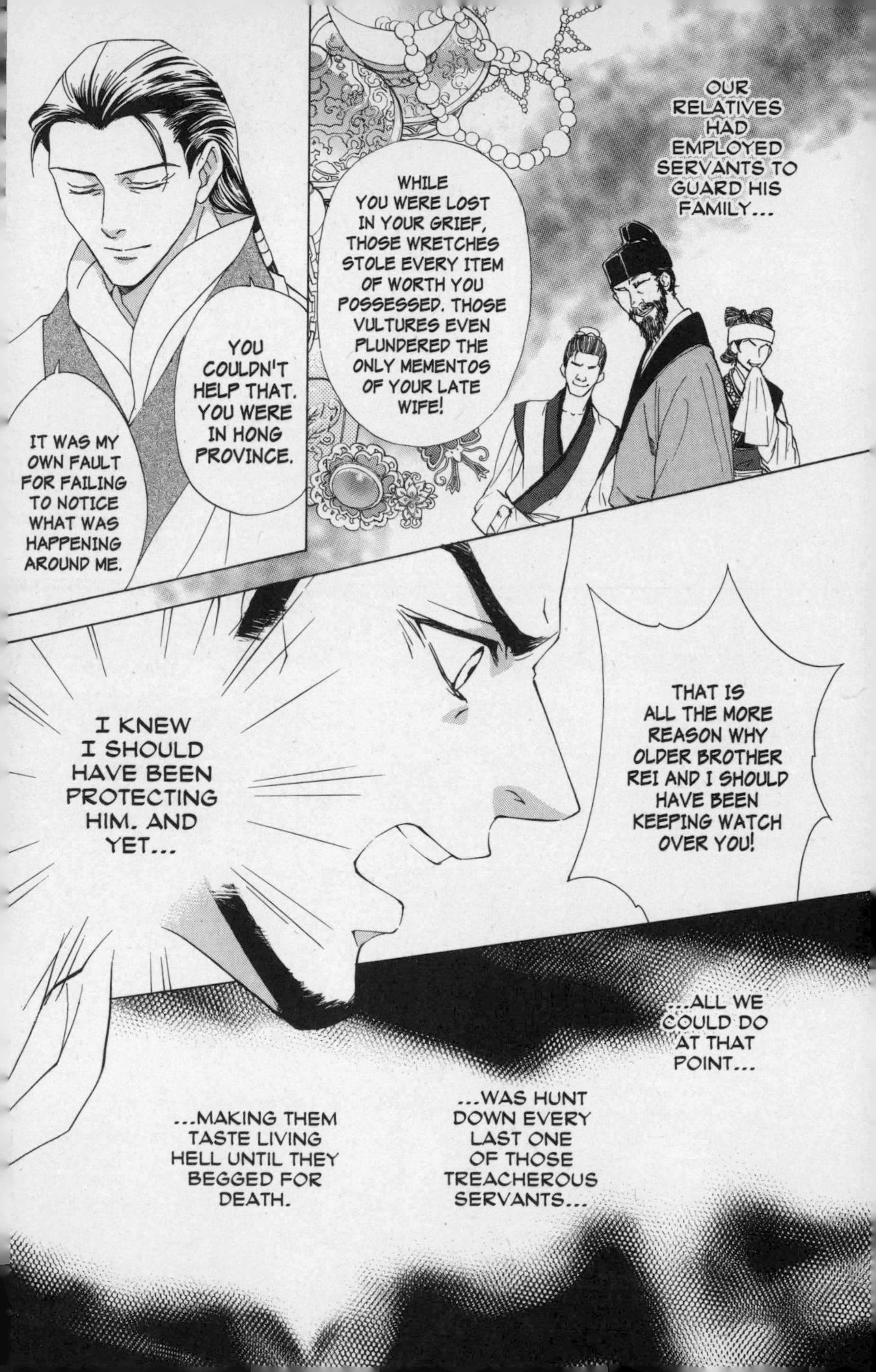
OUR RELATIVES HAD EMPLOYED SERVANTS TO GUARD HIS FAMILY...
WHILE YOU WERE LOST IN YOUR GRIEF, THOSE WRETCHES STOLE EVERY ITEM OF WORTH YOU POSSESSED. THOSE VULTURES EVEN PLUNDERED THE ONLY MEMENTOS OF YOUR LATE WIFE!
YOU COULDN'T HELP THAT. YOU WERE IN HONG PROVINCE.
IT WAS MY OWN FAULT FOR FAILING TO NOTICE WHAT WAS HAPPENING AROUND ME.
THAT IS ALL THE MORE REASON WHY OLDER BROTHER REI AND I SHOULD HAVE BEEN KEEPING WATCH OVER YOU!
I KNEW I SHOULD HAVE BEEN PROTECTING HIM. AND YET...
...ALL WE COULD DO AT THAT POINT...
...WAS HUNT DOWN EVERY LAST ONE OF THOSE TREACHEROUS SERVANTS...
...MAKING THEM TASTE LIVING HELL UNTIL THEY BEGGED FOR DEATH.

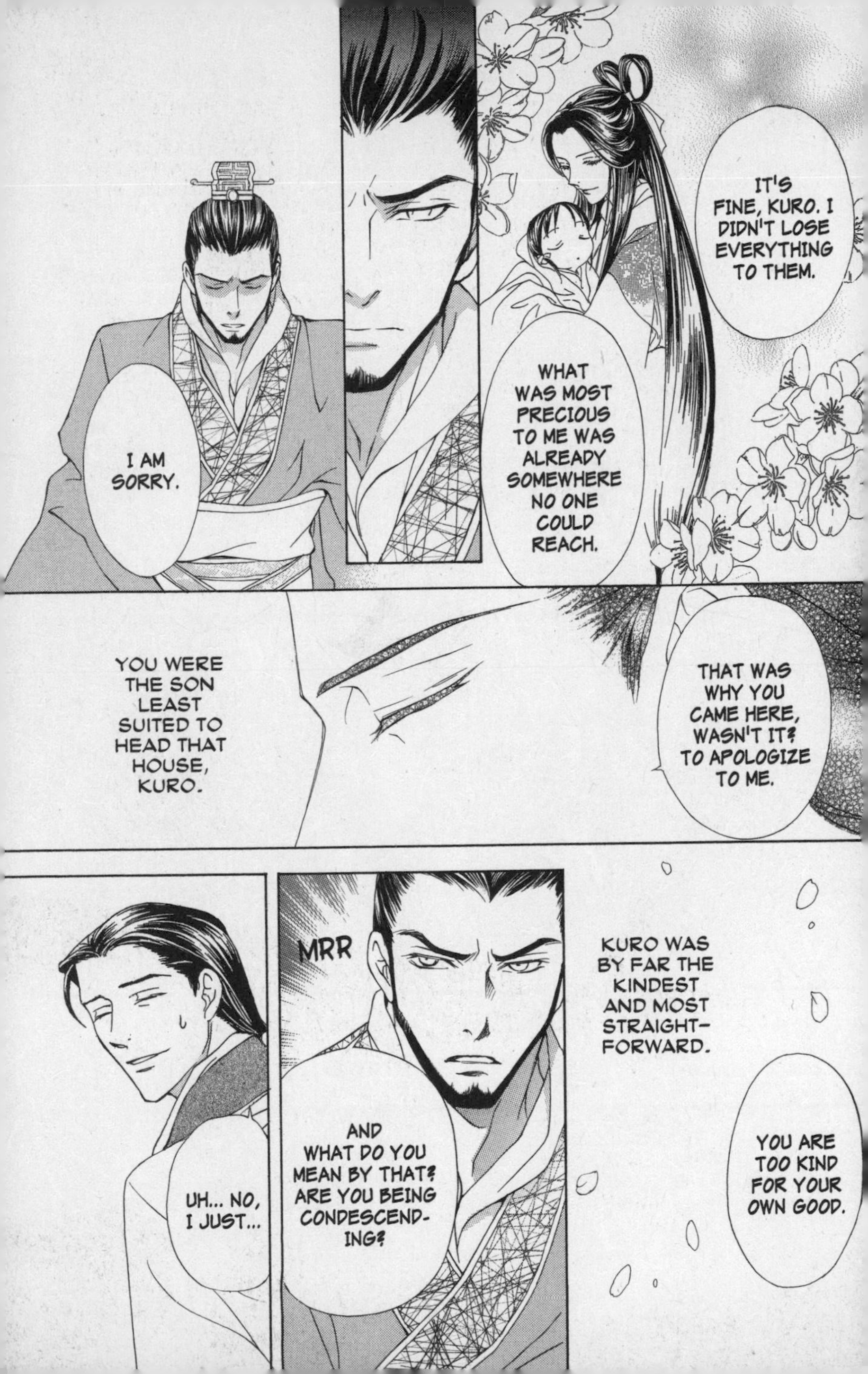
IT'S FINE, KURO. I DIDN'T LOSE EVERYTHING TO THEM.
WHAT WAS MOST PRECIOUS TO ME WAS ALREADY SOMEWHERE NO ONE COULD REACH.
I AM SORRY.
THAT WAS WHY YOU CAME HERE, WASN'T IT? TO APOLOGIZE TO ME.
YOU WERE THE SON LEAST SUITED TO HEAD THAT HOUSE, KURO.
KURO WAS BY FAR THE KINDEST AND MOST STRAIGHT-FORWARD.
YOU ARE TOO KIND FOR YOUR OWN GOOD.
MRR
AND WHAT DO YOU MEAN BY THAT? ARE YOU BEING CONDESCEND-ING?
UH... NO, I JUST...

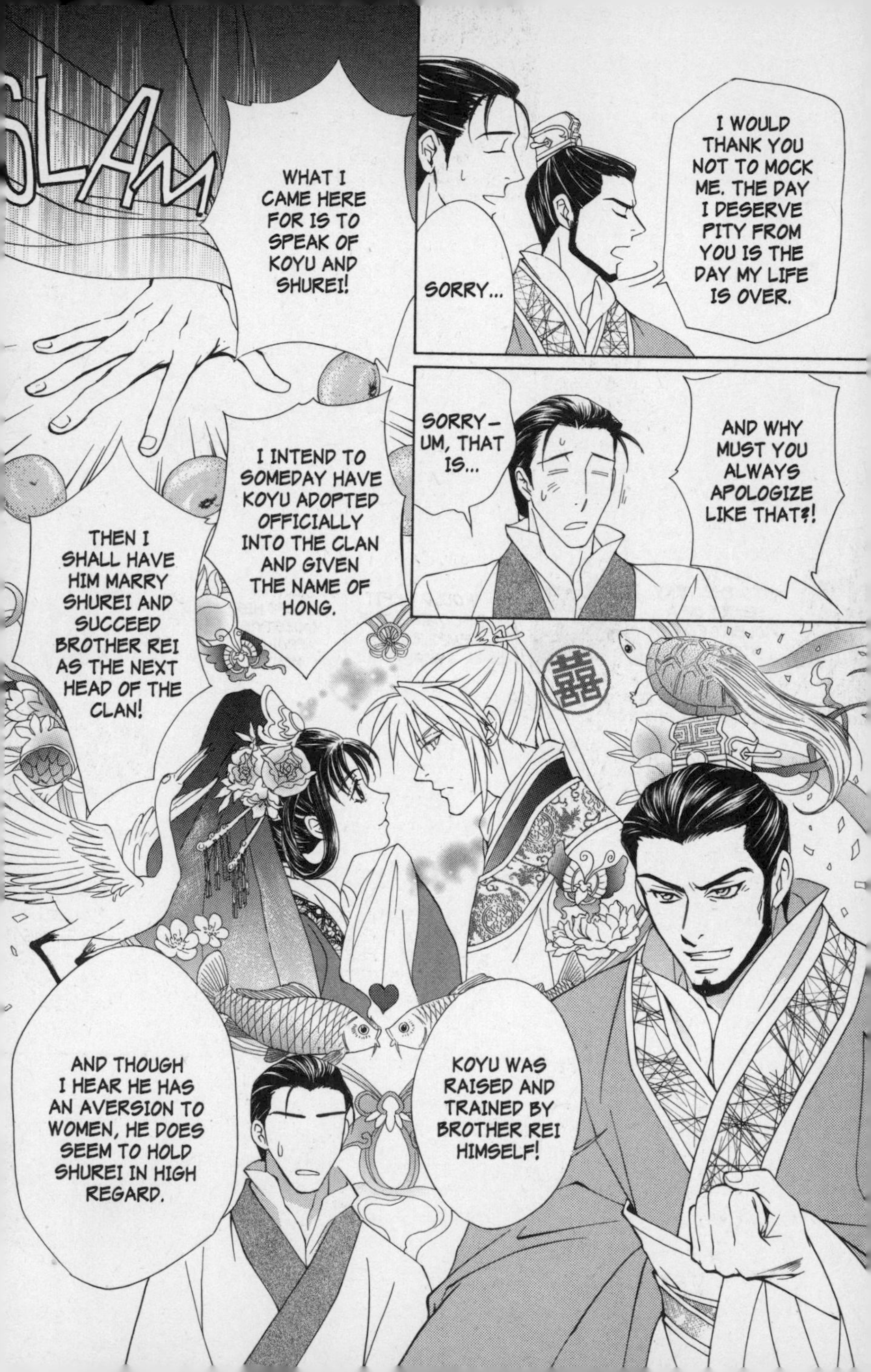
I WOULD THANK YOU NOT TO MOCK ME. THE DAY I DESERVE PITY FROM YOU IS THE DAY MY LIFE IS OVER.
SORRY...
AND WHY MUST YOU ALWAYS APOLOGIZE LIKE THAT?!
SORRY— UM, THAT IS...
SLAM
WHAT I CAME HERE FOR IS TO SPEAK OF KOYU AND SHUREI!
I INTEND TO SOMEDAY HAVE KOYU ADOPTED OFFICIALLY INTO THE CLAN AND GIVEN THE NAME OF HONG.
THEN I SHALL HAVE HIM MARRY SHUREI AND SUCCEED BROTHER REI AS THE NEXT HEAD OF THE CLAN!
KOYU WAS RAISED AND TRAINED BY BROTHER REI HIMSELF!
AND THOUGH I HEAR HE HAS AN AVERSION TO WOMEN, HE DOES SEEM TO HOLD SHUREI IN HIGH REGARD.

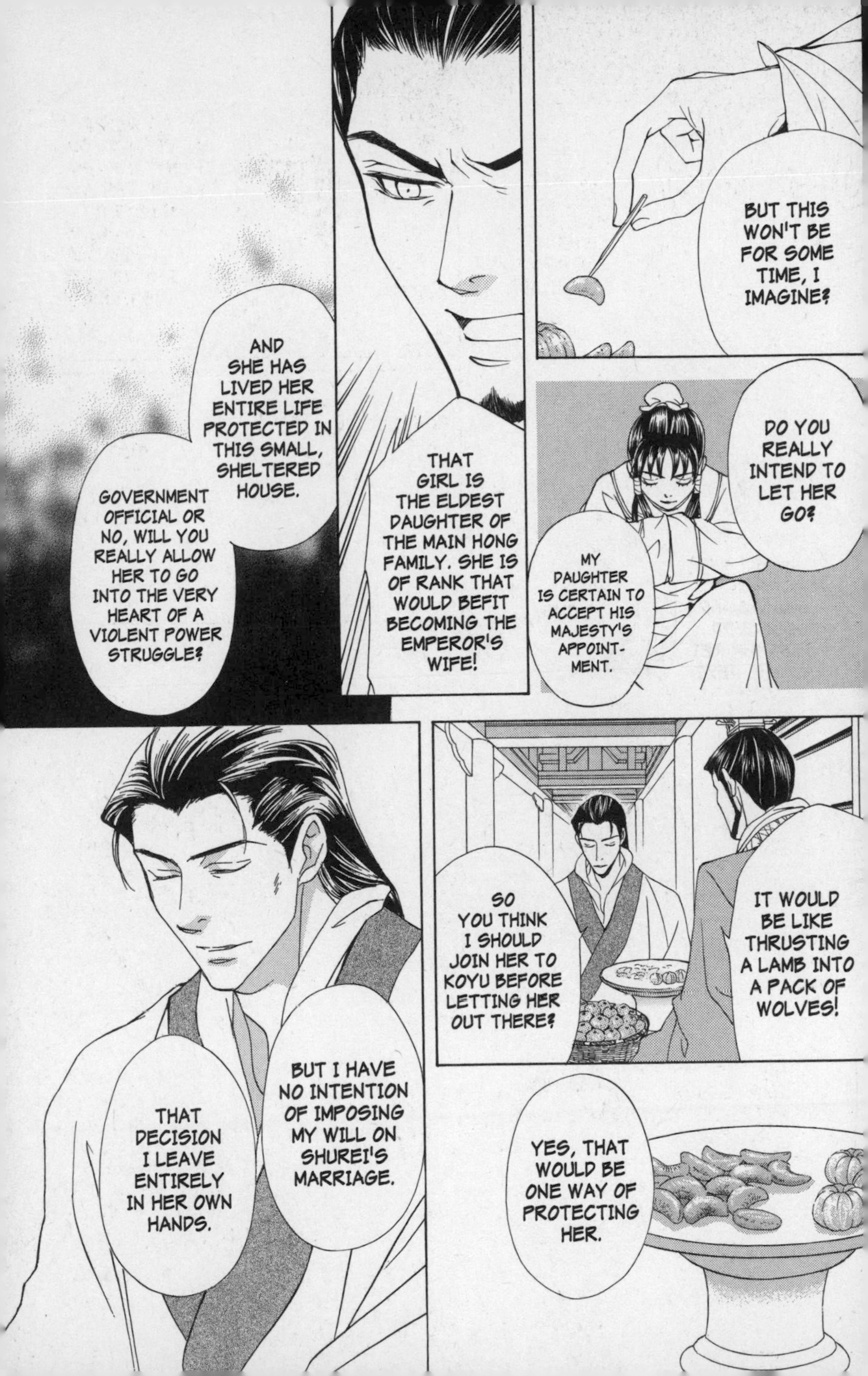
BUT THIS WON'T BE FOR SOME TIME, I IMAGINE?
DO YOU REALLY INTEND TO LET HER GO?
MY DAUGHTER IS CERTAIN TO ACCEPT HIS MAJESTY'S APPOINT-MENT.
THAT GIRL IS THE ELDEST DAUGHTER OF THE MAIN HONG FAMILY. SHE IS OF RANK THAT WOULD BEFIT BECOMING THE EMPEROR'S WIFE!
AND SHE HAS LIVED HER ENTIRE LIFE PROTECTED IN THIS SMALL, SHELTERED HOUSE.
GOVERNMENT OFFICIAL OR NO, WILL YOU REALLY ALLOW HER TO GO INTO THE VERY HEART OF A VIOLENT POWER STRUGGLE?
IT WOULD BE LIKE THRUSTING A LAMB INTO A PACK OF WOLVES!
SO YOU THINK I SHOULD JOIN HER TO KOYU BEFORE LETTING HER OUT THERE?
YES, THAT WOULD BE ONE WAY OF PROTECTING HER.
BUT I HAVE NO INTENTION OF IMPOSING MY WILL ON SHUREI'S MARRIAGE.
THAT DECISION I LEAVE ENTIRELY IN HER OWN HANDS.

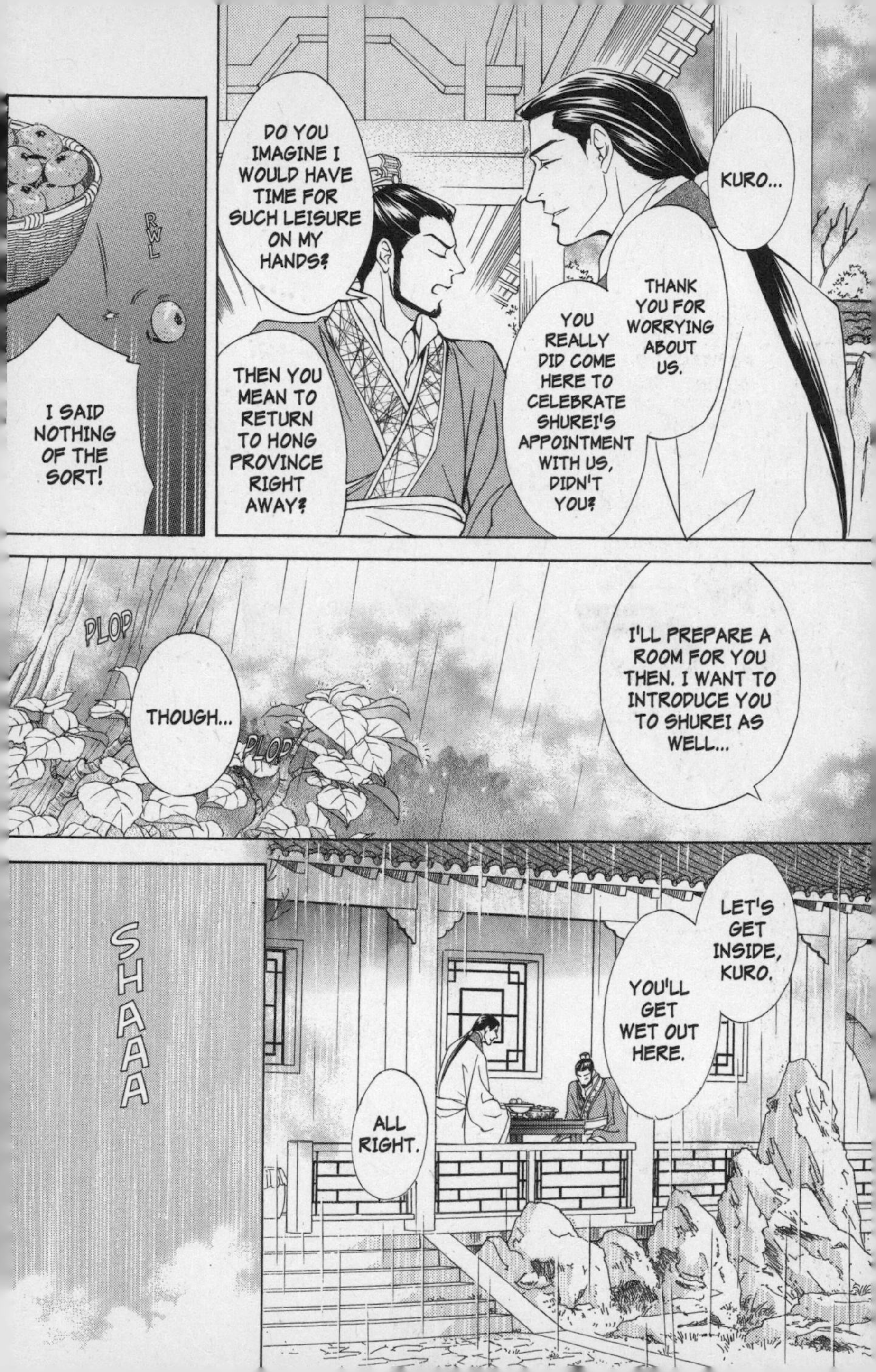
KURO...
THANK YOU FOR WORRYING ABOUT US.
YOU REALLY DID COME HERE TO CELEBRATE SHUREI'S APPOINTMENT WITH US, DIDN'T YOU?
DO YOU IMAGINE I WOULD HAVE TIME FOR SUCH LEISURE ON MY HANDS?
THEN YOU MEAN TO RETURN TO HONG PROVINCE RIGHT AWAY?
RWL
I SAID NOTHING OF THE SORT!
I'LL PREPARE A ROOM FOR YOU THEN. I WANT TO INTRODUCE YOU TO SHUREI AS WELL...
PLOP
THOUGH...
PLOP
LET'S GET INSIDE, KURO.
YOU'LL GET WET OUT HERE.
ALL RIGHT.
SHAAA

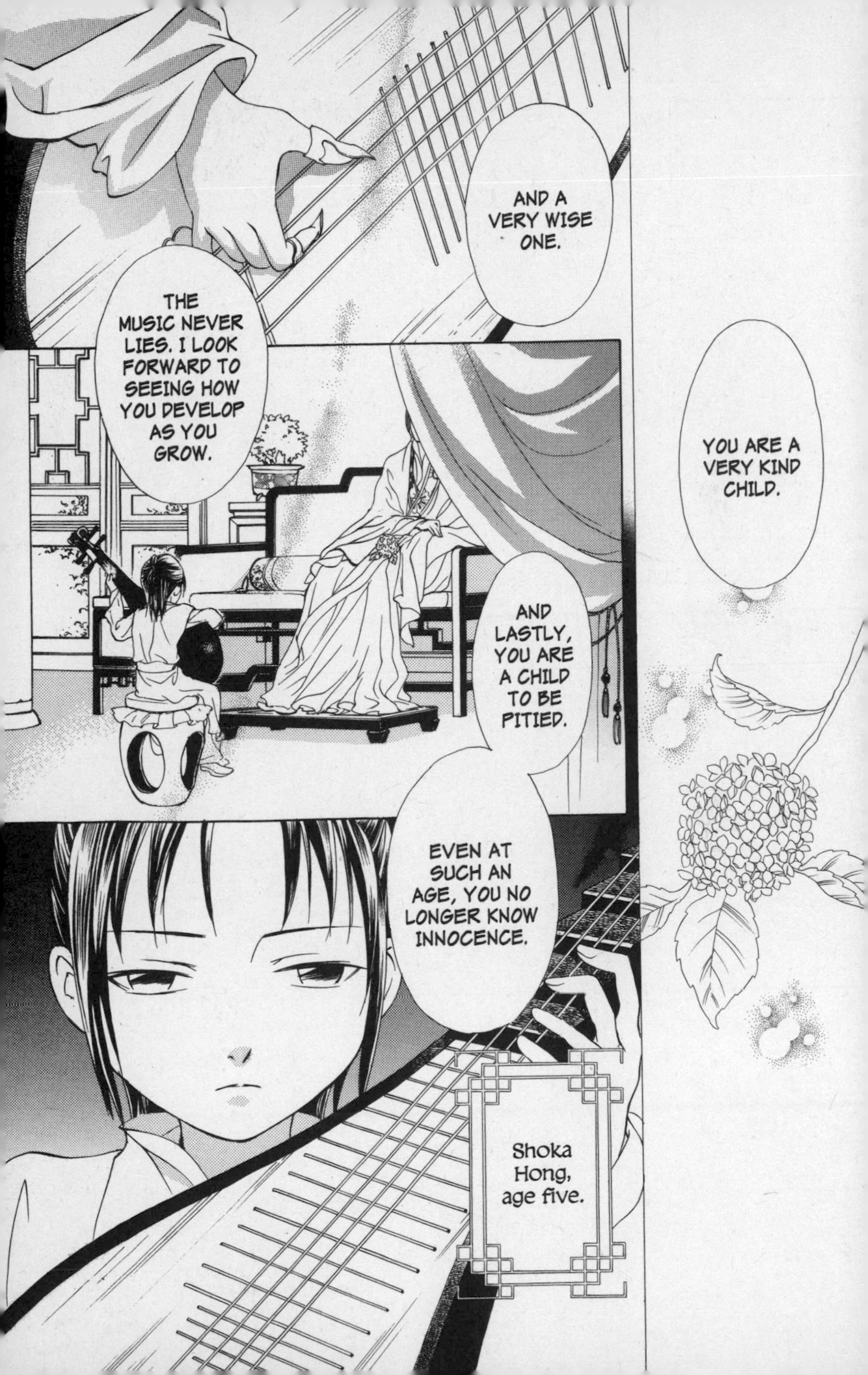
YOU ARE A VERY KIND CHILD.
AND A VERY WISE ONE.
THE MUSIC NEVER LIES. I LOOK FORWARD TO SEEING HOW YOU DEVELOP AS YOU GROW.
AND LASTLY, YOU ARE A CHILD TO BE PITIED.
EVEN AT SUCH AN AGE, YOU NO LONGER KNOW INNOCENCE.
Shoka Hong, age five.

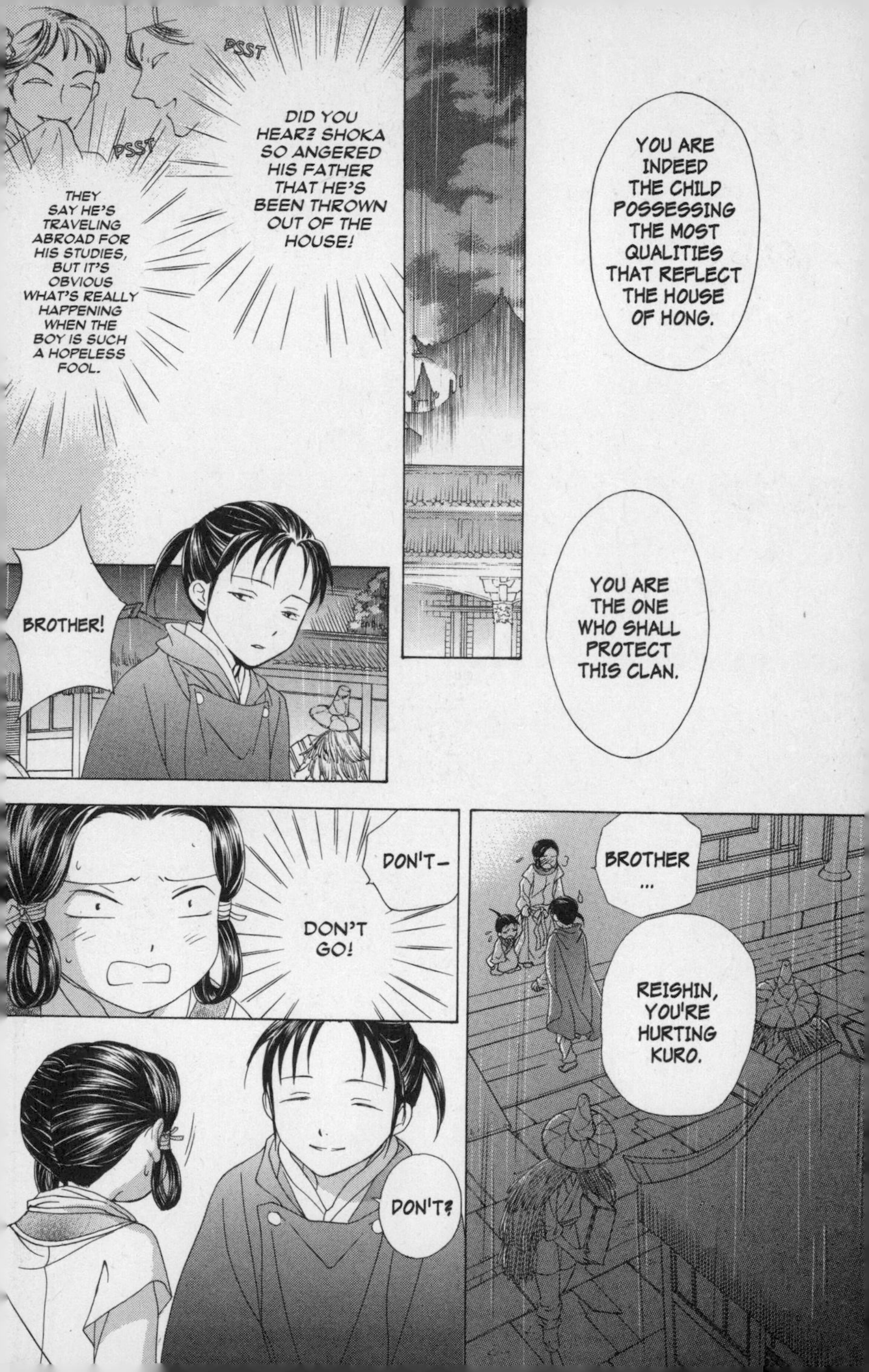
YOU ARE INDEED THE CHILD POSSESSING THE MOST QUALITIES THAT REFLECT THE HOUSE OF HONG.
YOU ARE THE ONE WHO SHALL PROTECT THIS CLAN.
PSST
PSST
DID YOU HEAR? SHOKA SO ANGERED HIS FATHER THAT HE'S BEEN THROWN OUT OF THE HOUSE!
THEY SAY HE'S TRAVELING ABROAD FOR HIS STUDIES, BUT IT'S OBVIOUS WHAT'S REALLY HAPPENING WHEN THE BOY IS SUCH A HOPELESS FOOL.
BROTHER!
BROTHER ...
REISHIN, YOU'RE HURTING KURO.
DON'T—
DON'T GO!
DON'T?

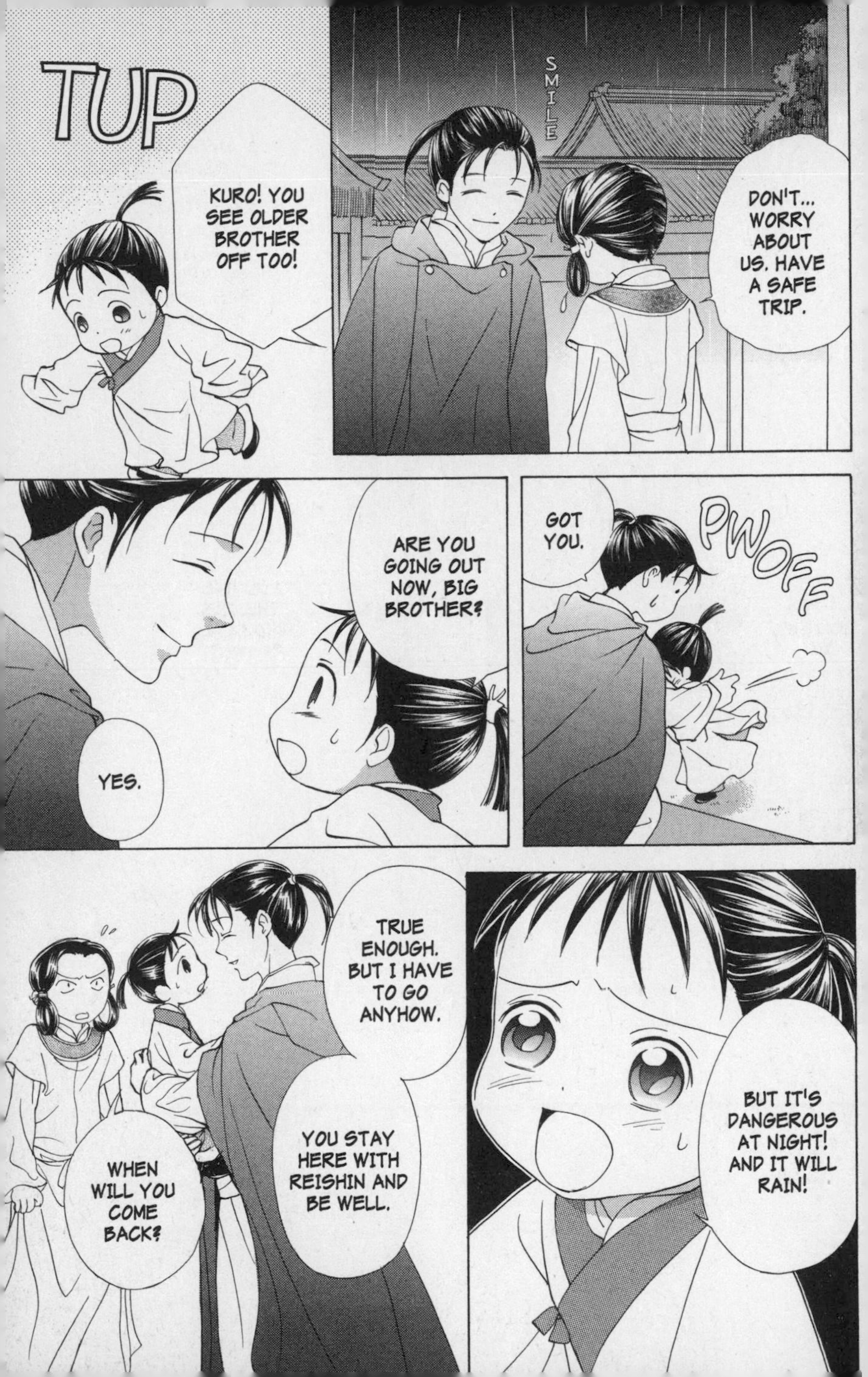
DON'T... WORRY ABOUT US. HAVE A SAFE TRIP.
SMILE
TUP
KURO! YOU SEE OLDER BROTHER OFF TOO!
PWOFF
GOT YOU.
ARE YOU GOING OUT NOW, BIG BROTHER?
YES.
BUT IT'S DANGEROUS AT NIGHT! AND IT WILL RAIN!
TRUE ENOUGH. BUT I HAVE TO GO ANYHOW.
YOU STAY HERE WITH REISHIN AND BE WELL.
WHEN WILL YOU COME BACK?

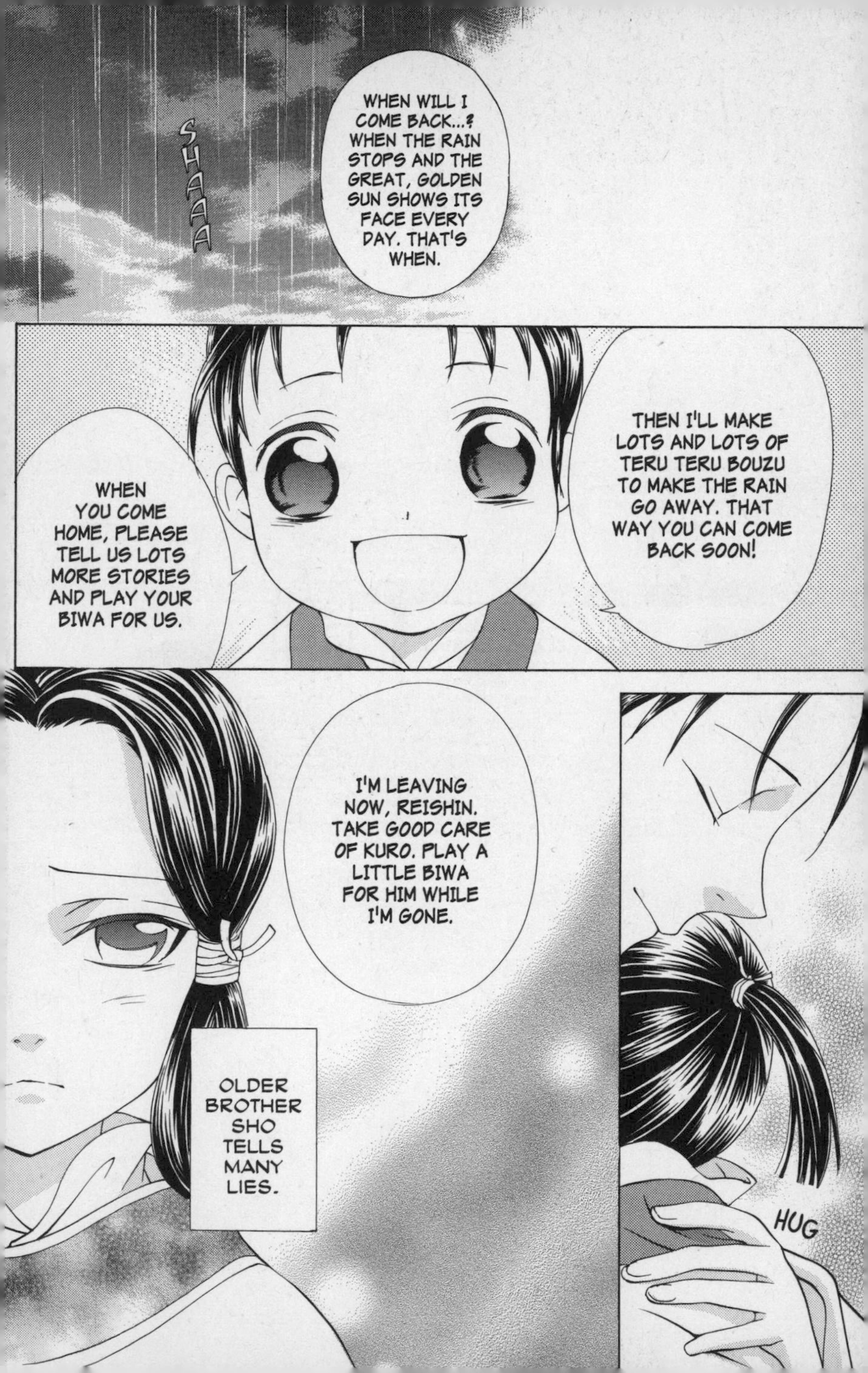
WHEN WILL I COME BACK...? WHEN THE RAIN STOPS AND THE GREAT, GOLDEN SUN SHOWS ITS FACE EVERY DAY. THAT'S WHEN.
SHAAAA
THEN I'LL MAKE LOTS AND LOTS OF TERU TERU BOUZU TO MAKE THE RAIN GO AWAY. THAT WAY YOU CAN COME BACK SOON!
WHEN YOU COME HOME, PLEASE TELL US LOTS MORE STORIES AND PLAY YOUR BIWA FOR US.
HUG
I'M LEAVING NOW, REISHIN. TAKE GOOD CARE OF KURO. PLAY A LITTLE BIWA FOR HIM WHILE I'M GONE.
OLDER BROTHER SHO TELLS MANY LIES.

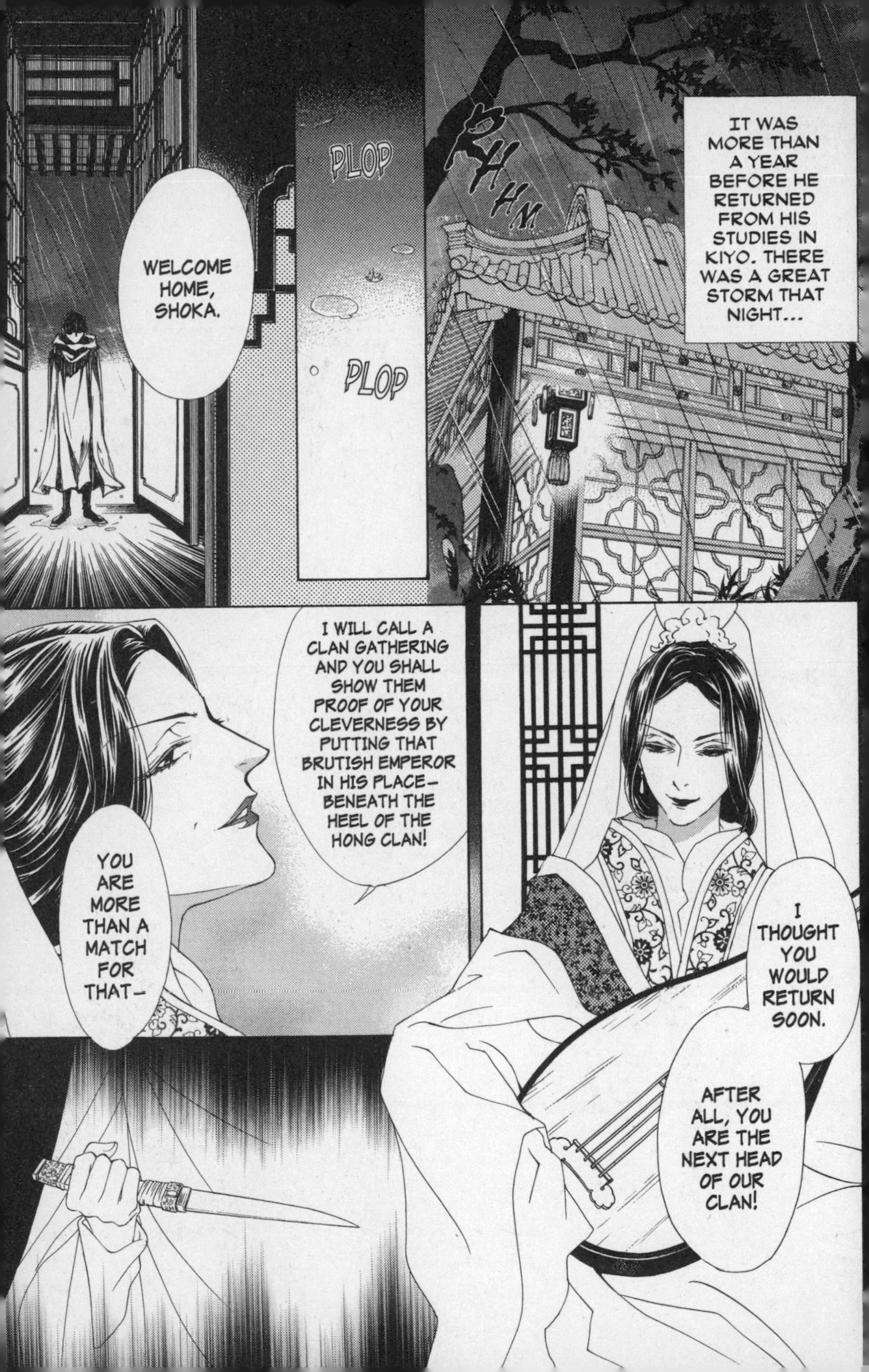
IT WAS MORE THAN A YEAR BEFORE HE RETURNED FROM HIS STUDIES IN KIYO. THERE WAS A GREAT STORM THAT NIGHT...
RHHN
PLOP
PLOP
WELCOME HOME, SHOKA.
I THOUGHT YOU WOULD RETURN SOON.
AFTER ALL, YOU ARE THE NEXT HEAD OF OUR CLAN!
I WILL CALL A CLAN GATHERING AND YOU SHALL SHOW THEM PROOF OF YOUR CLEVERNESS BY PUTTING THAT BRUTISH EMPEROR IN HIS PLACE— BENEATH THE HEEL OF THE HONG CLAN!
YOU ARE MORE THAN A MATCH FOR THAT—

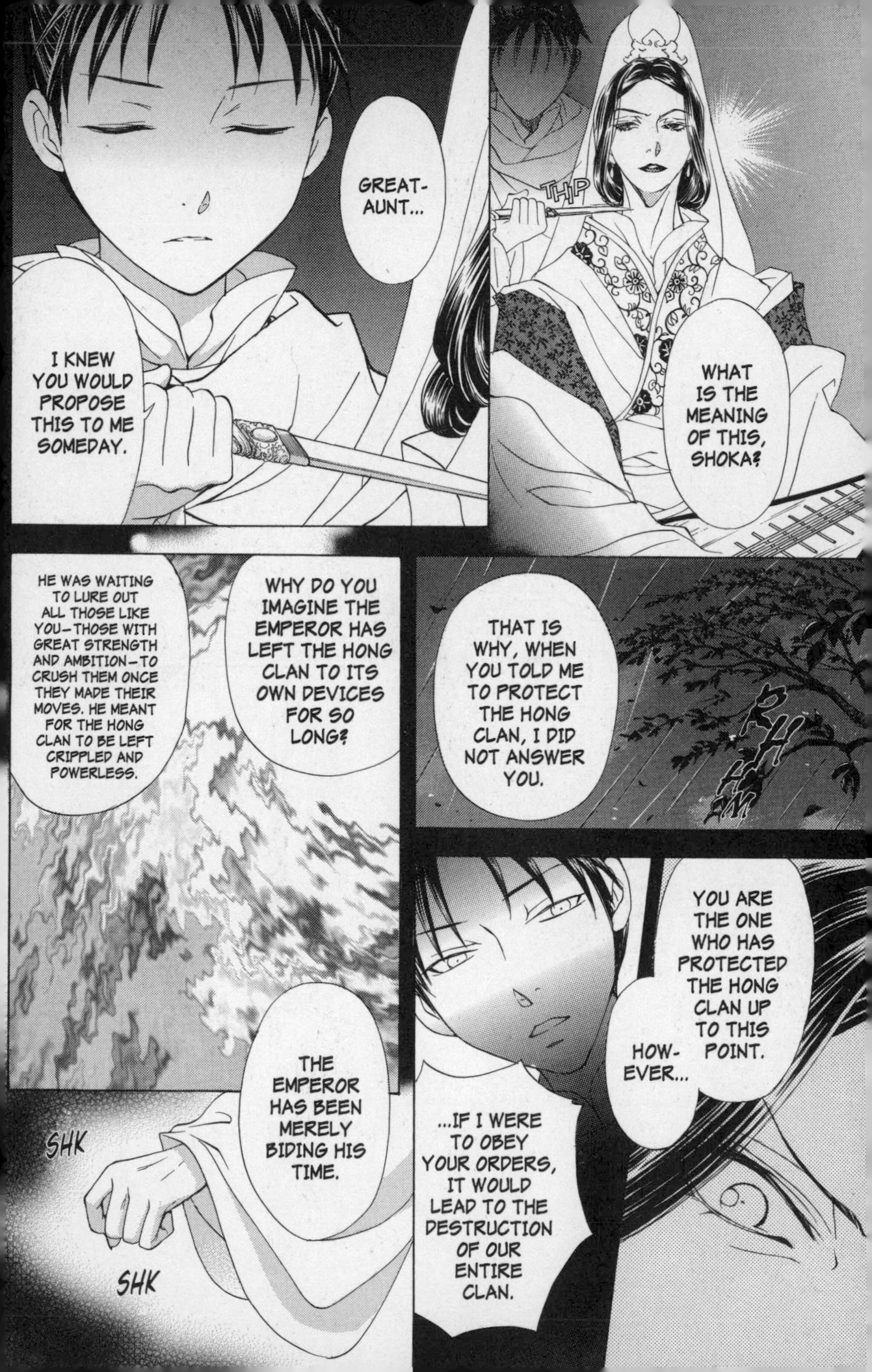
THP
WHAT IS THE MEANING OF THIS, SHOKA?
GREAT-AUNT...
I KNEW YOU WOULD PROPOSE THIS TO ME SOMEDAY.
THAT IS WHY, WHEN YOU TOLD ME TO PROTECT THE HONG CLAN, I DID NOT ANSWER YOU.
RHHM
YOU ARE THE ONE WHO HAS PROTECTED THE HONG CLAN UP TO THIS POINT.
HOW-EVER...
...IF I WERE TO OBEY YOUR ORDERS, IT WOULD LEAD TO THE DESTRUCTION OF OUR ENTIRE CLAN.
WHY DO YOU IMAGINE THE EMPEROR HAS LEFT THE HONG CLAN TO ITS OWN DEVICES FOR SO LONG?
HE WAS WAITING TO LURE OUT ALL THOSE LIKE YOU—THOSE WITH GREAT STRENGTH AND AMBITION—TO CRUSH THEM ONCE THEY MADE THEIR MOVES. HE MEANT FOR THE HONG CLAN TO BE LEFT CRIPPLED AND POWERLESS.
THE EMPEROR HAS BEEN MERELY BIDING HIS TIME.
SHK
SHK

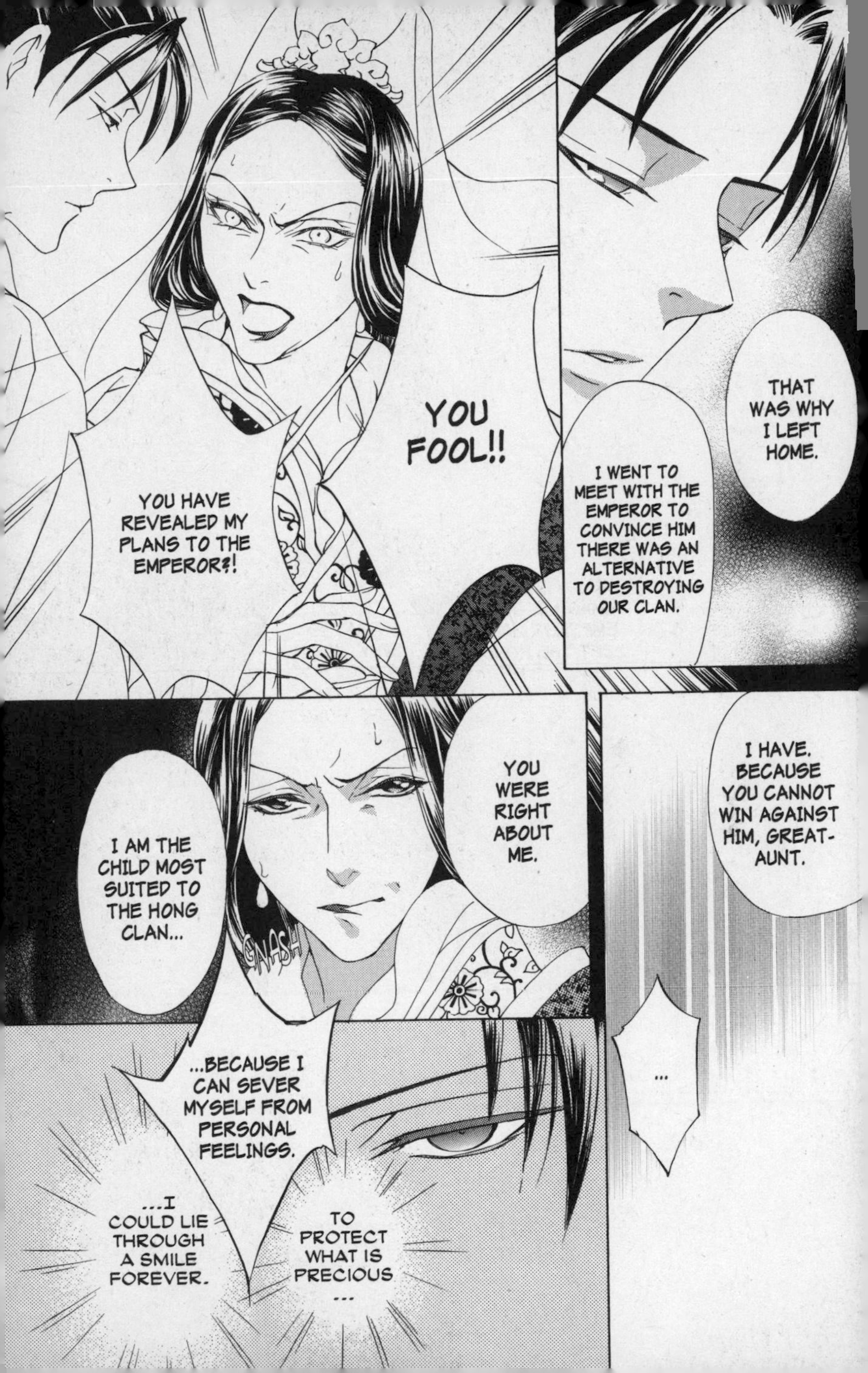
THAT WAS WHY I LEFT HOME.
I WENT TO MEET WITH THE EMPEROR TO CONVINCE HIM THERE WAS AN ALTERNATIVE TO DESTROYING OUR CLAN.
YOU FOOL!!
YOU HAVE REVEALED MY PLANS TO THE EMPEROR?!
I HAVE. BECAUSE YOU CANNOT WIN AGAINST HIM, GREAT-AUNT.
...
YOU WERE RIGHT ABOUT ME.
I AM THE CHILD MOST SUITED TO THE HONG CLAN...
GNASH
...BECAUSE I CAN SEVER MYSELF FROM PERSONAL FEELINGS.
TO PROTECT WHAT IS PRECIOUS...
...I COULD LIE THROUGH A SMILE FOREVER.

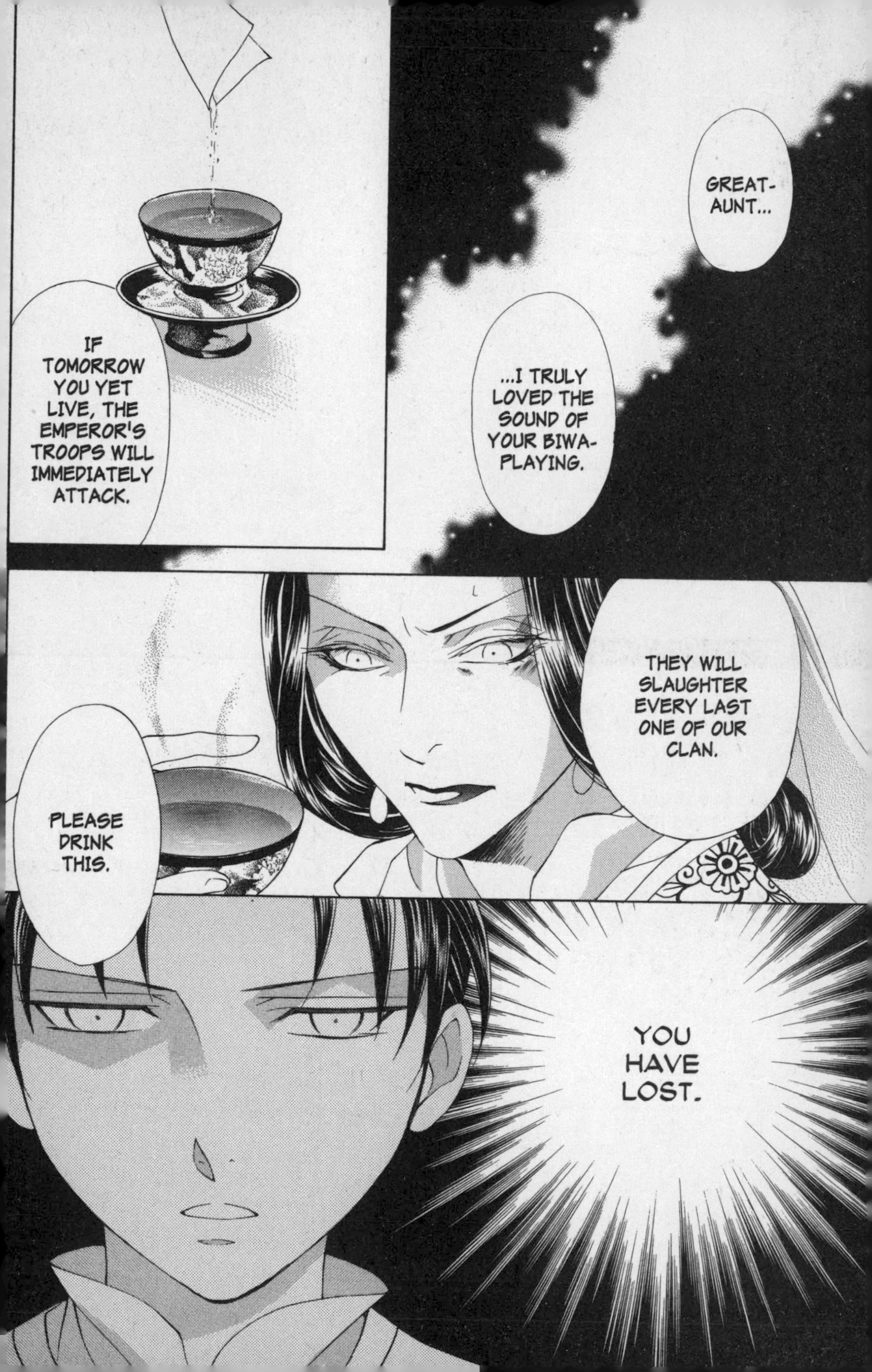
GREAT-AUNT...
...I TRULY LOVED THE SOUND OF YOUR BIWA-PLAYING.
IF TOMORROW YOU YET LIVE, THE EMPEROR'S TROOPS WILL IMMEDIATELY ATTACK.
THEY WILL SLAUGHTER EVERY LAST ONE OF OUR CLAN.
PLEASE DRINK THIS.
YOU HAVE LOST.

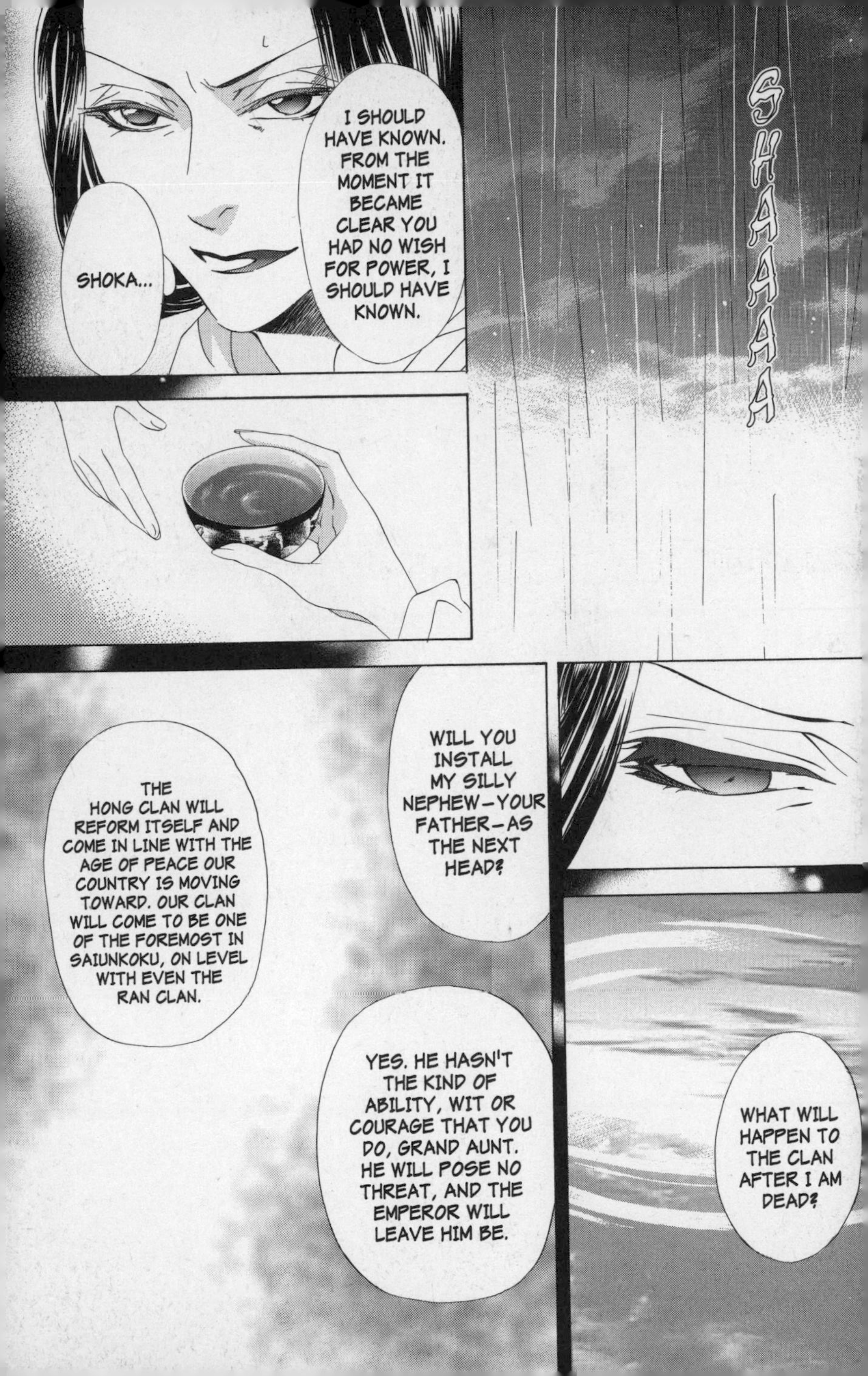
SHAAAAA
I SHOULD HAVE KNOWN. FROM THE MOMENT IT BECAME CLEAR YOU HAD NO WISH FOR POWER, I SHOULD HAVE KNOWN.
SHOKA...
WHAT WILL HAPPEN TO THE CLAN AFTER I AM DEAD?
WILL YOU INSTALL MY SILLY NEPHEW—YOUR FATHER—AS THE NEXT HEAD?
THE HONG CLAN WILL REFORM ITSELF AND COME IN LINE WITH THE AGE OF PEACE OUR COUNTRY IS MOVING TOWARD. OUR CLAN WILL COME TO BE ONE OF THE FOREMOST IN SAIUNKOKU, ON LEVEL WITH EVEN THE RAN CLAN.
YES. HE HASN'T THE KIND OF ABILITY, WIT OR COURAGE THAT YOU DO, GRAND AUNT. HE WILL POSE NO THREAT, AND THE EMPEROR WILL LEAVE HIM BE.

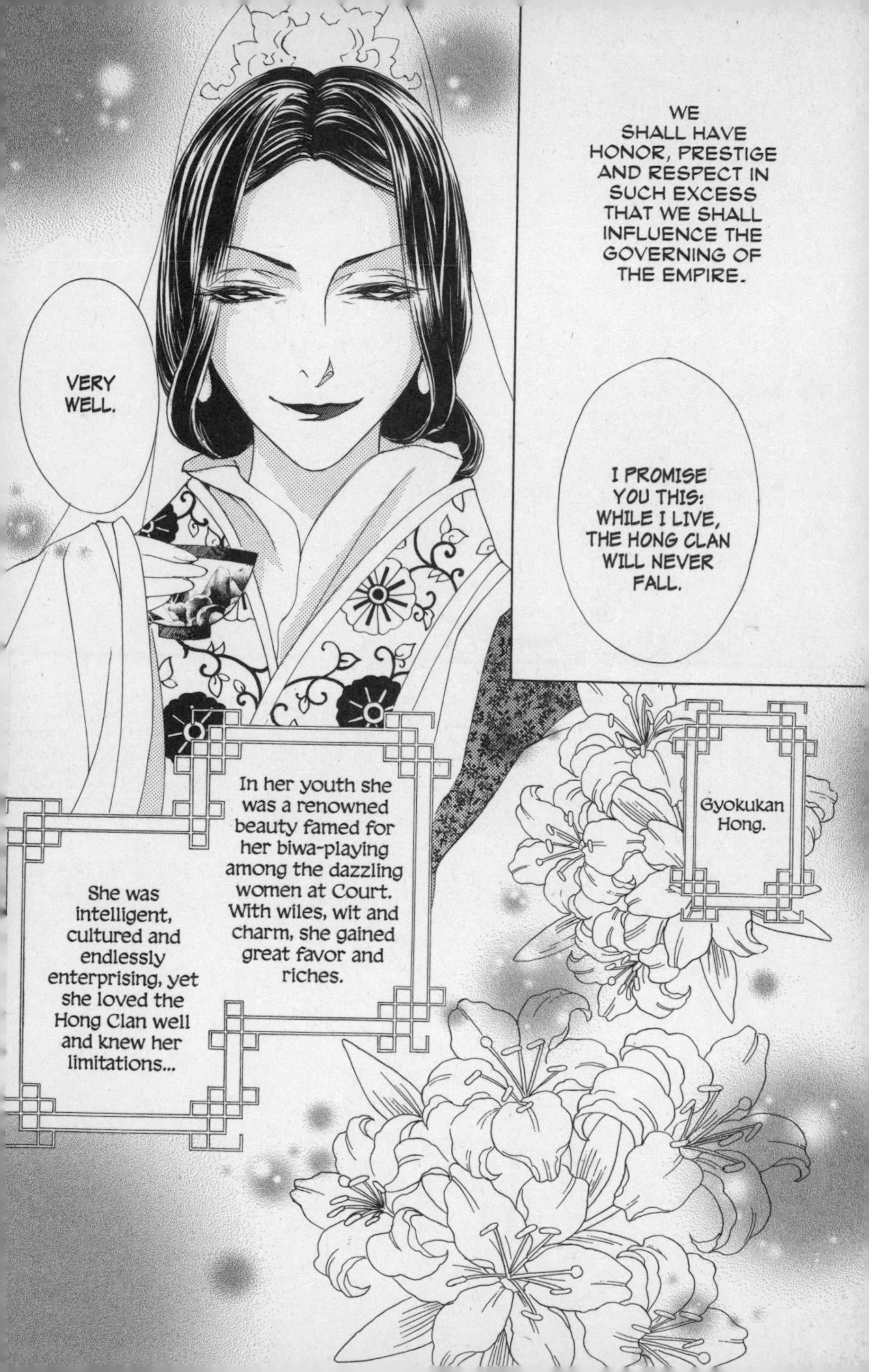
WE SHALL HAVE HONOR, PRESTIGE AND RESPECT IN SUCH EXCESS THAT WE SHALL INFLUENCE THE GOVERNING OF THE EMPIRE.
I PROMISE YOU THIS: WHILE I LIVE, THE HONG CLAN WILL NEVER FALL.
VERY WELL.
Gyokukan Hong.
In her youth she was a renowned beauty famed for her biwa-playing among the dazzling women at Court. With wiles, wit and charm, she gained great favor and riches.
She was intelligent, cultured and endlessly enterprising, yet she loved the Hong Clan well and knew her limitations...

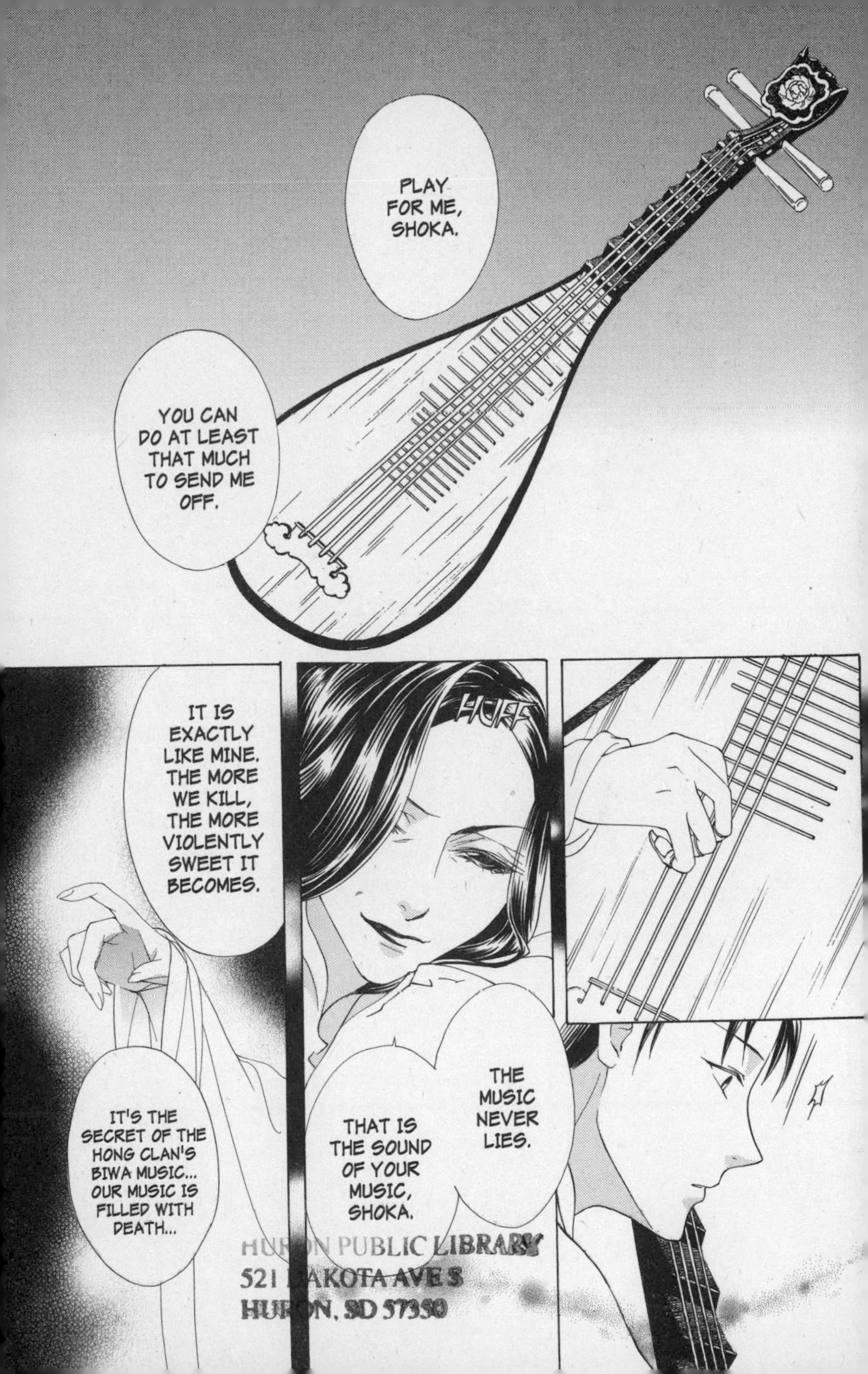
PLAY FOR ME, SHOKA.
YOU CAN DO AT LEAST THAT MUCH TO SEND ME OFF.
HUFF
IT IS EXACTLY LIKE MINE. THE MORE WE KILL, THE MORE VIOLENTLY SWEET IT BECOMES.
THE MUSIC NEVER LIES.
THAT IS THE SOUND OF YOUR MUSIC, SHOKA.
IT'S THE SECRET OF THE HONG CLAN'S BIWA MUSIC... OUR MUSIC IS FILLED WITH DEATH...

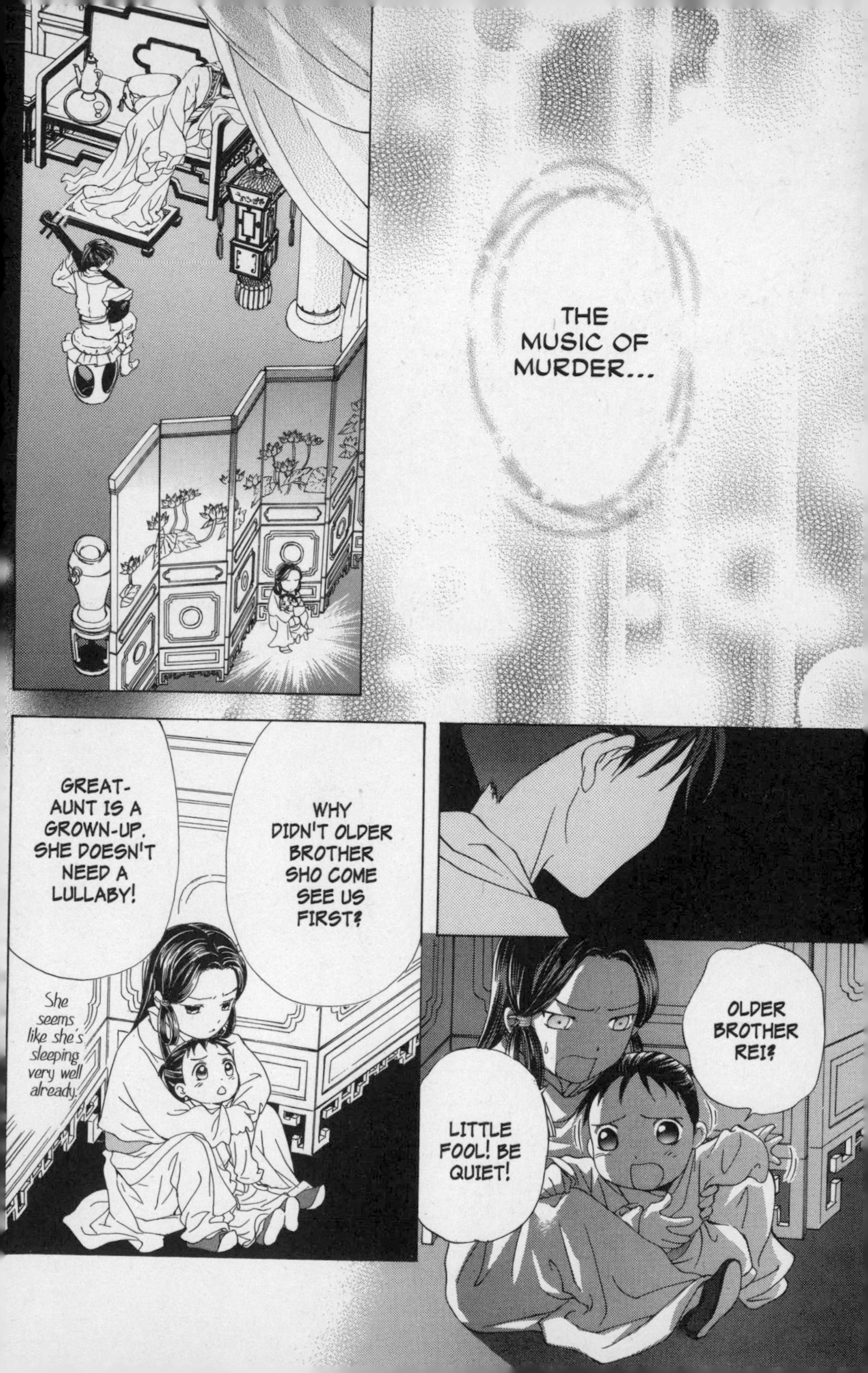
THE MUSIC OF MURDER...
OLDER BROTHER REI?
LITTLE FOOL! BE QUIET!
WHY DIDN'T OLDER BROTHER SHO COME SEE US FIRST?
GREAT-AUNT IS A GROWN-UP. SHE DOESN'T NEED A LULLABY!
She seems like she's sleeping very well already.

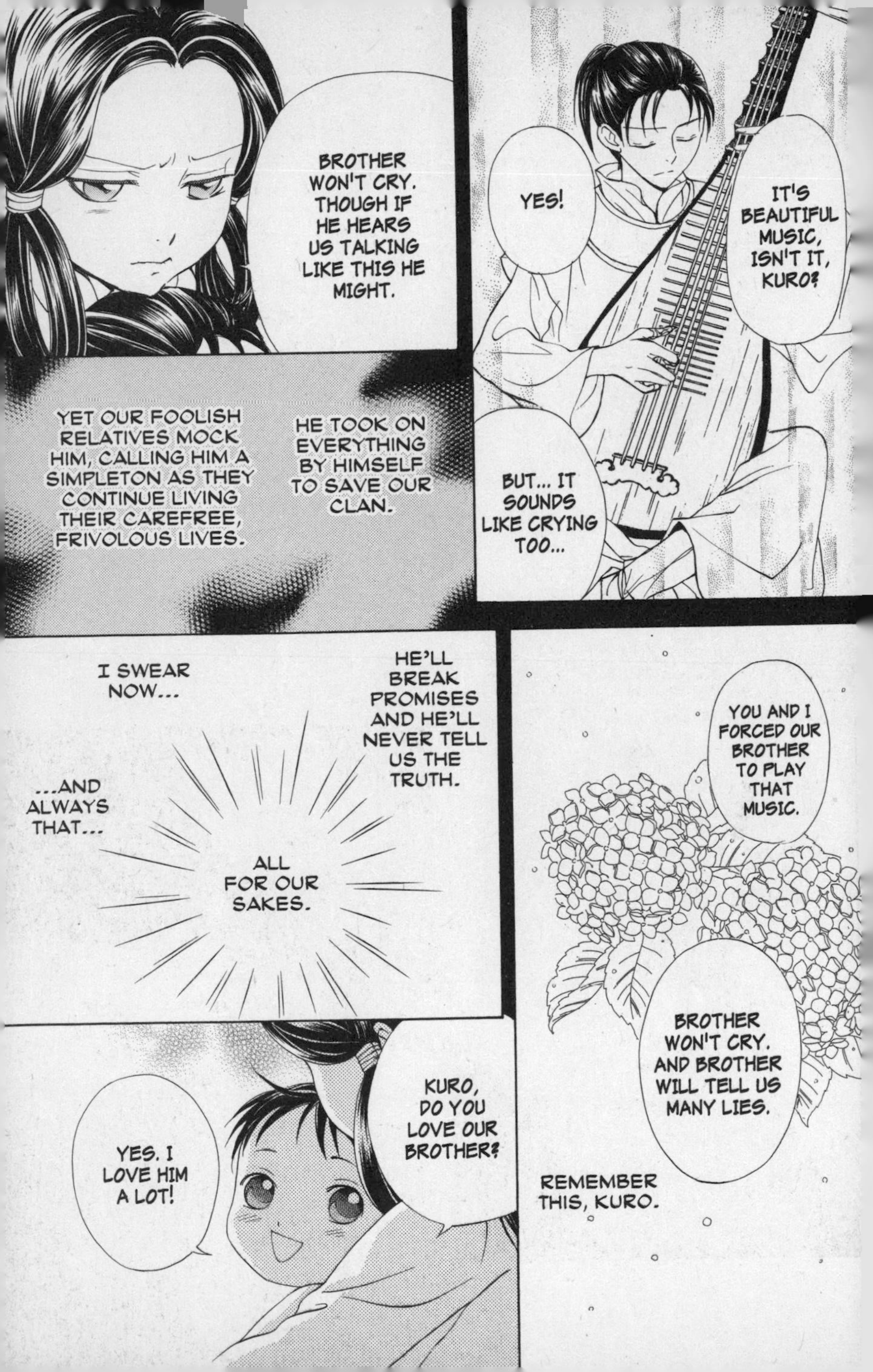
IT'S BEAUTIFUL MUSIC, ISN'T IT, KURO?
YES!
BUT... IT SOUNDS LIKE CRYING TOO...
BROTHER WON'T CRY. THOUGH IF HE HEARS US TALKING LIKE THIS HE MIGHT.
HE TOOK ON EVERYTHING BY HIMSELF TO SAVE OUR CLAN.
YET OUR FOOLISH RELATIVES MOCK HIM, CALLING HIM A SIMPLETON AS THEY CONTINUE LIVING THEIR CAREFREE, FRIVOLOUS LIVES.
YOU AND I FORCED OUR BROTHER TO PLAY THAT MUSIC.
BROTHER WON'T CRY. AND BROTHER WILL TELL US MANY LIES.
REMEMBER THIS, KURO.
HE'LL BREAK PROMISES AND HE'LL NEVER TELL US THE TRUTH.
I SWEAR NOW...
ALL FOR OUR SAKES.
...AND ALWAYS THAT...
KURO, DO YOU LOVE OUR BROTHER?
YES. I LOVE HIM A LOT!

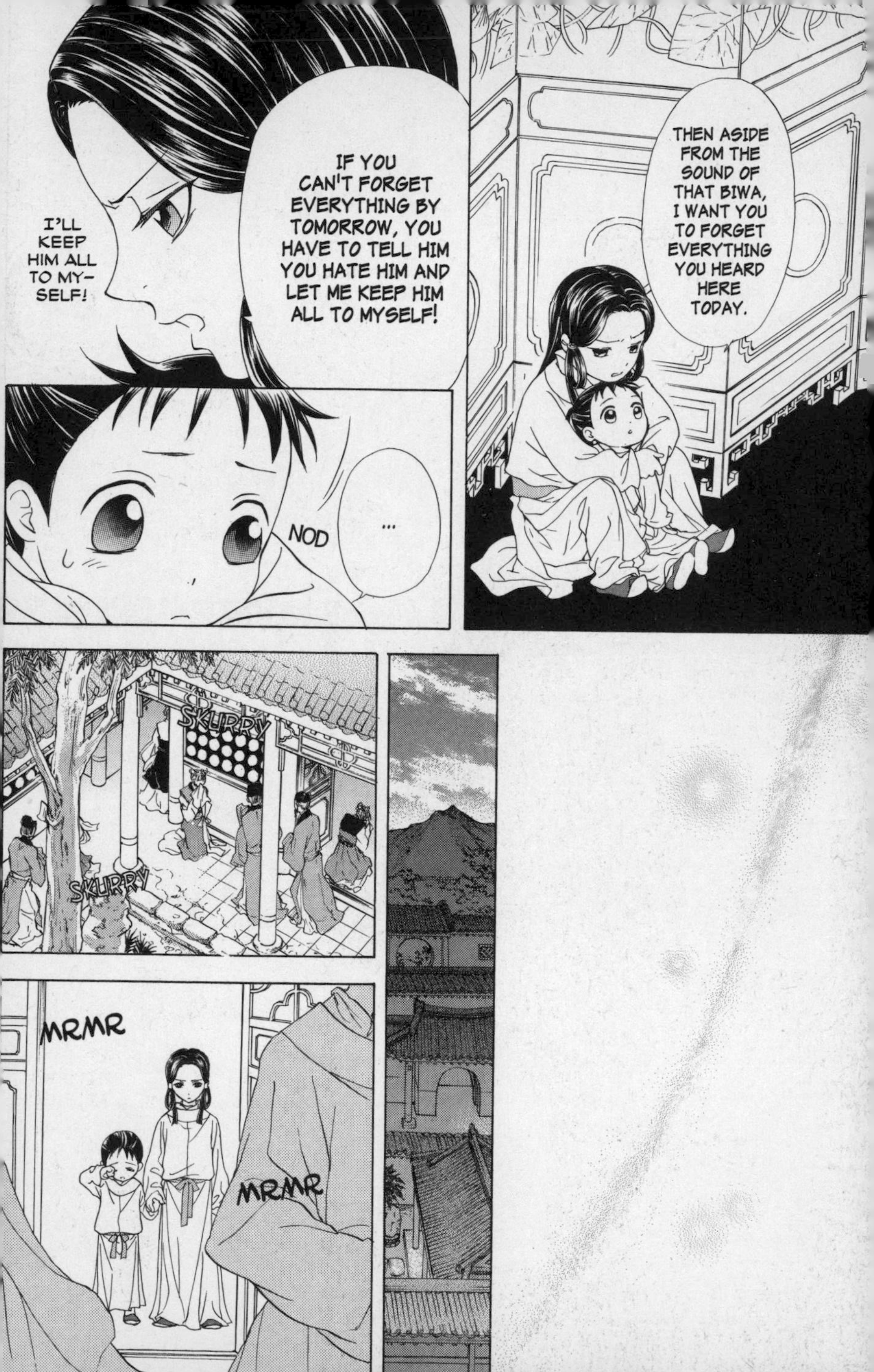
THEN ASIDE FROM THE SOUND OF THAT BIWA, I WANT YOU TO FORGET EVERYTHING YOU HEARD HERE TODAY.
IF YOU CAN'T FORGET EVERYTHING BY TOMORROW, YOU HAVE TO TELL HIM YOU HATE HIM AND LET ME KEEP HIM ALL TO MYSELF!
I'LL KEEP HIM ALL TO MY-SELF!
...
NOD
SKURRY
SKURRY
MRMR
MRMR

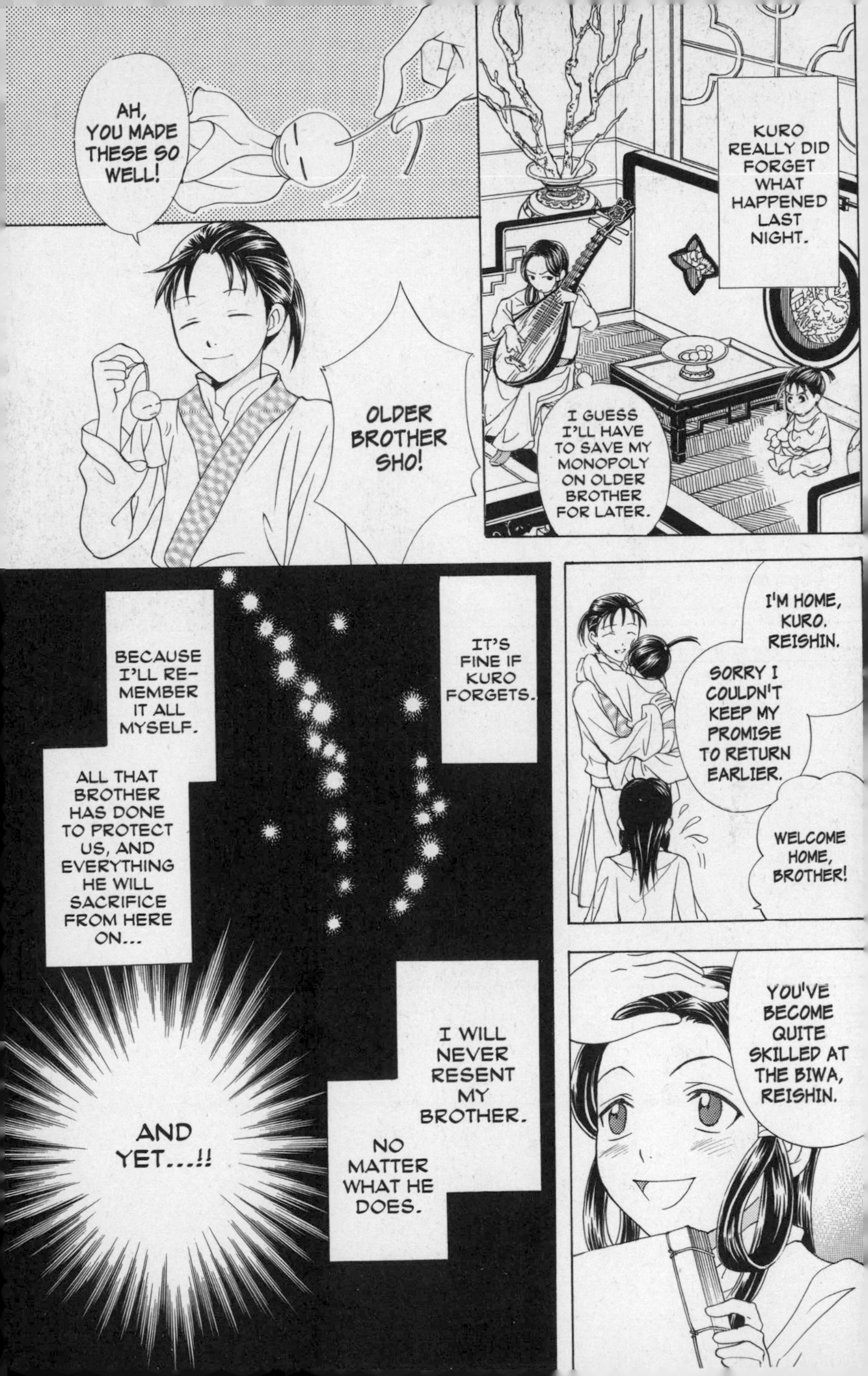
KURO REALLY DID FORGET WHAT HAPPENED LAST NIGHT.
I GUESS I'LL HAVE TO SAVE MY MONOPOLY ON OLDER BROTHER FOR LATER.
AH, YOU MADE THESE SO WELL!
OLDER BROTHER SHO!
I'M HOME, KURO. REISHIN.
SORRY I COULDN'T KEEP MY PROMISE TO RETURN EARLIER.
WELCOME HOME, BROTHER!
YOU'VE BECOME QUITE SKILLED AT THE BIWA, REISHIN.
IT'S FINE IF KURO FORGETS.
BECAUSE I'LL RE-MEMBER IT ALL MYSELF.
ALL THAT BROTHER HAS DONE TO PROTECT US, AND EVERYTHING HE WILL SACRIFICE FROM HERE ON...
I WILL NEVER RESENT MY BROTHER.
NO MATTER WHAT HE DOES.
AND YET...!!

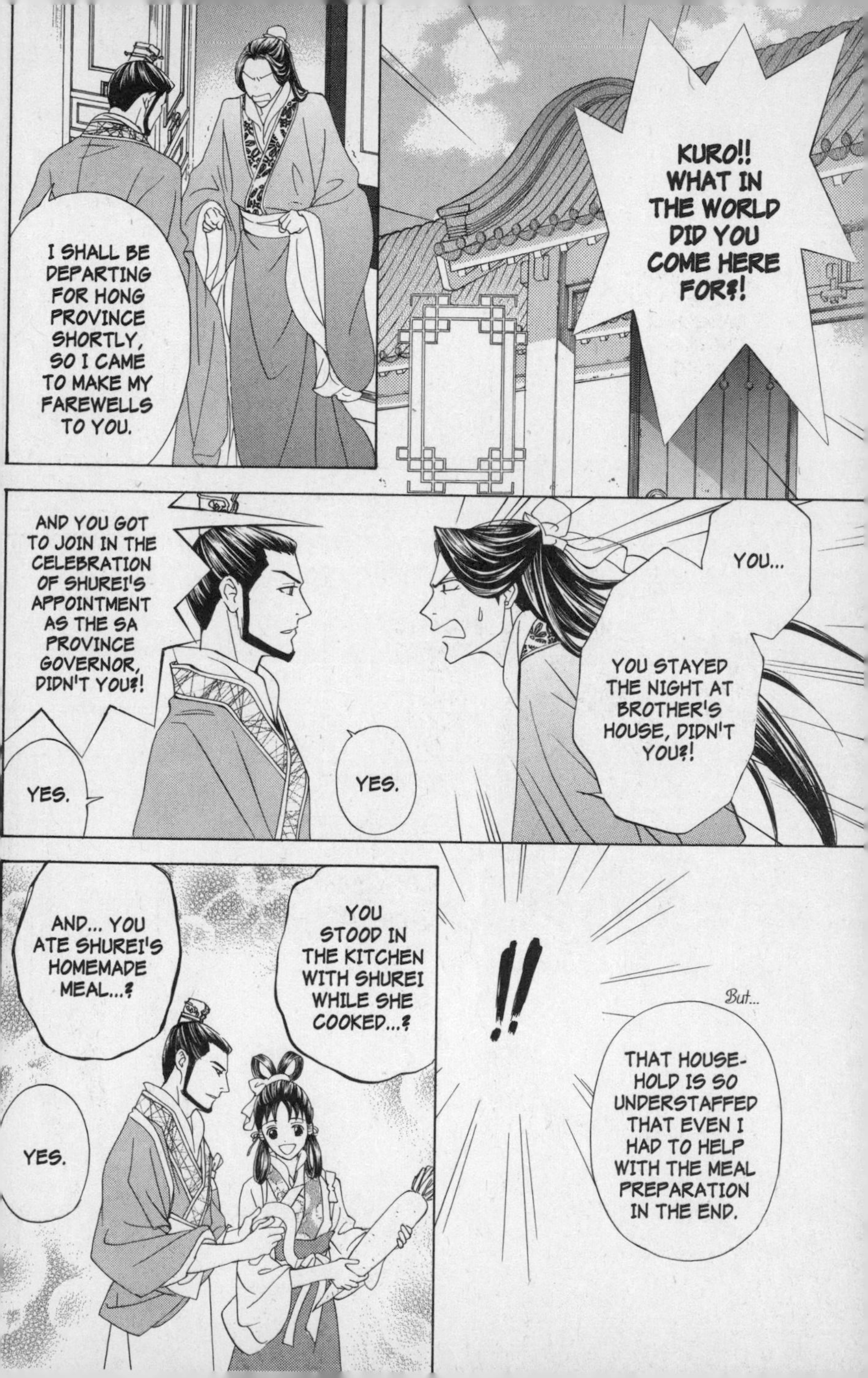
KURO!! WHAT IN THE WORLD DID YOU COME HERE FOR?!
I SHALL BE DEPARTING FOR HONG PROVINCE SHORTLY, SO I CAME TO MAKE MY FAREWELLS TO YOU.
YOU...
YOU STAYED THE NIGHT AT BROTHER'S HOUSE, DIDN'T YOU?!
AND YOU GOT TO JOIN IN THE CELEBRATION OF SHUREI'S APPOINTMENT AS THE SA PROVINCE GOVERNOR, DIDN'T YOU?!
YES.
YES.
!!
But...
THAT HOUSE-HOLD IS SO UNDERSTAFFED THAT EVEN I HAD TO HELP WITH THE MEAL PREPARATION IN THE END.
YOU STOOD IN THE KITCHEN WITH SHUREI WHILE SHE COOKED...?
AND... YOU ATE SHUREI'S HOMEMADE MEAL...?
YES.

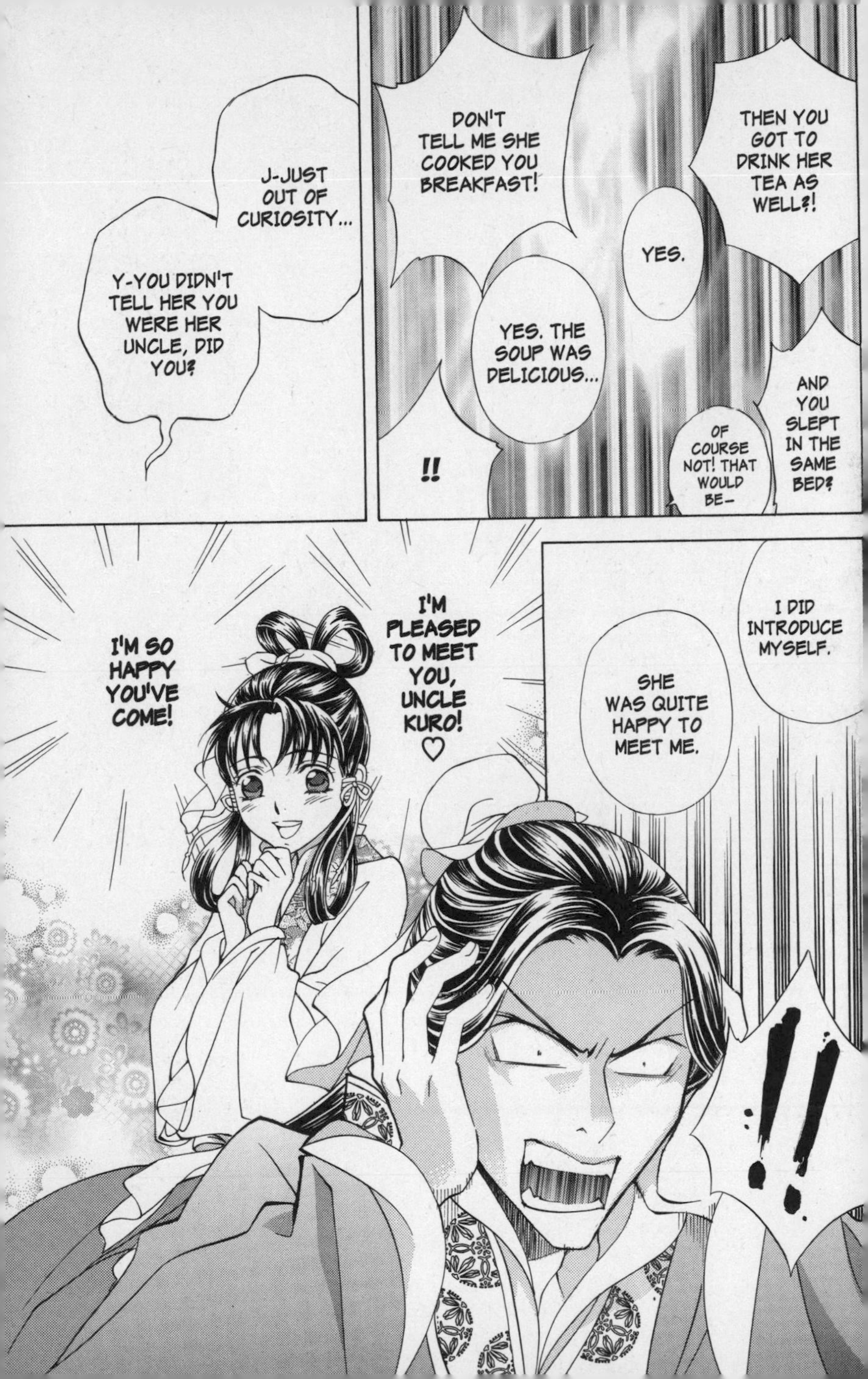
DON'T TELL ME SHE COOKED YOU BREAKFAST!
YES. THE SOUP WAS DELICIOUS...
THEN YOU GOT TO DRINK HER TEA AS WELL?!
YES.
AND YOU SLEPT IN THE SAME BED?
OF COURSE NOT! THAT WOULD BE-
!!
J-JUST OUT OF CURIOSITY...
Y-YOU DIDN'T TELL HER YOU WERE HER UNCLE, DID YOU?
I DID INTRODUCE MYSELF.
SHE WAS QUITE HAPPY TO MEET ME.
I'M PLEASED TO MEET YOU, UNCLE KURO! ♡
I'M SO HAPPY YOU'VE COME!
!!

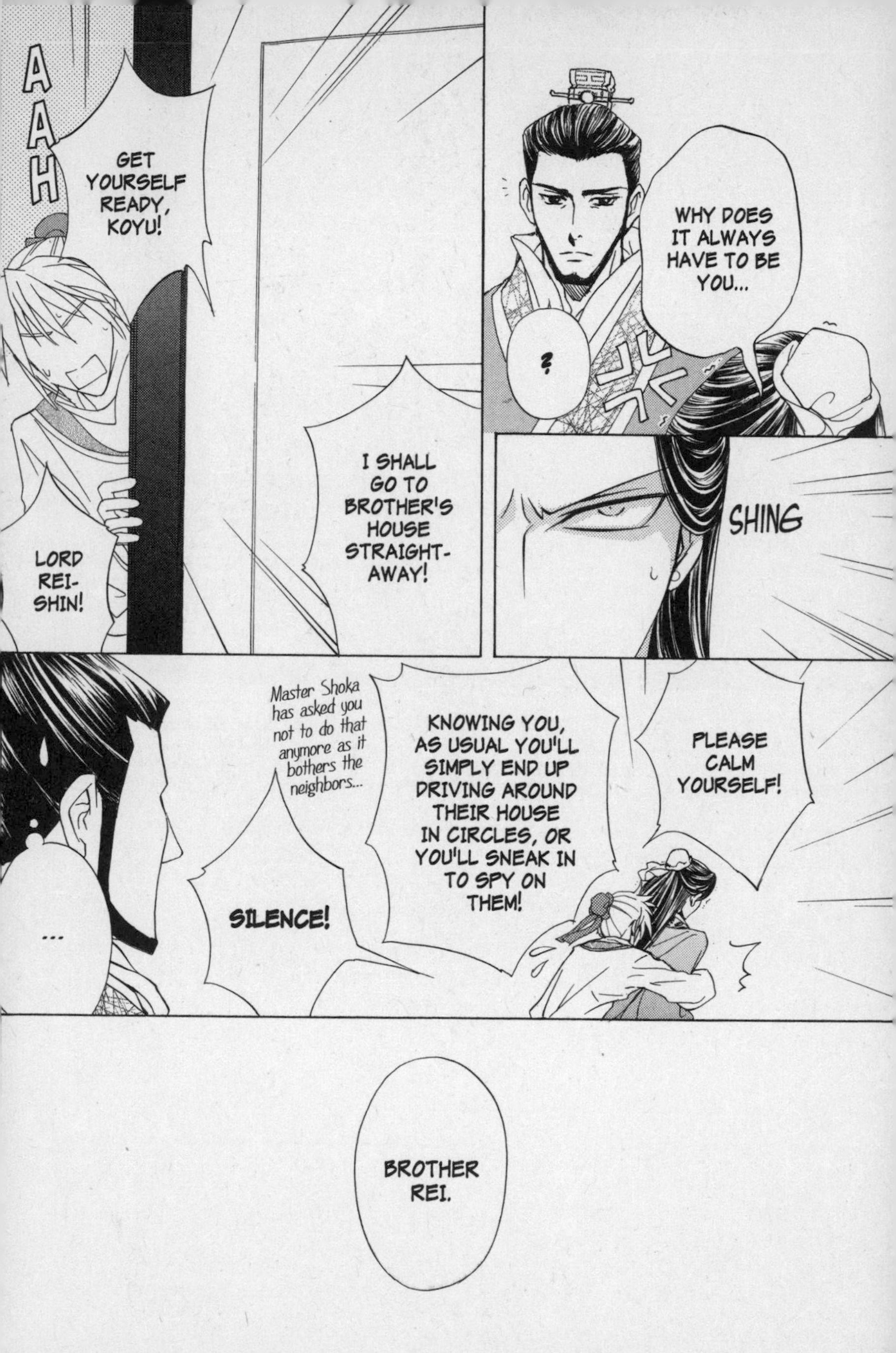
WHY DOES IT ALWAYS HAVE TO BE YOU...
?
SHING
I SHALL GO TO BROTHER'S HOUSE STRAIGHT-AWAY!
GET YOURSELF READY, KOYU!
AAAH
LORD REI-SHIN!
PLEASE CALM YOURSELF!
KNOWING YOU, AS USUAL YOU'LL SIMPLY END UP DRIVING AROUND THEIR HOUSE IN CIRCLES, OR YOU'LL SNEAK IN TO SPY ON THEM!
Master Shoka has asked you not to do that anymore as it bothers the neighbors...
SILENCE!
...
BROTHER REI.

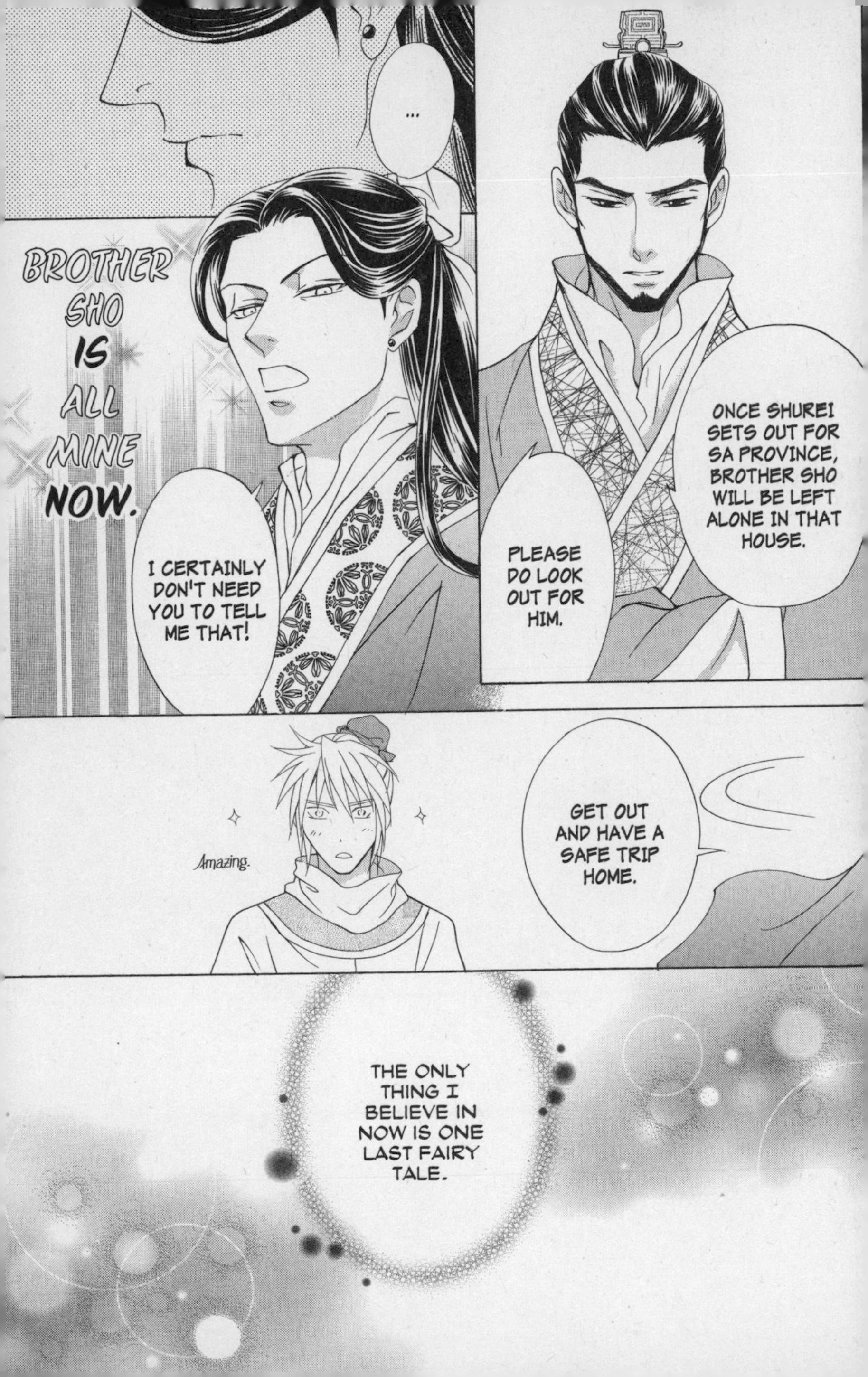
ONCE SHUREI SETS OUT FOR SA PROVINCE, BROTHER SHO WILL BE LEFT ALONE IN THAT HOUSE.
PLEASE DO LOOK OUT FOR HIM.
...
I CERTAINLY DON'T NEED YOU TO TELL ME THAT!
BROTHER SHO IS ALL MINE NOW.
GET OUT AND HAVE A SAFE TRIP HOME.
Amazing.
THE ONLY THING I BELIEVE IN NOW IS ONE LAST FAIRY TALE.

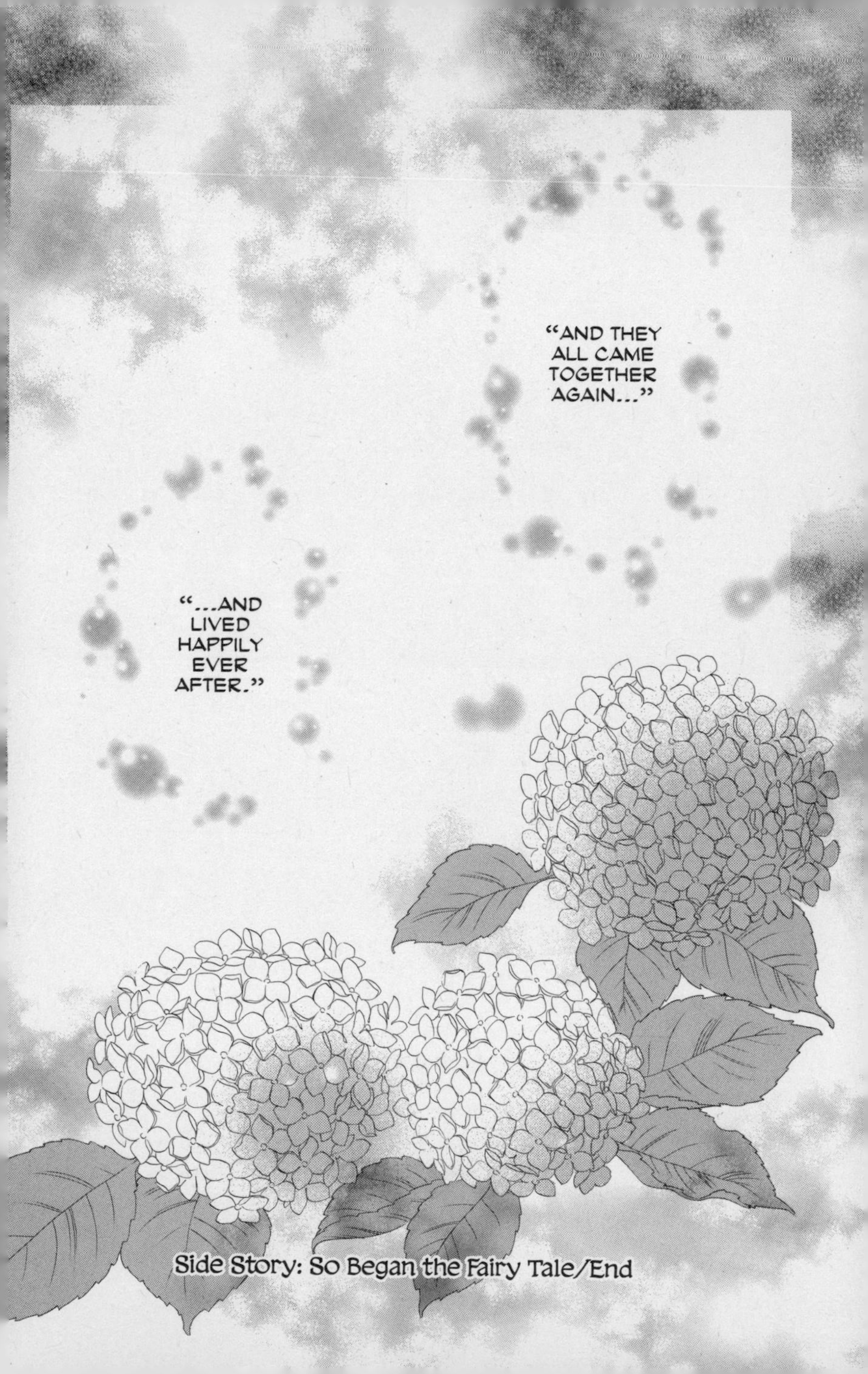
"AND THEY ALL CAME TOGETHER AGAIN..."
"...AND LIVED HAPPILY EVER AFTER."
Side Story: So Began the Fairy Tale/End

The Story of SAIUNKOKU

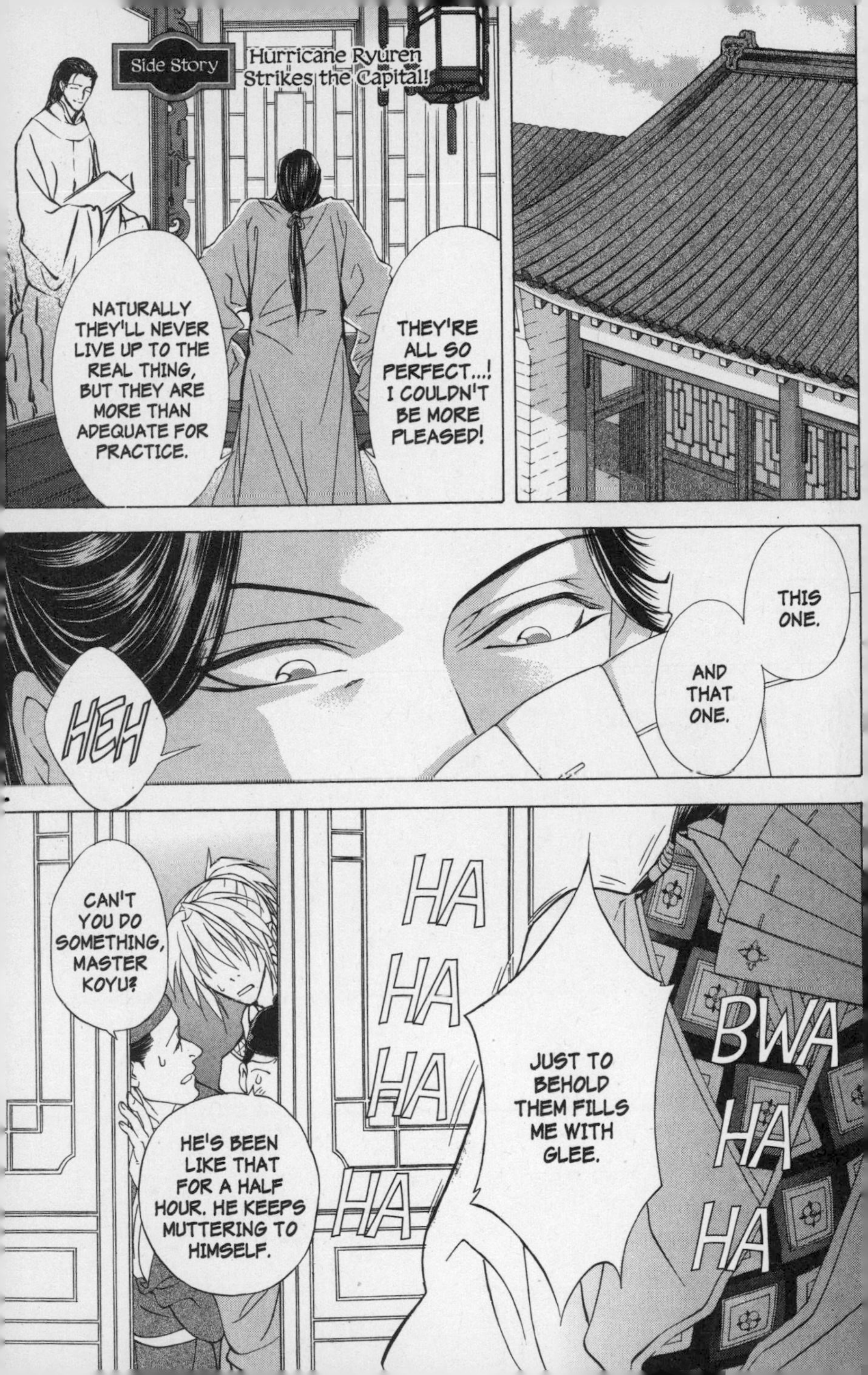
Side Story
Hurricane Ryuren Strikes the Capital!
THEY'RE ALL SO PERFECT...! I COULDN'T BE MORE PLEASED!
NATURALLY THEY'LL NEVER LIVE UP TO THE REAL THING, BUT THEY ARE MORE THAN ADEQUATE FOR PRACTICE.
THIS ONE.
AND THAT ONE.
HEH
BWA HA HA HA
JUST TO BEHOLD THEM FILLS ME WITH GLEE.
HA HA HA HA
CAN'T YOU DO SOMETHING, MASTER KOYU?
HE'S BEEN LIKE THAT FOR A HALF HOUR. HE KEEPS MUTTERING TO HIMSELF.

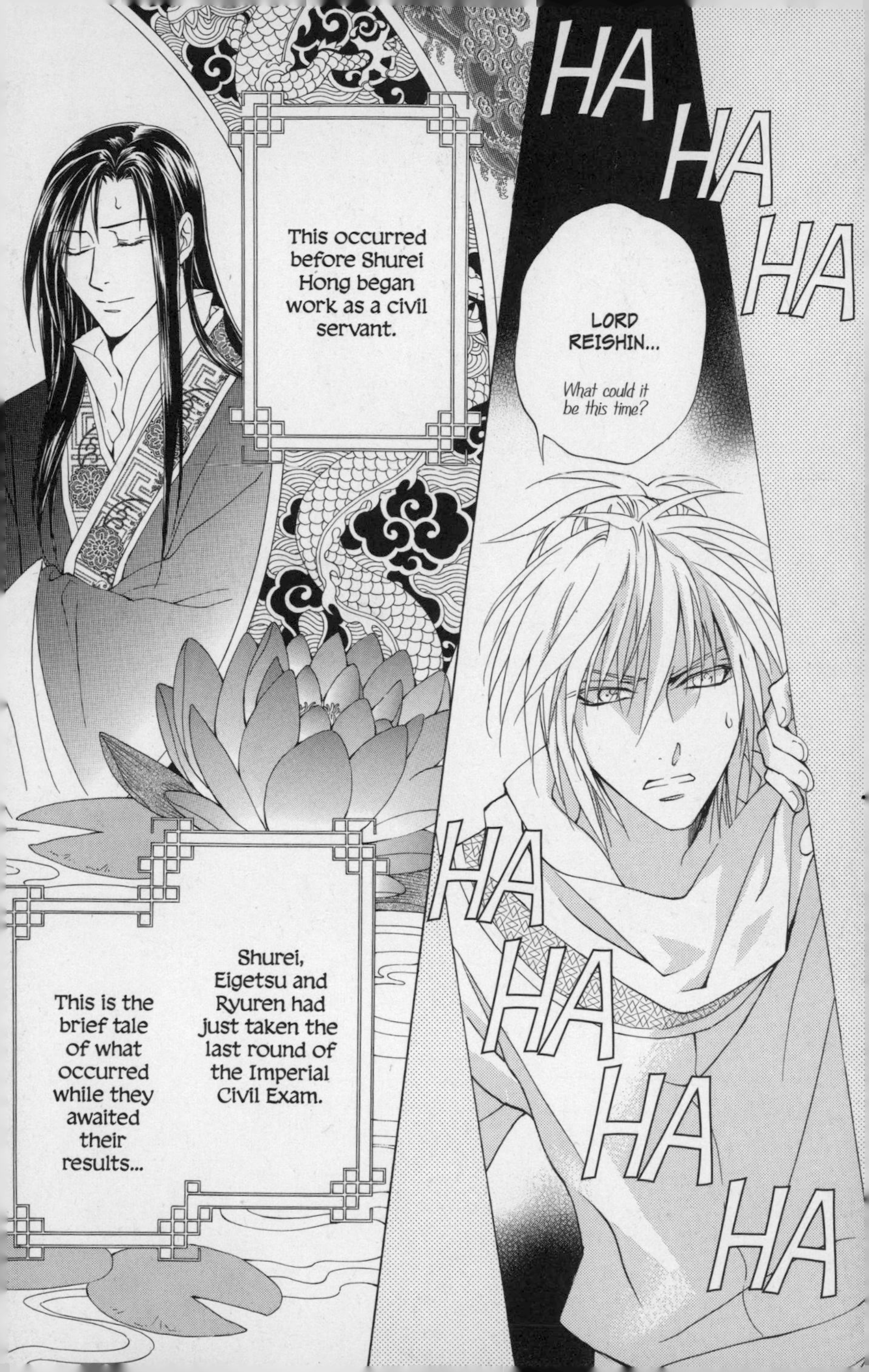
HA HA HA HA
LORD REISHIN...
What could it be this time?
HA HA HA HA
This occurred before Shurei Hong began work as a civil servant.
Shurei, Eigetsu and Ryuren had just taken the last round of the Imperial Civil Exam.
This is the brief tale of what occurred while they awaited their results...

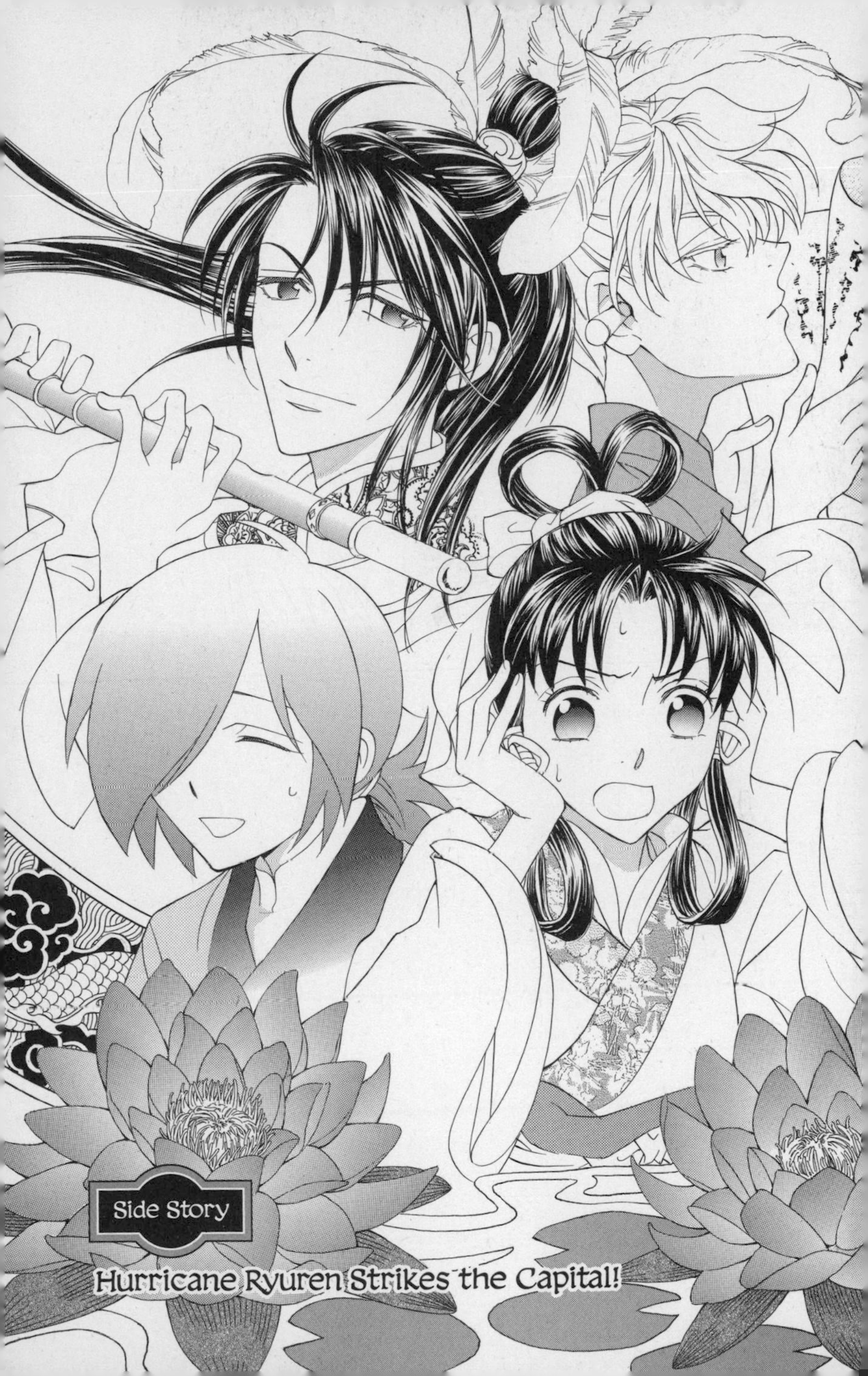
Side Story
Hurricane Ryuren Strikes the Capital!

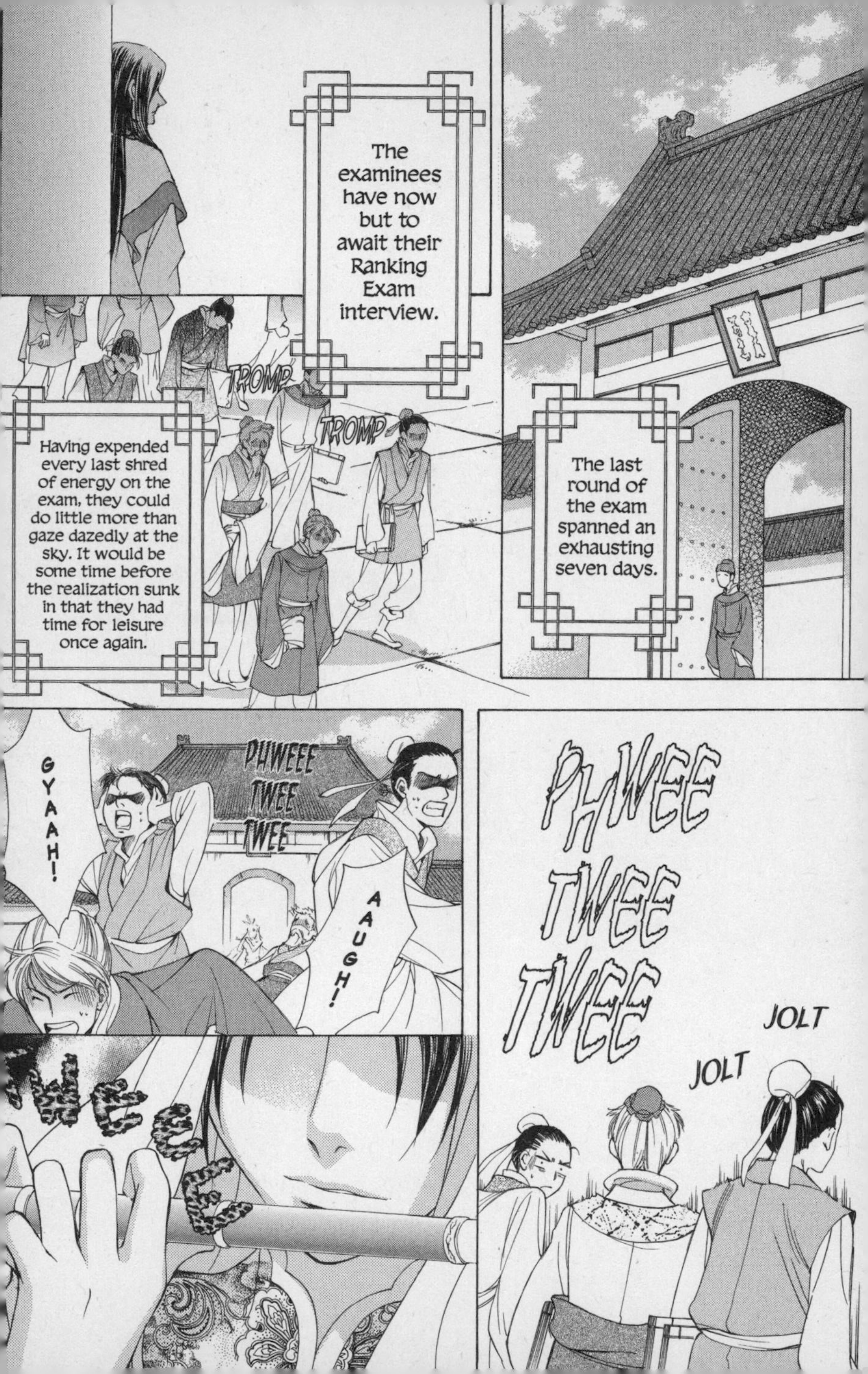
The last round of the exam spanned an exhausting seven days.
The examinees have now but to await their Ranking Exam interview.
TROMP
TROMP
Having expended every last shred of energy on the exam, they could do little more than gaze dazedly at the sky. It would be some time before the realization sunk in that they had time for leisure once again.
PHWEE TWEE TWEE
JOLT
JOLT
PHWEEE TWEE TWEE
AAUGH!
GYAAH!

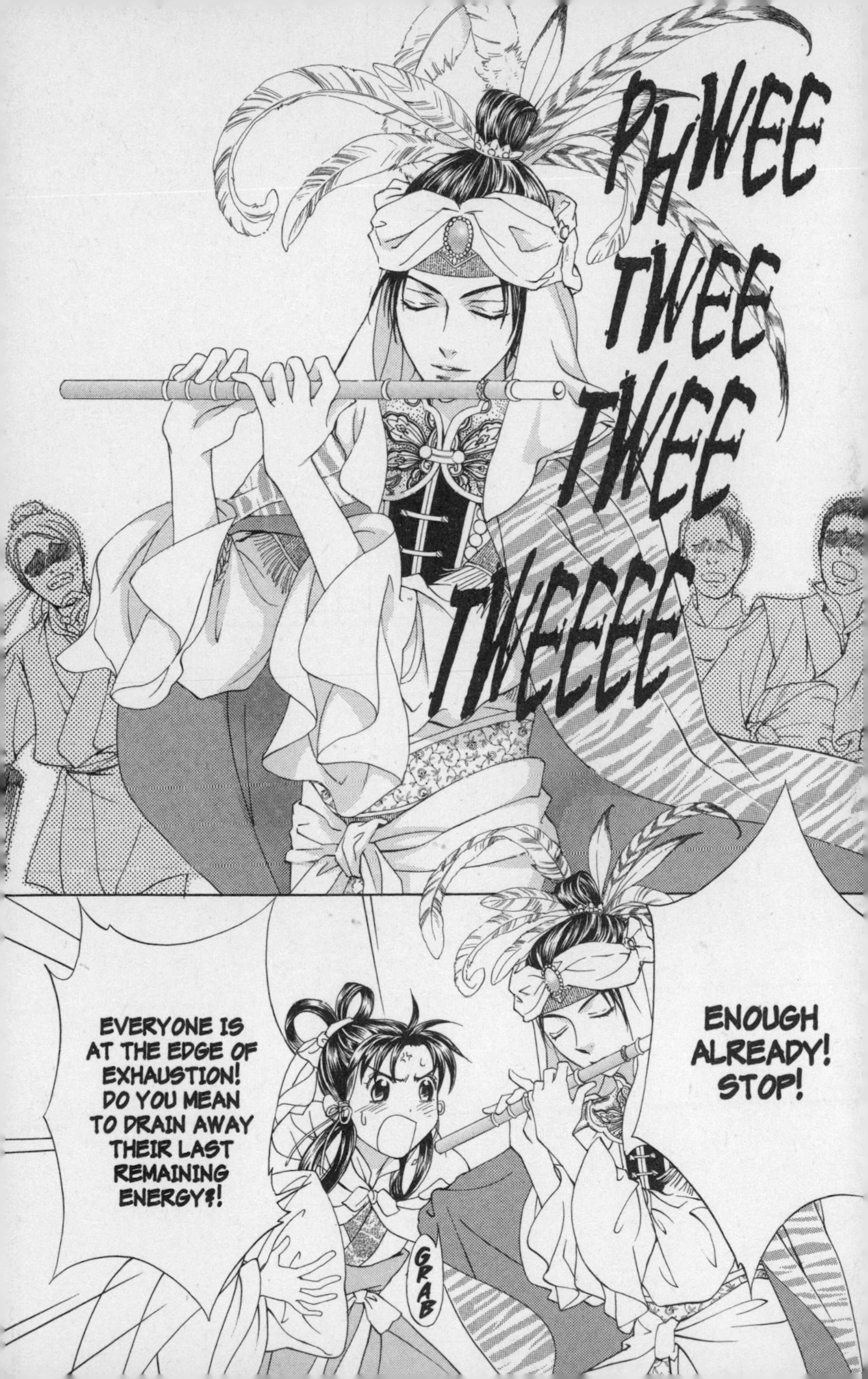
PHWEE TWEE TWEE TWEEEEE
ENOUGH ALREADY! STOP!
EVERYONE IS AT THE EDGE OF EXHAUSTION! DO YOU MEAN TO DRAIN AWAY THEIR LAST REMAINING ENERGY?!
GRAB

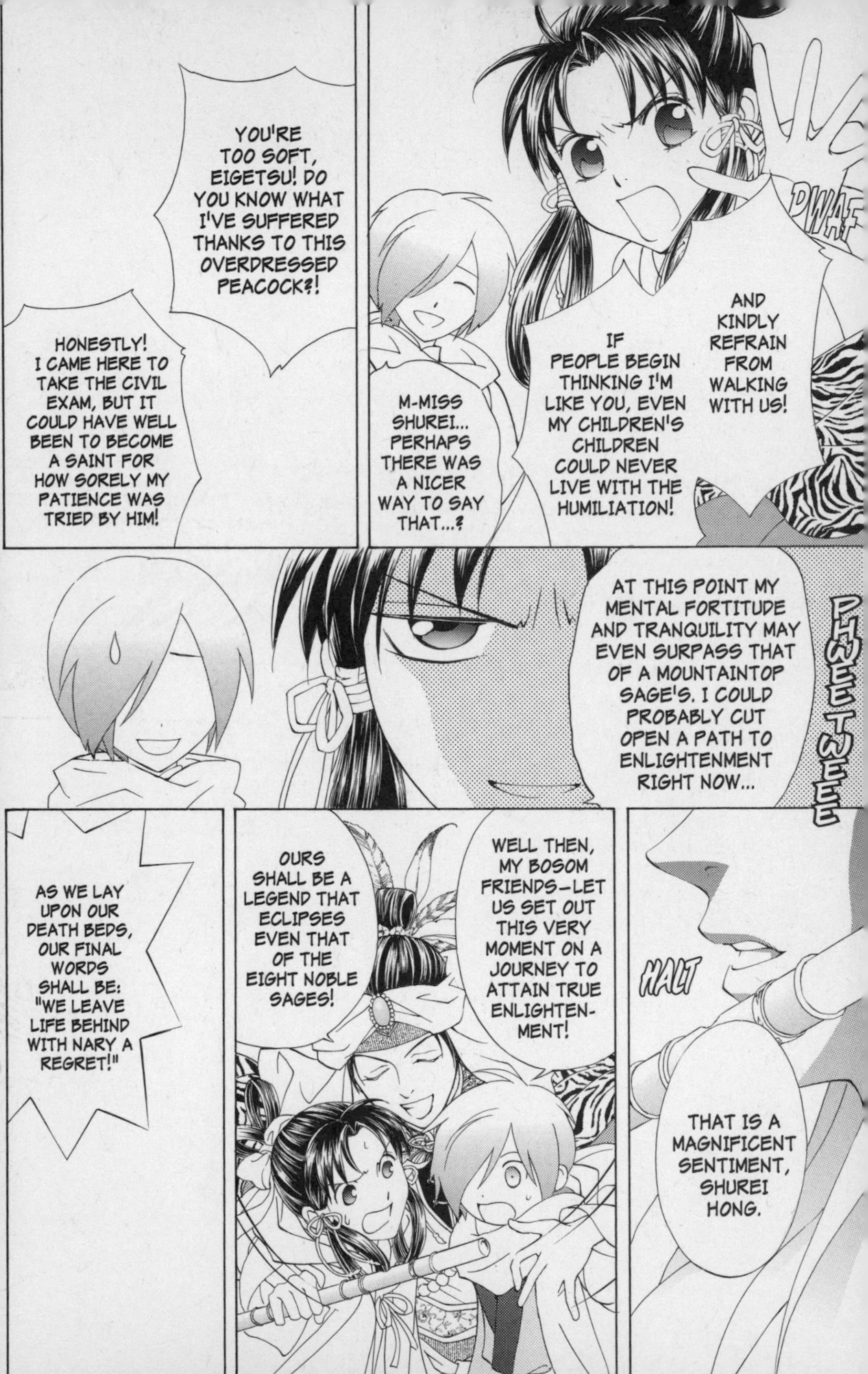

AND KINDLY REFRAIN FROM WALKING WITH US!
DWAF
IF PEOPLE BEGIN THINKING I'M LIKE YOU, EVEN MY CHILDREN'S CHILDREN COULD NEVER LIVE WITH THE HUMILIATION!
M-MISS SHUREI... PERHAPS THERE WAS A NICER WAY TO SAY THAT...?
YOU'RE TOO SOFT, EIGETSU! DO YOU KNOW WHAT I'VE SUFFERED THANKS TO THIS OVERDRESSED PEACOCK?!
HONESTLY! I CAME HERE TO TAKE THE CIVIL EXAM, BUT IT COULD HAVE WELL BEEN TO BECOME A SAINT FOR HOW SORELY MY PATIENCE WAS TRIED BY HIM!
PHWEE TWEE
AT THIS POINT MY MENTAL FORTITUDE AND TRANQUILITY MAY EVEN SURPASS THAT OF A MOUNTAINTOP SAGE'S. I COULD PROBABLY CUT OPEN A PATH TO ENLIGHTENMENT RIGHT NOW...
HALT
THAT IS A MAGNIFICENT SENTIMENT, SHUREI HONG.
WELL THEN, MY BOSOM FRIENDS—LET US SET OUT THIS VERY MOMENT ON A JOURNEY TO ATTAIN TRUE ENLIGHTEN-MENT!
OURS SHALL BE A LEGEND THAT ECLIPSES EVEN THAT OF THE EIGHT NOBLE SAGES!
AS WE LAY UPON OUR DEATH BEDS, OUR FINAL WORDS SHALL BE: "WE LEAVE LIFE BEHIND WITH NARY A REGRET!"

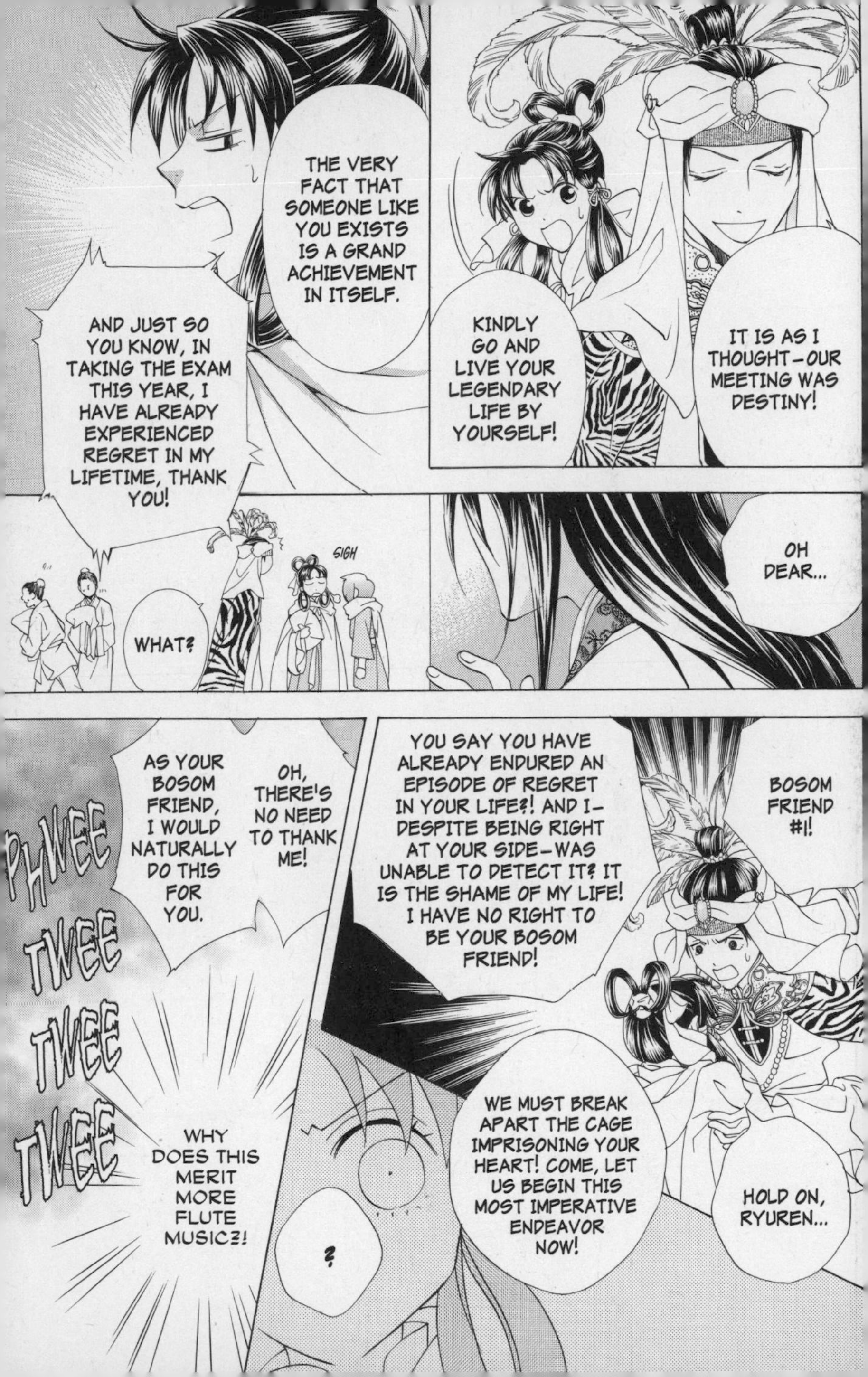
IT IS AS I THOUGHT—OUR MEETING WAS DESTINY!
KINDLY GO AND LIVE YOUR LEGENDARY LIFE BY YOURSELF!
THE VERY FACT THAT SOMEONE LIKE YOU EXISTS IS A GRAND ACHIEVEMENT IN ITSELF.
AND JUST SO YOU KNOW, IN TAKING THE EXAM THIS YEAR, I HAVE ALREADY EXPERIENCED REGRET IN MY LIFETIME, THANK YOU!
OH DEAR...
SIGH
WHAT?
BOSOM FRIEND #1!
YOU SAY YOU HAVE ALREADY ENDURED AN EPISODE OF REGRET IN YOUR LIFE?! AND I—DESPITE BEING RIGHT AT YOUR SIDE—WAS UNABLE TO DETECT IT? IT IS THE SHAME OF MY LIFE! I HAVE NO RIGHT TO BE YOUR BOSOM FRIEND!
HOLD ON, RYUREN...
WE MUST BREAK APART THE CAGE IMPRISONING YOUR HEART! COME, LET US BEGIN THIS MOST IMPERATIVE ENDEAVOR NOW!
?
OH, THERE'S NO NEED TO THANK ME!
AS YOUR BOSOM FRIEND, I WOULD NATURALLY DO THIS FOR YOU.
PHWEE TWEE TWEE TWEE
WHY DOES THIS MERIT MORE FLUTE MUSIC?!

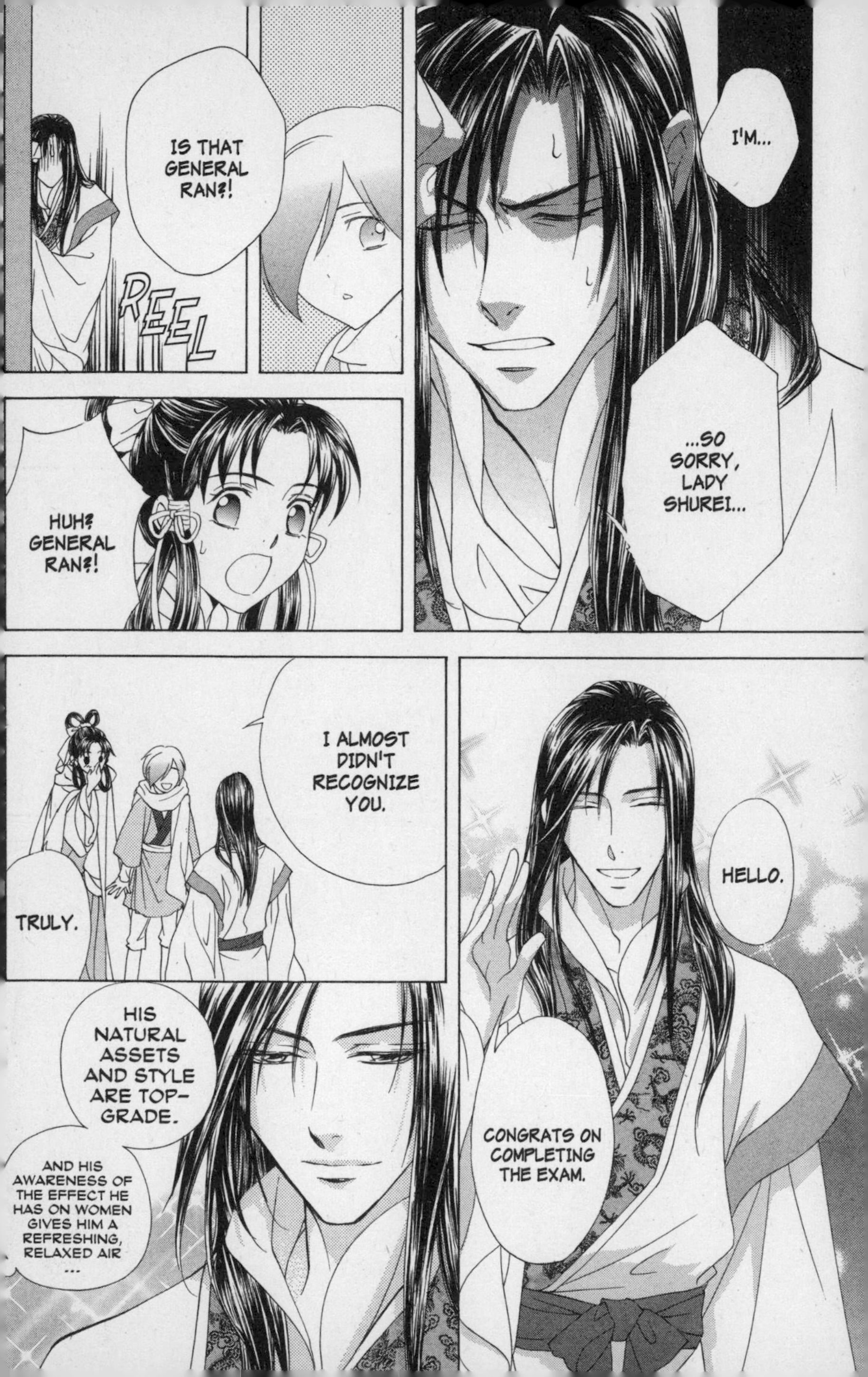
I'M...
...SO SORRY, LADY SHUREI...
IS THAT GENERAL RAN?!
REEL
HUH? GENERAL RAN?!
HELLO.
CONGRATS ON COMPLETING THE EXAM.
I ALMOST DIDN'T RECOGNIZE YOU.
TRULY.
HIS NATURAL ASSETS AND STYLE ARE TOP-GRADE.
AND HIS AWARENESS OF THE EFFECT HE HAS ON WOMEN GIVES HIM A REFRESHING, RELAXED AIR ...

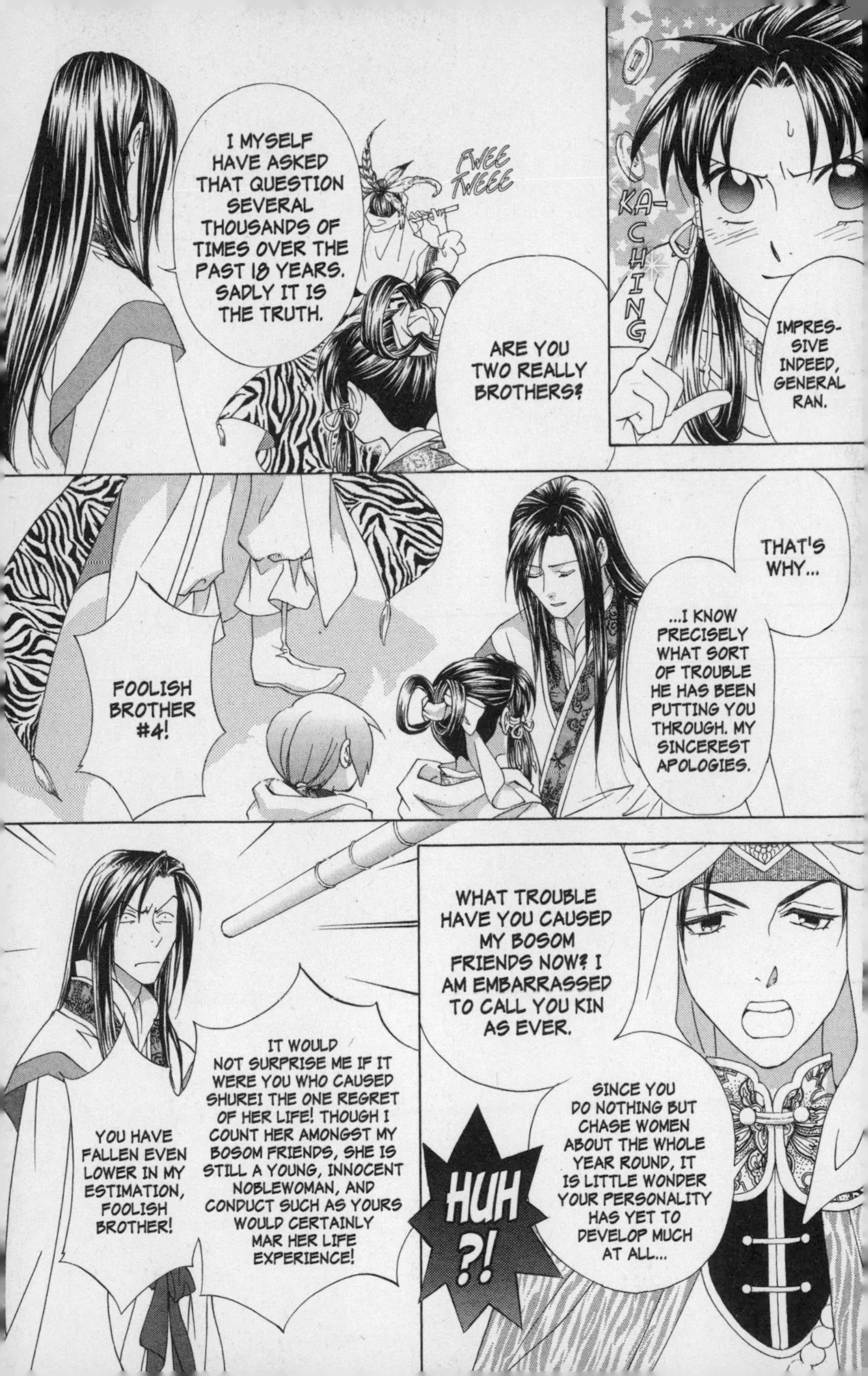
KA-CHING
IMPRES-SIVE INDEED, GENERAL RAN.
ARE YOU TWO REALLY BROTHERS?
FWEE TWEEE
I MYSELF HAVE ASKED THAT QUESTION SEVERAL THOUSANDS OF TIMES OVER THE PAST 18 YEARS. SADLY IT IS THE TRUTH.
THAT'S WHY...
...I KNOW PRECISELY WHAT SORT OF TROUBLE HE HAS BEEN PUTTING YOU THROUGH. MY SINCEREST APOLOGIES.
FOOLISH BROTHER #4!
WHAT TROUBLE HAVE YOU CAUSED MY BOSOM FRIENDS NOW? I AM EMBARRASSED TO CALL YOU KIN AS EVER.
SINCE YOU DO NOTHING BUT CHASE WOMEN ABOUT THE WHOLE YEAR ROUND, IT IS LITTLE WONDER YOUR PERSONALITY HAS YET TO DEVELOP MUCH AT ALL...
HUH ?!
IT WOULD NOT SURPRISE ME IF IT WERE YOU WHO CAUSED SHUREI THE ONE REGRET OF HER LIFE! THOUGH I COUNT HER AMONGST MY BOSOM FRIENDS, SHE IS STILL A YOUNG, INNOCENT NOBLEWOMAN, AND CONDUCT SUCH AS YOURS WOULD CERTAINLY MAR HER LIFE EXPERIENCE!
YOU HAVE FALLEN EVEN LOWER IN MY ESTIMATION, FOOLISH BROTHER!

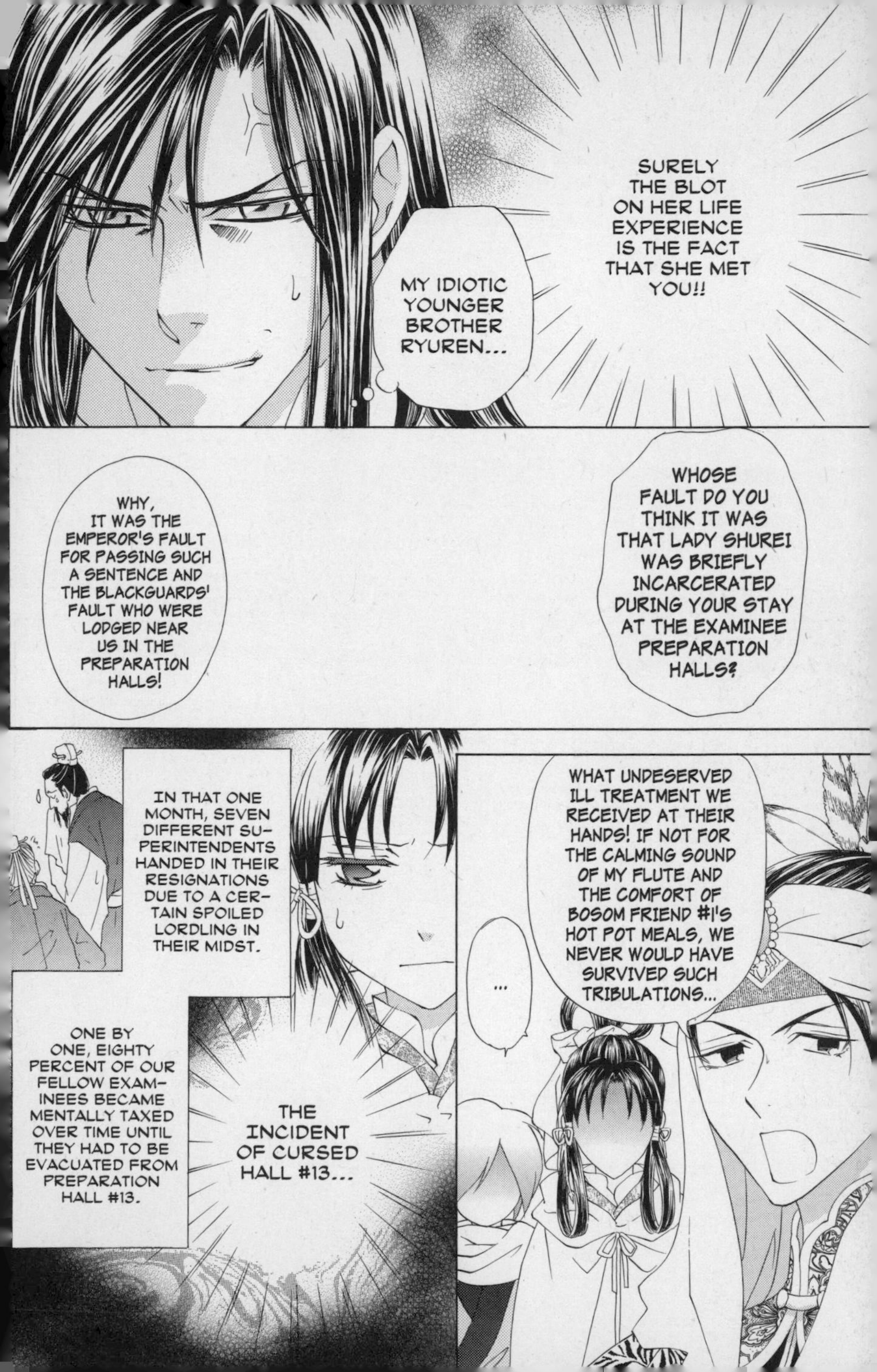

SURELY THE BLOT ON HER LIFE EXPERIENCE IS THE FACT THAT SHE MET YOU!!
MY IDIOTIC YOUNGER BROTHER RYUREN...
WHOSE FAULT DO YOU THINK IT WAS THAT LADY SHUREI WAS BRIEFLY INCARCERATED DURING YOUR STAY AT THE EXAMINEE PREPARATION HALLS?
WHY, IT WAS THE EMPEROR'S FAULT FOR PASSING SUCH A SENTENCE AND THE BLACKGUARDS' FAULT WHO WERE LODGED NEAR US IN THE PREPARATION HALLS!
WHAT UNDESERVED ILL TREATMENT WE RECEIVED AT THEIR HANDS! IF NOT FOR THE CALMING SOUND OF MY FLUTE AND THE COMFORT OF BOSOM FRIEND #1'S HOT POT MEALS, WE NEVER WOULD HAVE SURVIVED SUCH TRIBULATIONS...
...
IN THAT ONE MONTH, SEVEN DIFFERENT SUPERINTENDENTS HANDED IN THEIR RESIGNATIONS DUE TO A CERTAIN SPOILED LORDLING IN THEIR MIDST.
ONE BY ONE, EIGHTY PERCENT OF OUR FELLOW EXAMINEES BECAME MENTALLY TAXED OVER TIME UNTIL THEY HAD TO BE EVACUATED FROM PREPARATION HALL #13.
THE INCIDENT OF CURSED HALL #13...

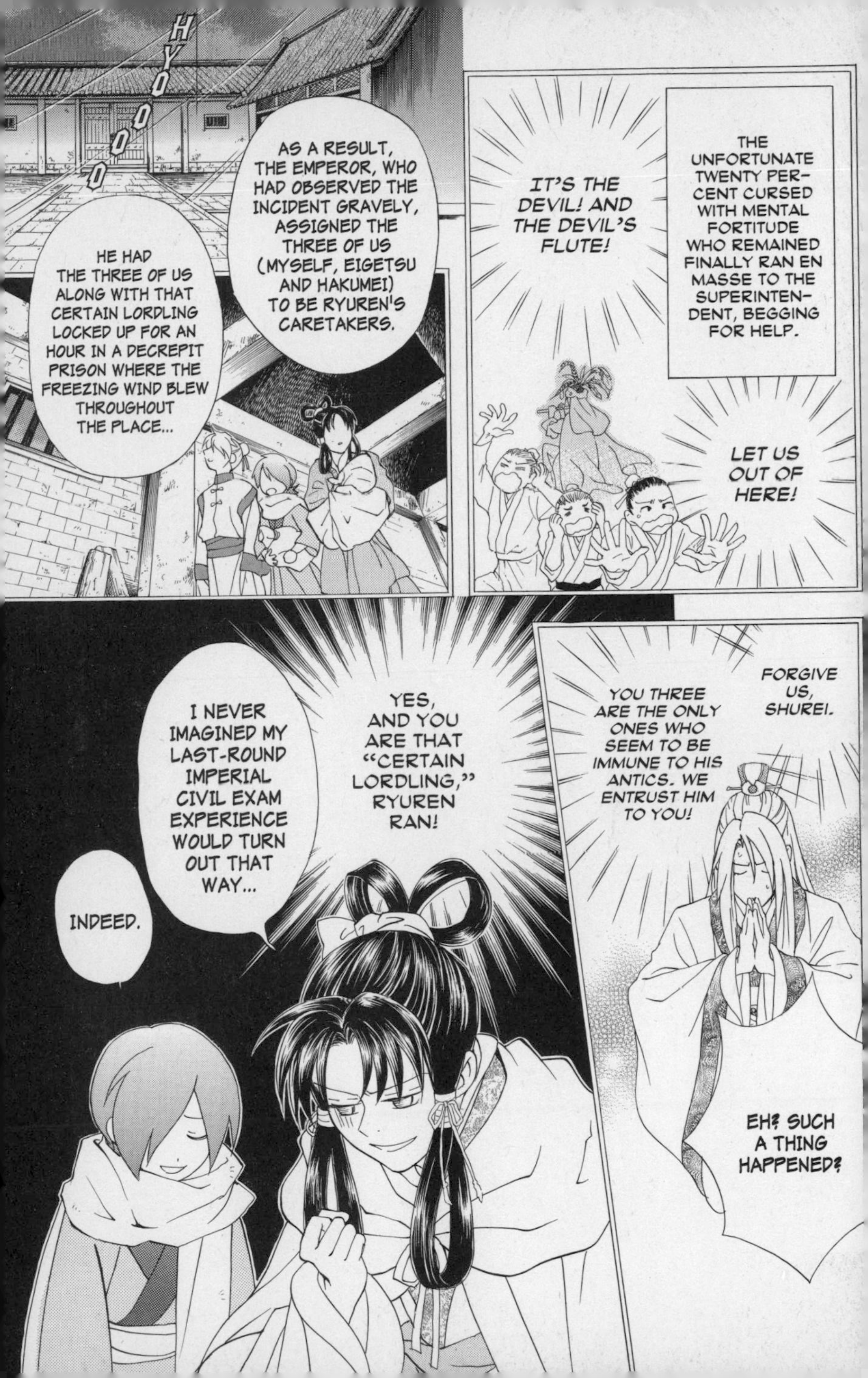
THE UNFORTUNATE TWENTY PERCENT CURSED WITH MENTAL FORTITUDE WHO REMAINED FINALLY RAN EN MASSE TO THE SUPERINTENDENT, BEGGING FOR HELP.
IT'S THE DEVIL! AND THE DEVIL'S FLUTE!
LET US OUT OF HERE!
HYOOOOO
AS A RESULT, THE EMPEROR, WHO HAD OBSERVED THE INCIDENT GRAVELY, ASSIGNED THE THREE OF US (MYSELF, EIGETSU AND HAKUMEI) TO BE RYUREN'S CARETAKERS.
HE HAD THE THREE OF US ALONG WITH THAT CERTAIN LORDLING LOCKED UP FOR AN HOUR IN A DECREPIT PRISON WHERE THE FREEZING WIND BLEW THROUGHOUT THE PLACE...
FORGIVE US, SHUREI.
YOU THREE ARE THE ONLY ONES WHO SEEM TO BE IMMUNE TO HIS ANTICS. WE ENTRUST HIM TO YOU!
EH? SUCH A THING HAPPENED?
YES, AND YOU ARE THAT "CERTAIN LORDLING," RYUREN RAN!
I NEVER IMAGINED MY LAST-ROUND IMPERIAL CIVIL EXAM EXPERIENCE WOULD TURN OUT THAT WAY...
INDEED.

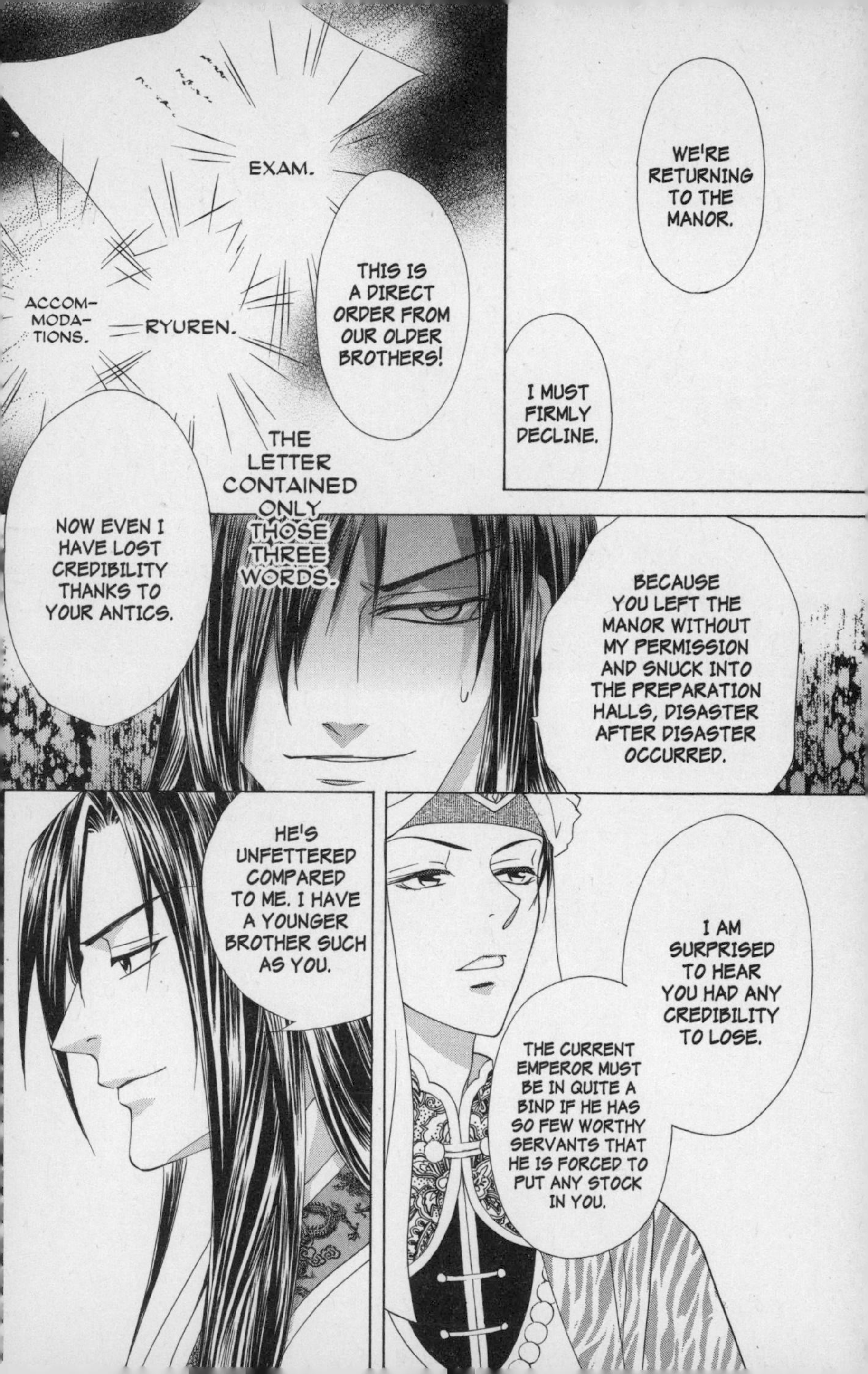
WE'RE RETURNING TO THE MANOR.
I MUST FIRMLY DECLINE.
THIS IS A DIRECT ORDER FROM OUR OLDER BROTHERS!
EXAM.
RYUREN.
ACCOM-MODA-TIONS.
THE LETTER CONTAINED ONLY THOSE THREE WORDS.
BECAUSE YOU LEFT THE MANOR WITHOUT MY PERMISSION AND SNUCK INTO THE PREPARATION HALLS, DISASTER AFTER DISASTER OCCURRED.
NOW EVEN I HAVE LOST CREDIBILITY THANKS TO YOUR ANTICS.
I AM SURPRISED TO HEAR YOU HAD ANY CREDIBILITY TO LOSE.
THE CURRENT EMPEROR MUST BE IN QUITE A BIND IF HE HAS SO FEW WORTHY SERVANTS THAT HE IS FORCED TO PUT ANY STOCK IN YOU.
HE'S UNFETTERED COMPARED TO ME. I HAVE A YOUNGER BROTHER SUCH AS YOU.

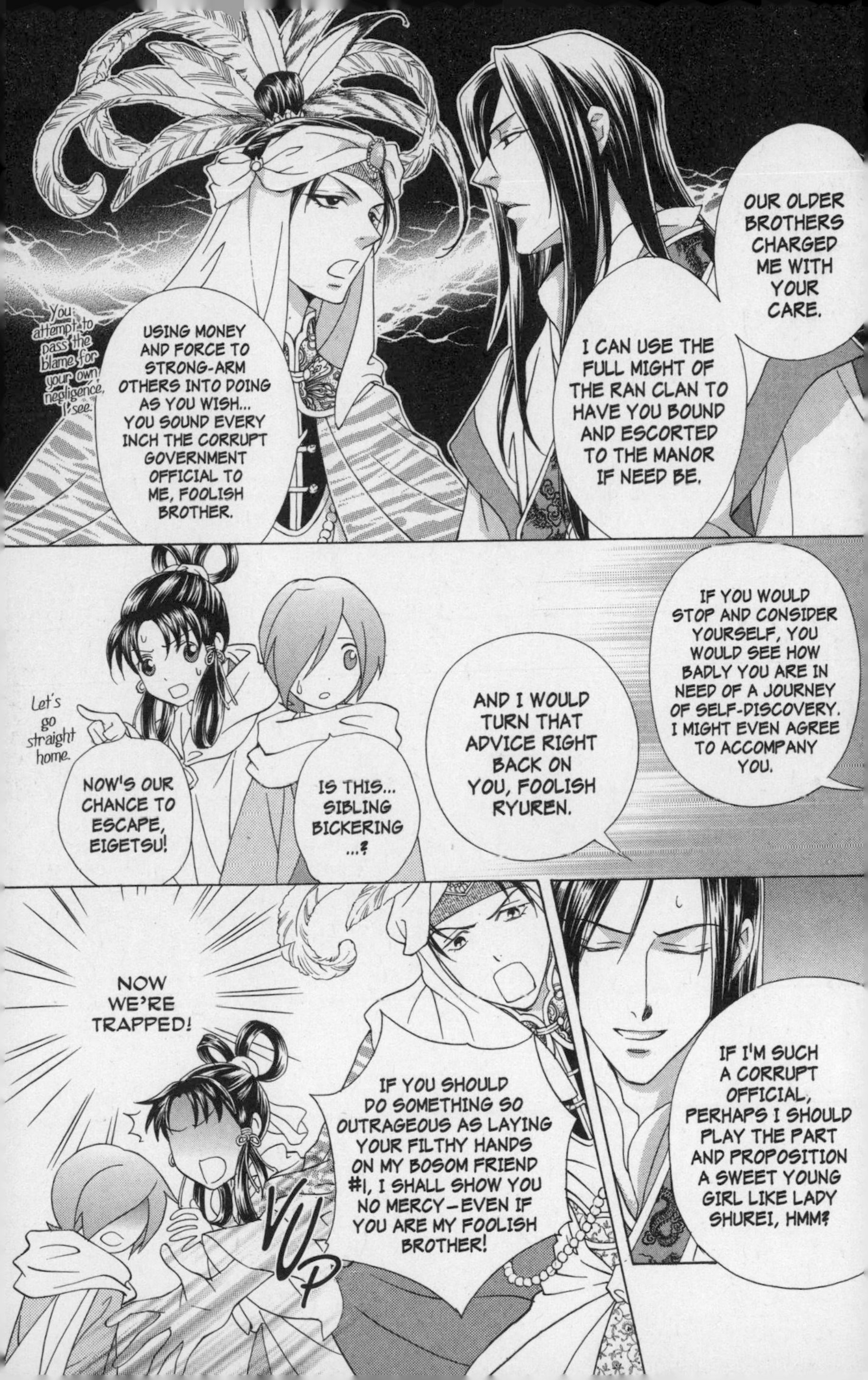
OUR OLDER BROTHERS CHARGED ME WITH YOUR CARE.
I CAN USE THE FULL MIGHT OF THE RAN CLAN TO HAVE YOU BOUND AND ESCORTED TO THE MANOR IF NEED BE.
USING MONEY AND FORCE TO STRONG-ARM OTHERS INTO DOING AS YOU WISH... YOU SOUND EVERY INCH THE CORRUPT GOVERNMENT OFFICIAL TO ME, FOOLISH BROTHER.
You attempt to pass the blame for your own negligence, I see.
IF YOU WOULD STOP AND CONSIDER YOURSELF, YOU WOULD SEE HOW BADLY YOU ARE IN NEED OF A JOURNEY OF SELF-DISCOVERY. I MIGHT EVEN AGREE TO ACCOMPANY YOU.
AND I WOULD TURN THAT ADVICE RIGHT BACK ON YOU, FOOLISH RYUREN.
IS THIS... SIBLING BICKERING ...?
Let's go straight home.
NOW'S OUR CHANCE TO ESCAPE, EIGETSU!
IF I'M SUCH A CORRUPT OFFICIAL, PERHAPS I SHOULD PLAY THE PART AND PROPOSITION A SWEET YOUNG GIRL LIKE LADY SHUREI, HMM?
IF YOU SHOULD DO SOMETHING SO OUTRAGEOUS AS LAYING YOUR FILTHY HANDS ON MY BOSOM FRIEND #1, I SHALL SHOW YOU NO MERCY—EVEN IF YOU ARE MY FOOLISH BROTHER!
VUP
NOW WE'RE TRAPPED!

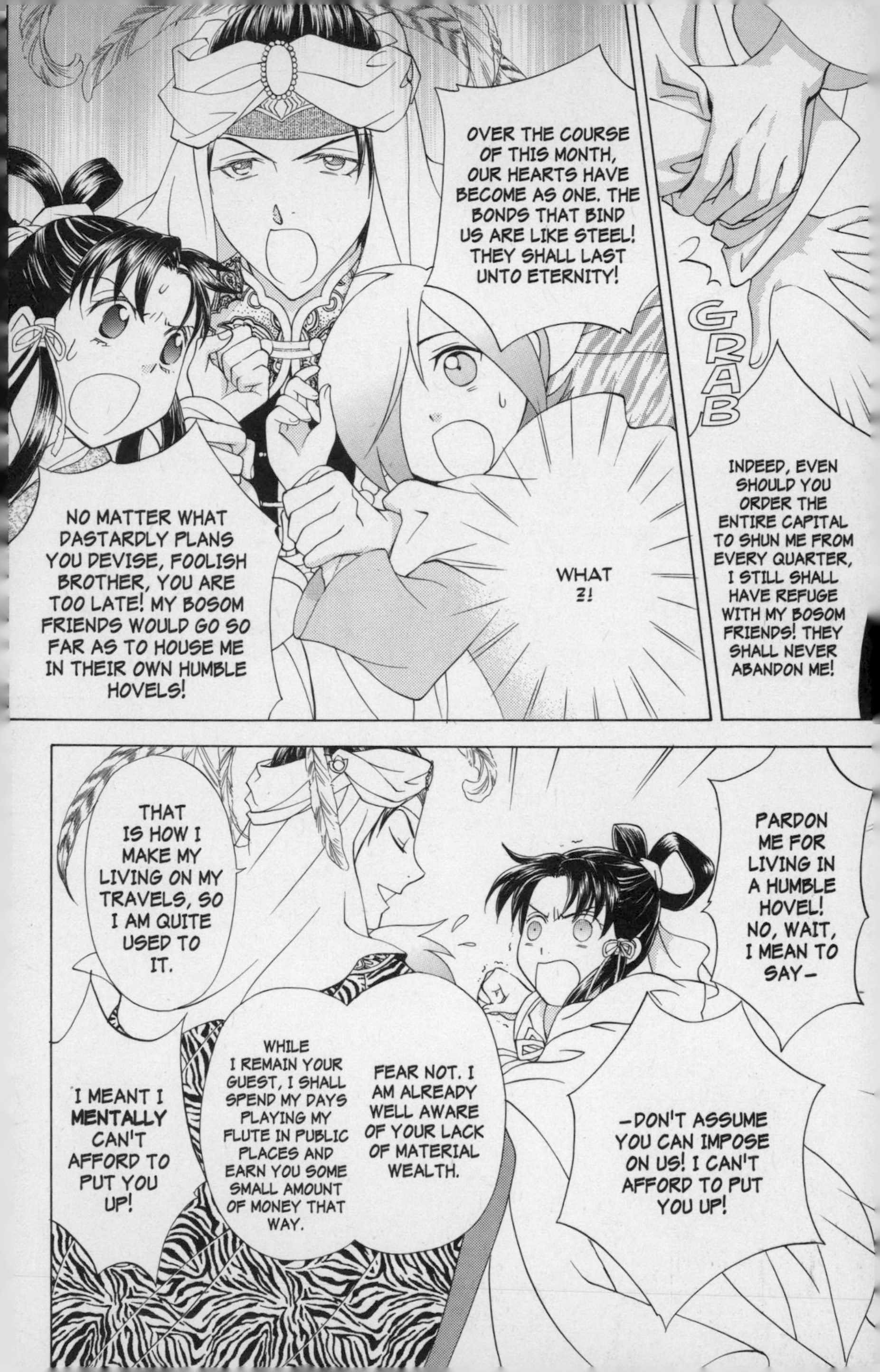
GRAB
INDEED, EVEN SHOULD YOU ORDER THE ENTIRE CAPITAL TO SHUN ME FROM EVERY QUARTER, I STILL SHALL HAVE REFUGE WITH MY BOSOM FRIENDS! THEY SHALL NEVER ABANDON ME!
OVER THE COURSE OF THIS MONTH, OUR HEARTS HAVE BECOME AS ONE. THE BONDS THAT BIND US ARE LIKE STEEL! THEY SHALL LAST UNTO ETERNITY!
WHAT?!
NO MATTER WHAT DASTARDLY PLANS YOU DEVISE, FOOLISH BROTHER, YOU ARE TOO LATE! MY BOSOM FRIENDS WOULD GO SO FAR AS TO HOUSE ME IN THEIR OWN HUMBLE HOVELS!
PARDON ME FOR LIVING IN A HUMBLE HOVEL! NO, WAIT, I MEAN TO SAY—
—DON'T ASSUME YOU CAN IMPOSE ON US! I CAN'T AFFORD TO PUT YOU UP!
FEAR NOT. I AM ALREADY WELL AWARE OF YOUR LACK OF MATERIAL WEALTH.
WHILE I REMAIN YOUR GUEST, I SHALL SPEND MY DAYS PLAYING MY FLUTE IN PUBLIC PLACES AND EARN YOU SOME SMALL AMOUNT OF MONEY THAT WAY.
THAT IS HOW I MAKE MY LIVING ON MY TRAVELS, SO I AM QUITE USED TO IT.
I MEANT I MENTALLY CAN'T AFFORD TO PUT YOU UP!

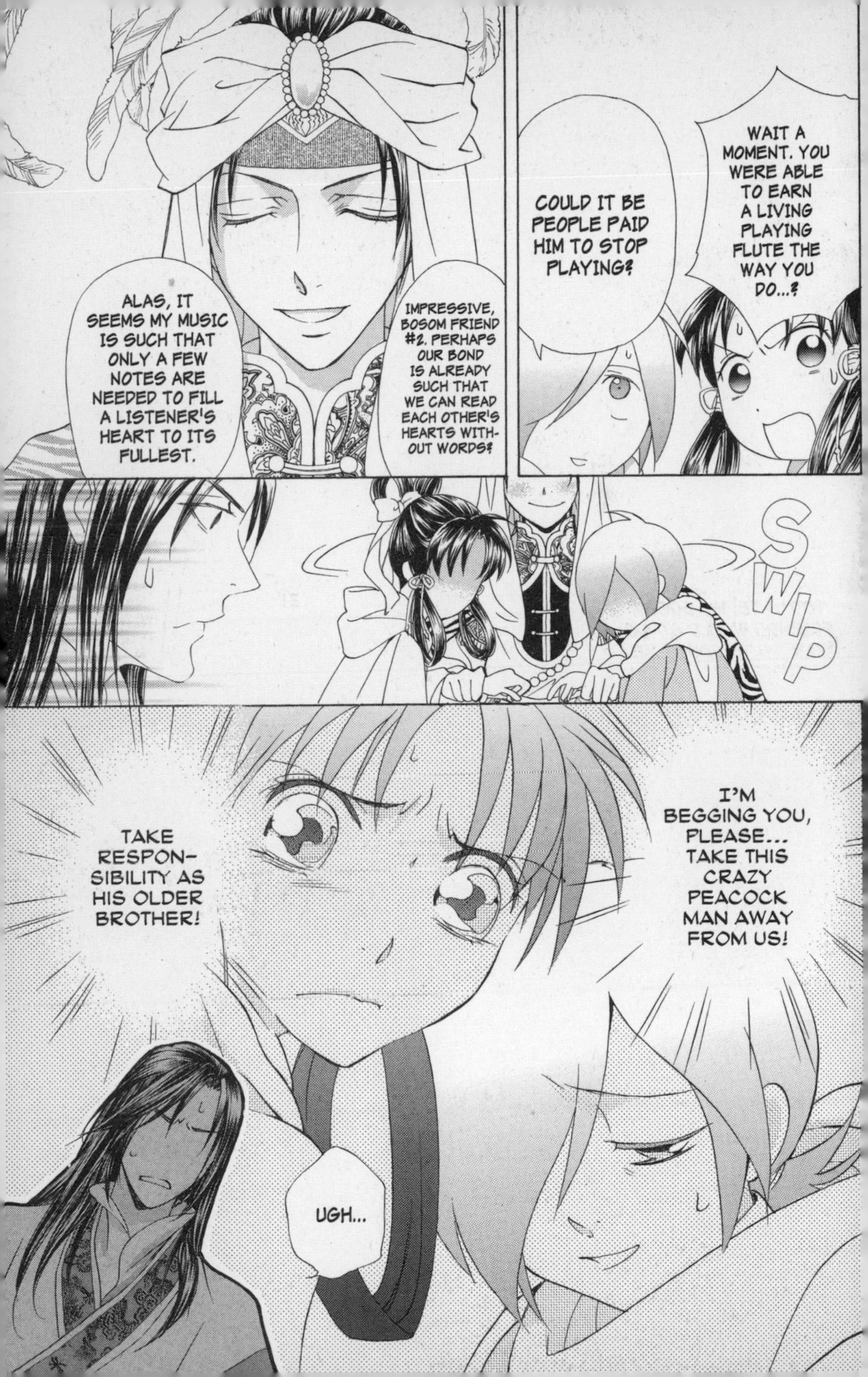
WAIT A MOMENT. YOU WERE ABLE TO EARN A LIVING PLAYING FLUTE THE WAY YOU DO...?
COULD IT BE PEOPLE PAID HIM TO STOP PLAYING?
IMPRESSIVE, BOSOM FRIEND #2. PERHAPS OUR BOND IS ALREADY SUCH THAT WE CAN READ EACH OTHER'S HEARTS WITHOUT WORDS?
ALAS, IT SEEMS MY MUSIC IS SUCH THAT ONLY A FEW NOTES ARE NEEDED TO FILL A LISTENER'S HEART TO ITS FULLEST.
SWIP
I'M BEGGING YOU, PLEASE... TAKE THIS CRAZY PEACOCK MAN AWAY FROM US!
TAKE RESPONSIBILITY AS HIS OLDER BROTHER!
UGH...

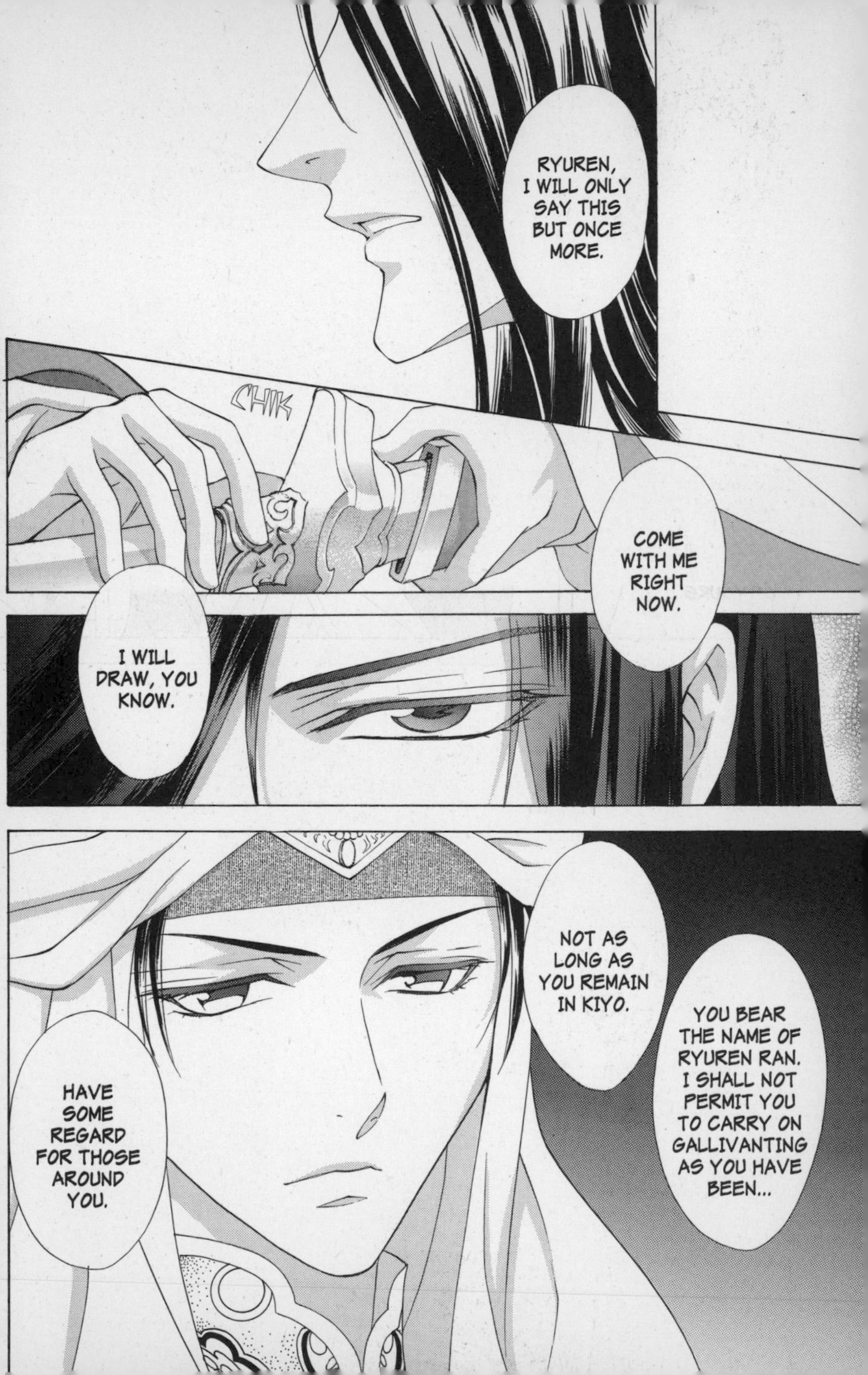
RYUREN, I WILL ONLY SAY THIS BUT ONCE MORE.
CHIK
COME WITH ME RIGHT NOW.
I WILL DRAW, YOU KNOW.
NOT AS LONG AS YOU REMAIN IN KIYO.
YOU BEAR THE NAME OF RYUREN RAN. I SHALL NOT PERMIT YOU TO CARRY ON GALLIVANTING AS YOU HAVE BEEN...
HAVE SOME REGARD FOR THOSE AROUND YOU.

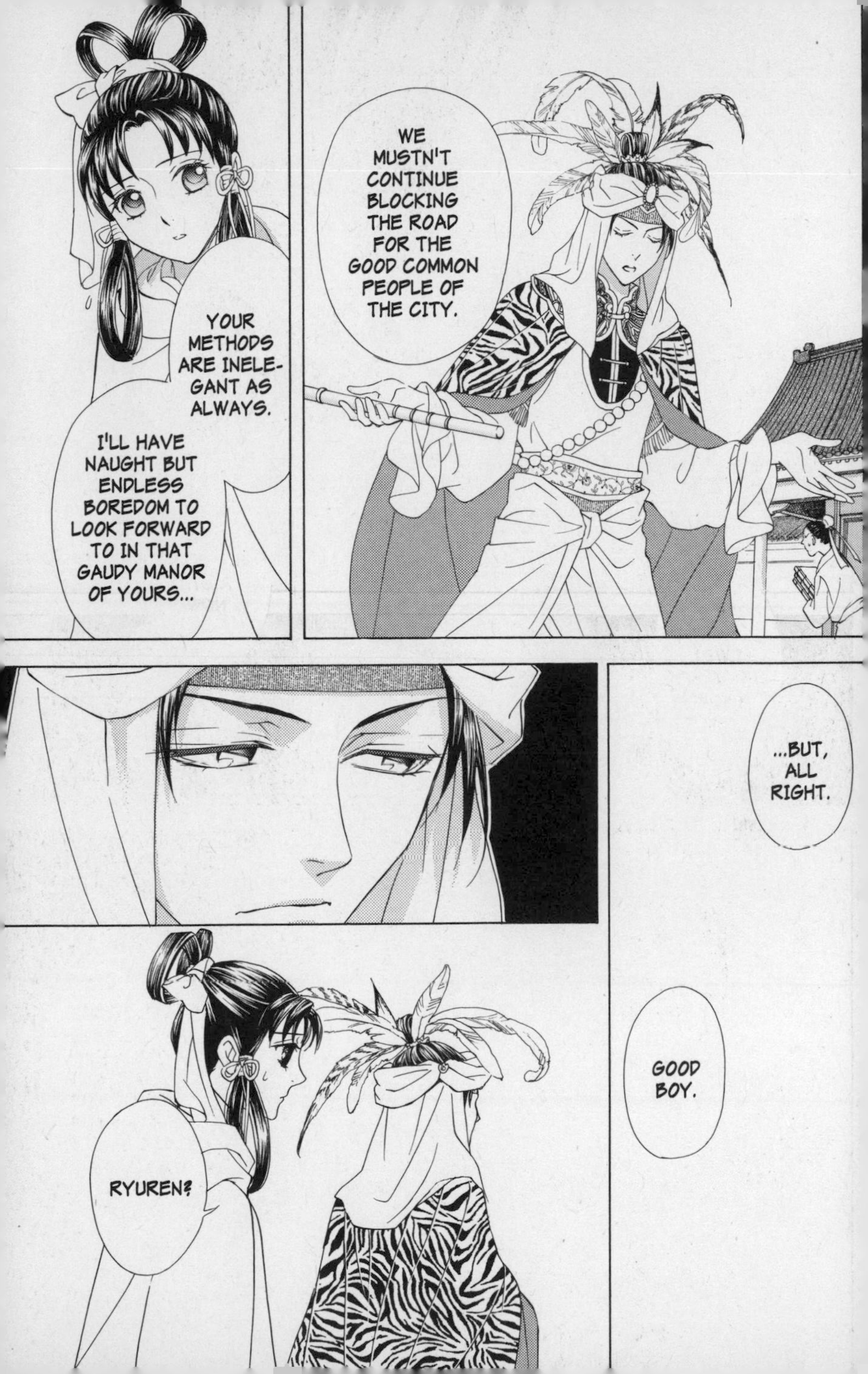
WE MUSTN'T CONTINUE BLOCKING THE ROAD FOR THE GOOD COMMON PEOPLE OF THE CITY.
YOUR METHODS ARE INELE-GANT AS ALWAYS.
I'LL HAVE NAUGHT BUT ENDLESS BOREDOM TO LOOK FORWARD TO IN THAT GAUDY MANOR OF YOURS...
...BUT, ALL RIGHT.
GOOD BOY.
RYUREN?

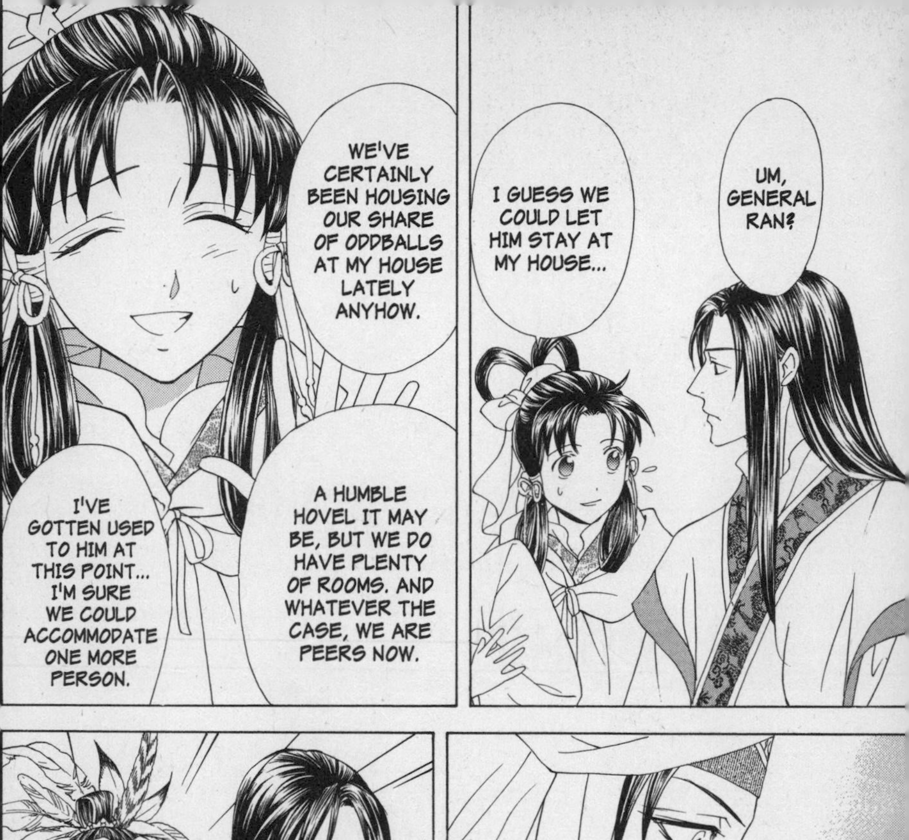
UM, GENERAL RAN?
I GUESS WE COULD LET HIM STAY AT MY HOUSE...
WE'VE CERTAINLY BEEN HOUSING OUR SHARE OF ODDBALLS AT MY HOUSE LATELY ANYHOW.
A HUMBLE HOVEL IT MAY BE, BUT WE DO HAVE PLENTY OF ROOMS. AND WHATEVER THE CASE, WE ARE PEERS NOW.
I'VE GOTTEN USED TO HIM AT THIS POINT... I'M SURE WE COULD ACCOMMODATE ONE MORE PERSON.
IT'S ALL RIGHT. I COULDN'T BEAR TO TROUBLE YOU THAT MUCH, LADY SHUREI.
IN FACT, HEARING YOU CARE THAT MUCH ABOUT HIM ACTUALLY MAKES ME A BIT JEALOUS.
DON'T YOU DARE TAINT OUR PURE FRIENDSHIP WITH YOUR FILTHY THOUGHTS, FOOLISH BROTHER!

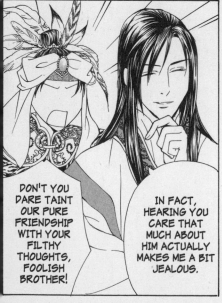

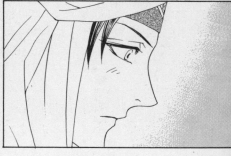

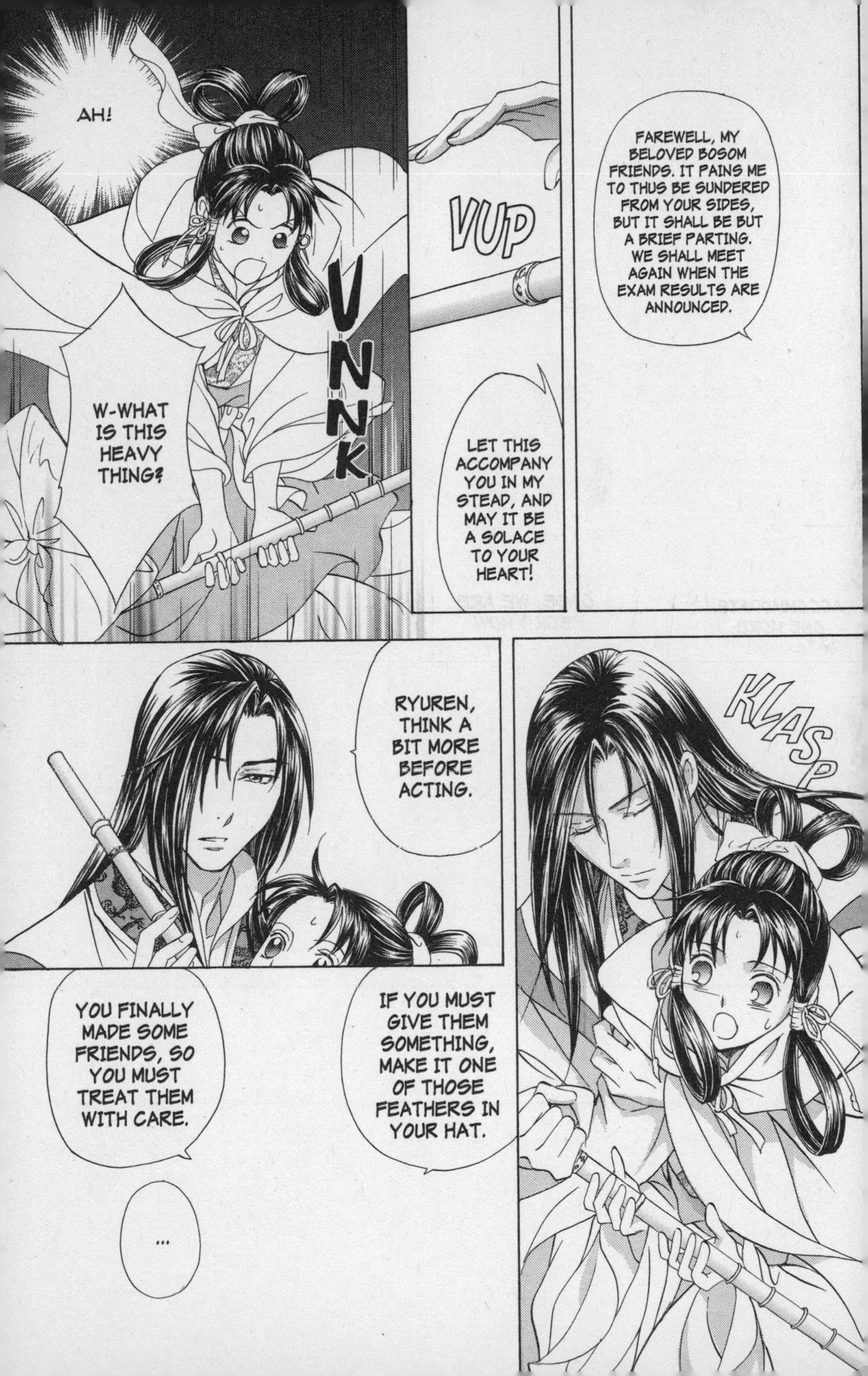
FAREWELL, MY BELOVED BOSOM FRIENDS. IT PAINS ME TO THUS BE SUNDERED FROM YOUR SIDES, BUT IT SHALL BE BUT A BRIEF PARTING. WE SHALL MEET AGAIN WHEN THE EXAM RESULTS ARE ANNOUNCED.
VUP
LET THIS ACCOMPANY YOU IN MY STEAD, AND MAY IT BE A SOLACE TO YOUR HEART!
AH!
VUNNK
W-WHAT IS THIS HEAVY THING?
KLASP
RYUREN, THINK A BIT MORE BEFORE ACTING.
IF YOU MUST GIVE THEM SOMETHING, MAKE IT ONE OF THOSE FEATHERS IN YOUR HAT.
YOU FINALLY MADE SOME FRIENDS, SO YOU MUST TREAT THEM WITH CARE.
...

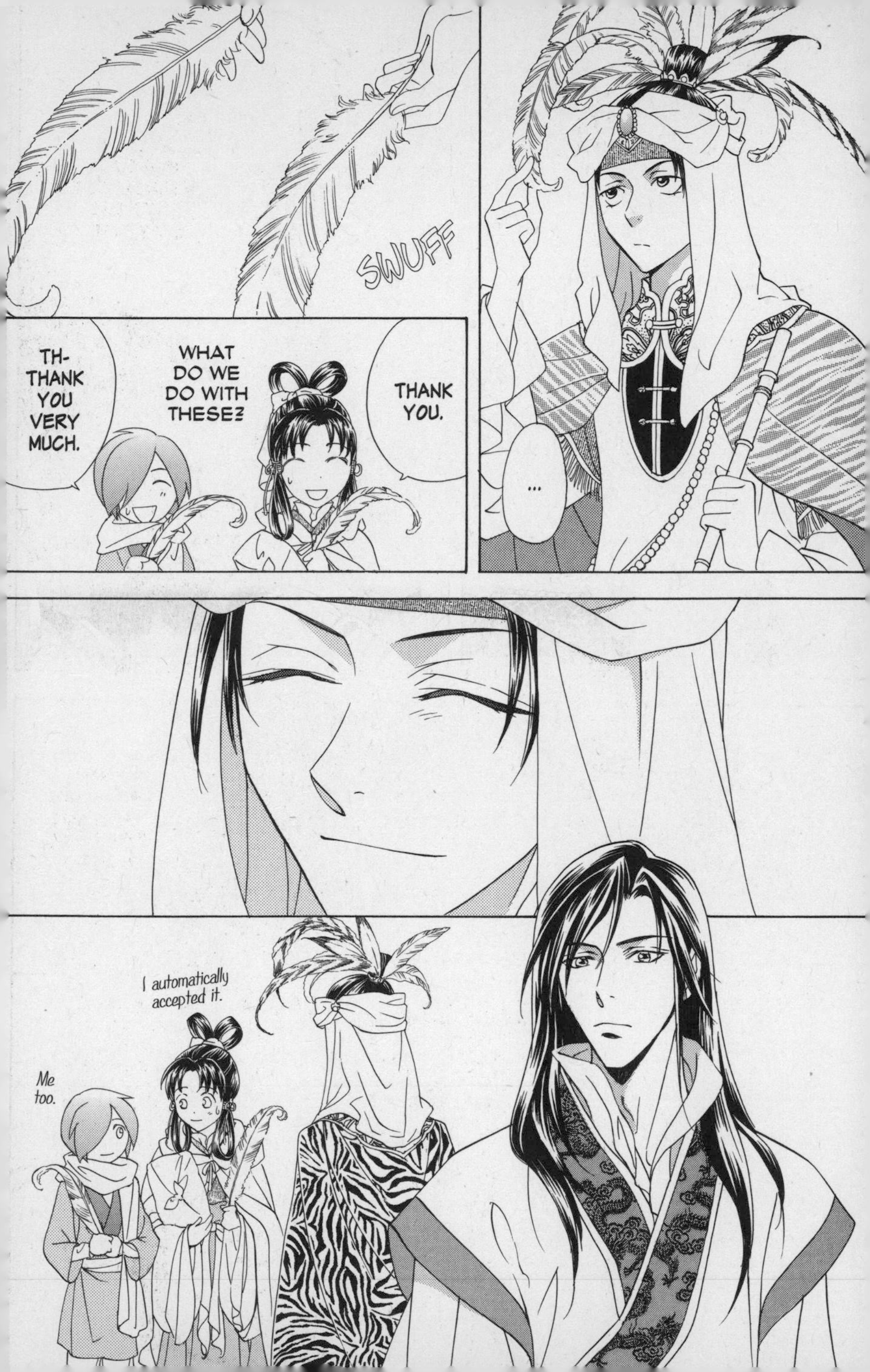
...
SWUFF
THANK YOU.
WHAT DO WE DO WITH THESE?
TH-THANK YOU VERY MUCH.
I automatically accepted it.
Me too.

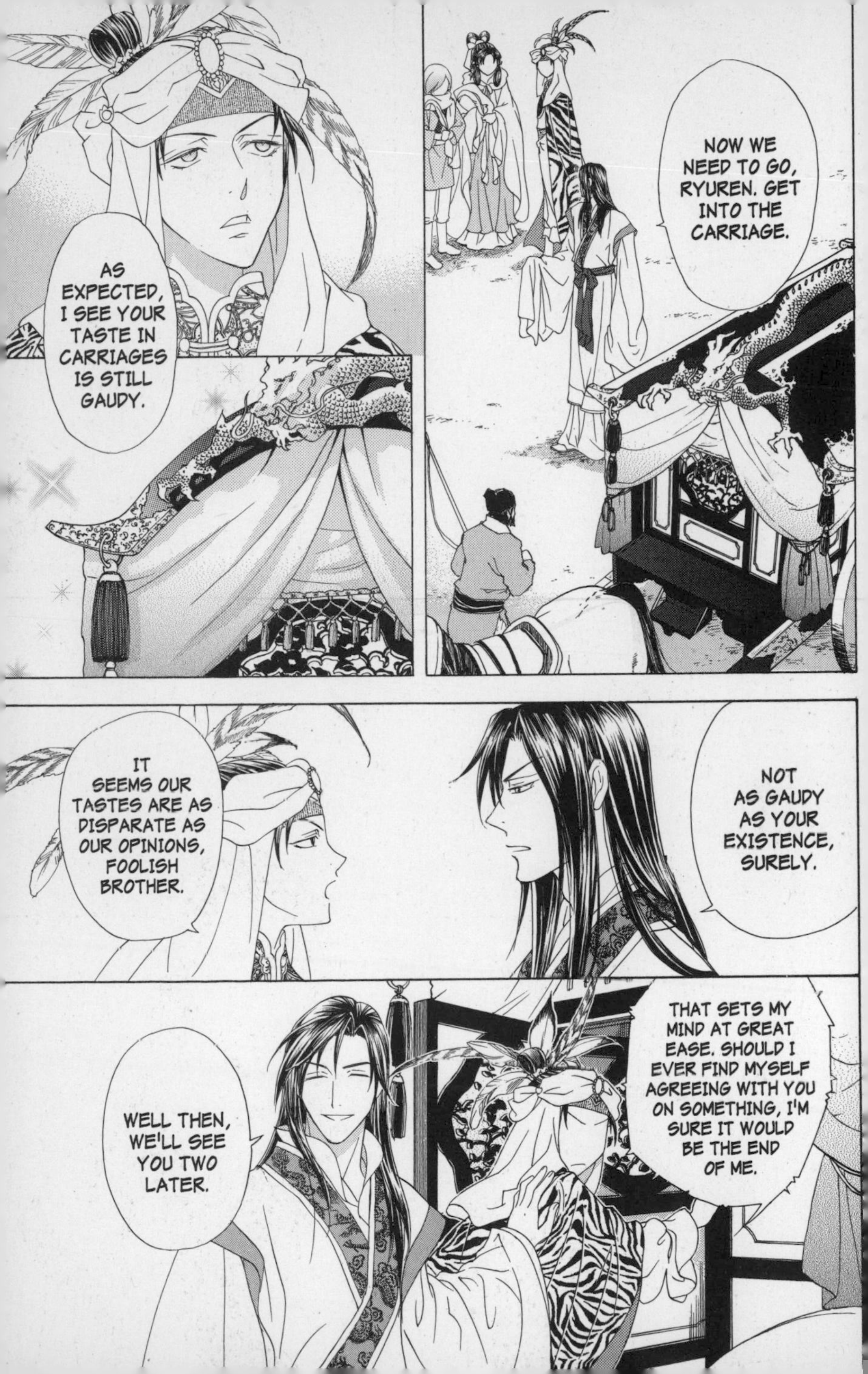
NOW WE NEED TO GO, RYUREN. GET INTO THE CARRIAGE.
AS EXPECTED, I SEE YOUR TASTE IN CARRIAGES IS STILL GAUDY.
NOT AS GAUDY AS YOUR EXISTENCE, SURELY.
IT SEEMS OUR TASTES ARE AS DISPARATE AS OUR OPINIONS, FOOLISH BROTHER.
THAT SETS MY MIND AT GREAT EASE. SHOULD I EVER FIND MYSELF AGREEING WITH YOU ON SOMETHING, I'M SURE IT WOULD BE THE END OF ME.
WELL THEN, WE'LL SEE YOU TWO LATER.

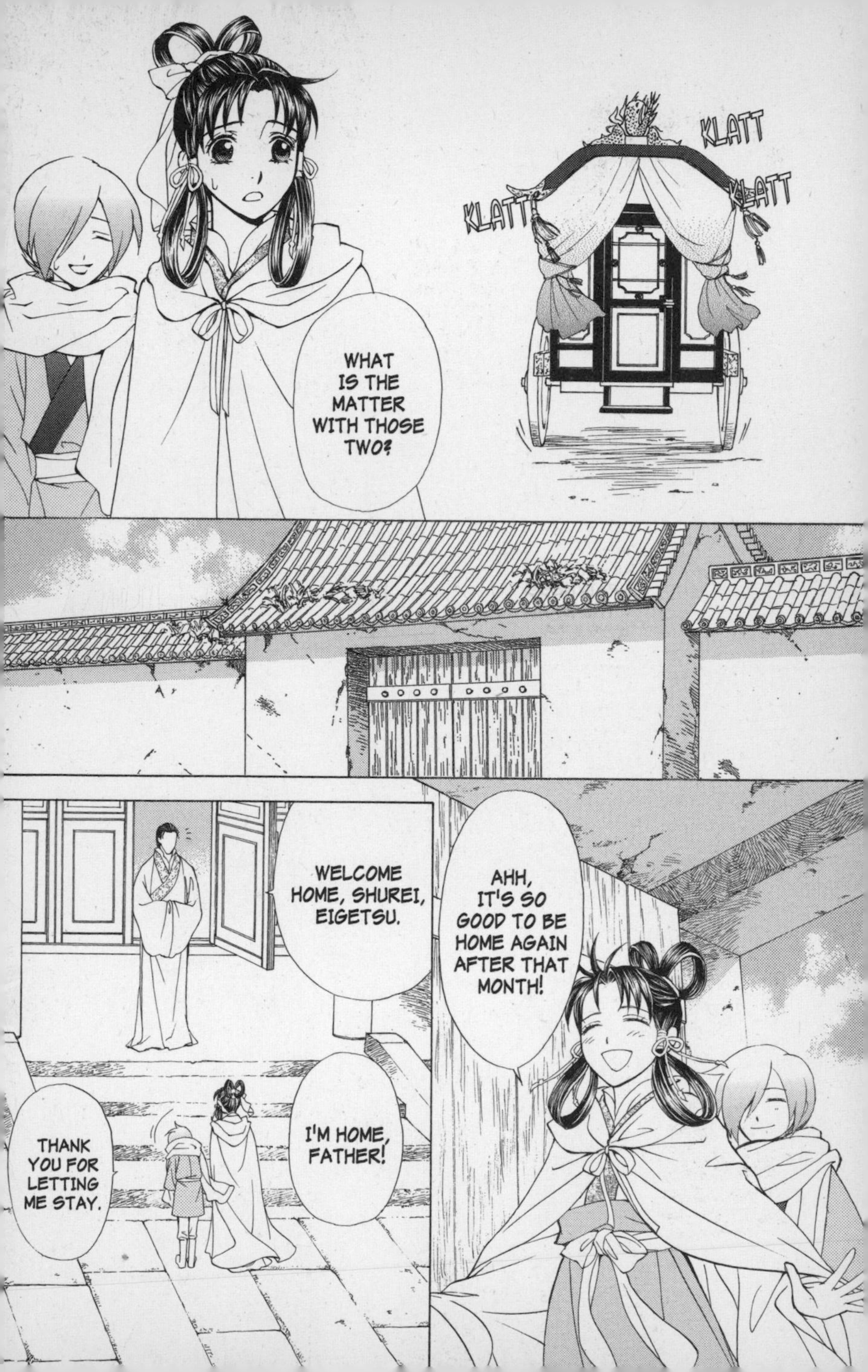
KLATT
KLATT
KLATT
WHAT IS THE MATTER WITH THOSE TWO?
AHH, IT'S SO GOOD TO BE HOME AGAIN AFTER THAT MONTH!
WELCOME HOME, SHUREI, EIGETSU.
I'M HOME, FATHER!
THANK YOU FOR LETTING ME STAY.

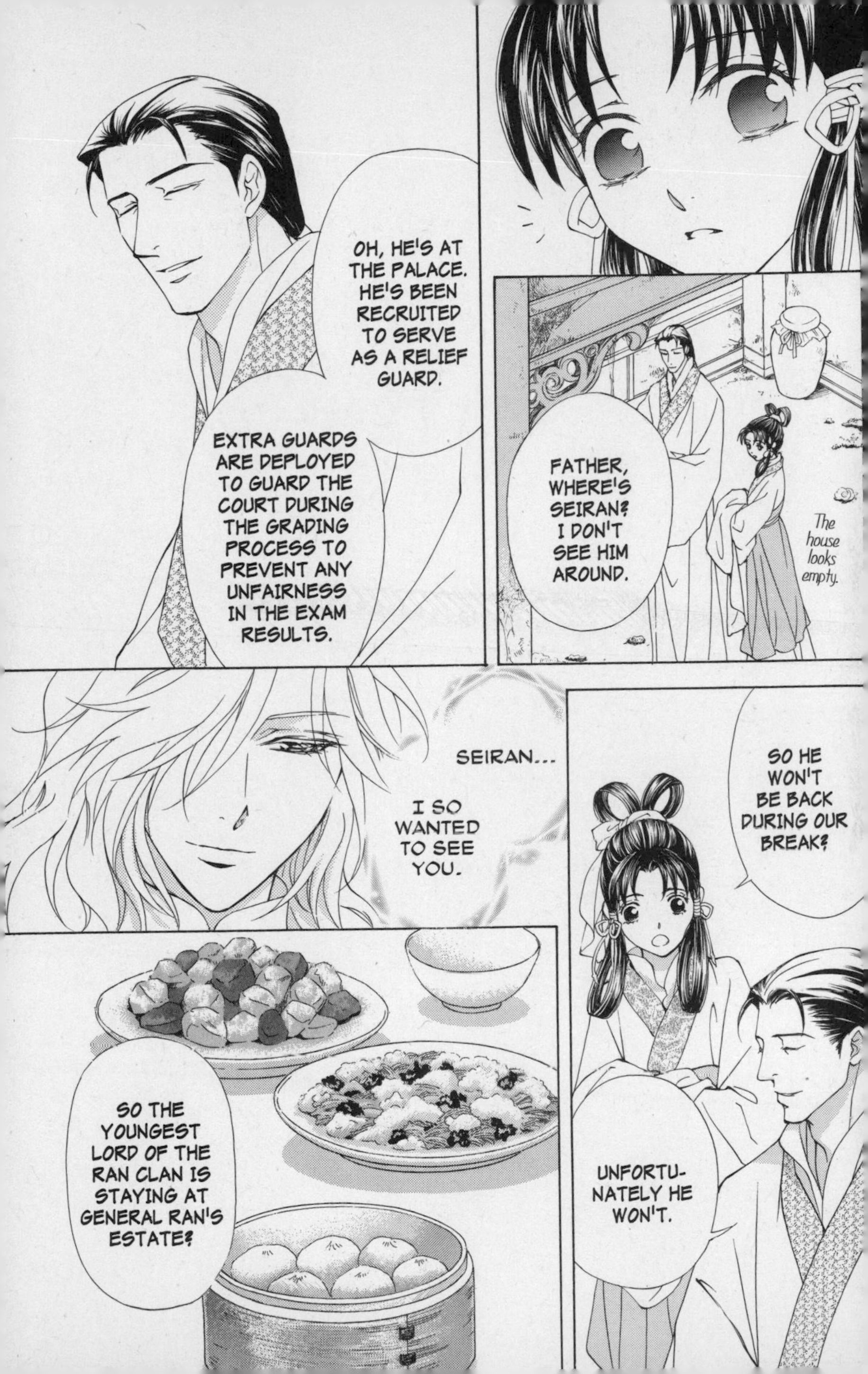
FATHER, WHERE'S SEIRAN? I DON'T SEE HIM AROUND.
The house looks empty.
OH, HE'S AT THE PALACE. HE'S BEEN RECRUITED TO SERVE AS A RELIEF GUARD.
EXTRA GUARDS ARE DEPLOYED TO GUARD THE COURT DURING THE GRADING PROCESS TO PREVENT ANY UNFAIRNESS IN THE EXAM RESULTS.
SO HE WON'T BE BACK DURING OUR BREAK?
UNFORTU-NATELY HE WON'T.
SEIRAN...
I SO WANTED TO SEE YOU.
SO THE YOUNGEST LORD OF THE RAN CLAN IS STAYING AT GENERAL RAN'S ESTATE?

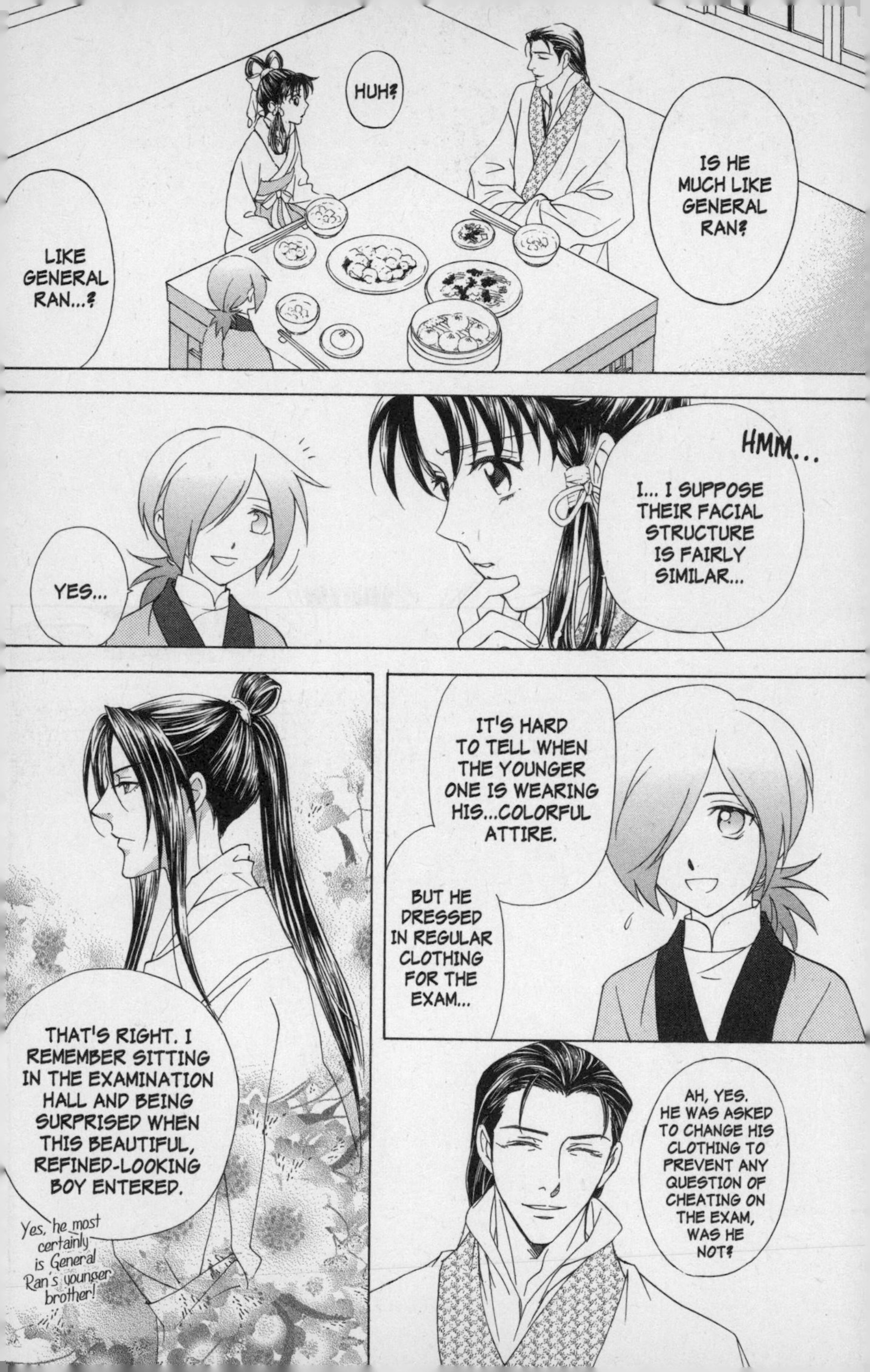
IS HE MUCH LIKE GENERAL RAN?
HUH?
LIKE GENERAL RAN...?
HMM...
I... I SUPPOSE THEIR FACIAL STRUCTURE IS FAIRLY SIMILAR...
YES...
IT'S HARD TO TELL WHEN THE YOUNGER ONE IS WEARING HIS...COLORFUL ATTIRE.
BUT HE DRESSED IN REGULAR CLOTHING FOR THE EXAM...
AH, YES. HE WAS ASKED TO CHANGE HIS CLOTHING TO PREVENT ANY QUESTION OF CHEATING ON THE EXAM, WAS HE NOT?
THAT'S RIGHT. I REMEMBER SITTING IN THE EXAMINATION HALL AND BEING SURPRISED WHEN THIS BEAUTIFUL, REFINED-LOOKING BOY ENTERED.
Yes, he most certainly is General Ran's younger brother!

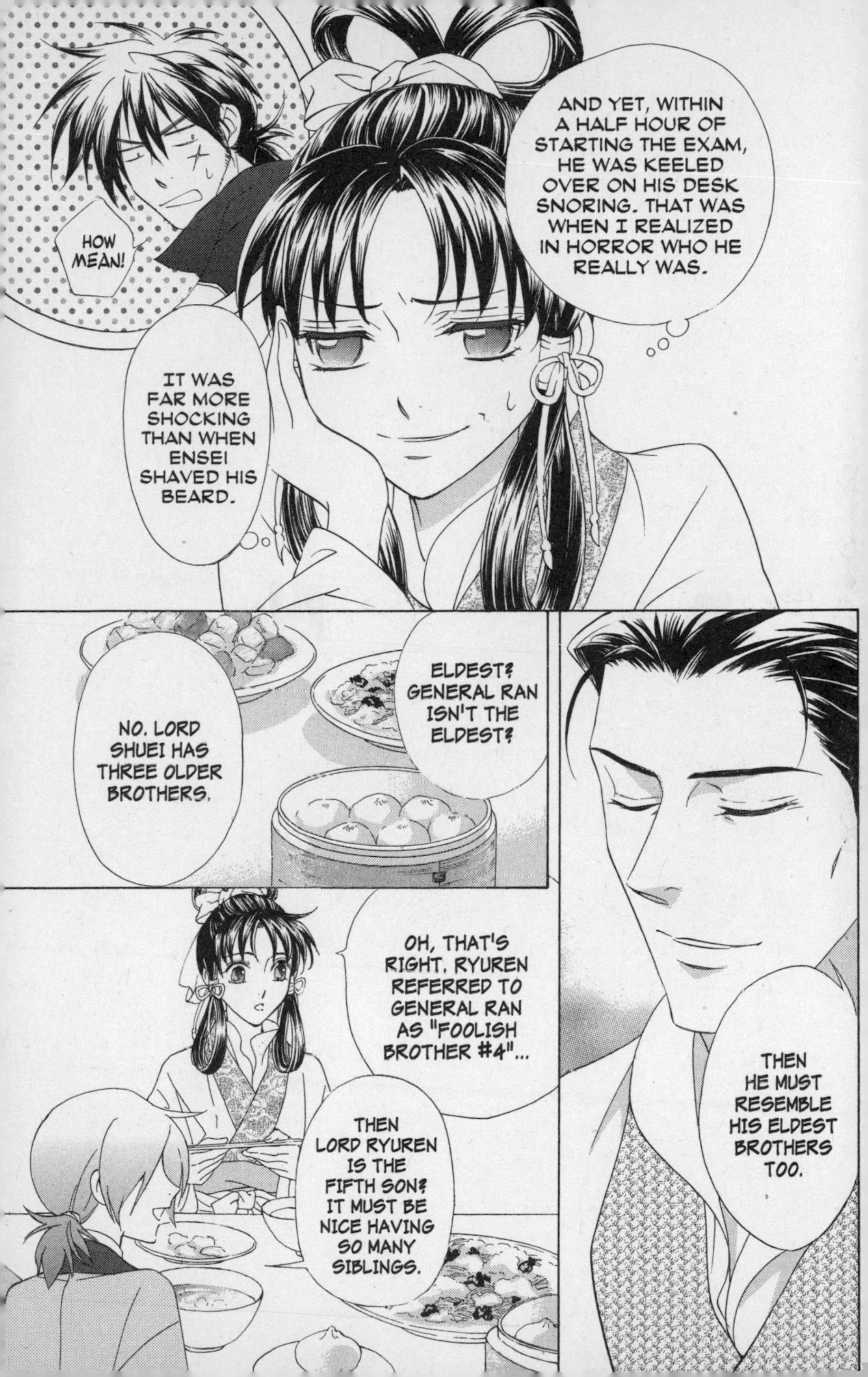
AND YET, WITHIN A HALF HOUR OF STARTING THE EXAM, HE WAS KEELED OVER ON HIS DESK SNORING. THAT WAS WHEN I REALIZED IN HORROR WHO HE REALLY WAS.
HOW MEAN!
IT WAS FAR MORE SHOCKING THAN WHEN ENSEI SHAVED HIS BEARD.
ELDEST? GENERAL RAN ISN'T THE ELDEST?
NO. LORD SHUEI HAS THREE OLDER BROTHERS.
OH, THAT'S RIGHT. RYUREN REFERRED TO GENERAL RAN AS "FOOLISH BROTHER #4"...
THEN LORD RYUREN IS THE FIFTH SON? IT MUST BE NICE HAVING SO MANY SIBLINGS.
THEN HE MUST RESEMBLE HIS ELDEST BROTHERS TOO.

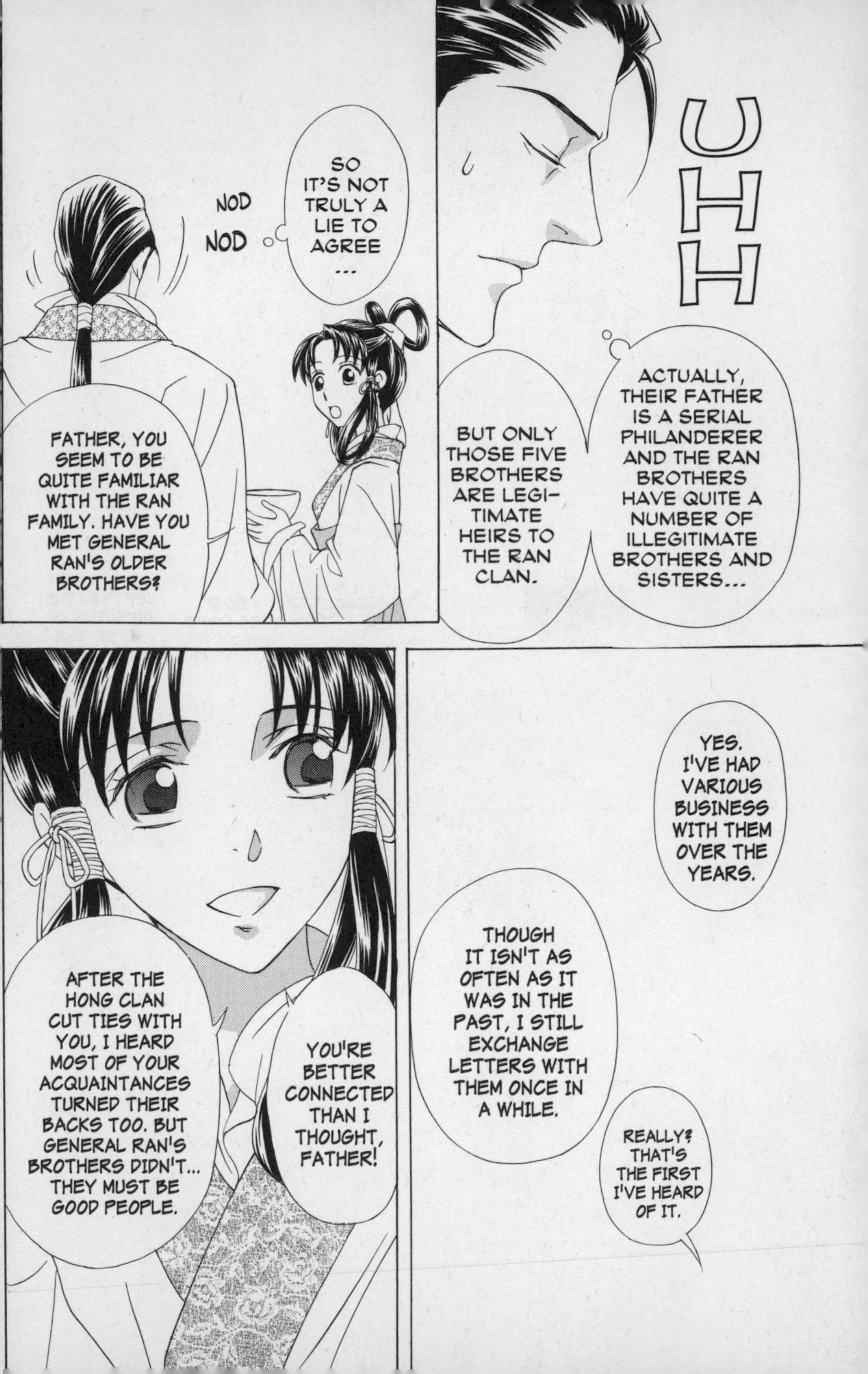
UHH
ACTUALLY, THEIR FATHER IS A SERIAL PHILANDERER AND THE RAN BROTHERS HAVE QUITE A NUMBER OF ILLEGITIMATE BROTHERS AND SISTERS...
BUT ONLY THOSE FIVE BROTHERS ARE LEGI-TIMATE HEIRS TO THE RAN CLAN.
SO IT'S NOT TRULY A LIE TO AGREE...
NOD NOD
FATHER, YOU SEEM TO BE QUITE FAMILIAR WITH THE RAN FAMILY. HAVE YOU MET GENERAL RAN'S OLDER BROTHERS?
YES. I'VE HAD VARIOUS BUSINESS WITH THEM OVER THE YEARS.
THOUGH IT ISN'T AS OFTEN AS IT WAS IN THE PAST, I STILL EXCHANGE LETTERS WITH THEM ONCE IN A WHILE.
REALLY? THAT'S THE FIRST I'VE HEARD OF IT.
YOU'RE BETTER CONNECTED THAN I THOUGHT, FATHER!
AFTER THE HONG CLAN CUT TIES WITH YOU, I HEARD MOST OF YOUR ACQUAINTANCES TURNED THEIR BACKS TOO. BUT GENERAL RAN'S BROTHERS DIDN'T... THEY MUST BE GOOD PEOPLE.

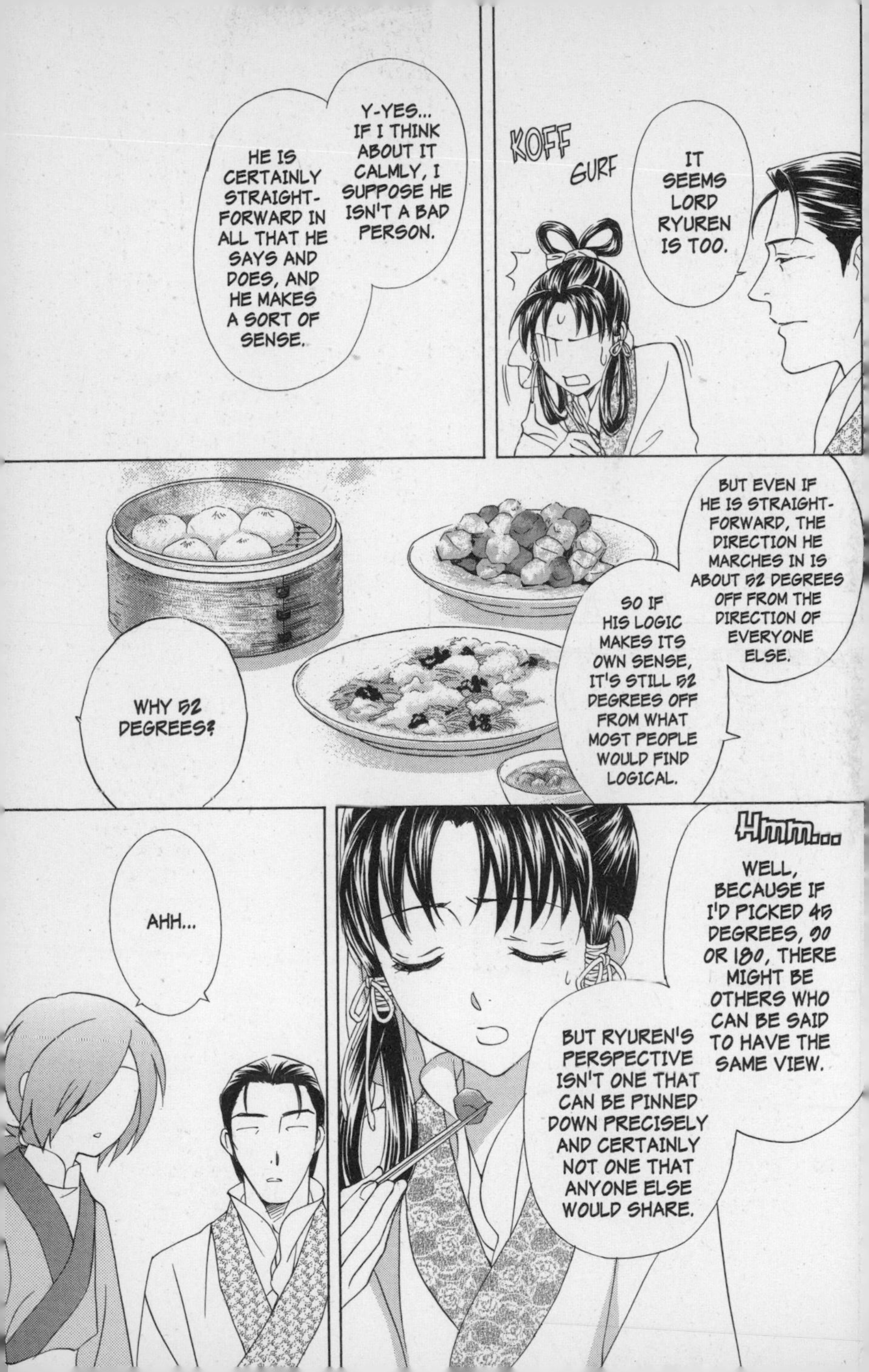
KOFF
GURF
IT SEEMS LORD RYUREN IS TOO.
Y-YES... IF I THINK ABOUT IT CALMLY, I SUPPOSE HE ISN'T A BAD PERSON.
HE IS CERTAINLY STRAIGHT-FORWARD IN ALL THAT HE SAYS AND DOES, AND HE MAKES A SORT OF SENSE.
BUT EVEN IF HE IS STRAIGHT-FORWARD, THE DIRECTION HE MARCHES IN IS ABOUT 52 DEGREES OFF FROM THE DIRECTION OF EVERYONE ELSE.
SO IF HIS LOGIC MAKES ITS OWN SENSE, IT'S STILL 52 DEGREES OFF FROM WHAT MOST PEOPLE WOULD FIND LOGICAL.
WHY 52 DEGREES?
Hmm...
WELL, BECAUSE IF I'D PICKED 45 DEGREES, 90 OR 180, THERE MIGHT BE OTHERS WHO CAN BE SAID TO HAVE THE SAME VIEW.
BUT RYUREN'S PERSPECTIVE ISN'T ONE THAT CAN BE PINNED DOWN PRECISELY AND CERTAINLY NOT ONE THAT ANYONE ELSE WOULD SHARE.
AHH...

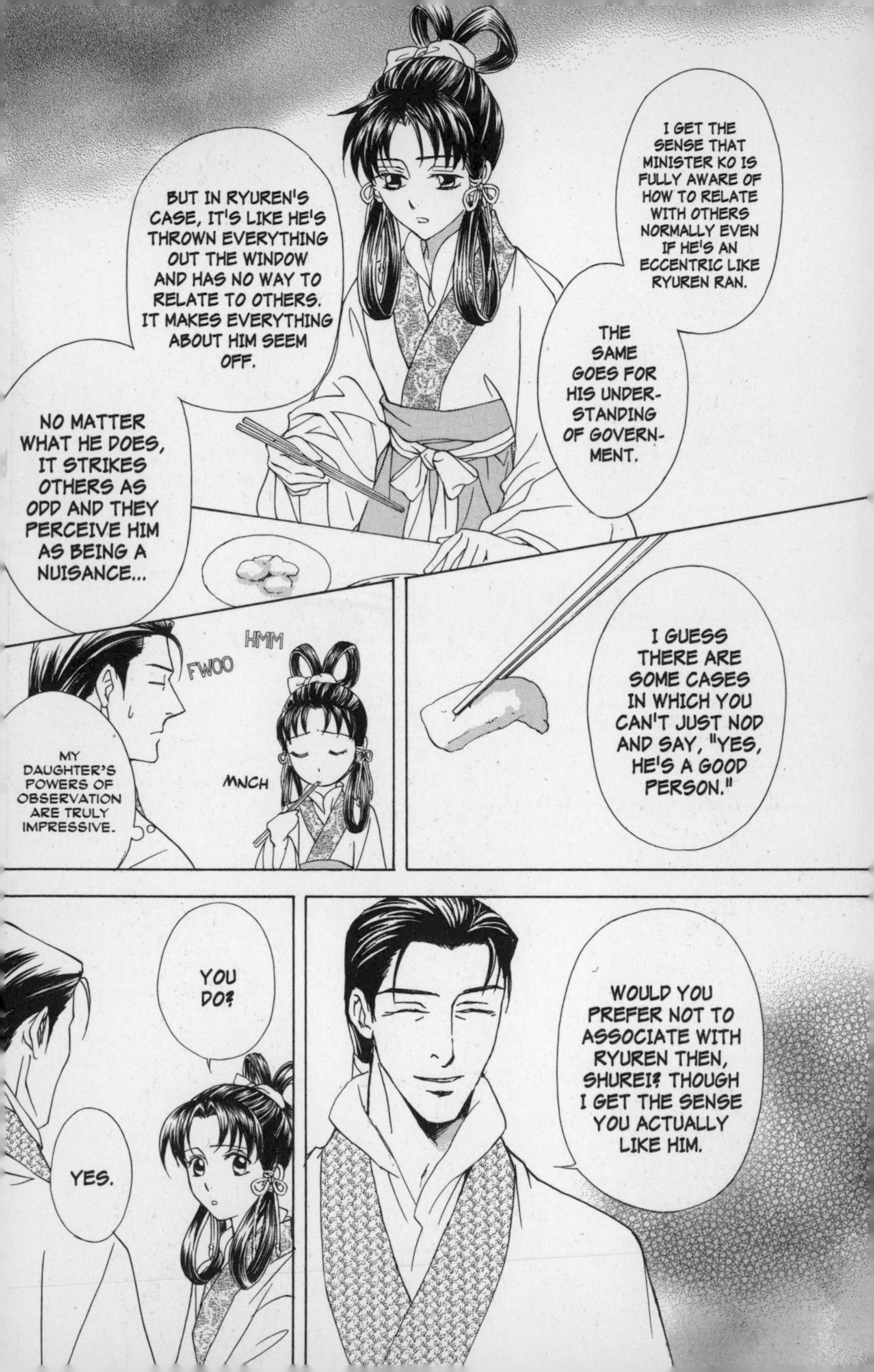
I GET THE SENSE THAT MINISTER KO IS FULLY AWARE OF HOW TO RELATE WITH OTHERS NORMALLY EVEN IF HE'S AN ECCENTRIC LIKE RYUREN RAN.
THE SAME GOES FOR HIS UNDER-STANDING OF GOVERN-MENT.
BUT IN RYUREN'S CASE, IT'S LIKE HE'S THROWN EVERYTHING OUT THE WINDOW AND HAS NO WAY TO RELATE TO OTHERS. IT MAKES EVERYTHING ABOUT HIM SEEM OFF.
NO MATTER WHAT HE DOES, IT STRIKES OTHERS AS ODD AND THEY PERCEIVE HIM AS BEING A NUISANCE...
I GUESS THERE ARE SOME CASES IN WHICH YOU CAN'T JUST NOD AND SAY, "YES, HE'S A GOOD PERSON."
HMM
FWOO
MNCH
MY DAUGHTER'S POWERS OF OBSERVATION ARE TRULY IMPRESSIVE.
WOULD YOU PREFER NOT TO ASSOCIATE WITH RYUREN THEN, SHUREI? THOUGH I GET THE SENSE YOU ACTUALLY LIKE HIM.
YOU DO?
YES.

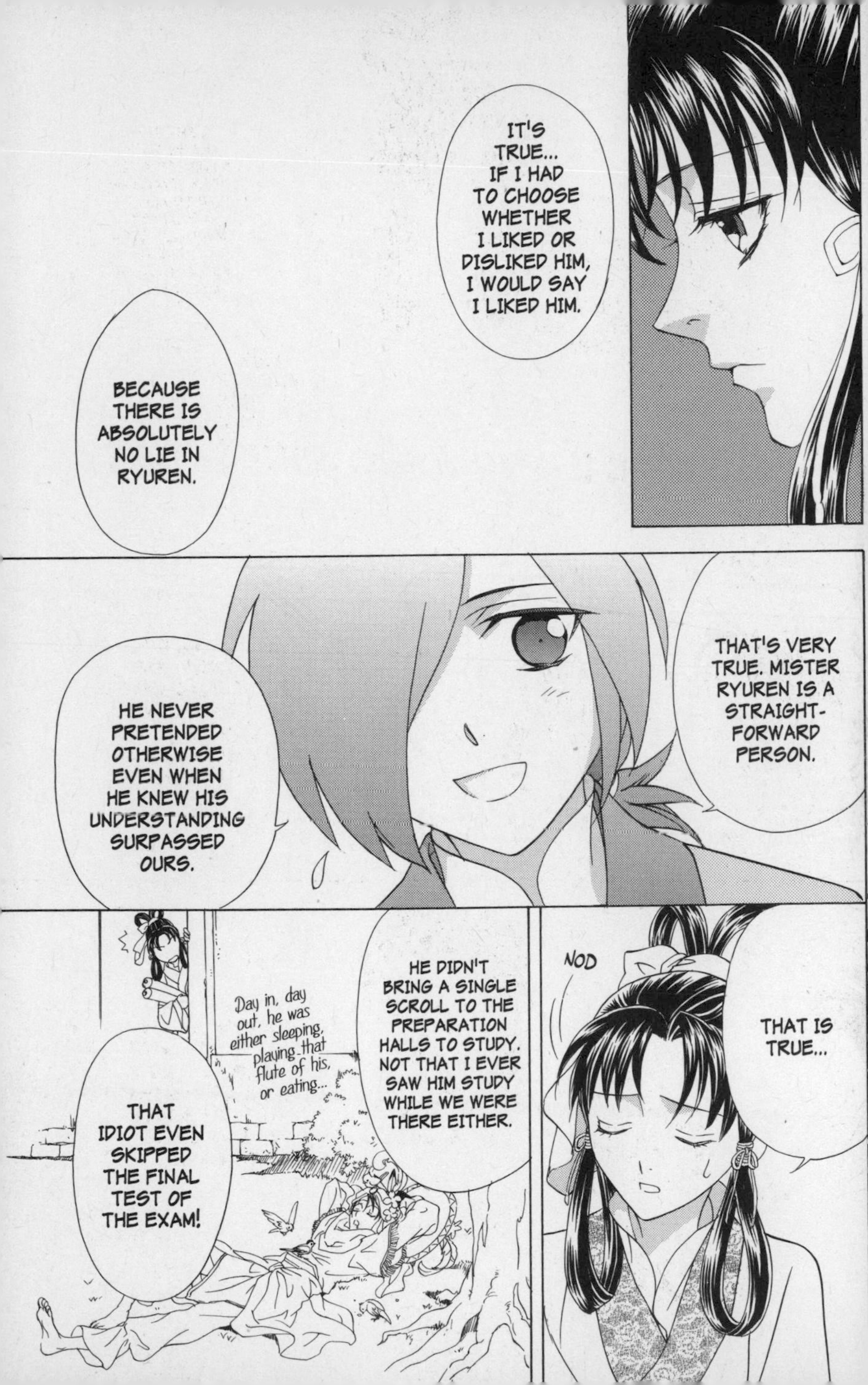
IT'S TRUE... IF I HAD TO CHOOSE WHETHER I LIKED OR DISLIKED HIM, I WOULD SAY I LIKED HIM.
BECAUSE THERE IS ABSOLUTELY NO LIE IN RYUREN.
THAT'S VERY TRUE. MISTER RYUREN IS A STRAIGHT-FORWARD PERSON.
HE NEVER PRETENDED OTHERWISE EVEN WHEN HE KNEW HIS UNDERSTANDING SURPASSED OURS.
NOD
THAT IS TRUE...
HE DIDN'T BRING A SINGLE SCROLL TO THE PREPARATION HALLS TO STUDY. NOT THAT I EVER SAW HIM STUDY WHILE WE WERE THERE EITHER.
Day in, day out, he was either sleeping, playing that flute of his, or eating...
THAT IDIOT EVEN SKIPPED THE FINAL TEST OF THE EXAM!

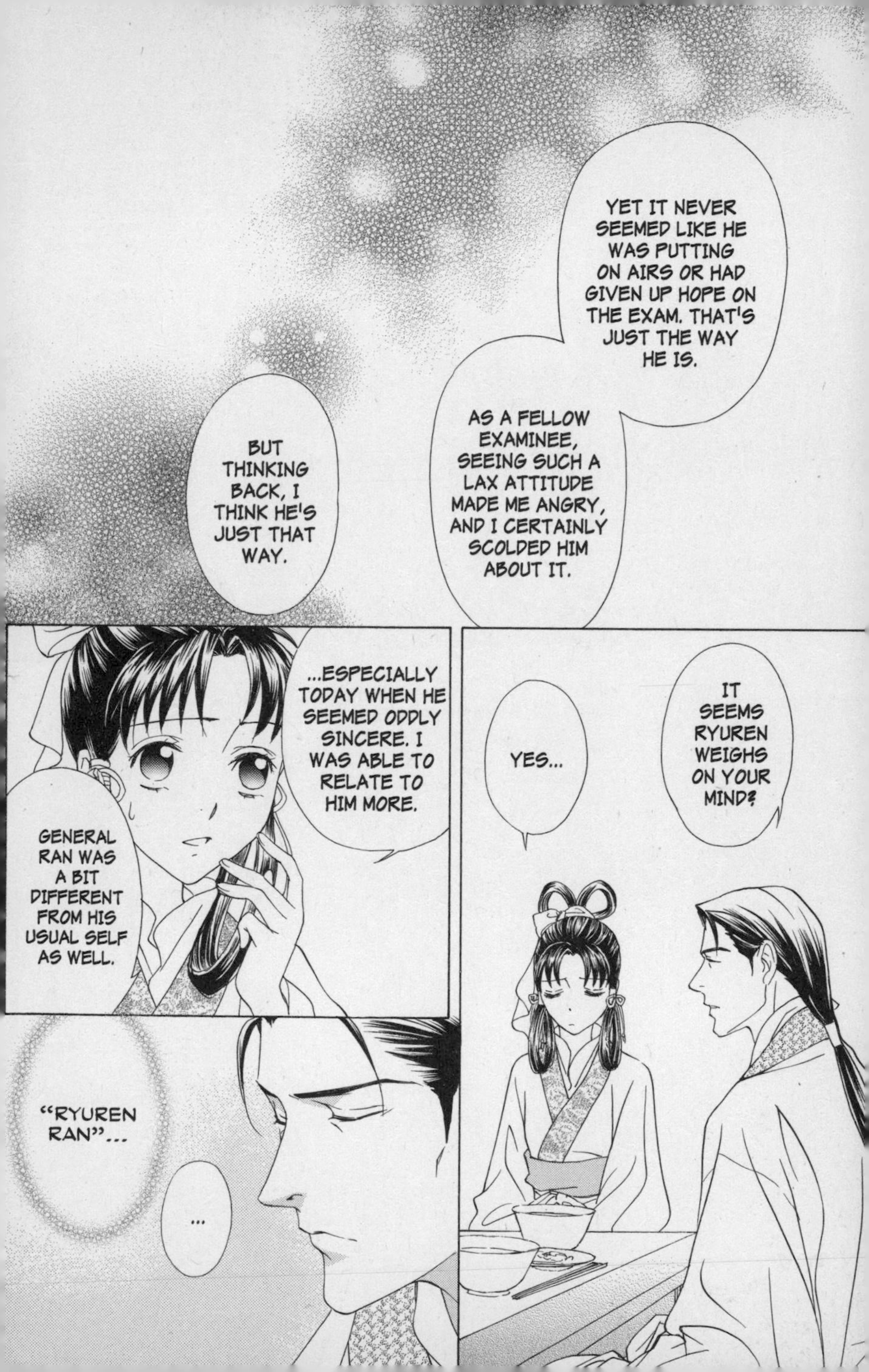
YET IT NEVER SEEMED LIKE HE WAS PUTTING ON AIRS OR HAD GIVEN UP HOPE ON THE EXAM. THAT'S JUST THE WAY HE IS.
AS A FELLOW EXAMINEE, SEEING SUCH A LAX ATTITUDE MADE ME ANGRY, AND I CERTAINLY SCOLDED HIM ABOUT IT.
BUT THINKING BACK, I THINK HE'S JUST THAT WAY.
IT SEEMS RYUREN WEIGHS ON YOUR MIND?
YES...
...ESPECIALLY TODAY WHEN HE SEEMED ODDLY SINCERE. I WAS ABLE TO RELATE TO HIM MORE.
GENERAL RAN WAS A BIT DIFFERENT FROM HIS USUAL SELF AS WELL.
"RYUREN RAN"...
...

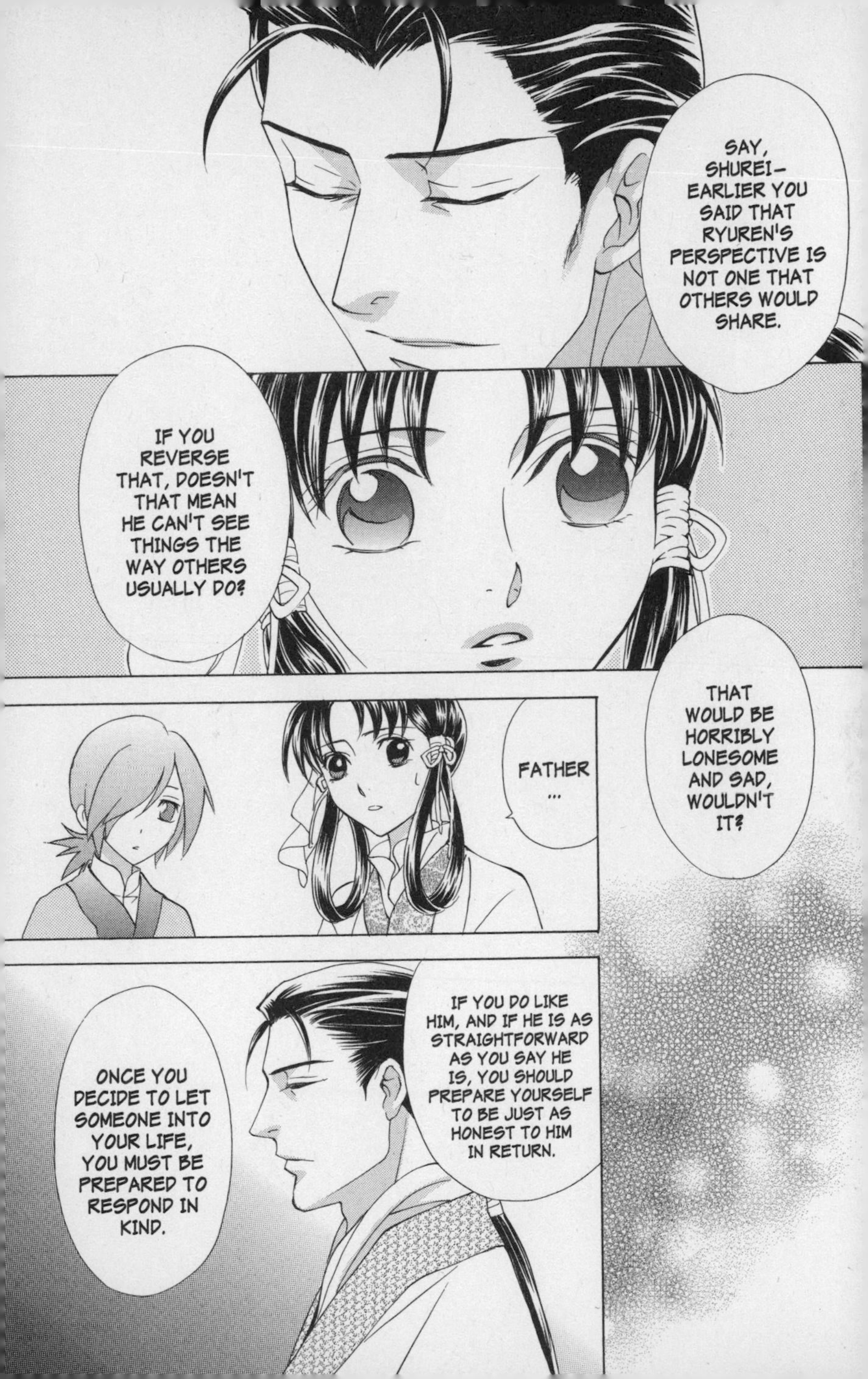
SAY, SHUREI— EARLIER YOU SAID THAT RYUREN'S PERSPECTIVE IS NOT ONE THAT OTHERS WOULD SHARE.
IF YOU REVERSE THAT, DOESN'T THAT MEAN HE CAN'T SEE THINGS THE WAY OTHERS USUALLY DO?
THAT WOULD BE HORRIBLY LONESOME AND SAD, WOULDN'T IT?
FATHER ...
IF YOU DO LIKE HIM, AND IF HE IS AS STRAIGHTFORWARD AS YOU SAY HE IS, YOU SHOULD PREPARE YOURSELF TO BE JUST AS HONEST TO HIM IN RETURN.
ONCE YOU DECIDE TO LET SOMEONE INTO YOUR LIFE, YOU MUST BE PREPARED TO RESPOND IN KIND.

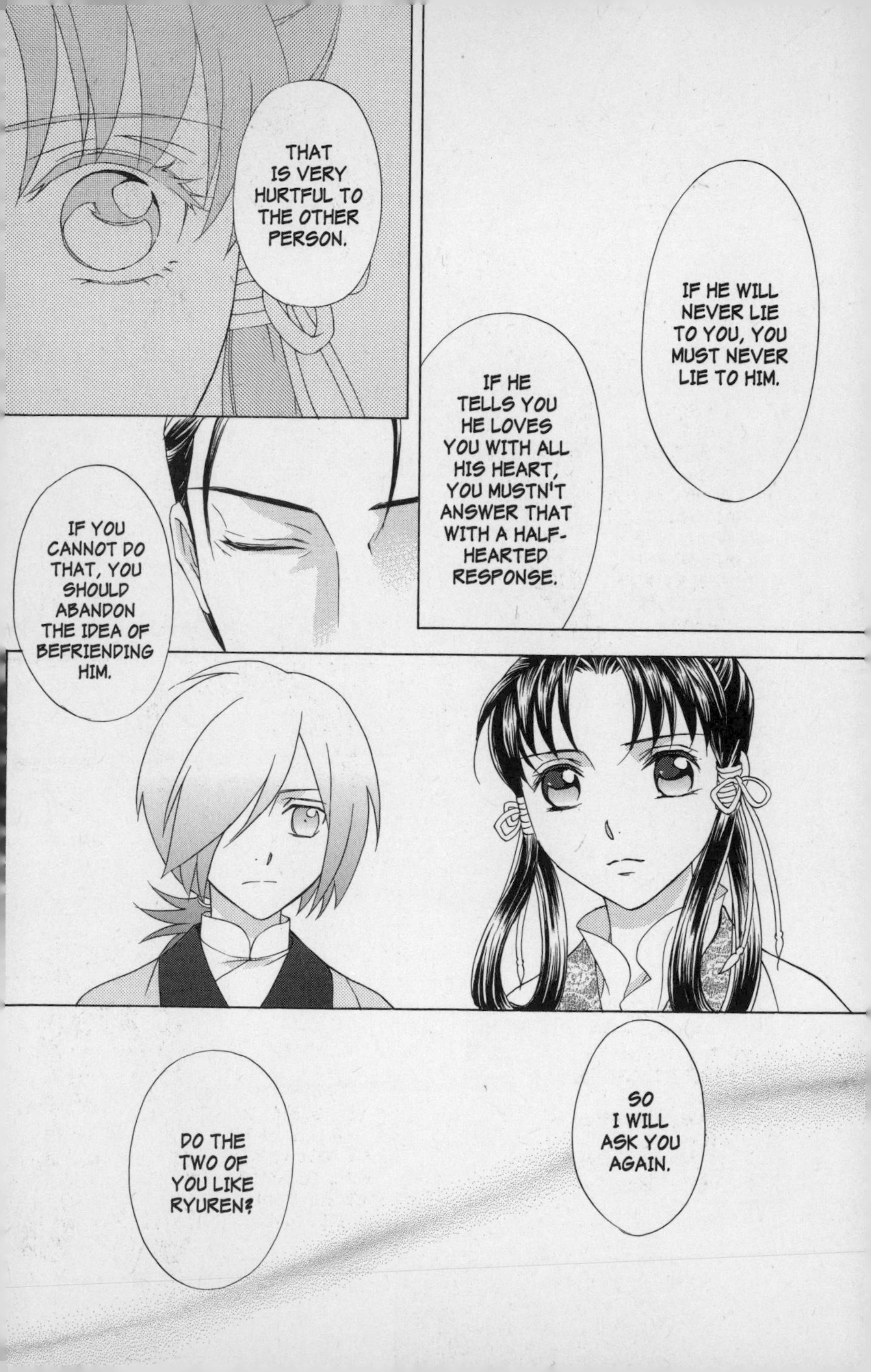
IF HE WILL NEVER LIE TO YOU, YOU MUST NEVER LIE TO HIM.
IF HE TELLS YOU HE LOVES YOU WITH ALL HIS HEART, YOU MUSTN'T ANSWER THAT WITH A HALF-HEARTED RESPONSE.
THAT IS VERY HURTFUL TO THE OTHER PERSON.
IF YOU CANNOT DO THAT, YOU SHOULD ABANDON THE IDEA OF BEFRIENDING HIM.
SO I WILL ASK YOU AGAIN.
DO THE TWO OF YOU LIKE RYUREN?

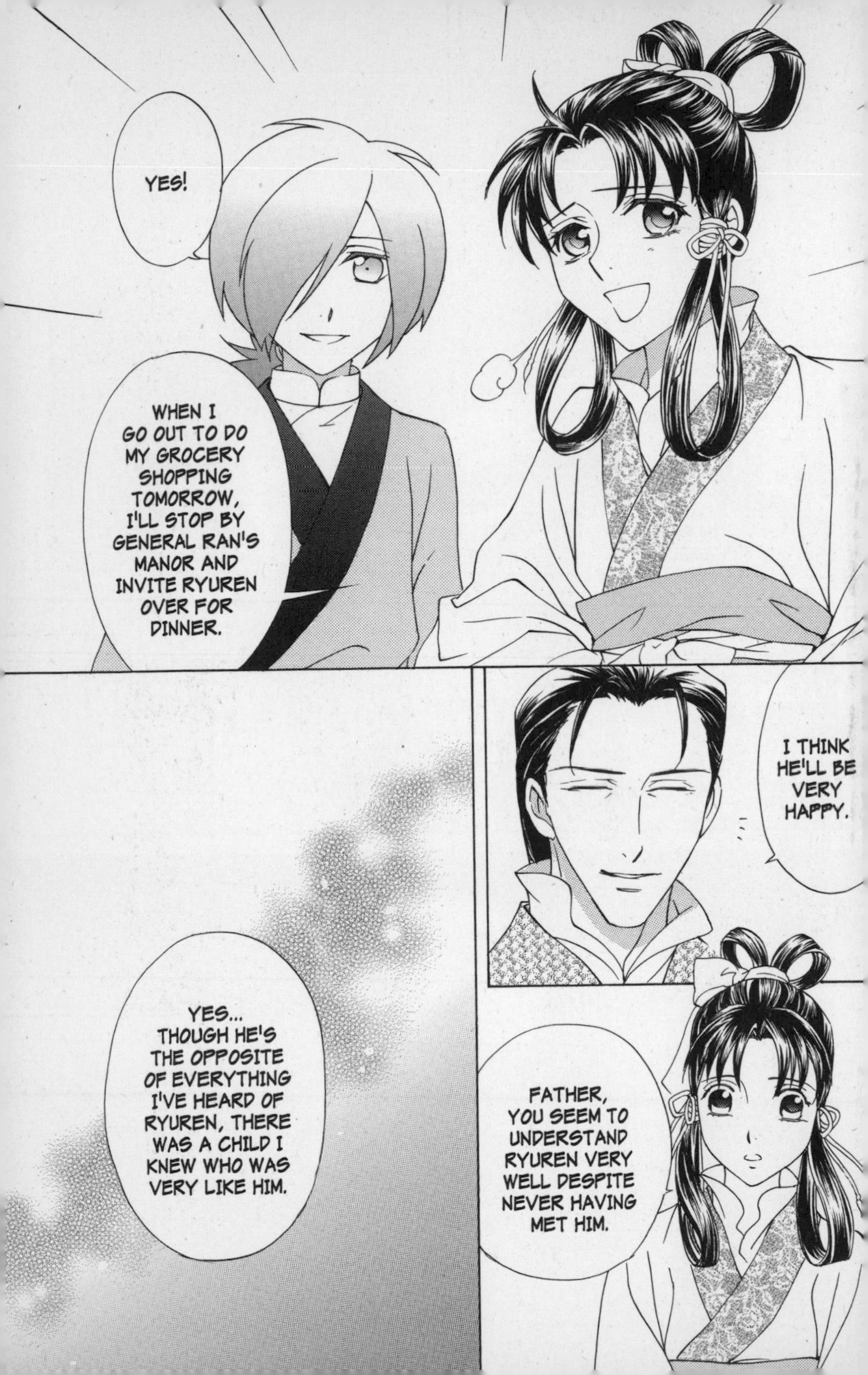
YES!
WHEN I GO OUT TO DO MY GROCERY SHOPPING TOMORROW, I'LL STOP BY GENERAL RAN'S MANOR AND INVITE RYUREN OVER FOR DINNER.
I THINK HE'LL BE VERY HAPPY.
FATHER, YOU SEEM TO UNDERSTAND RYUREN VERY WELL DESPITE NEVER HAVING MET HIM.
YES... THOUGH HE'S THE OPPOSITE OF EVERYTHING I'VE HEARD OF RYUREN, THERE WAS A CHILD I KNEW WHO WAS VERY LIKE HIM.

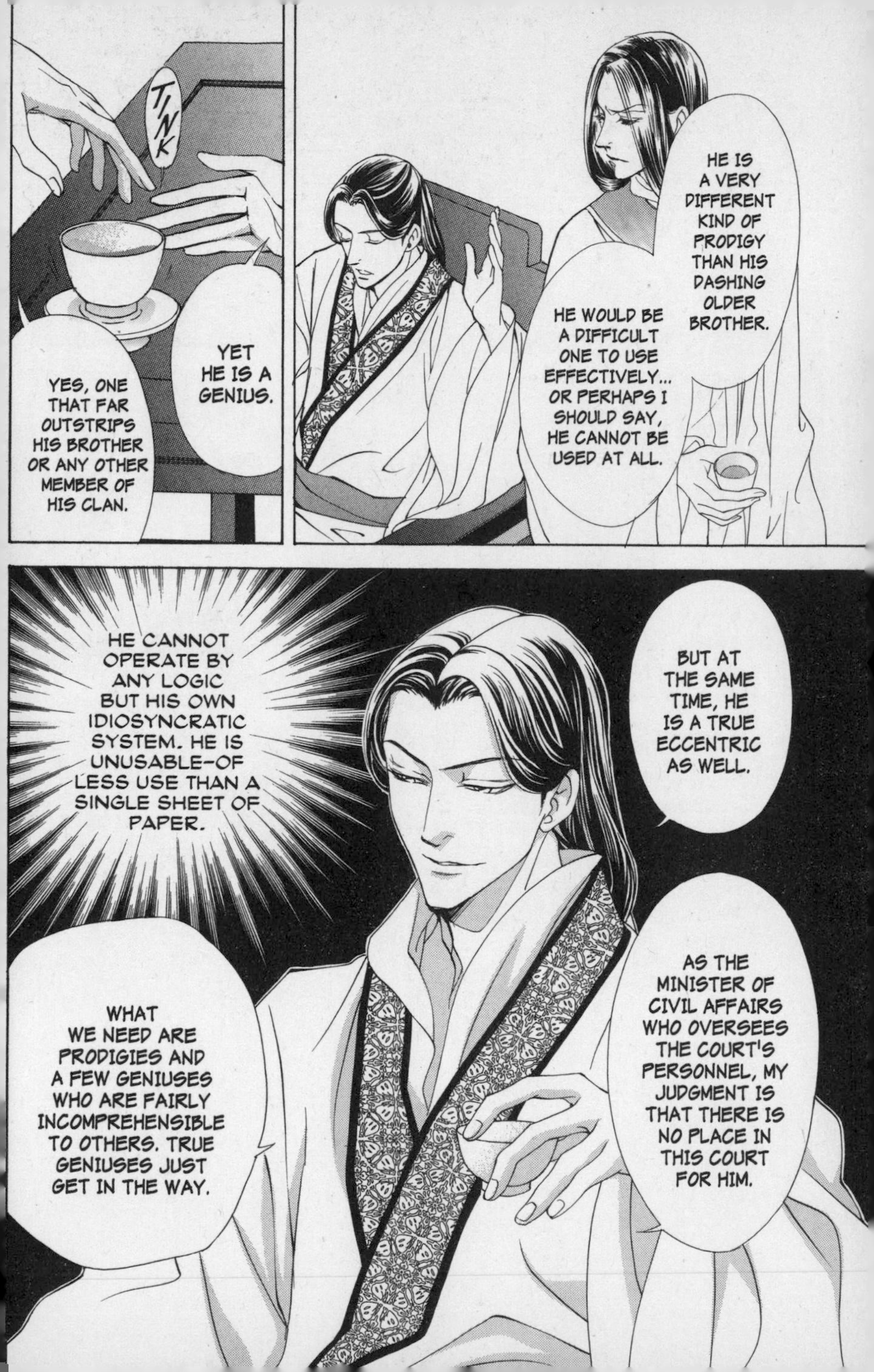
HE IS A VERY DIFFERENT KIND OF PRODIGY THAN HIS DASHING OLDER BROTHER.
HE WOULD BE A DIFFICULT ONE TO USE EFFECTIVELY... OR PERHAPS I SHOULD SAY, HE CANNOT BE USED AT ALL.
TINK
YET HE IS A GENIUS.
YES, ONE THAT FAR OUTSTRIPS HIS BROTHER OR ANY OTHER MEMBER OF HIS CLAN.
BUT AT THE SAME TIME, HE IS A TRUE ECCENTRIC AS WELL.
HE CANNOT OPERATE BY ANY LOGIC BUT HIS OWN IDIOSYNCRATIC SYSTEM. HE IS UNUSABLE—OF LESS USE THAN A SINGLE SHEET OF PAPER.
AS THE MINISTER OF CIVIL AFFAIRS WHO OVERSEES THE COURT'S PERSONNEL, MY JUDGMENT IS THAT THERE IS NO PLACE IN THIS COURT FOR HIM.
WHAT WE NEED ARE PRODIGIES AND A FEW GENIUSES WHO ARE FAIRLY INCOMPREHENSIBLE TO OTHERS. TRUE GENIUSES JUST GET IN THE WAY.

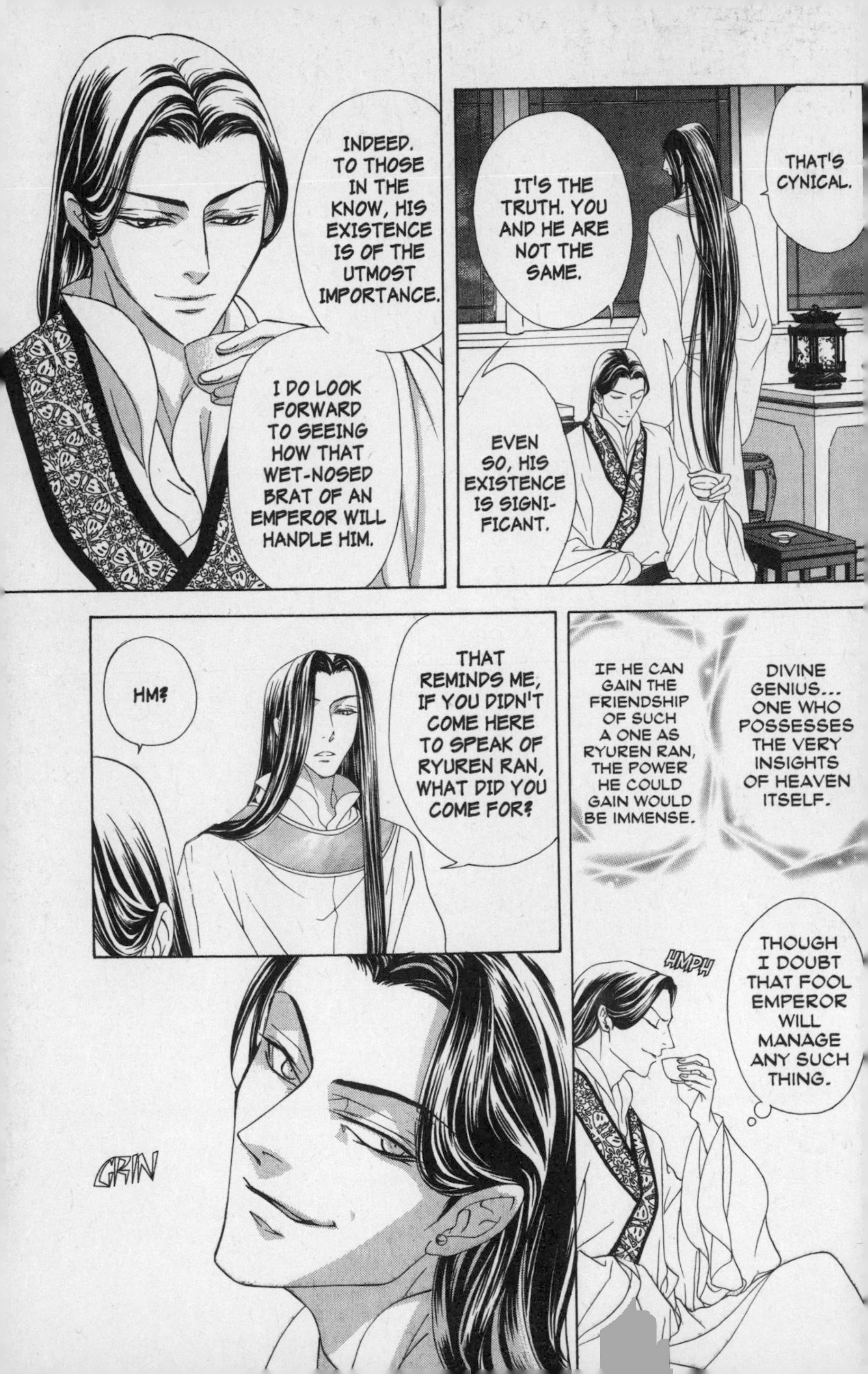
THAT'S CYNICAL.
IT'S THE TRUTH. YOU AND HE ARE NOT THE SAME.
EVEN SO, HIS EXISTENCE IS SIGNIFICANT.
INDEED. TO THOSE IN THE KNOW, HIS EXISTENCE IS OF THE UTMOST IMPORTANCE.
I DO LOOK FORWARD TO SEEING HOW THAT WET-NOSED BRAT OF AN EMPEROR WILL HANDLE HIM.
DIVINE GENIUS... ONE WHO POSSESSES THE VERY INSIGHTS OF HEAVEN ITSELF.
IF HE CAN GAIN THE FRIENDSHIP OF SUCH A ONE AS RYUREN RAN, THE POWER HE COULD GAIN WOULD BE IMMENSE.
THAT REMINDS ME, IF YOU DIDN'T COME HERE TO SPEAK OF RYUREN RAN, WHAT DID YOU COME FOR?
HM?
THOUGH I DOUBT THAT FOOL EMPEROR WILL MANAGE ANY SUCH THING.
HMPH
GRIN

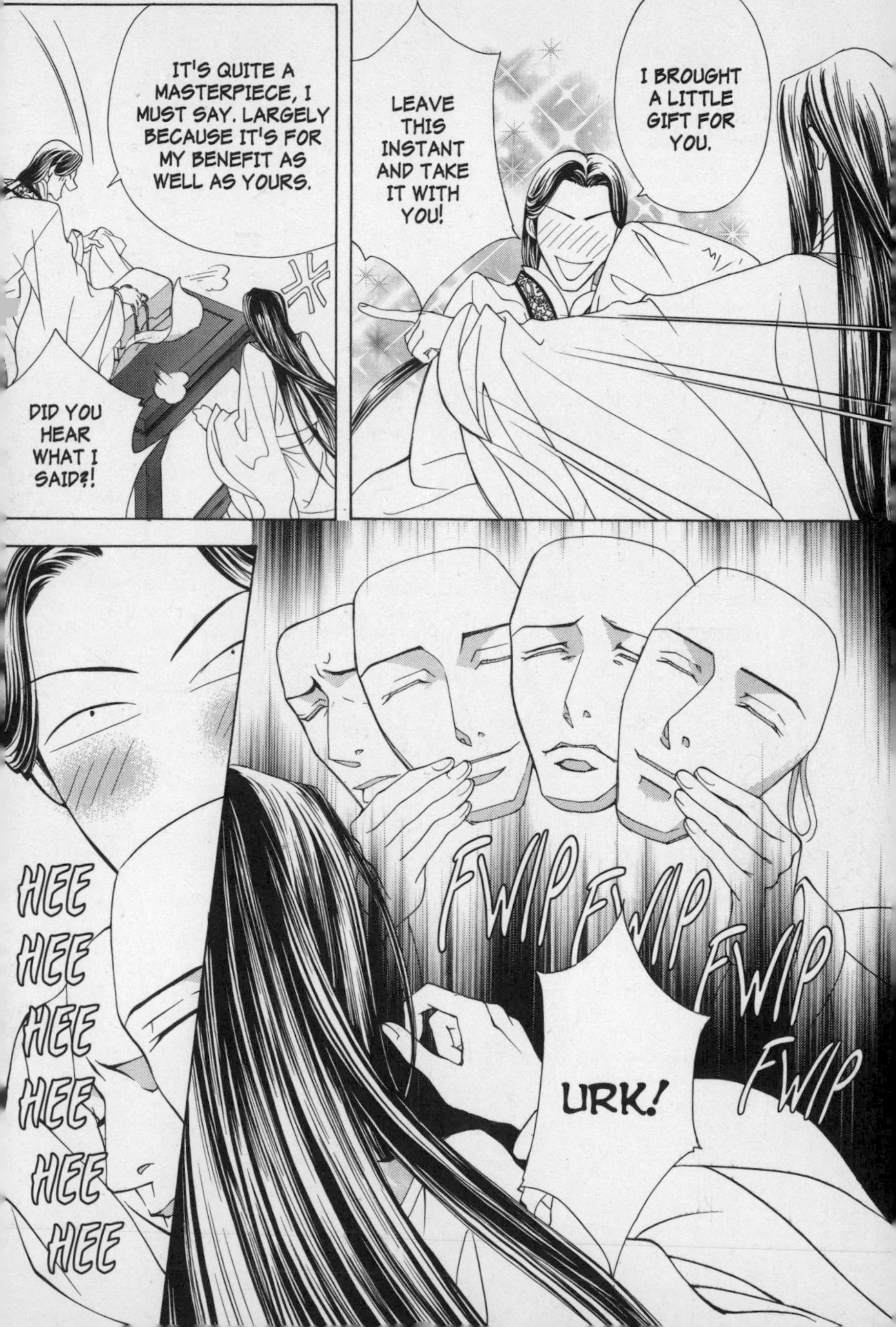
I BROUGHT A LITTLE GIFT FOR YOU.
LEAVE THIS INSTANT AND TAKE IT WITH YOU!
IT'S QUITE A MASTERPIECE, I MUST SAY. LARGELY BECAUSE IT'S FOR MY BENEFIT AS WELL AS YOURS.
DID YOU HEAR WHAT I SAID?!
FWIP FWIP FWIP FWIP
URK!
HEE HEE HEE HEE HEE HEE

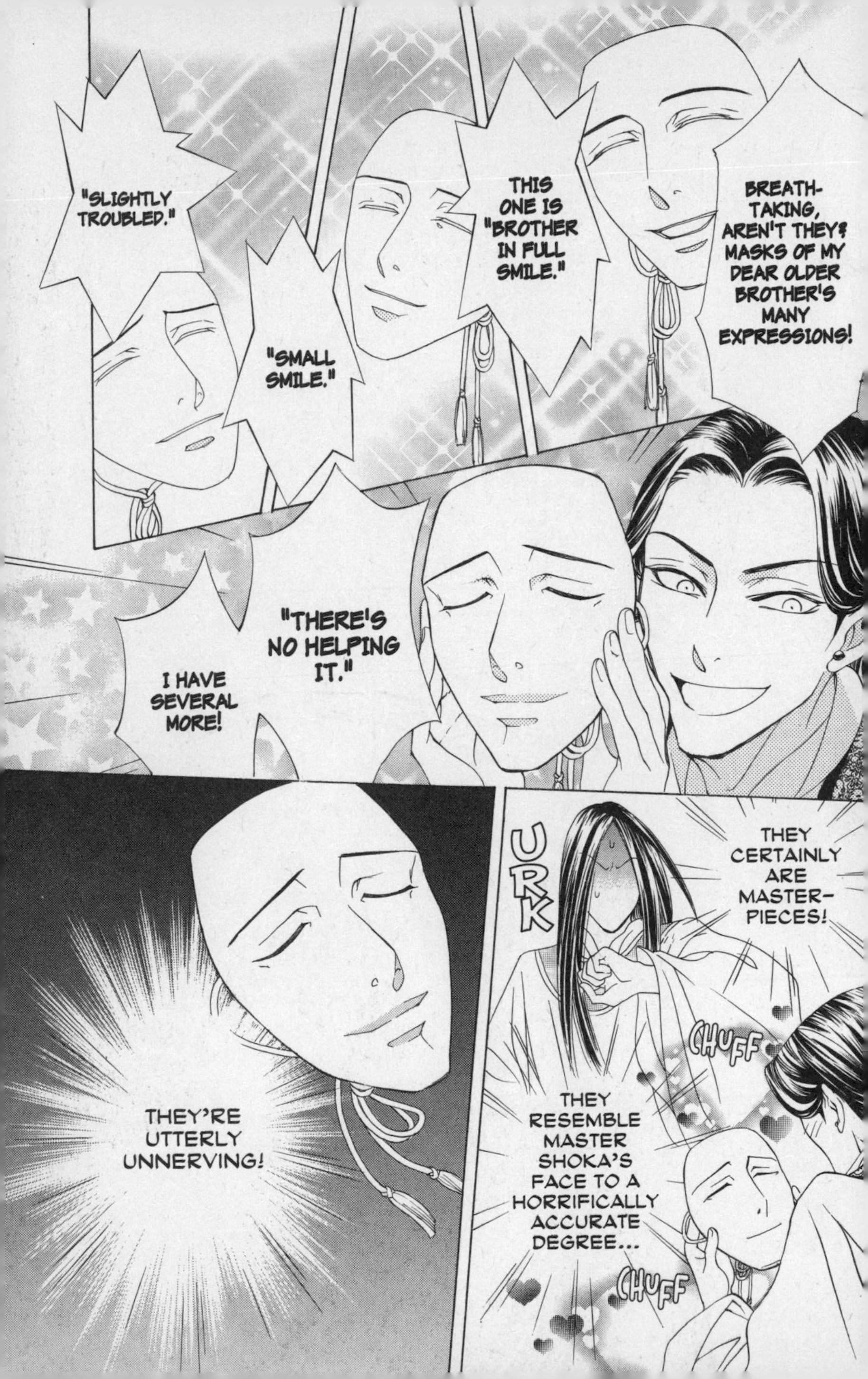
BREATH-TAKING, AREN'T THEY? MASKS OF MY DEAR OLDER BROTHER'S MANY EXPRESSIONS!
THIS ONE IS "BROTHER IN FULL SMILE."
"SMALL SMILE."
"SLIGHTLY TROUBLED."
"THERE'S NO HELPING IT."
I HAVE SEVERAL MORE!
THEY CERTAINLY ARE MASTER-PIECES!
URK
CHUFF
THEY RESEMBLE MASTER SHOKA'S FACE TO A HORRIFICALLY ACCURATE DEGREE...
CHUFF
THEY'RE UTTERLY UNNERVING!

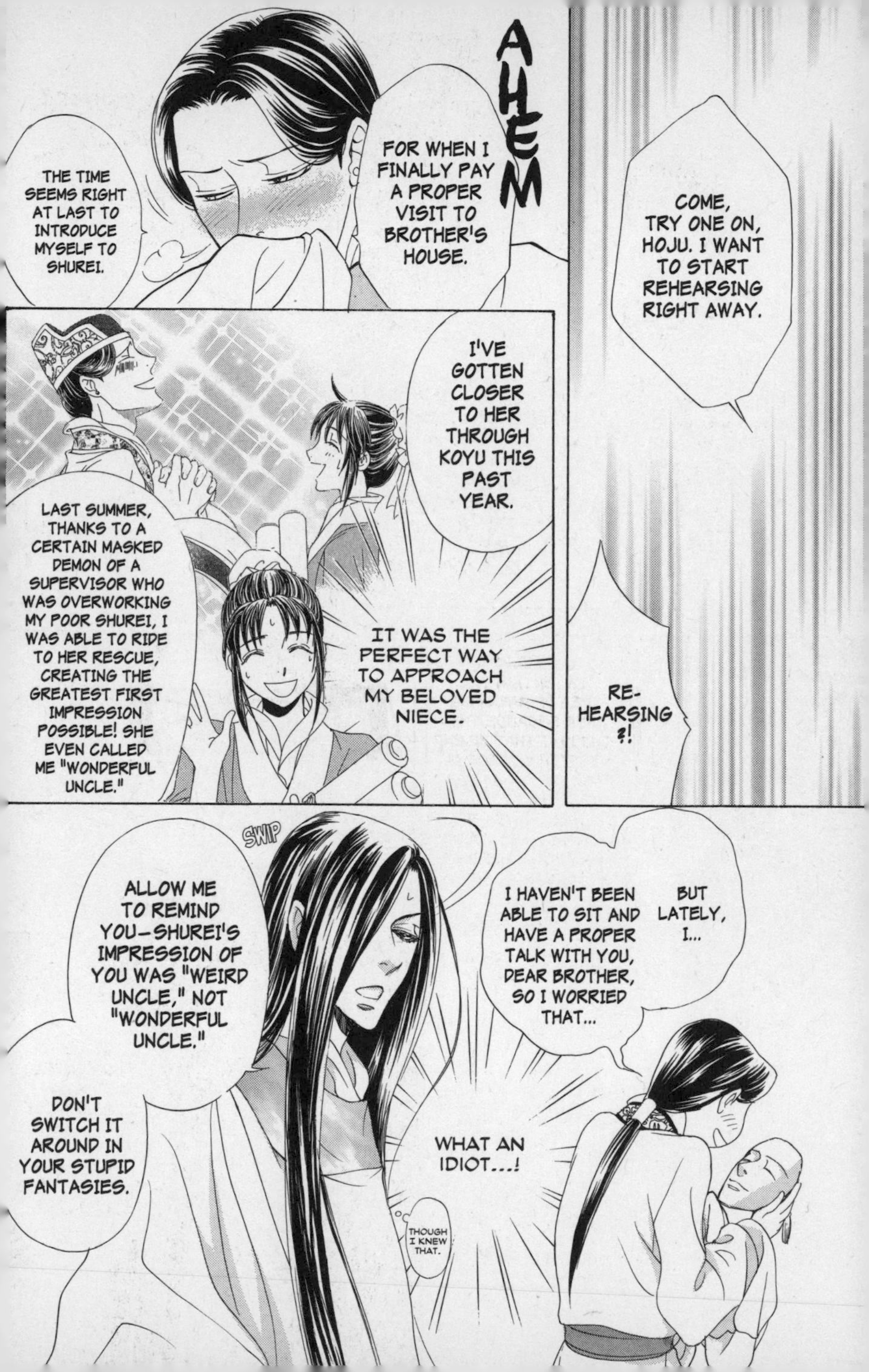
COME, TRY ONE ON, HOJU. I WANT TO START REHEARSING RIGHT AWAY.
RE-HEARSING?!
AHEM
FOR WHEN I FINALLY PAY A PROPER VISIT TO BROTHER'S HOUSE.
THE TIME SEEMS RIGHT AT LAST TO INTRODUCE MYSELF TO SHUREI.
I'VE GOTTEN CLOSER TO HER THROUGH KOYU THIS PAST YEAR.
LAST SUMMER, THANKS TO A CERTAIN MASKED DEMON OF A SUPERVISOR WHO WAS OVERWORKING MY POOR SHUREI, I WAS ABLE TO RIDE TO HER RESCUE, CREATING THE GREATEST FIRST IMPRESSION POSSIBLE! SHE EVEN CALLED ME "WONDERFUL UNCLE."
IT WAS THE PERFECT WAY TO APPROACH MY BELOVED NIECE.
SWIP
BUT LATELY, I...
I HAVEN'T BEEN ABLE TO SIT AND HAVE A PROPER TALK WITH YOU, DEAR BROTHER, SO I WORRIED THAT...
ALLOW ME TO REMIND YOU—SHUREI'S IMPRESSION OF YOU WAS "WEIRD UNCLE," NOT "WONDERFUL UNCLE."
WHAT AN IDIOT...!
THOUGH I KNEW THAT.
DON'T SWITCH IT AROUND IN YOUR STUPID FANTASIES.

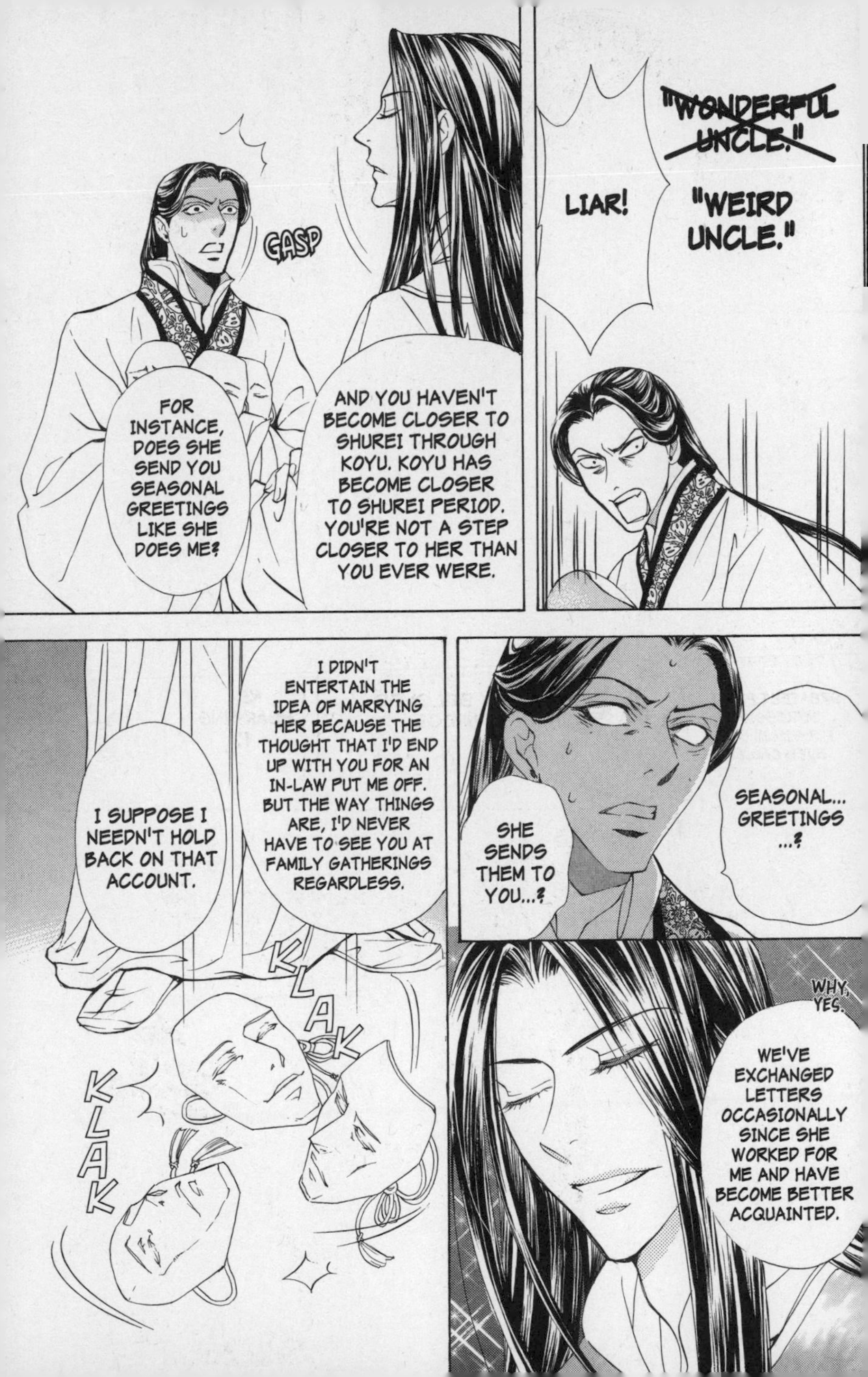
~~"WONDERFUL UNCLE."~~
"WEIRD UNCLE."
LIAR!
GASP
AND YOU HAVEN'T BECOME CLOSER TO SHUREI THROUGH KOYU. KOYU HAS BECOME CLOSER TO SHUREI PERIOD. YOU'RE NOT A STEP CLOSER TO HER THAN YOU EVER WERE.
FOR INSTANCE, DOES SHE SEND YOU SEASONAL GREETINGS LIKE SHE DOES ME?
SEASONAL... GREETINGS ...?
SHE SENDS THEM TO YOU...?
WHY, YES.
WE'VE EXCHANGED LETTERS OCCASIONALLY SINCE SHE WORKED FOR ME AND HAVE BECOME BETTER ACQUAINTED.
I DIDN'T ENTERTAIN THE IDEA OF MARRYING HER BECAUSE THE THOUGHT THAT I'D END UP WITH YOU FOR AN IN-LAW PUT ME OFF. BUT THE WAY THINGS ARE, I'D NEVER HAVE TO SEE YOU AT FAMILY GATHERINGS REGARDLESS.
I SUPPOSE I NEEDN'T HOLD BACK ON THAT ACCOUNT.
KLAK
KLAK

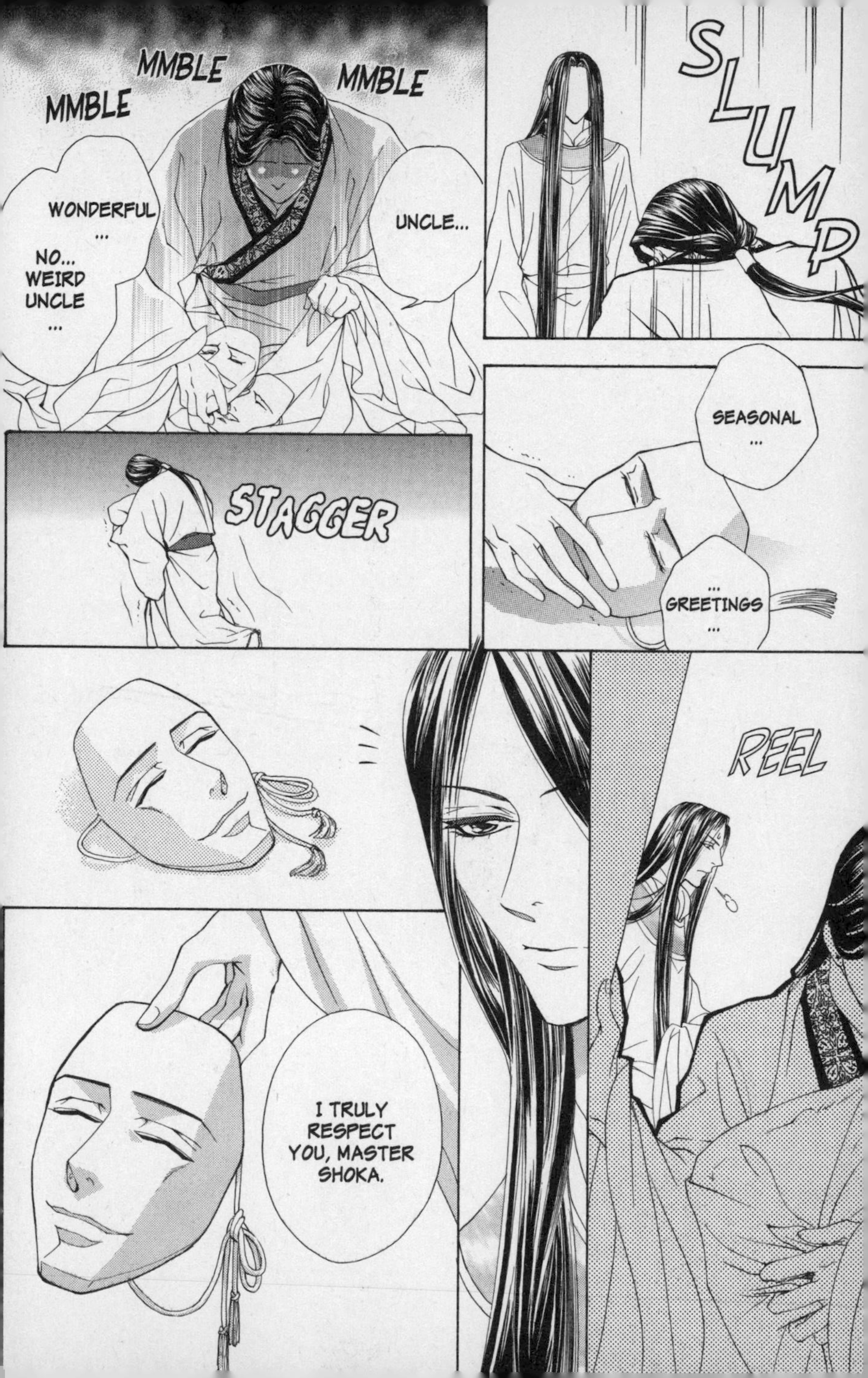
SLUMP
MMBLE
MMBLE
UNCLE...
MMBLE
WONDERFUL ...
NO... WEIRD UNCLE ...
SEASONAL ...
... GREETINGS ...
STAGGER
REEL
I TRULY RESPECT YOU, MASTER SHOKA.

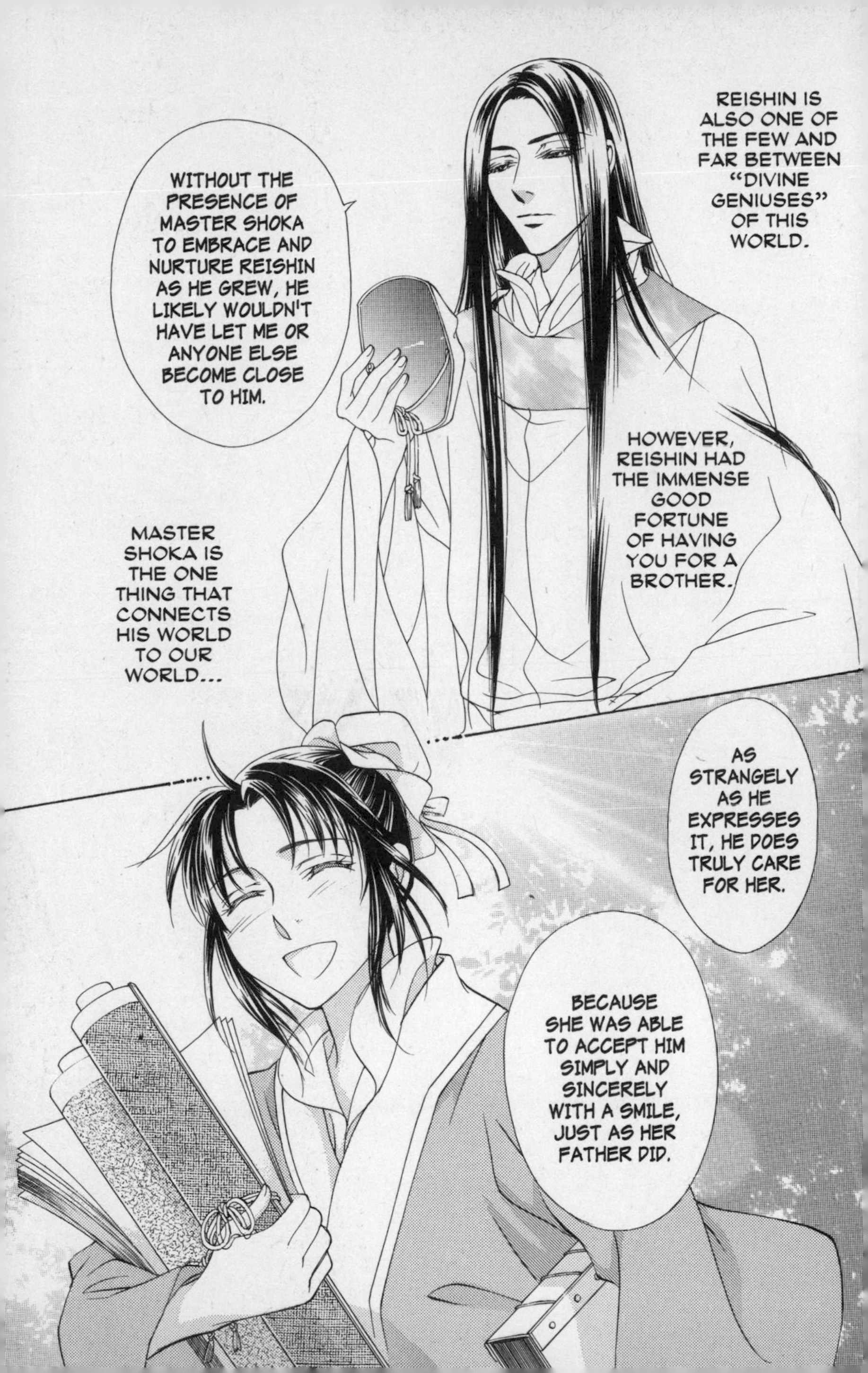
REISHIN IS ALSO ONE OF THE FEW AND FAR BETWEEN "DIVINE GENIUSES" OF THIS WORLD.
HOWEVER, REISHIN HAD THE IMMENSE GOOD FORTUNE OF HAVING YOU FOR A BROTHER.
MASTER SHOKA IS THE ONE THING THAT CONNECTS HIS WORLD TO OUR WORLD...
WITHOUT THE PRESENCE OF MASTER SHOKA TO EMBRACE AND NURTURE REISHIN AS HE GREW, HE LIKELY WOULDN'T HAVE LET ME OR ANYONE ELSE BECOME CLOSE TO HIM.
AS STRANGELY AS HE EXPRESSES IT, HE DOES TRULY CARE FOR HER.
BECAUSE SHE WAS ABLE TO ACCEPT HIM SIMPLY AND SINCERELY WITH A SMILE, JUST AS HER FATHER DID.

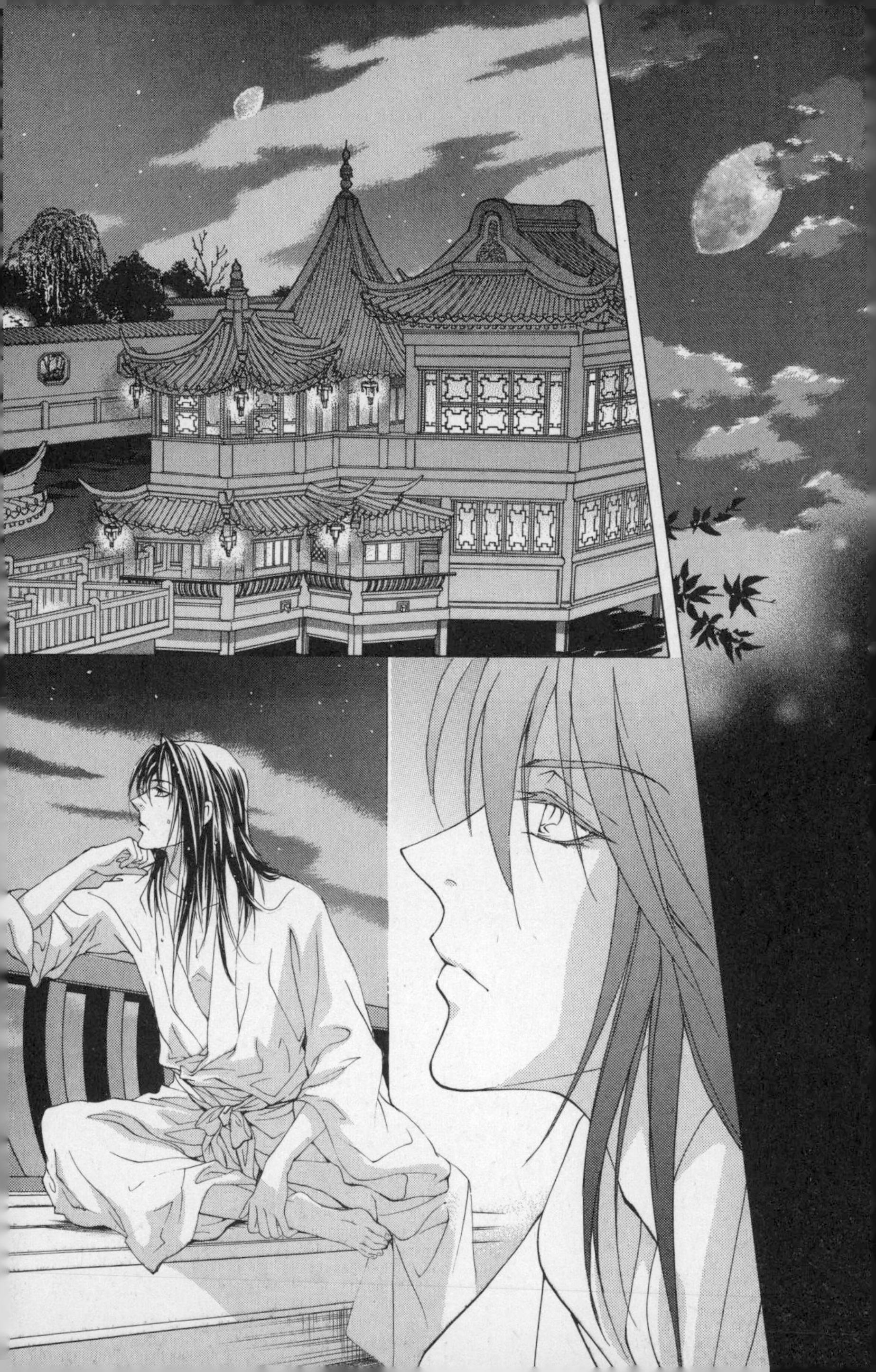

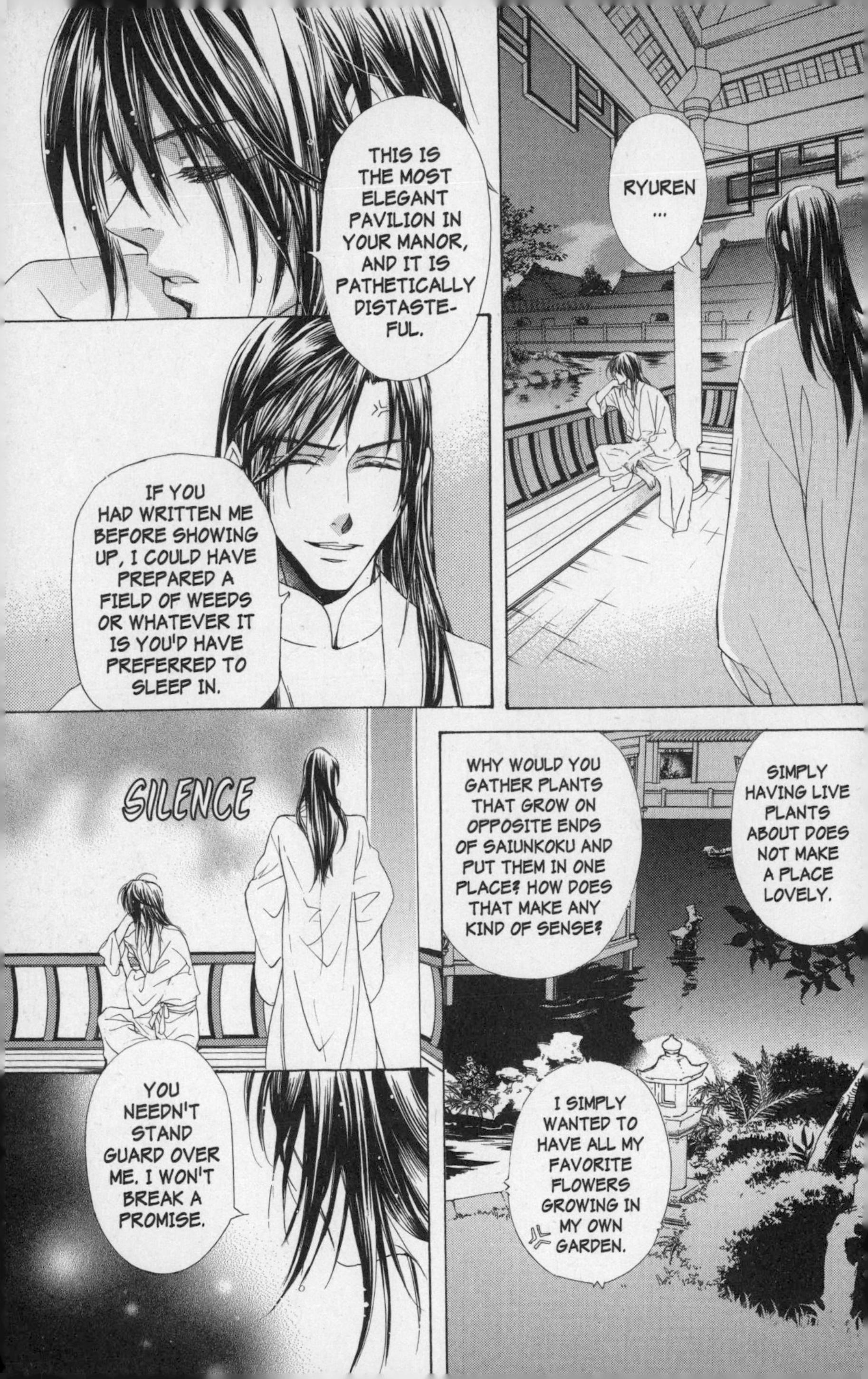
RYUREN ...
THIS IS THE MOST ELEGANT PAVILION IN YOUR MANOR, AND IT IS PATHETICALLY DISTASTE-FUL.
IF YOU HAD WRITTEN ME BEFORE SHOWING UP, I COULD HAVE PREPARED A FIELD OF WEEDS OR WHATEVER IT IS YOU'D HAVE PREFERRED TO SLEEP IN.
SIMPLY HAVING LIVE PLANTS ABOUT DOES NOT MAKE A PLACE LOVELY.
WHY WOULD YOU GATHER PLANTS THAT GROW ON OPPOSITE ENDS OF SAIUNKOKU AND PUT THEM IN ONE PLACE? HOW DOES THAT MAKE ANY KIND OF SENSE?
I SIMPLY WANTED TO HAVE ALL MY FAVORITE FLOWERS GROWING IN MY OWN GARDEN.
SILENCE
YOU NEEDN'T STAND GUARD OVER ME. I WON'T BREAK A PROMISE.

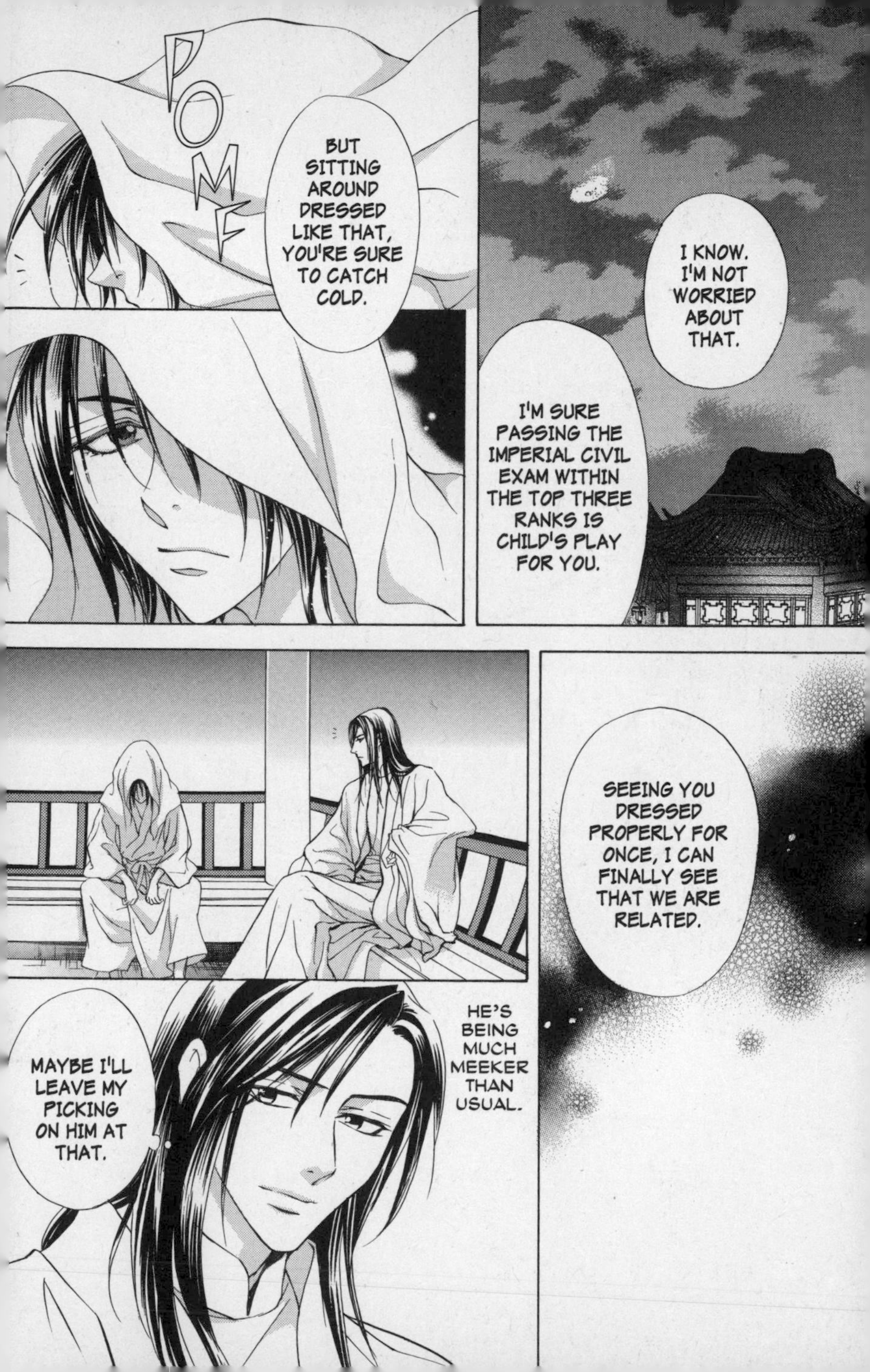
I KNOW. I'M NOT WORRIED ABOUT THAT.
I'M SURE PASSING THE IMPERIAL CIVIL EXAM WITHIN THE TOP THREE RANKS IS CHILD'S PLAY FOR YOU.
POMF
BUT SITTING AROUND DRESSED LIKE THAT, YOU'RE SURE TO CATCH COLD.
SEEING YOU DRESSED PROPERLY FOR ONCE, I CAN FINALLY SEE THAT WE ARE RELATED.
HE'S BEING MUCH MEEKER THAN USUAL.
MAYBE I'LL LEAVE MY PICKING ON HIM AT THAT.

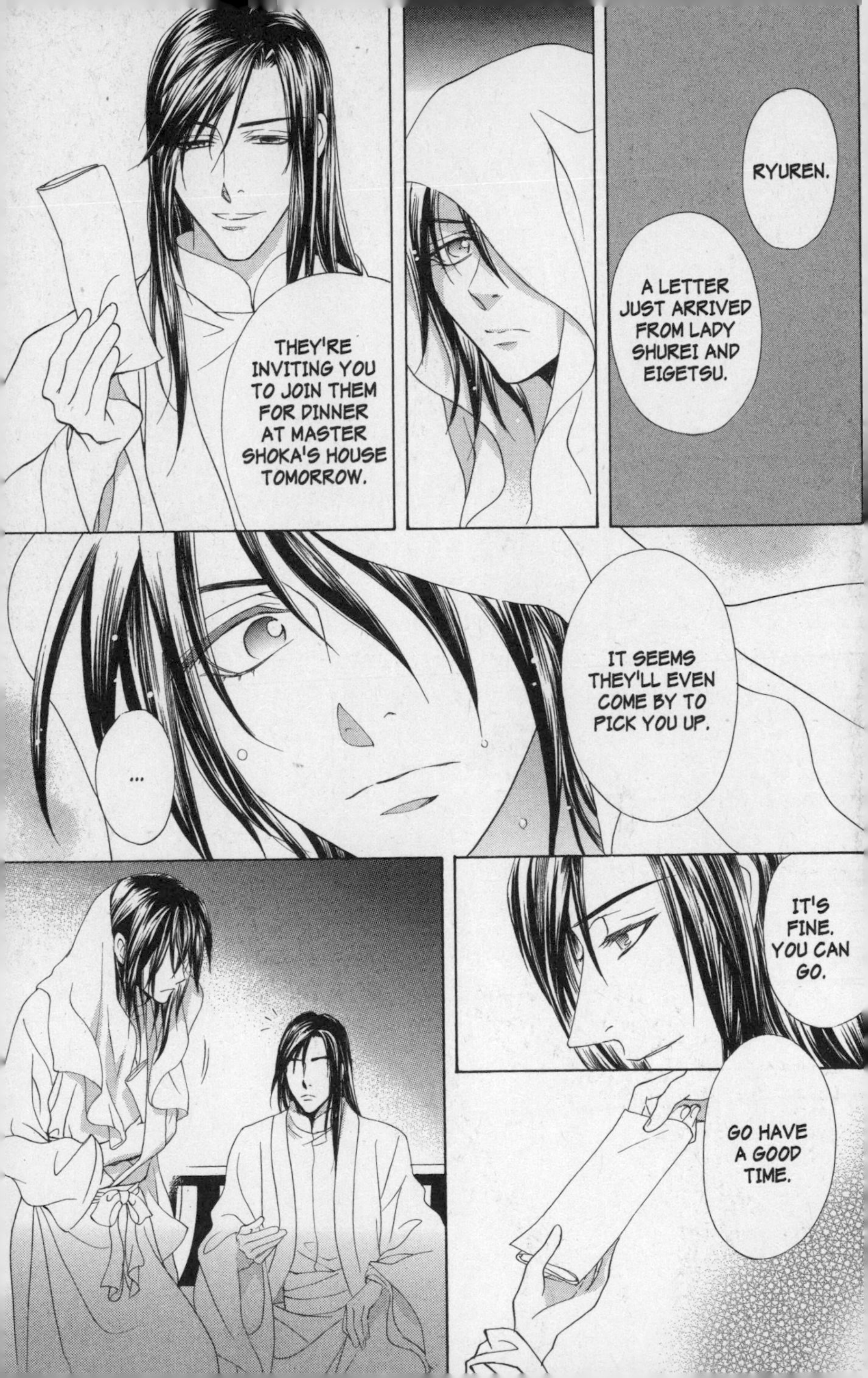
RYUREN.
A LETTER JUST ARRIVED FROM LADY SHUREI AND EIGETSU.
THEY'RE INVITING YOU TO JOIN THEM FOR DINNER AT MASTER SHOKA'S HOUSE TOMORROW.
IT SEEMS THEY'LL EVEN COME BY TO PICK YOU UP.
...
IT'S FINE. YOU CAN GO.
GO HAVE A GOOD TIME.

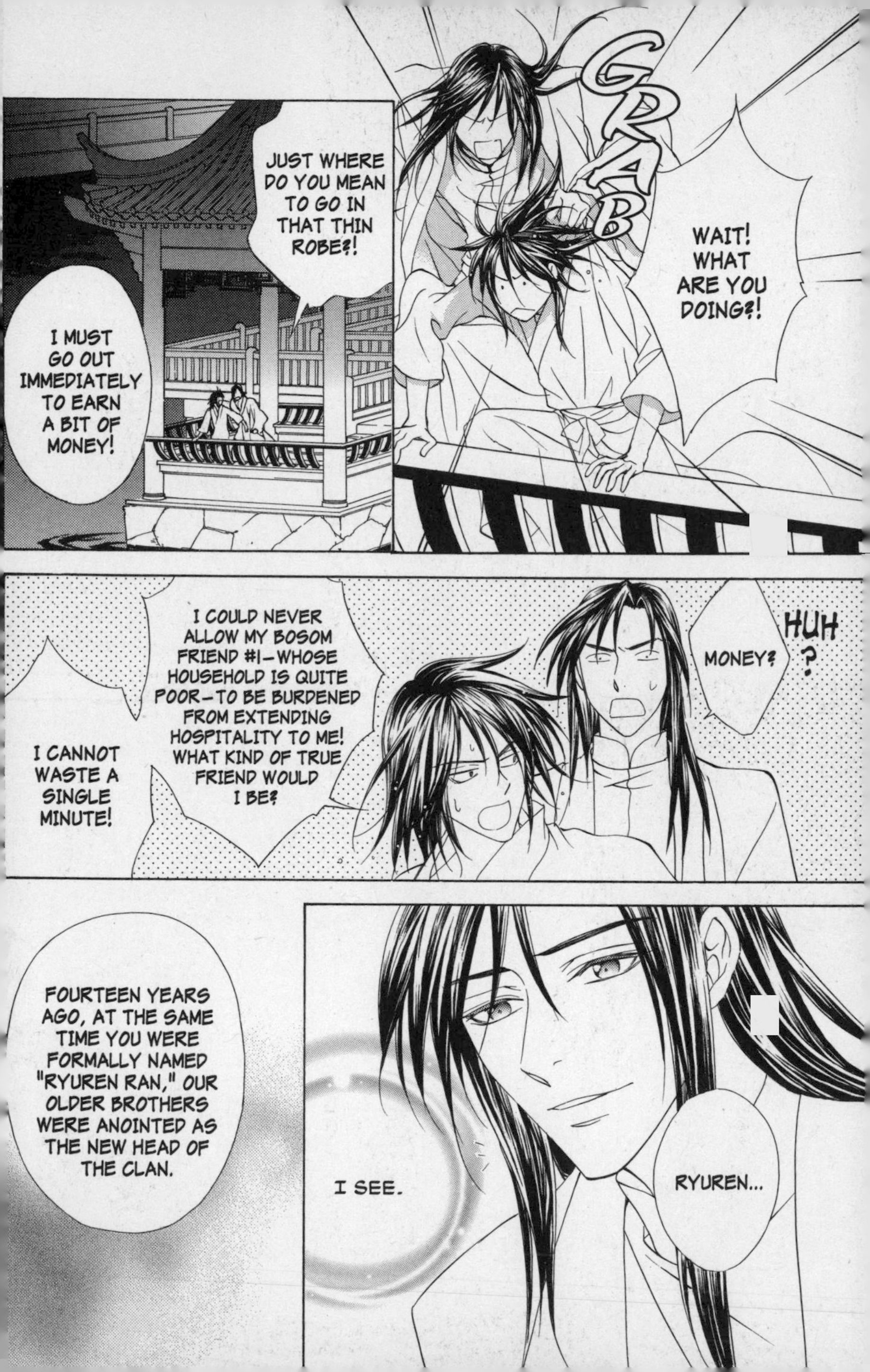
GRAB
WAIT! WHAT ARE YOU DOING?!
JUST WHERE DO YOU MEAN TO GO IN THAT THIN ROBE?!
I MUST GO OUT IMMEDIATELY TO EARN A BIT OF MONEY!
HUH?
MONEY?
I COULD NEVER ALLOW MY BOSOM FRIEND #1—WHOSE HOUSEHOLD IS QUITE POOR—TO BE BURDENED FROM EXTENDING HOSPITALITY TO ME! WHAT KIND OF TRUE FRIEND WOULD I BE?
I CANNOT WASTE A SINGLE MINUTE!
RYUREN...
I SEE.
FOURTEEN YEARS AGO, AT THE SAME TIME YOU WERE FORMALLY NAMED "RYUREN RAN," OUR OLDER BROTHERS WERE ANOINTED AS THE NEW HEAD OF THE CLAN.

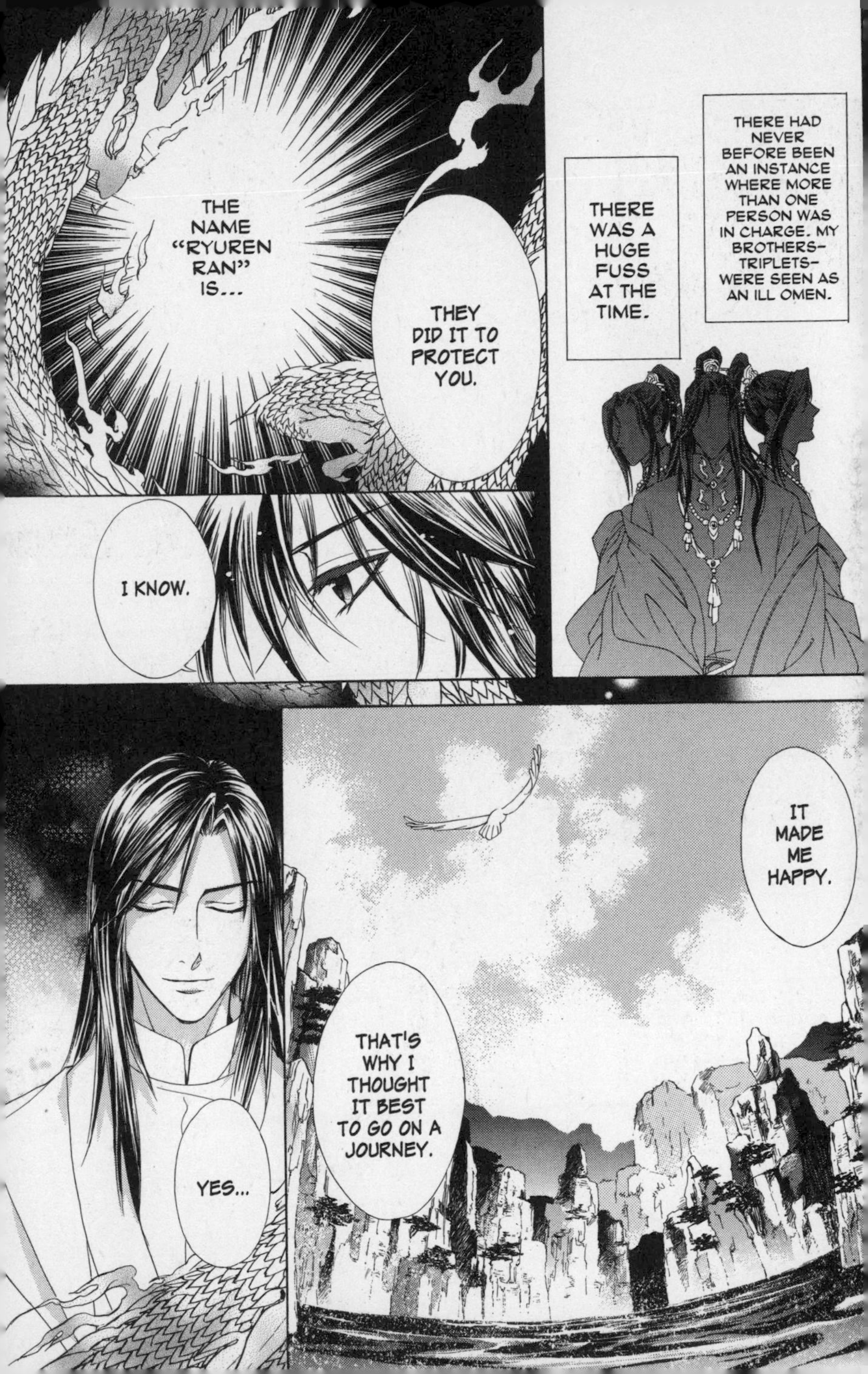
THERE HAD NEVER BEFORE BEEN AN INSTANCE WHERE MORE THAN ONE PERSON WAS IN CHARGE. MY BROTHERS—TRIPLETS—WERE SEEN AS AN ILL OMEN.
THERE WAS A HUGE FUSS AT THE TIME.
THE NAME "RYUREN RAN" IS...
THEY DID IT TO PROTECT YOU.
I KNOW.
IT MADE ME HAPPY.
THAT'S WHY I THOUGHT IT BEST TO GO ON A JOURNEY.
YES...

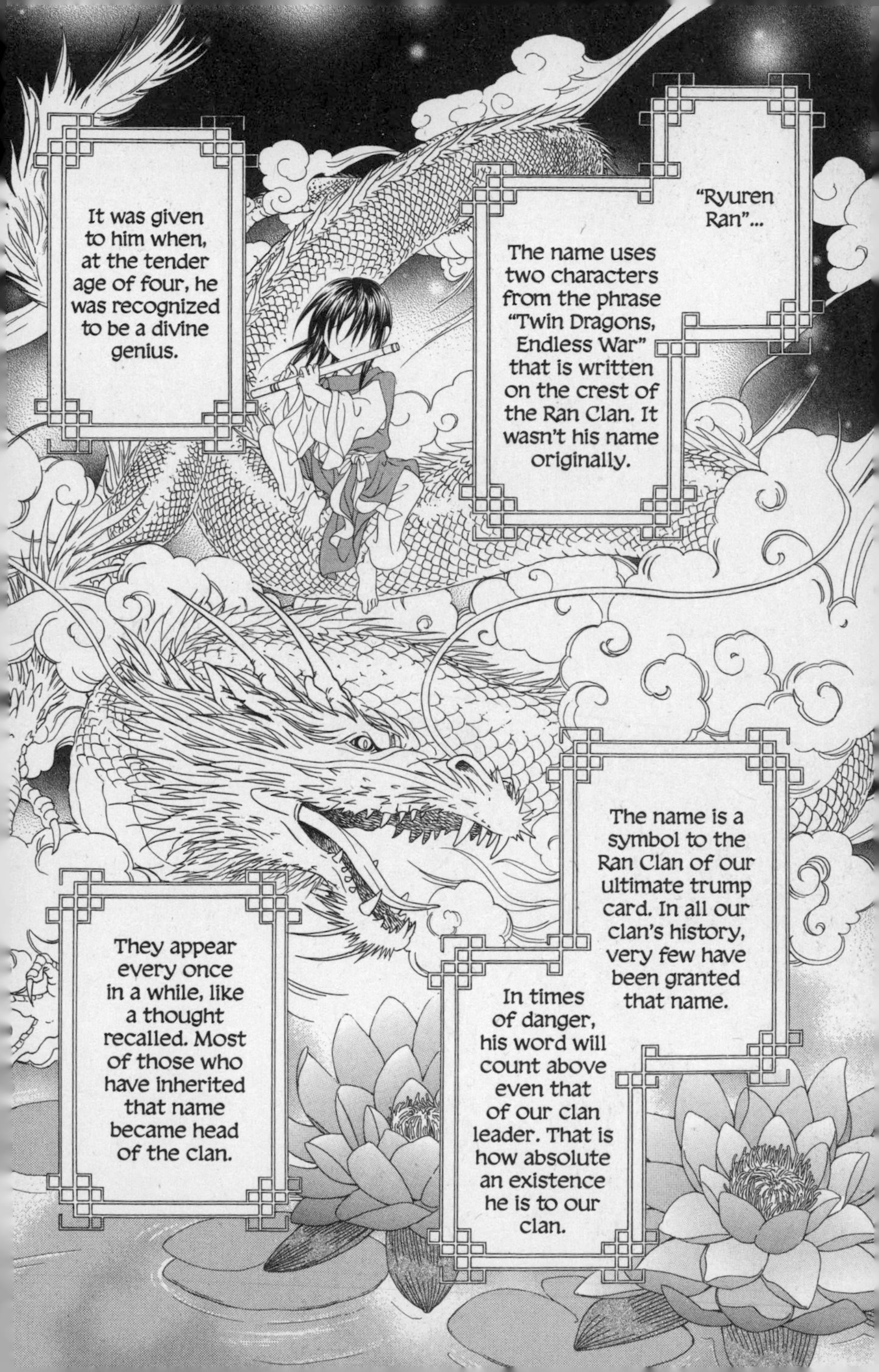
"Ryuren Ran"...
The name uses two characters from the phrase "Twin Dragons, Endless War" that is written on the crest of the Ran Clan. It wasn't his name originally.
It was given to him when, at the tender age of four, he was recognized to be a divine genius.
The name is a symbol to the Ran Clan of our ultimate trump card. In all our clan's history, very few have been granted that name.
In times of danger, his word will count above even that of our clan leader. That is how absolute an existence he is to our clan.
They appear every once in a while, like a thought recalled. Most of those who have inherited that name became head of the clan.

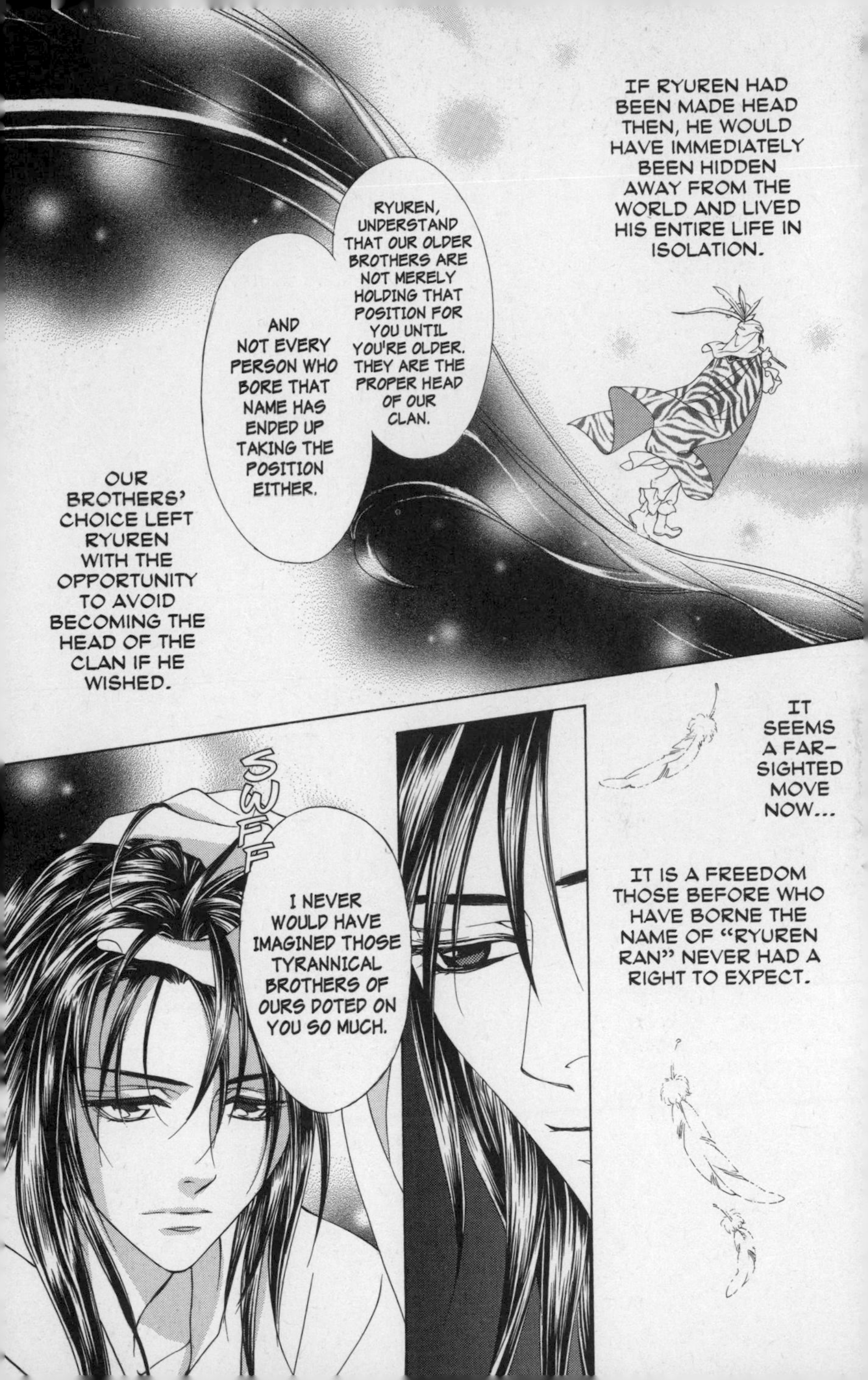
IF RYUREN HAD BEEN MADE HEAD THEN, HE WOULD HAVE IMMEDIATELY BEEN HIDDEN AWAY FROM THE WORLD AND LIVED HIS ENTIRE LIFE IN ISOLATION.
RYUREN, UNDERSTAND THAT OUR OLDER BROTHERS ARE NOT MERELY HOLDING THAT POSITION FOR YOU UNTIL YOU'RE OLDER. THEY ARE THE PROPER HEAD OF OUR CLAN.
AND NOT EVERY PERSON WHO BORE THAT NAME HAS ENDED UP TAKING THE POSITION EITHER.
OUR BROTHERS' CHOICE LEFT RYUREN WITH THE OPPORTUNITY TO AVOID BECOMING THE HEAD OF THE CLAN IF HE WISHED.
IT SEEMS A FAR-SIGHTED MOVE NOW...
IT IS A FREEDOM THOSE BEFORE WHO HAVE BORNE THE NAME OF "RYUREN RAN" NEVER HAD A RIGHT TO EXPECT.
SWFF
I NEVER WOULD HAVE IMAGINED THOSE TYRANNICAL BROTHERS OF OURS DOTED ON YOU SO MUCH.

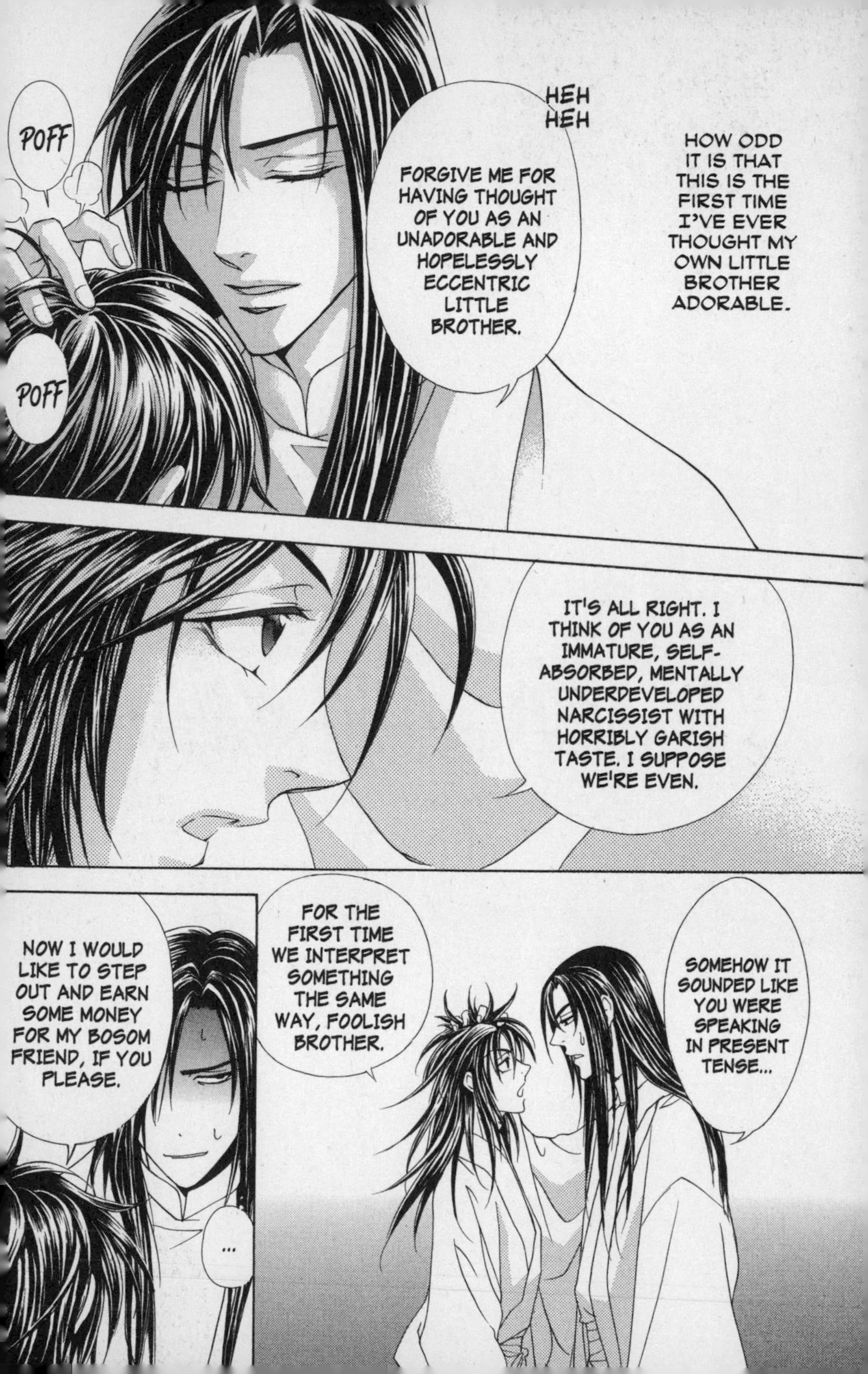
HOW ODD IT IS THAT THIS IS THE FIRST TIME I'VE EVER THOUGHT MY OWN LITTLE BROTHER ADORABLE.
HEH HEH
FORGIVE ME FOR HAVING THOUGHT OF YOU AS AN UNADORABLE AND HOPELESSLY ECCENTRIC LITTLE BROTHER.
POFF
POFF
IT'S ALL RIGHT. I THINK OF YOU AS AN IMMATURE, SELF-ABSORBED, MENTALLY UNDERDEVELOPED NARCISSIST WITH HORRIBLY GARISH TASTE. I SUPPOSE WE'RE EVEN.
SOMEHOW IT SOUNDED LIKE YOU WERE SPEAKING IN PRESENT TENSE...
FOR THE FIRST TIME WE INTERPRET SOMETHING THE SAME WAY, FOOLISH BROTHER.
NOW I WOULD LIKE TO STEP OUT AND EARN SOME MONEY FOR MY BOSOM FRIEND, IF YOU PLEASE.
...

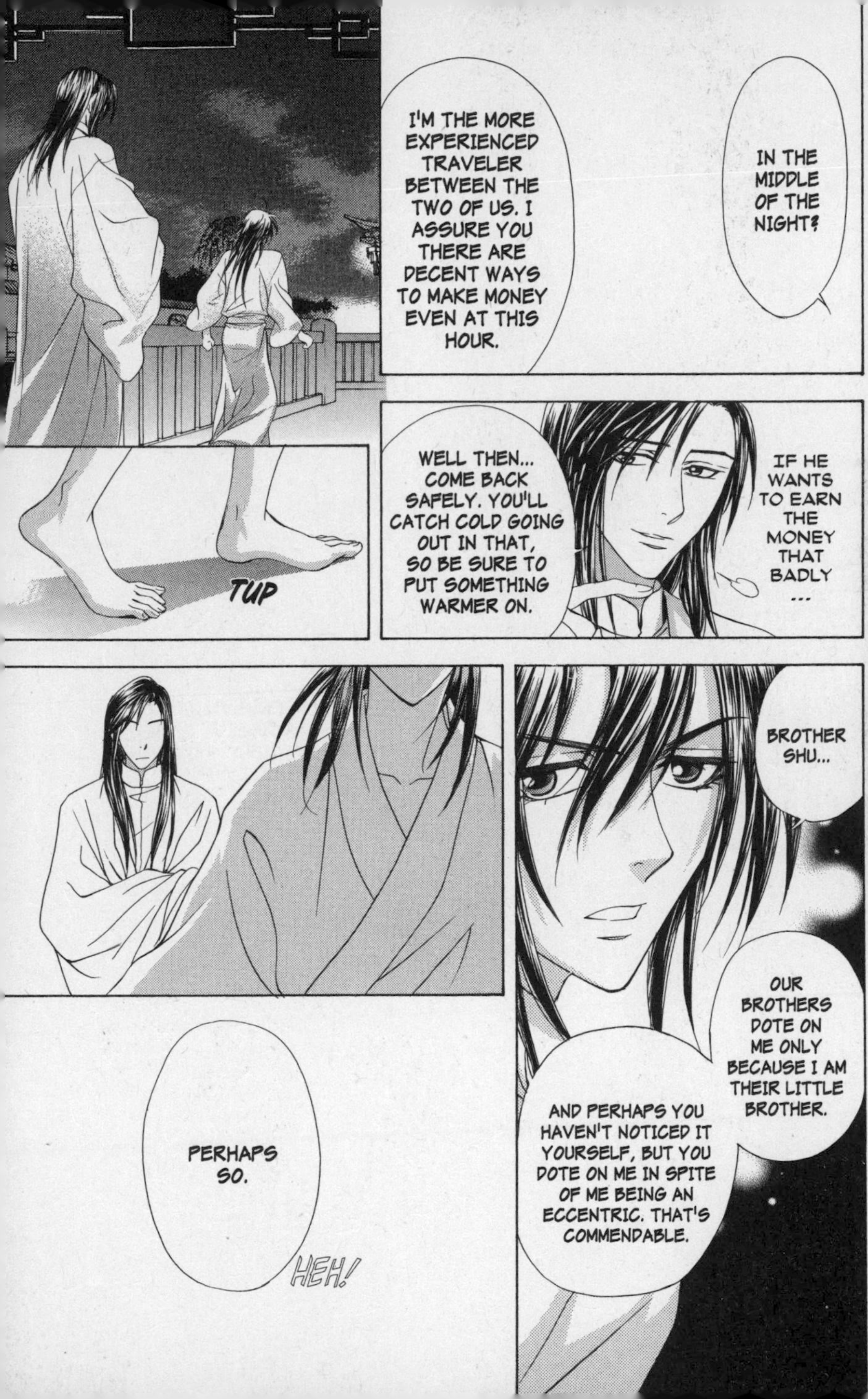
IN THE MIDDLE OF THE NIGHT?
I'M THE MORE EXPERIENCED TRAVELER BETWEEN THE TWO OF US. I ASSURE YOU THERE ARE DECENT WAYS TO MAKE MONEY EVEN AT THIS HOUR.
IF HE WANTS TO EARN THE MONEY THAT BADLY ...
WELL THEN... COME BACK SAFELY. YOU'LL CATCH COLD GOING OUT IN THAT, SO BE SURE TO PUT SOMETHING WARMER ON.
TUP
BROTHER SHU...
OUR BROTHERS DOTE ON ME ONLY BECAUSE I AM THEIR LITTLE BROTHER.
AND PERHAPS YOU HAVEN'T NOTICED IT YOURSELF, BUT YOU DOTE ON ME IN SPITE OF ME BEING AN ECCENTRIC. THAT'S COMMENDABLE.
PERHAPS SO.
HEH!

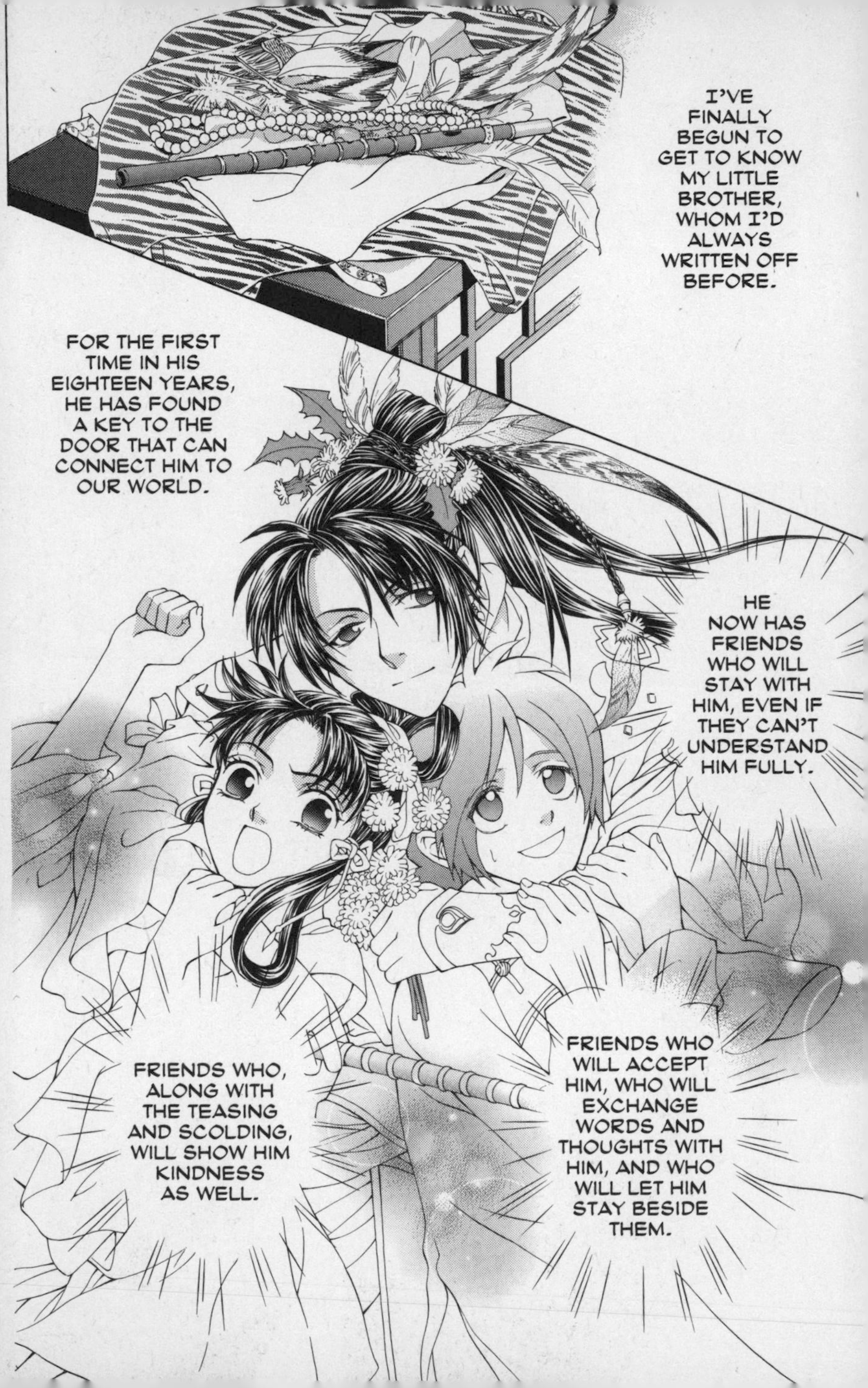
I'VE FINALLY BEGUN TO GET TO KNOW MY LITTLE BROTHER, WHOM I'D ALWAYS WRITTEN OFF BEFORE.
FOR THE FIRST TIME IN HIS EIGHTEEN YEARS, HE HAS FOUND A KEY TO THE DOOR THAT CAN CONNECT HIM TO OUR WORLD.
HE NOW HAS FRIENDS WHO WILL STAY WITH HIM, EVEN IF THEY CAN'T UNDERSTAND HIM FULLY.
FRIENDS WHO WILL ACCEPT HIM, WHO WILL EXCHANGE WORDS AND THOUGHTS WITH HIM, AND WHO WILL LET HIM STAY BESIDE THEM.
FRIENDS WHO, ALONG WITH THE TEASING AND SCOLDING, WILL SHOW HIM KINDNESS AS WELL.

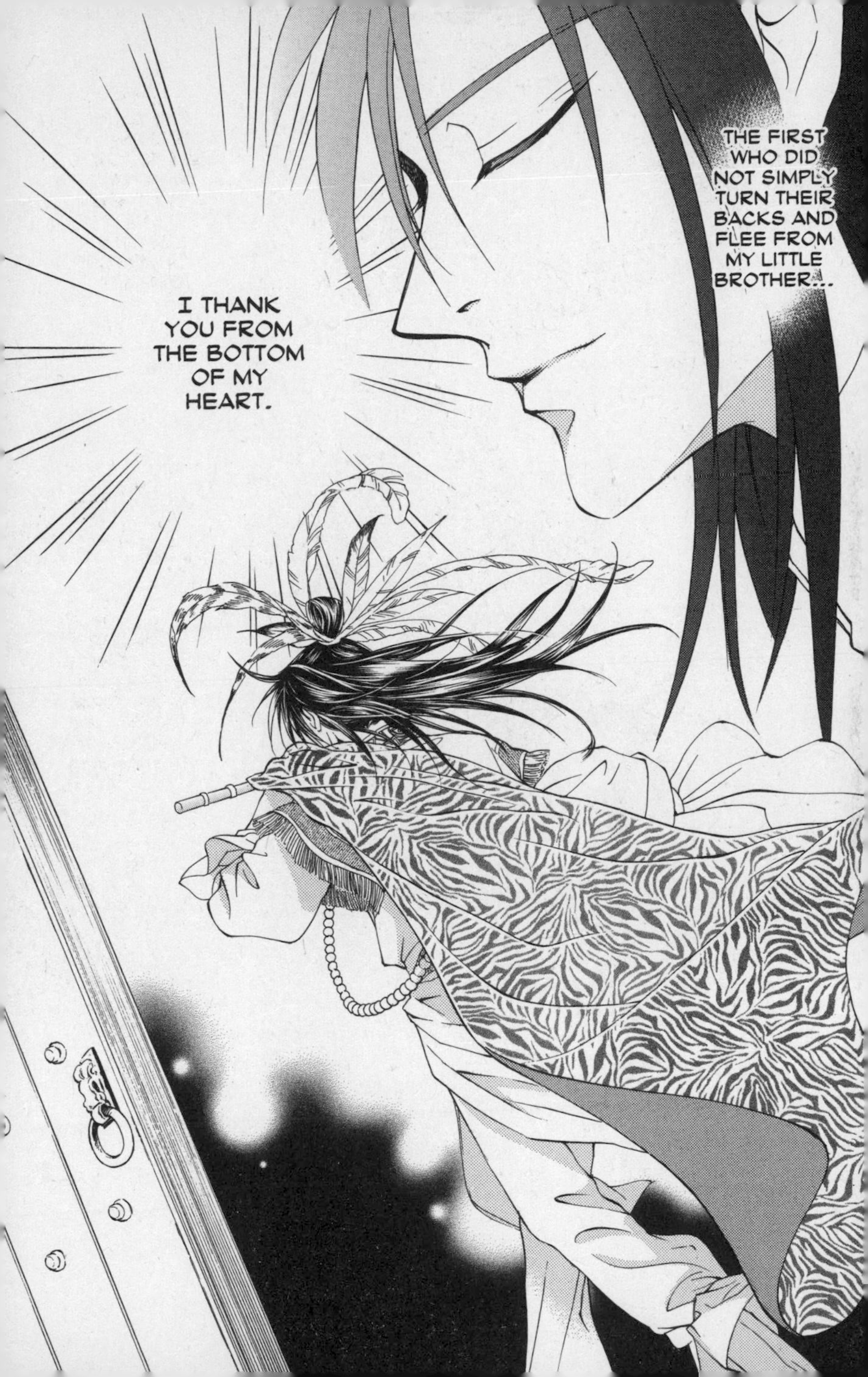
THE FIRST WHO DID NOT SIMPLY TURN THEIR BACKS AND FLEE FROM MY LITTLE BROTHER...
I THANK YOU FROM THE BOTTOM OF MY HEART.

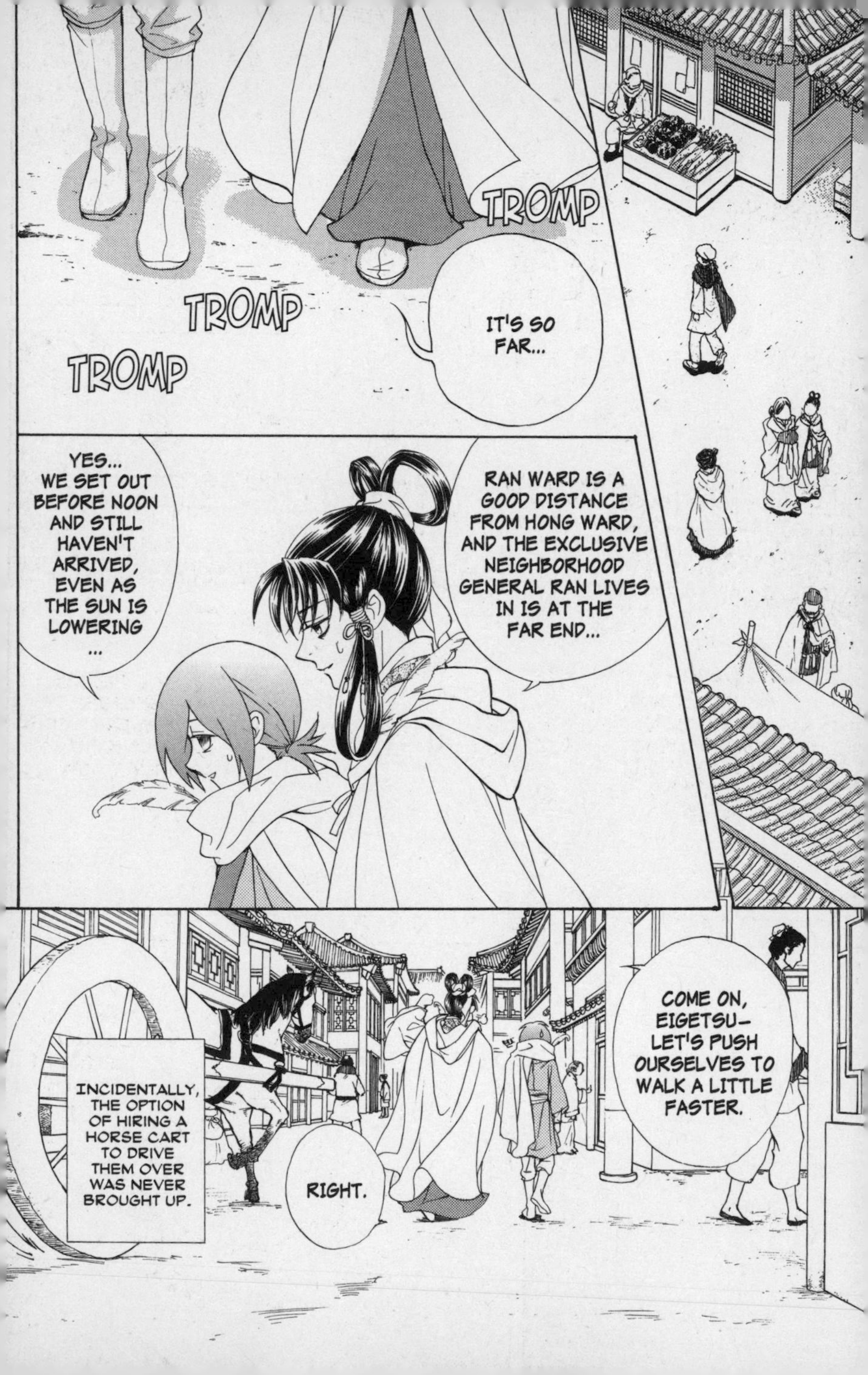
TROMP
TROMP
TROMP
IT'S SO FAR...
RAN WARD IS A GOOD DISTANCE FROM HONG WARD, AND THE EXCLUSIVE NEIGHBORHOOD GENERAL RAN LIVES IN IS AT THE FAR END...
YES... WE SET OUT BEFORE NOON AND STILL HAVEN'T ARRIVED, EVEN AS THE SUN IS LOWERING...
COME ON, EIGETSU—LET'S PUSH OURSELVES TO WALK A LITTLE FASTER.
RIGHT.
INCIDENTALLY, THE OPTION OF HIRING A HORSE CART TO DRIVE THEM OVER WAS NEVER BROUGHT UP.

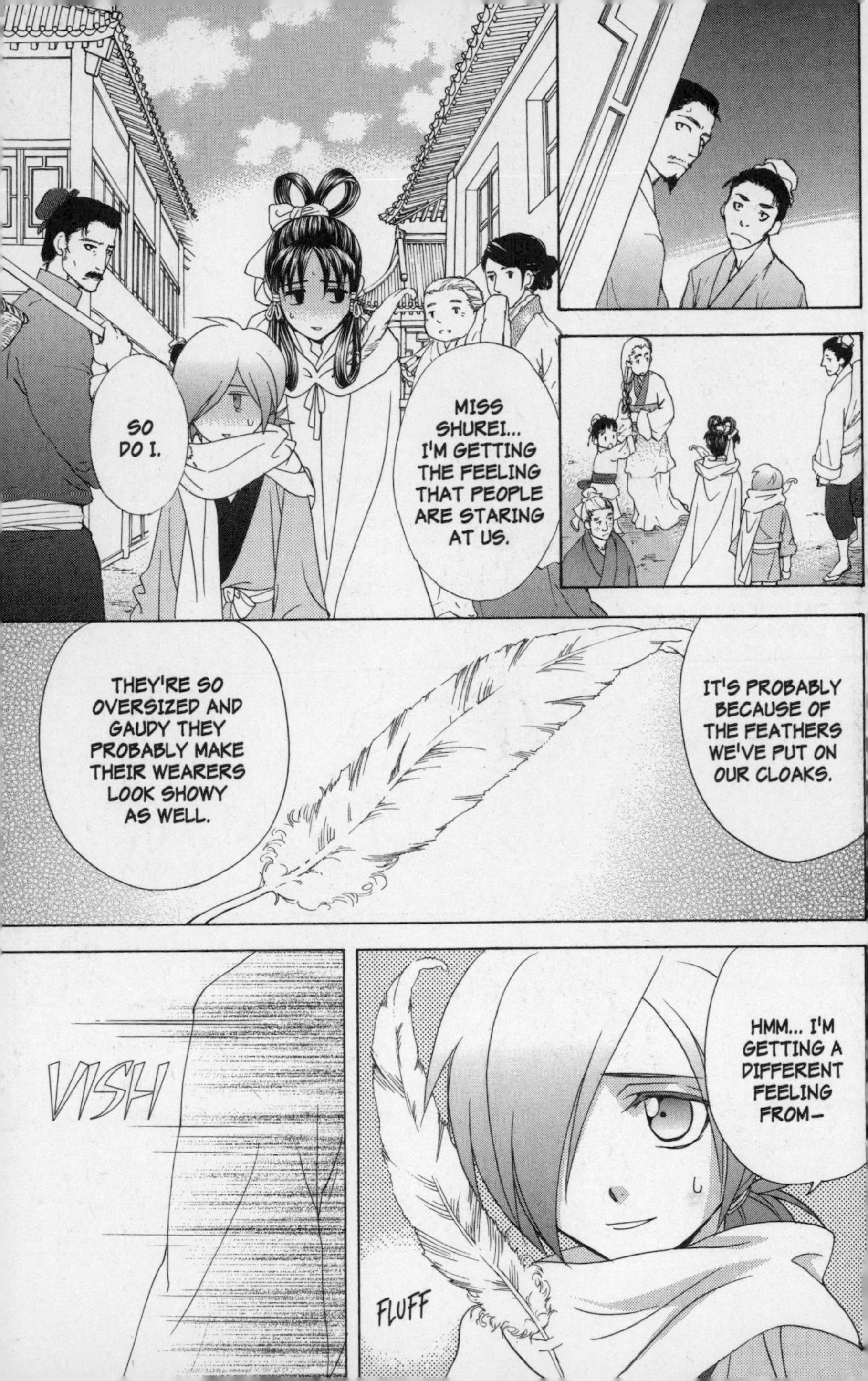
MISS SHUREI... I'M GETTING THE FEELING THAT PEOPLE ARE STARING AT US.
SO DO I.
IT'S PROBABLY BECAUSE OF THE FEATHERS WE'VE PUT ON OUR CLOAKS.
THEY'RE SO OVERSIZED AND GAUDY THEY PROBABLY MAKE THEIR WEARERS LOOK SHOWY AS WELL.
HMM... I'M GETTING A DIFFERENT FEELING FROM—
FLUFF
VISH

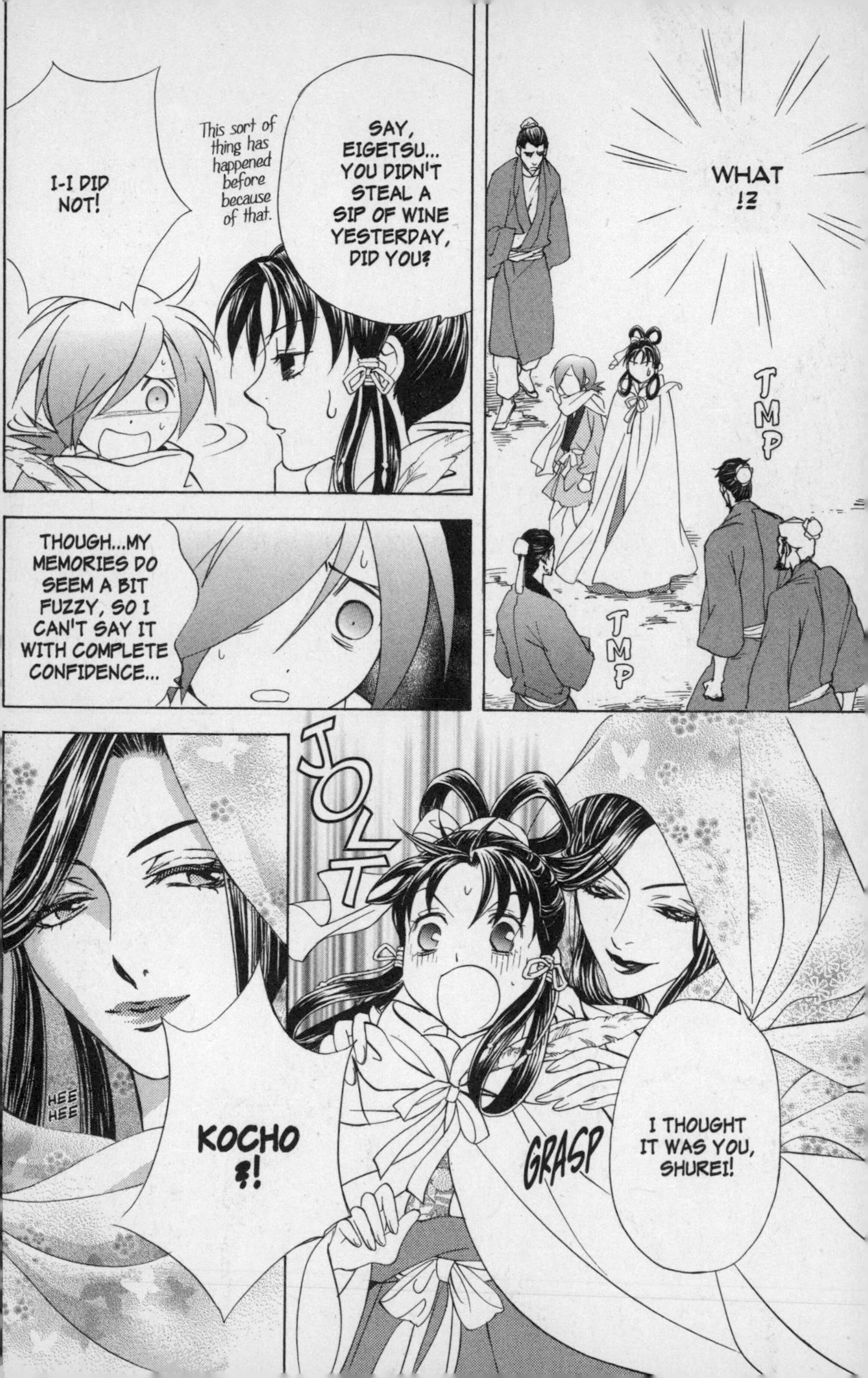
WHAT!?
TMP TMP
TMP TMP
SAY, EIGETSU... YOU DIDN'T STEAL A SIP OF WINE YESTERDAY, DID YOU?
This sort of thing has happened before because of that.
I-I DID NOT!
THOUGH...MY MEMORIES DO SEEM A BIT FUZZY, SO I CAN'T SAY IT WITH COMPLETE CONFIDENCE...
JOLT
I THOUGHT IT WAS YOU, SHUREI!
GRASP
KOCHO?!
HEE HEE

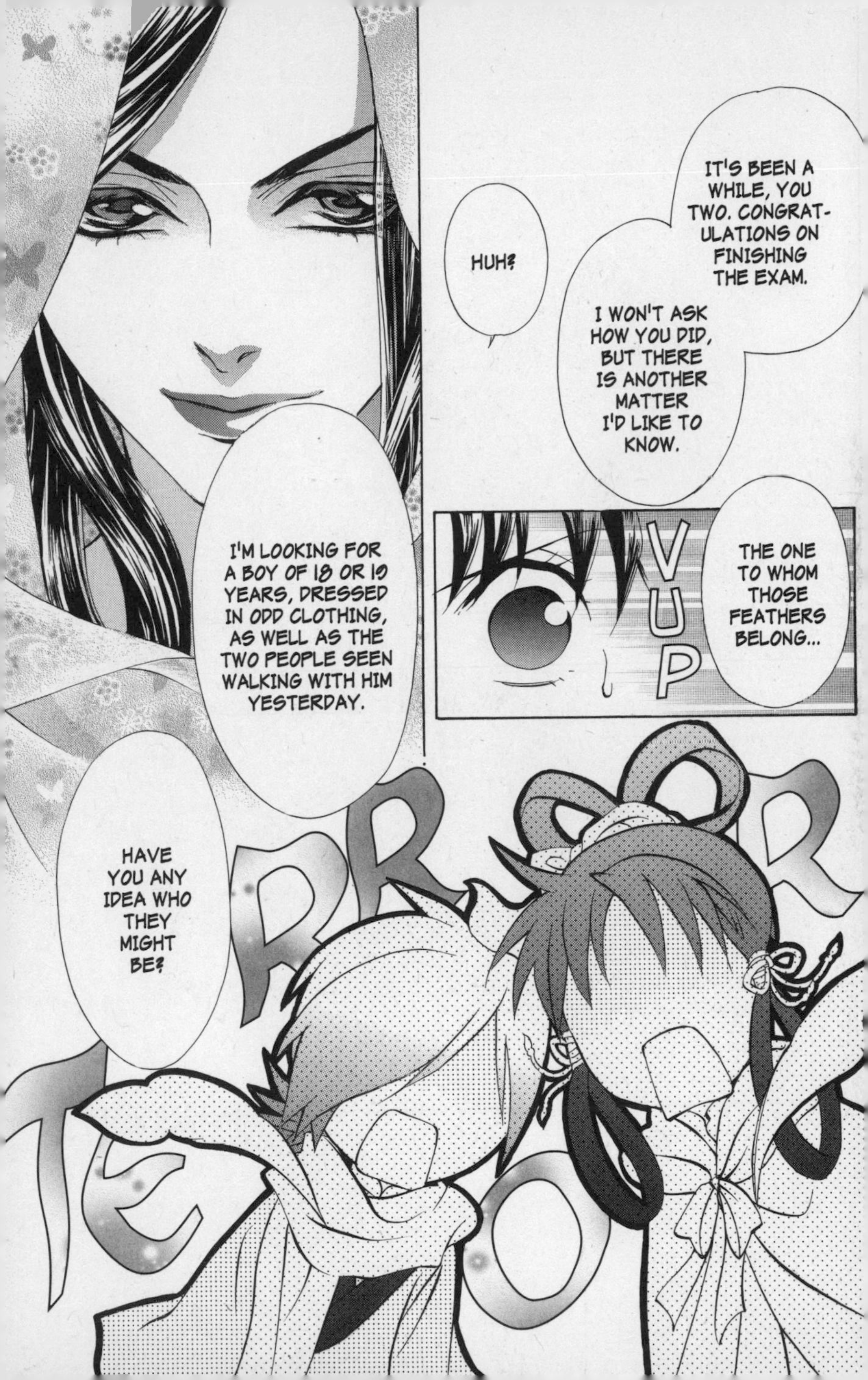
IT'S BEEN A WHILE, YOU TWO. CONGRAT-ULATIONS ON FINISHING THE EXAM.
HUH?
I WON'T ASK HOW YOU DID, BUT THERE IS ANOTHER MATTER I'D LIKE TO KNOW.
THE ONE TO WHOM THOSE FEATHERS BELONG...
VUP
I'M LOOKING FOR A BOY OF 18 OR 19 YEARS, DRESSED IN ODD CLOTHING, AS WELL AS THE TWO PEOPLE SEEN WALKING WITH HIM YESTERDAY.
HAVE YOU ANY IDEA WHO THEY MIGHT BE?

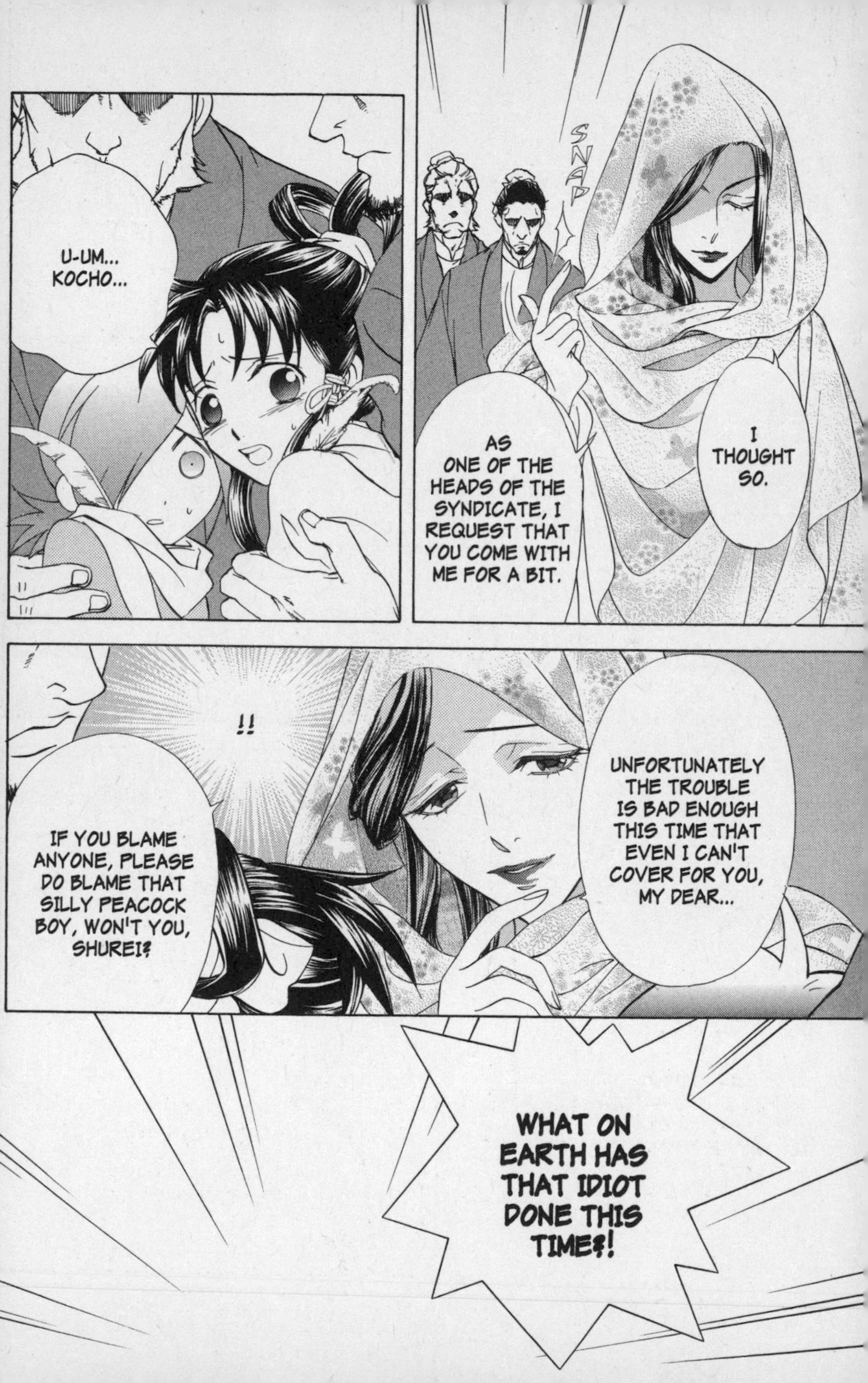
SNAP
I THOUGHT SO.
AS ONE OF THE HEADS OF THE SYNDICATE, I REQUEST THAT YOU COME WITH ME FOR A BIT.
U-UM... KOCHO...
UNFORTUNATELY THE TROUBLE IS BAD ENOUGH THIS TIME THAT EVEN I CAN'T COVER FOR YOU, MY DEAR...
!!
IF YOU BLAME ANYONE, PLEASE DO BLAME THAT SILLY PEACOCK BOY, WON'T YOU, SHUREI?
WHAT ON EARTH HAS THAT IDIOT DONE THIS TIME?!

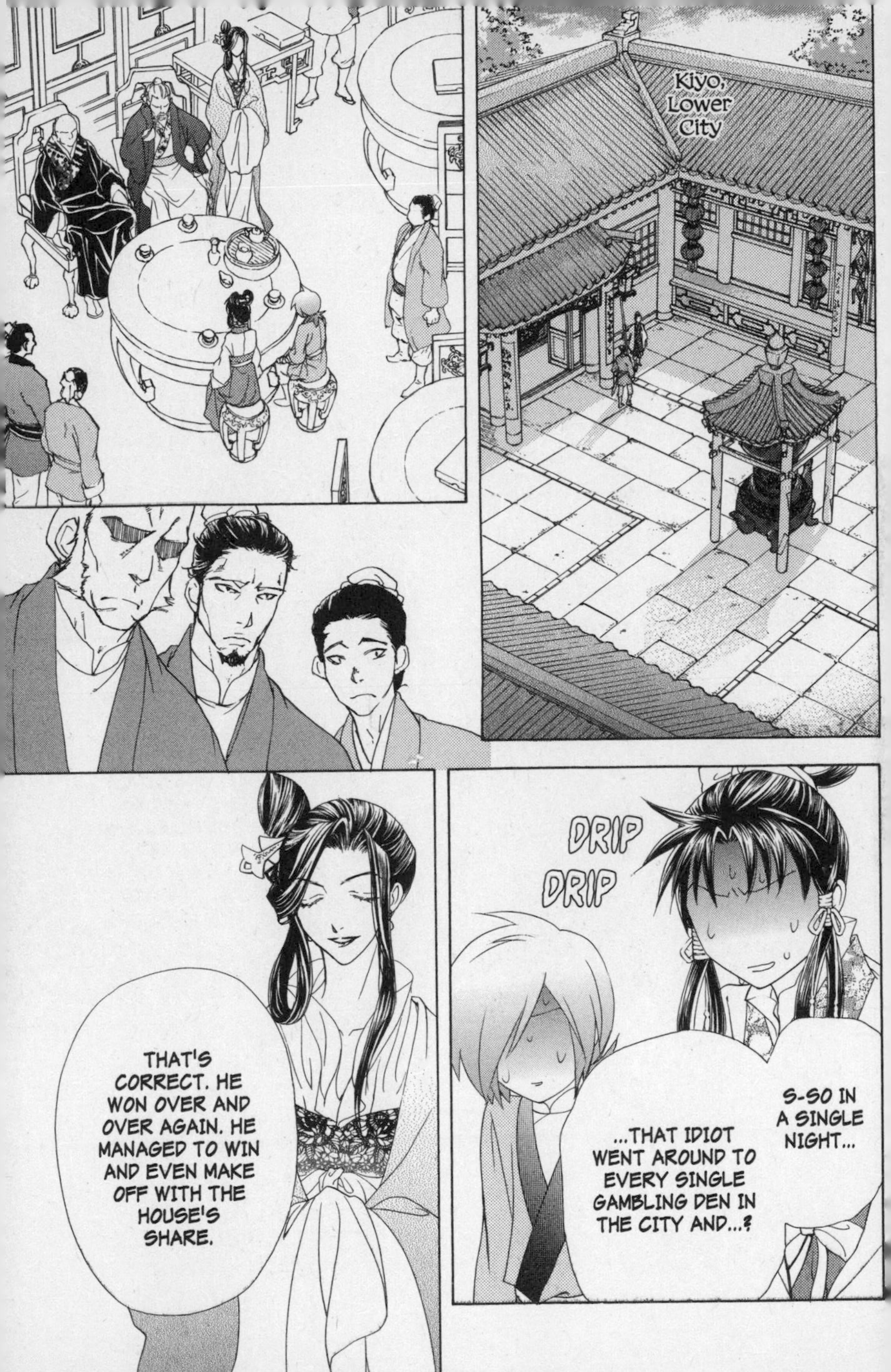
Kiyo, Lower City
DRIP
DRIP
S-SO IN A SINGLE NIGHT...
...THAT IDIOT WENT AROUND TO EVERY SINGLE GAMBLING DEN IN THE CITY AND...?
THAT'S CORRECT. HE WON OVER AND OVER AGAIN. HE MANAGED TO WIN AND EVEN MAKE OFF WITH THE HOUSE'S SHARE.

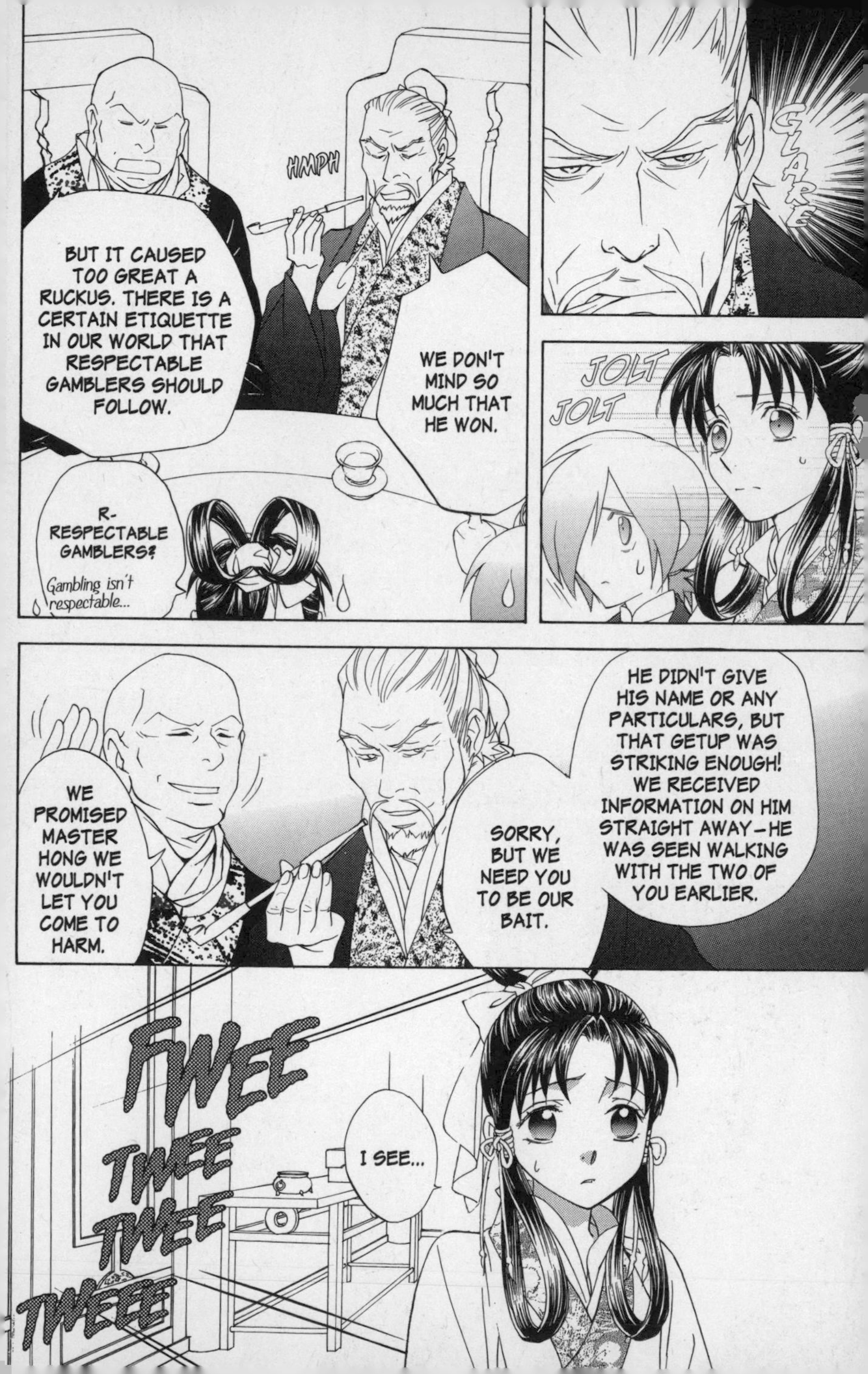
GLARE
JOLT
JOLT
HMPH
WE DON'T MIND SO MUCH THAT HE WON.
BUT IT CAUSED TOO GREAT A RUCKUS. THERE IS A CERTAIN ETIQUETTE IN OUR WORLD THAT RESPECTABLE GAMBLERS SHOULD FOLLOW.
R-RESPECTABLE GAMBLERS?
Gambling isn't respectable...
HE DIDN'T GIVE HIS NAME OR ANY PARTICULARS, BUT THAT GETUP WAS STRIKING ENOUGH! WE RECEIVED INFORMATION ON HIM STRAIGHT AWAY—HE WAS SEEN WALKING WITH THE TWO OF YOU EARLIER.
SORRY, BUT WE NEED YOU TO BE OUR BAIT.
WE PROMISED MASTER HONG WE WOULDN'T LET YOU COME TO HARM.
FWEE
TWEE
TWEE
TWEEE
I SEE...

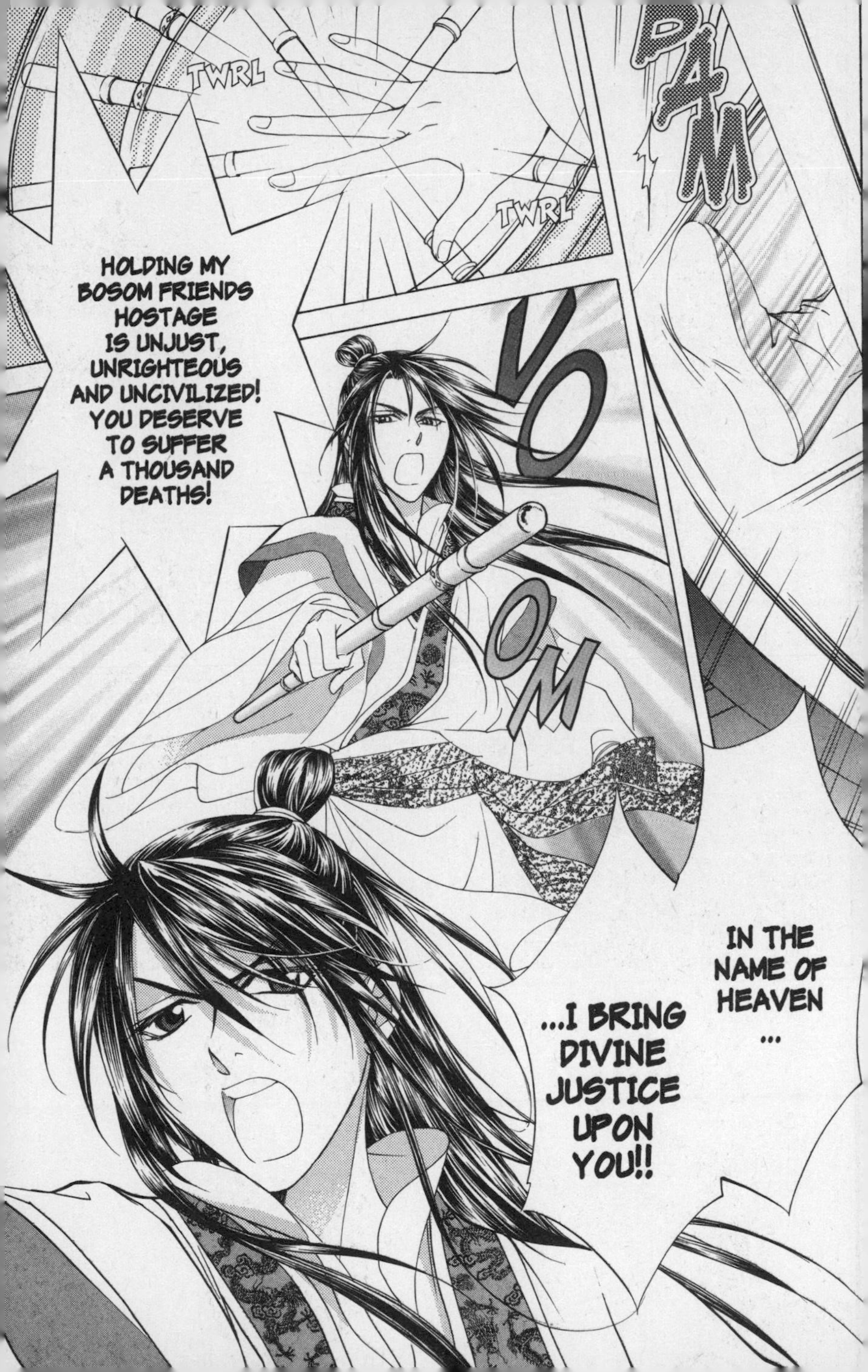
BAM
TWRL
TWRL
VOOM
HOLDING MY BOSOM FRIENDS HOSTAGE IS UNJUST, UNRIGHTEOUS AND UNCIVILIZED! YOU DESERVE TO SUFFER A THOUSAND DEATHS!
IN THE NAME OF HEAVEN ...
...I BRING DIVINE JUSTICE UPON YOU!!

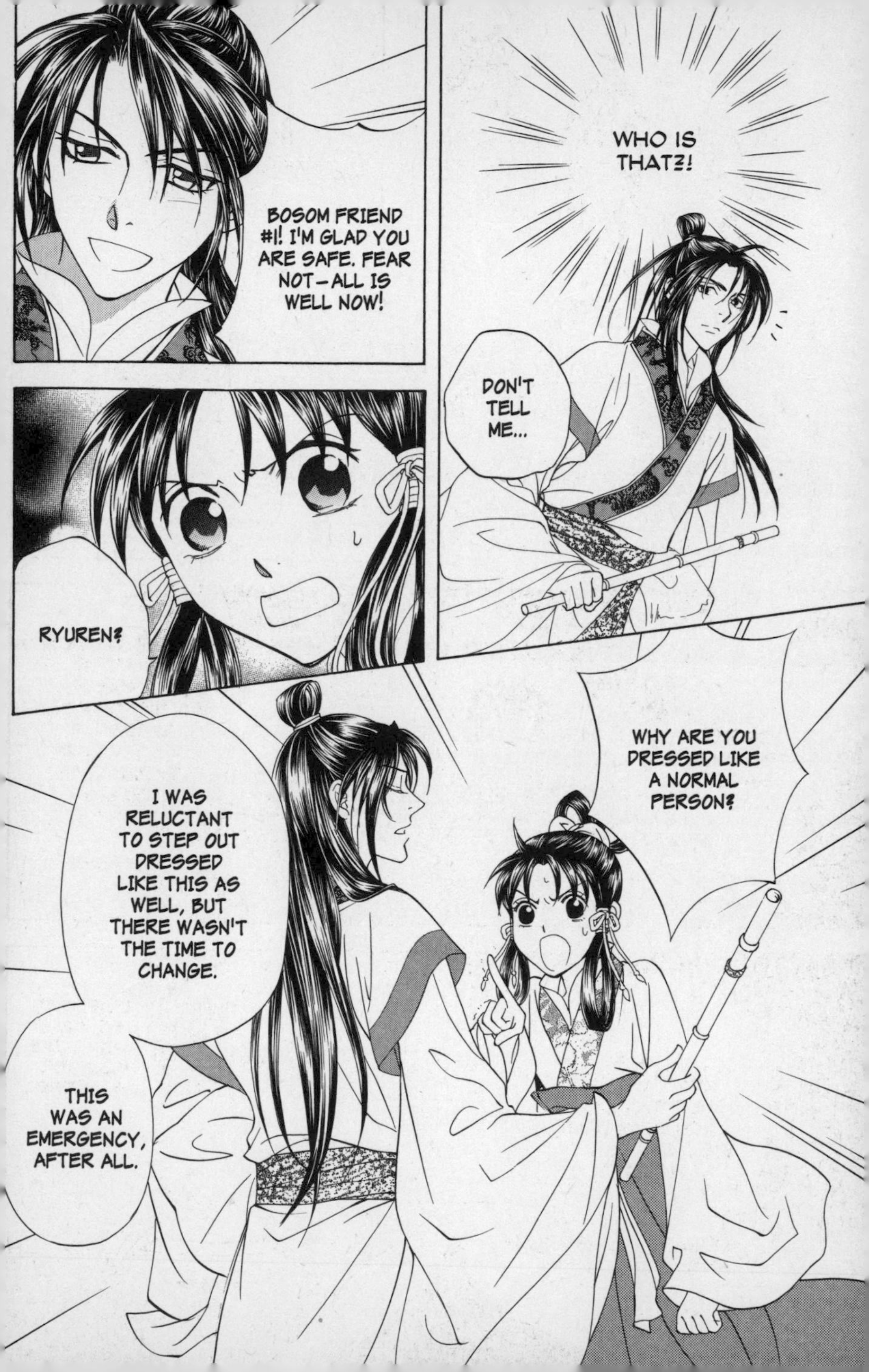
WHO IS THAT?!
DON'T TELL ME...
BOSOM FRIEND #1! I'M GLAD YOU ARE SAFE. FEAR NOT—ALL IS WELL NOW!
RYUREN?
WHY ARE YOU DRESSED LIKE A NORMAL PERSON?
I WAS RELUCTANT TO STEP OUT DRESSED LIKE THIS AS WELL, BUT THERE WASN'T THE TIME TO CHANGE.
THIS WAS AN EMERGENCY, AFTER ALL.

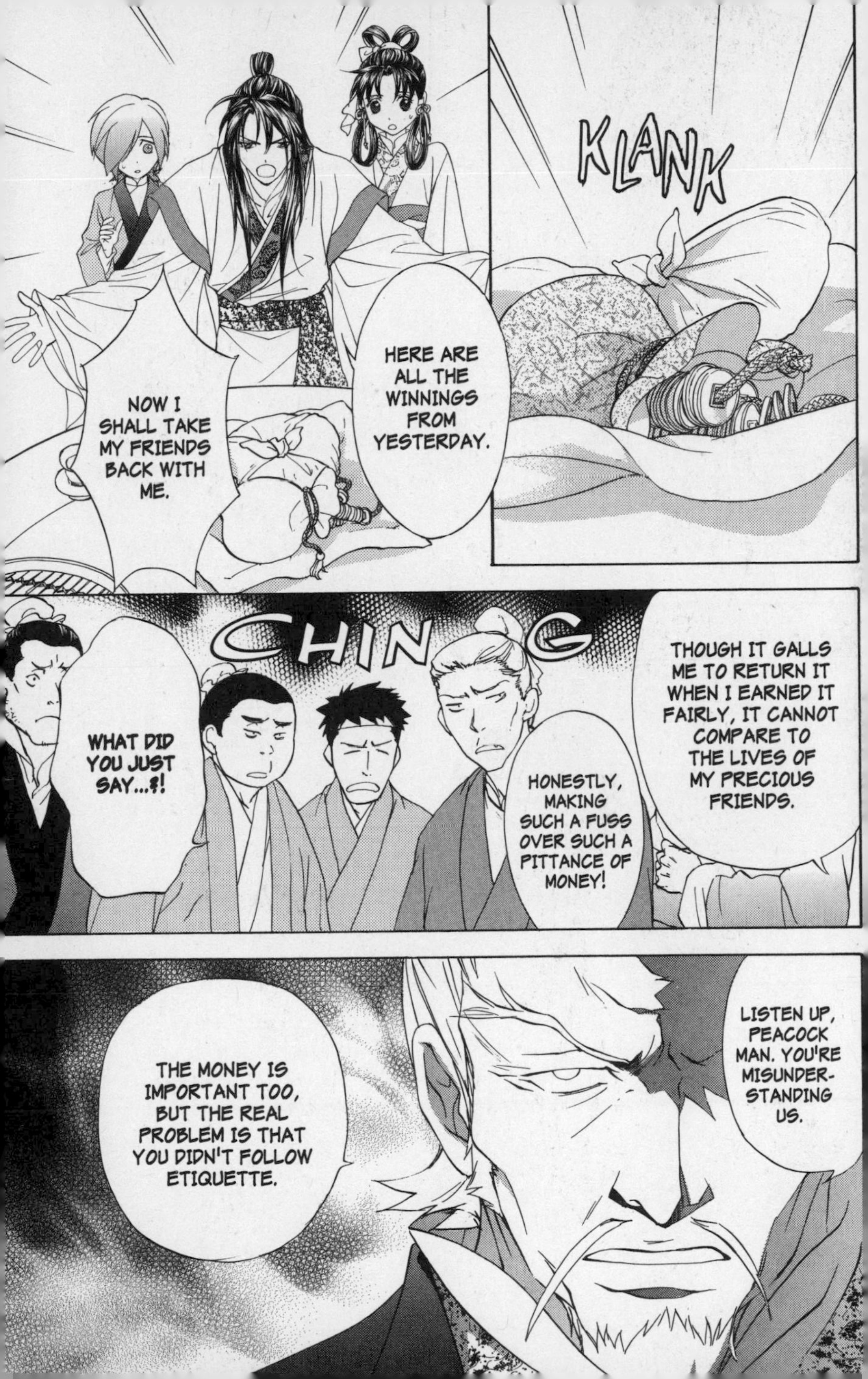
KLANK
HERE ARE ALL THE WINNINGS FROM YESTERDAY.
NOW I SHALL TAKE MY FRIENDS BACK WITH ME.
THOUGH IT GALLS ME TO RETURN IT WHEN I EARNED IT FAIRLY, IT CANNOT COMPARE TO THE LIVES OF MY PRECIOUS FRIENDS.
CHING
HONESTLY, MAKING SUCH A FUSS OVER SUCH A PITTANCE OF MONEY!
WHAT DID YOU JUST SAY...?!
LISTEN UP, PEACOCK MAN. YOU'RE MISUNDER-STANDING US.
THE MONEY IS IMPORTANT TOO, BUT THE REAL PROBLEM IS THAT YOU DIDN'T FOLLOW ETIQUETTE.

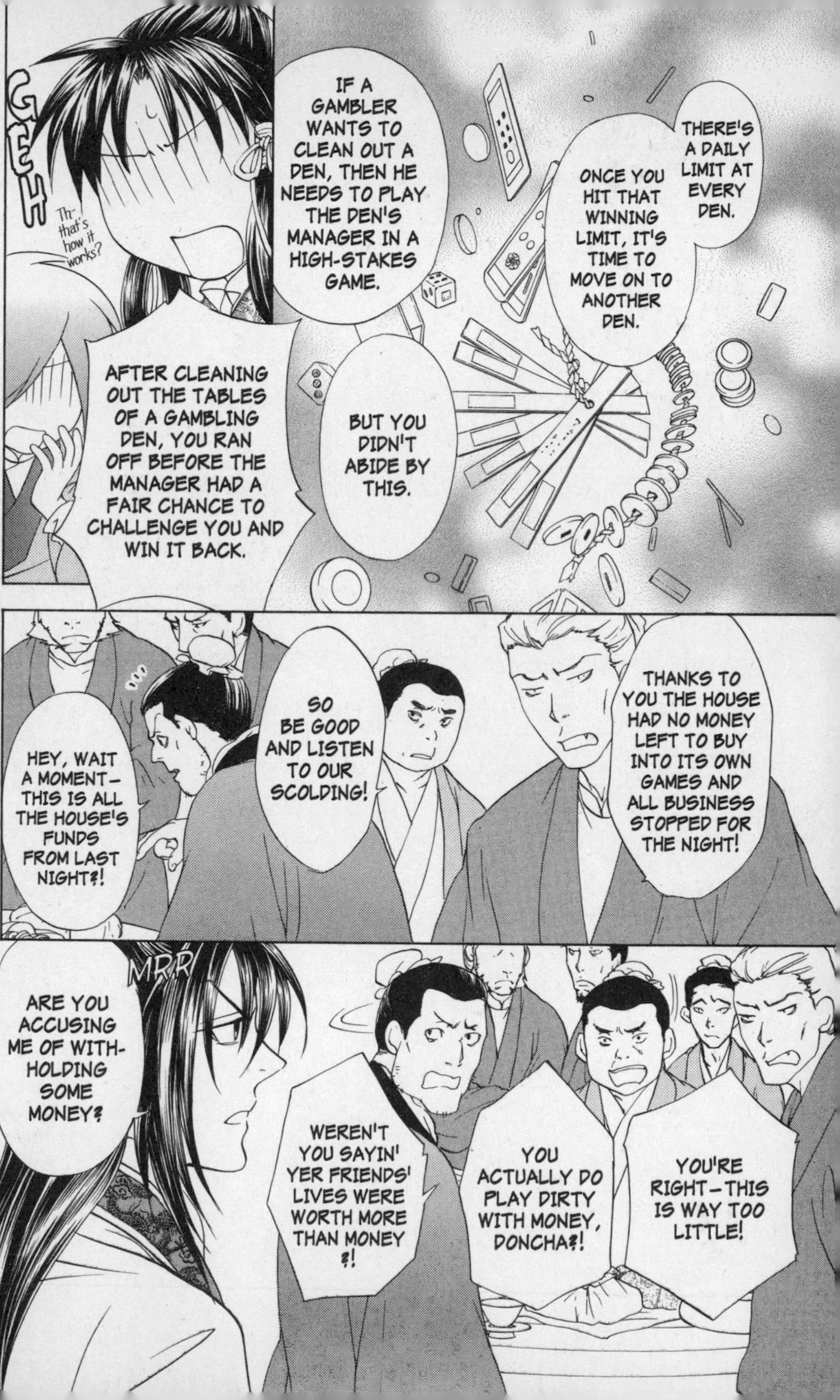
THERE'S A DAILY LIMIT AT EVERY DEN.
ONCE YOU HIT THAT WINNING LIMIT, IT'S TIME TO MOVE ON TO ANOTHER DEN.
IF A GAMBLER WANTS TO CLEAN OUT A DEN, THEN HE NEEDS TO PLAY THE DEN'S MANAGER IN A HIGH-STAKES GAME.
GEH
Th-that's how it works?
BUT YOU DIDN'T ABIDE BY THIS.
AFTER CLEANING OUT THE TABLES OF A GAMBLING DEN, YOU RAN OFF BEFORE THE MANAGER HAD A FAIR CHANCE TO CHALLENGE YOU AND WIN IT BACK.
THANKS TO YOU THE HOUSE HAD NO MONEY LEFT TO BUY INTO ITS OWN GAMES AND ALL BUSINESS STOPPED FOR THE NIGHT!
SO BE GOOD AND LISTEN TO OUR SCOLDING!
HEY, WAIT A MOMENT—THIS IS ALL THE HOUSE'S FUNDS FROM LAST NIGHT?!
YOU'RE RIGHT—THIS IS WAY TOO LITTLE!
YOU ACTUALLY DO PLAY DIRTY WITH MONEY, DONCHA?!
WEREN'T YOU SAYIN' YER FRIENDS' LIVES WERE WORTH MORE THAN MONEY?!
MRR
ARE YOU ACCUSING ME OF WITH-HOLDING SOME MONEY?

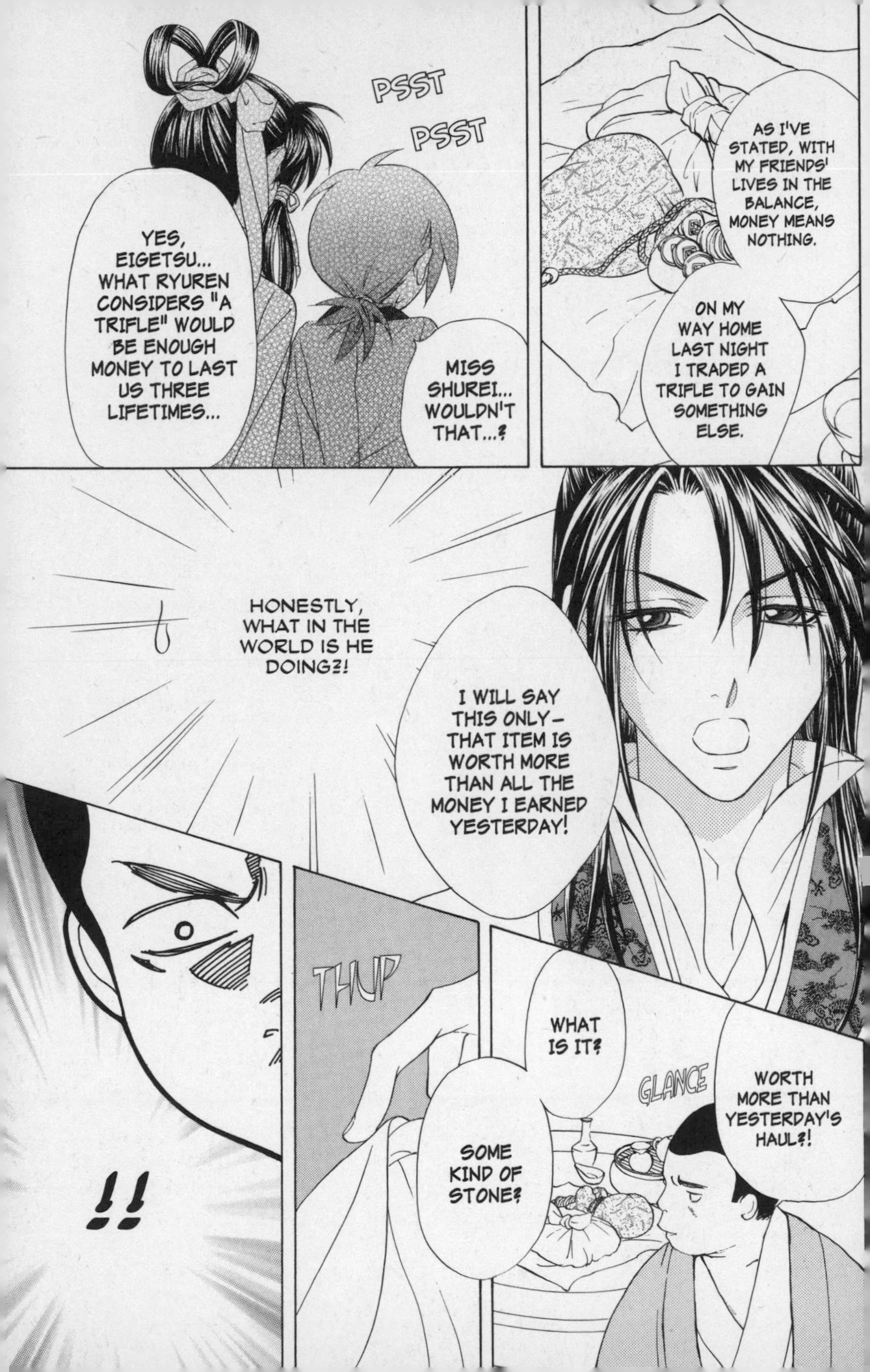
AS I'VE STATED, WITH MY FRIENDS' LIVES IN THE BALANCE, MONEY MEANS NOTHING.
ON MY WAY HOME LAST NIGHT I TRADED A TRIFLE TO GAIN SOMETHING ELSE.
PSST
PSST
MISS SHUREI... WOULDN'T THAT...?
YES, EIGETSU... WHAT RYUREN CONSIDERS "A TRIFLE" WOULD BE ENOUGH MONEY TO LAST US THREE LIFETIMES...
I WILL SAY THIS ONLY— THAT ITEM IS WORTH MORE THAN ALL THE MONEY I EARNED YESTERDAY!
HONESTLY, WHAT IN THE WORLD IS HE DOING?!
WORTH MORE THAN YESTERDAY'S HAUL?!
GLANCE
WHAT IS IT?
SOME KIND OF STONE?
THUP
!!

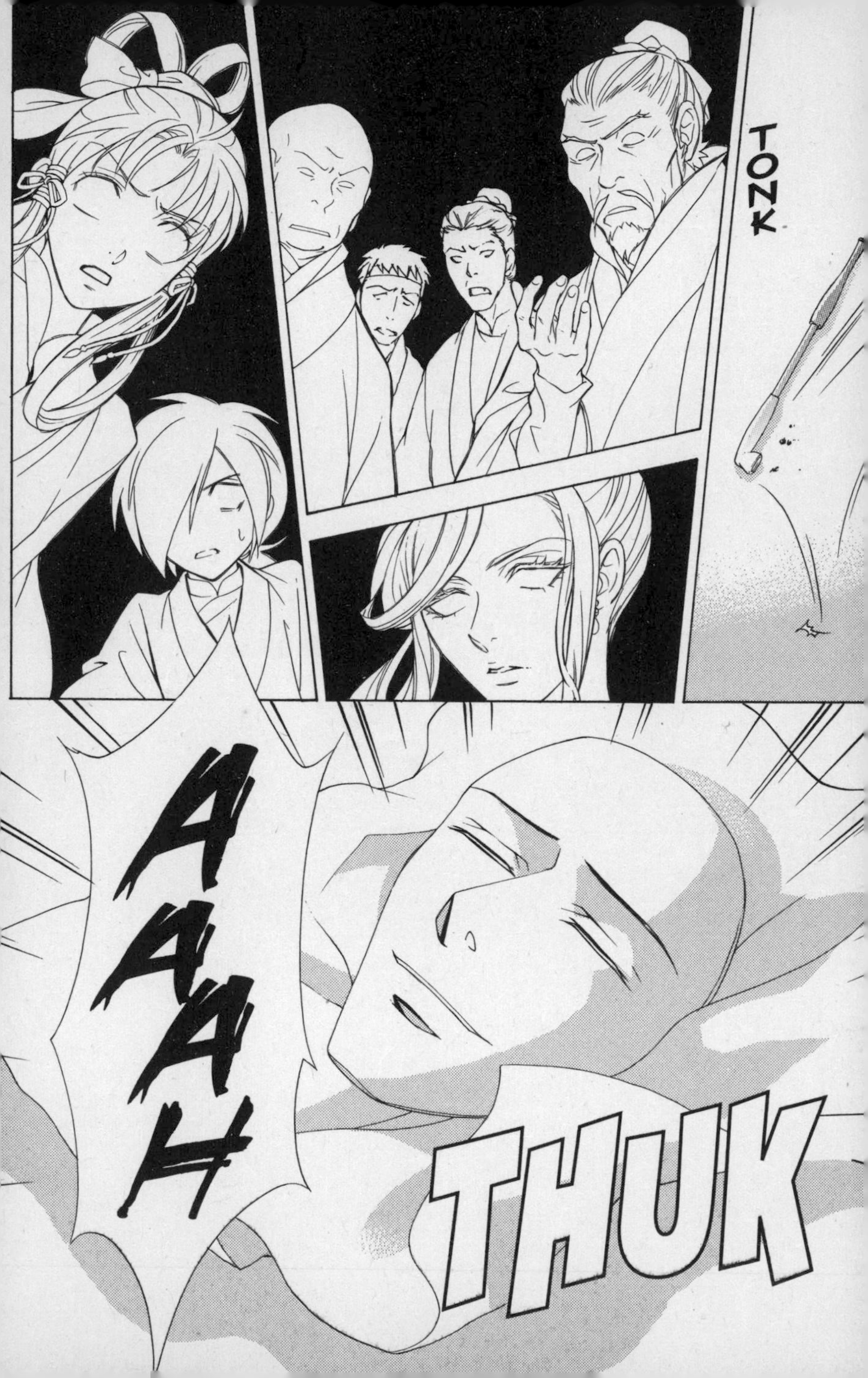
TONK
AAAAH
THUK

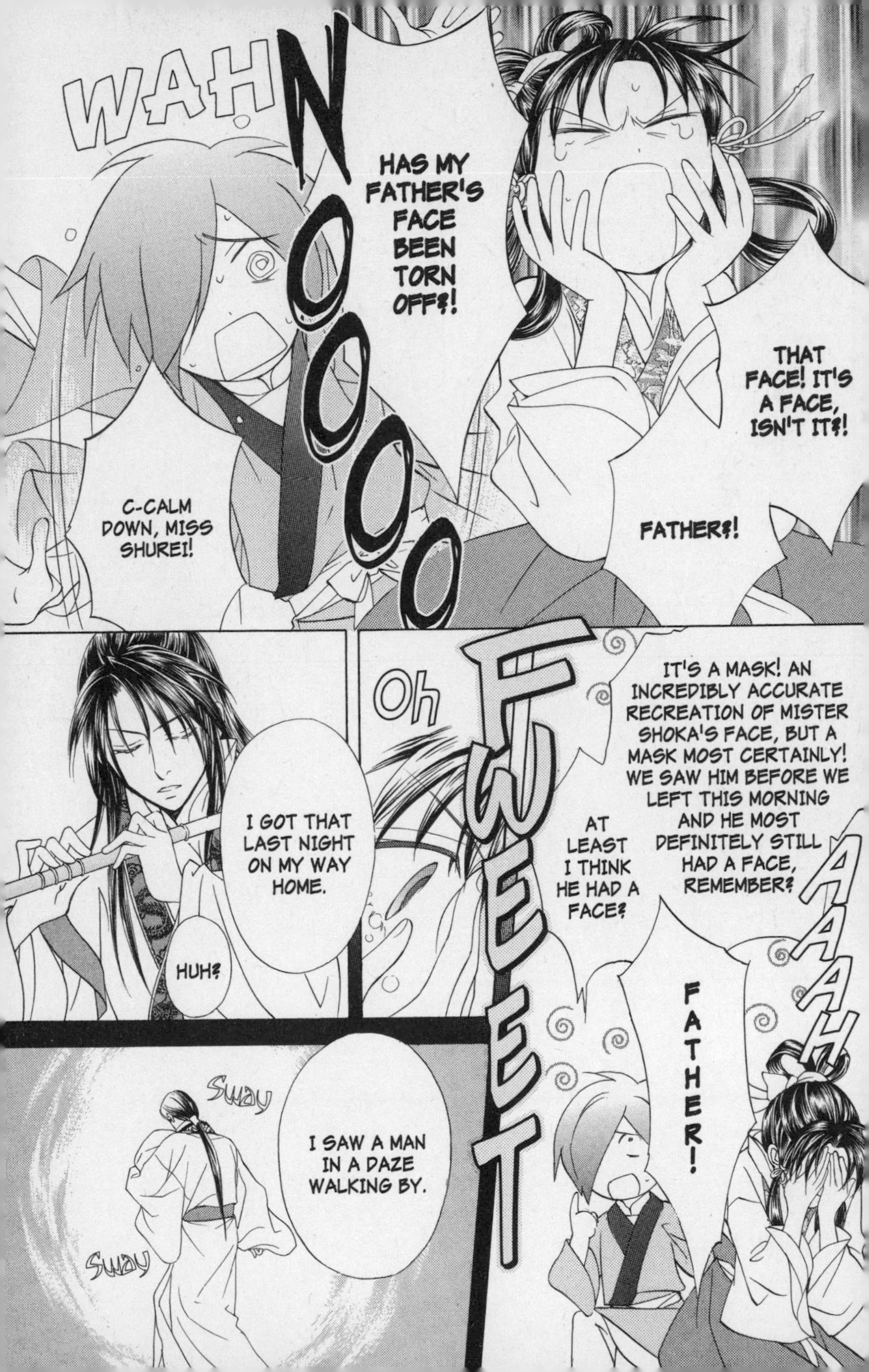
HAS MY FATHER'S FACE BEEN TORN OFF?!
THAT FACE! IT'S A FACE, ISN'T IT?!
FATHER?!
WAHNOOOOOO
C-CALM DOWN, MISS SHUREI!
IT'S A MASK! AN INCREDIBLY ACCURATE RECREATION OF MISTER SHOKA'S FACE, BUT A MASK MOST CERTAINLY! WE SAW HIM BEFORE WE LEFT THIS MORNING AND HE MOST DEFINITELY STILL HAD A FACE, REMEMBER?
AT LEAST I THINK HE HAD A FACE?
AAAAH
FATHER!
Oh
FWEEET
I GOT THAT LAST NIGHT ON MY WAY HOME.
HUH?
Sway
I SAW A MAN IN A DAZE WALKING BY.
Sway

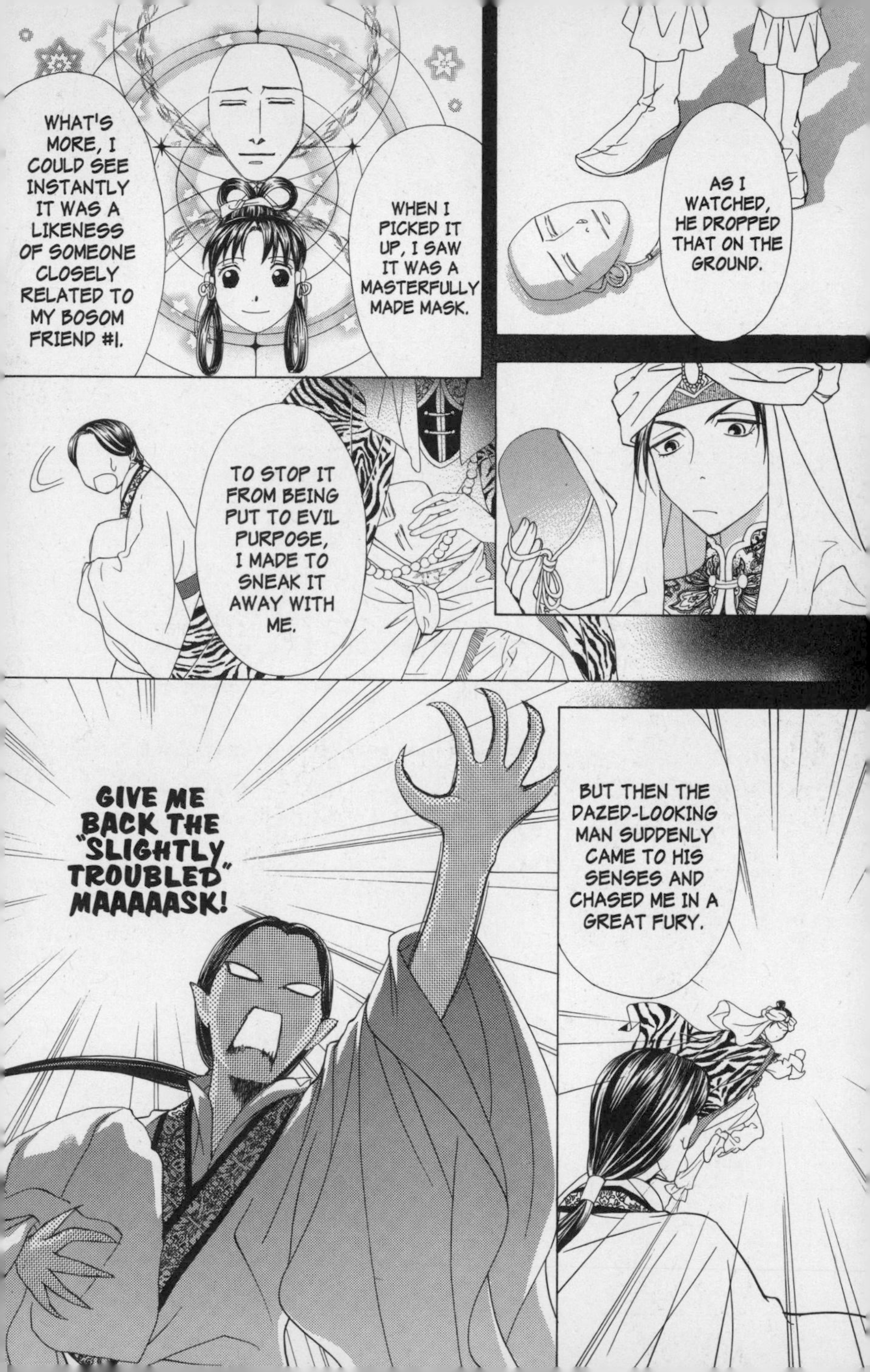
AS I WATCHED, HE DROPPED THAT ON THE GROUND.
WHEN I PICKED IT UP, I SAW IT WAS A MASTERFULLY MADE MASK.
WHAT'S MORE, I COULD SEE INSTANTLY IT WAS A LIKENESS OF SOMEONE CLOSELY RELATED TO MY BOSOM FRIEND #1.
TO STOP IT FROM BEING PUT TO EVIL PURPOSE, I MADE TO SNEAK IT AWAY WITH ME.
BUT THEN THE DAZED-LOOKING MAN SUDDENLY CAME TO HIS SENSES AND CHASED ME IN A GREAT FURY.
GIVE ME BACK THE "SLIGHTLY TROUBLED" MAAAAASK!

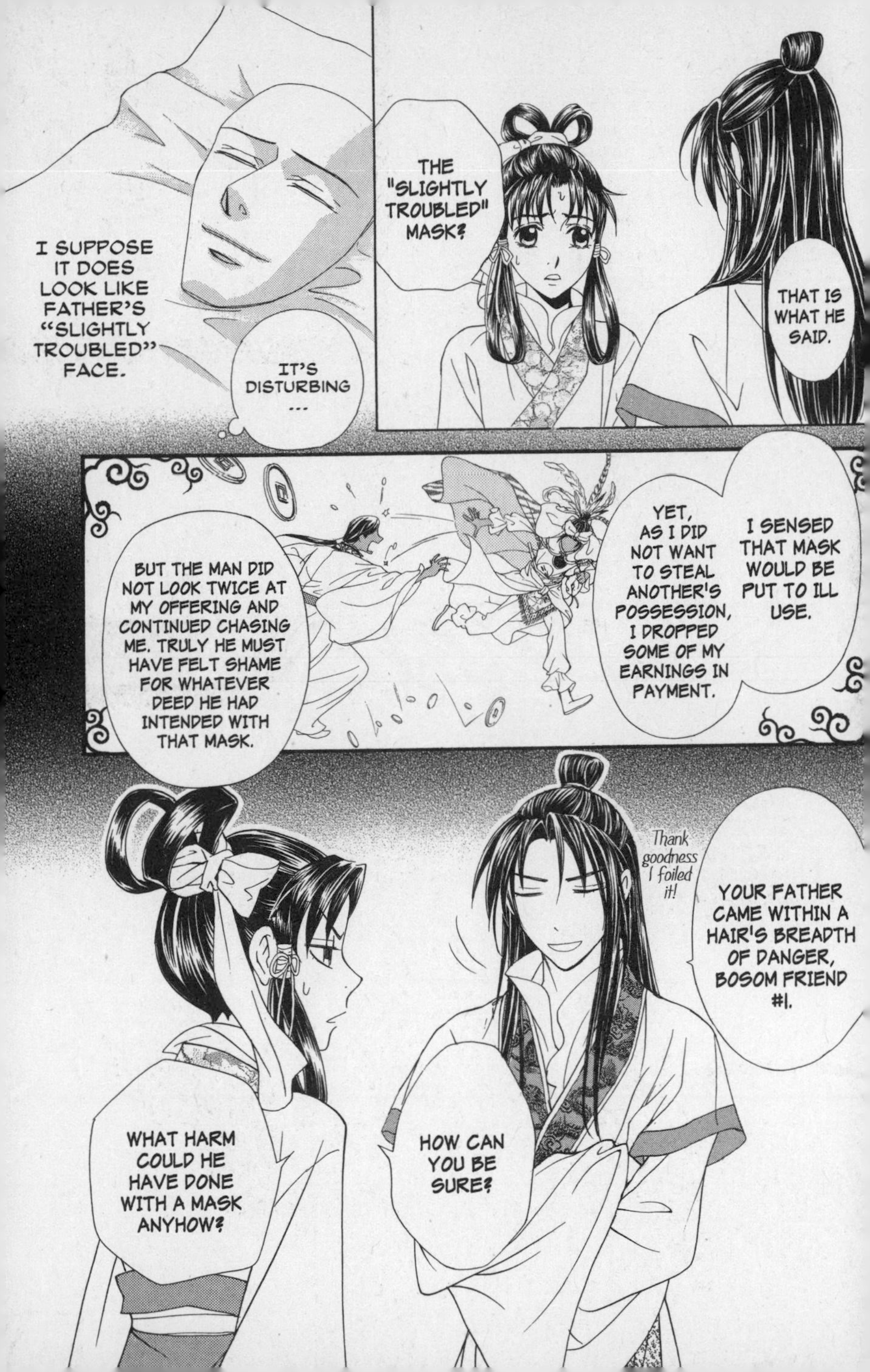
THE "SLIGHTLY TROUBLED" MASK?
THAT IS WHAT HE SAID.
I SUPPOSE IT DOES LOOK LIKE FATHER'S "SLIGHTLY TROUBLED" FACE.
IT'S DISTURBING ...
I SENSED THAT MASK WOULD BE PUT TO ILL USE.
YET, AS I DID NOT WANT TO STEAL ANOTHER'S POSSESSION, I DROPPED SOME OF MY EARNINGS IN PAYMENT.
BUT THE MAN DID NOT LOOK TWICE AT MY OFFERING AND CONTINUED CHASING ME. TRULY HE MUST HAVE FELT SHAME FOR WHATEVER DEED HE HAD INTENDED WITH THAT MASK.
YOUR FATHER CAME WITHIN A HAIR'S BREADTH OF DANGER, BOSOM FRIEND #1.
Thank goodness I foiled it!
HOW CAN YOU BE SURE?
WHAT HARM COULD HE HAVE DONE WITH A MASK ANYHOW?

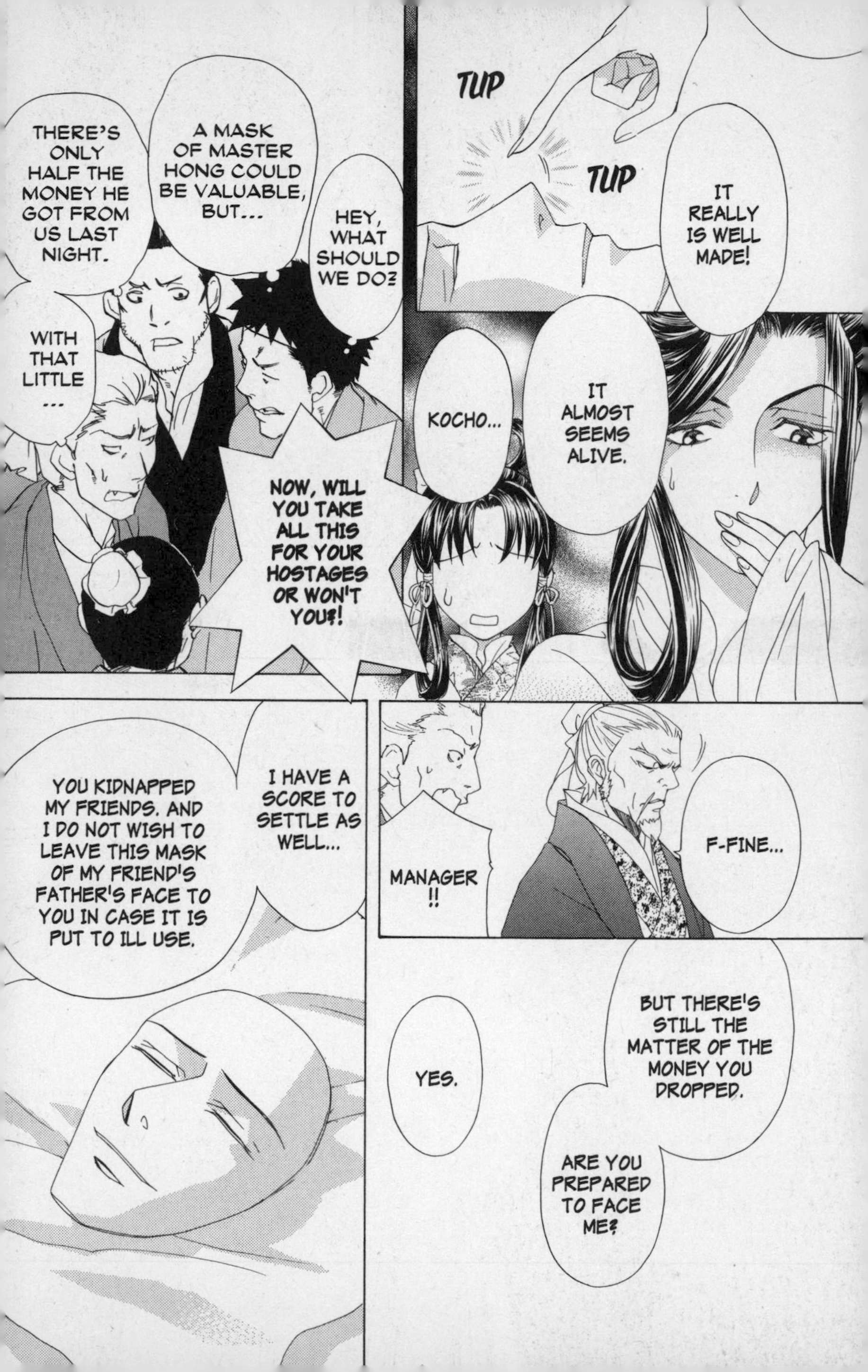
TUP
TUP
IT REALLY IS WELL MADE!
IT ALMOST SEEMS ALIVE.
KOCHO...
HEY, WHAT SHOULD WE DO?
A MASK OF MASTER HONG COULD BE VALUABLE, BUT...
THERE'S ONLY HALF THE MONEY HE GOT FROM US LAST NIGHT.
WITH THAT LITTLE...
NOW, WILL YOU TAKE ALL THIS FOR YOUR HOSTAGES OR WON'T YOU?!
F-FINE...
MANAGER!!
BUT THERE'S STILL THE MATTER OF THE MONEY YOU DROPPED.
YES.
ARE YOU PREPARED TO FACE ME?
I HAVE A SCORE TO SETTLE AS WELL...
YOU KIDNAPPED MY FRIENDS. AND I DO NOT WISH TO LEAVE THIS MASK OF MY FRIEND'S FATHER'S FACE TO YOU IN CASE IT IS PUT TO ILL USE.

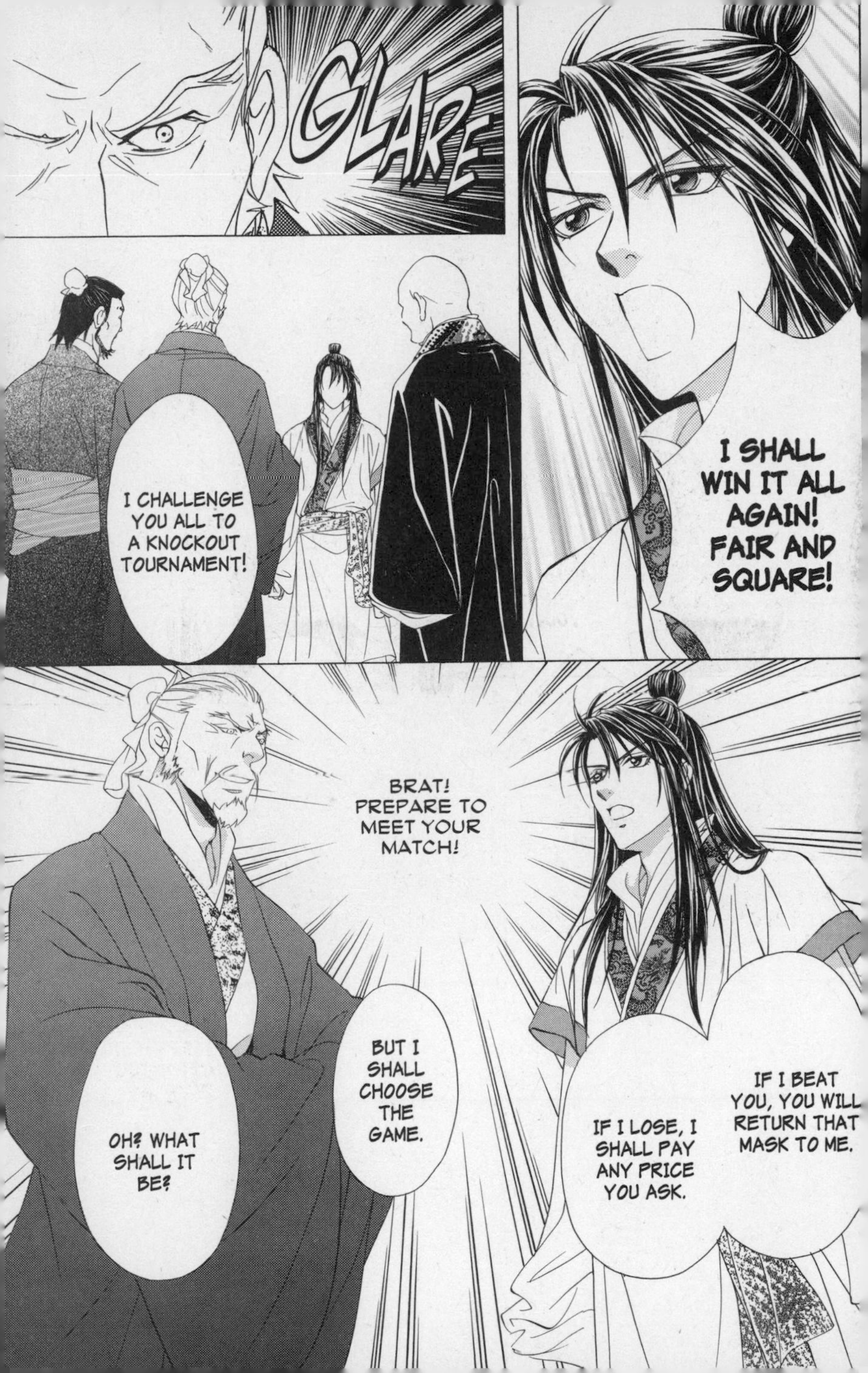
I SHALL WIN IT ALL AGAIN! FAIR AND SQUARE!
GLARE
I CHALLENGE YOU ALL TO A KNOCKOUT TOURNAMENT!
BRAT! PREPARE TO MEET YOUR MATCH!
IF I BEAT YOU, YOU WILL RETURN THAT MASK TO ME.
IF I LOSE, I SHALL PAY ANY PRICE YOU ASK.
BUT I SHALL CHOOSE THE GAME.
OH? WHAT SHALL IT BE?

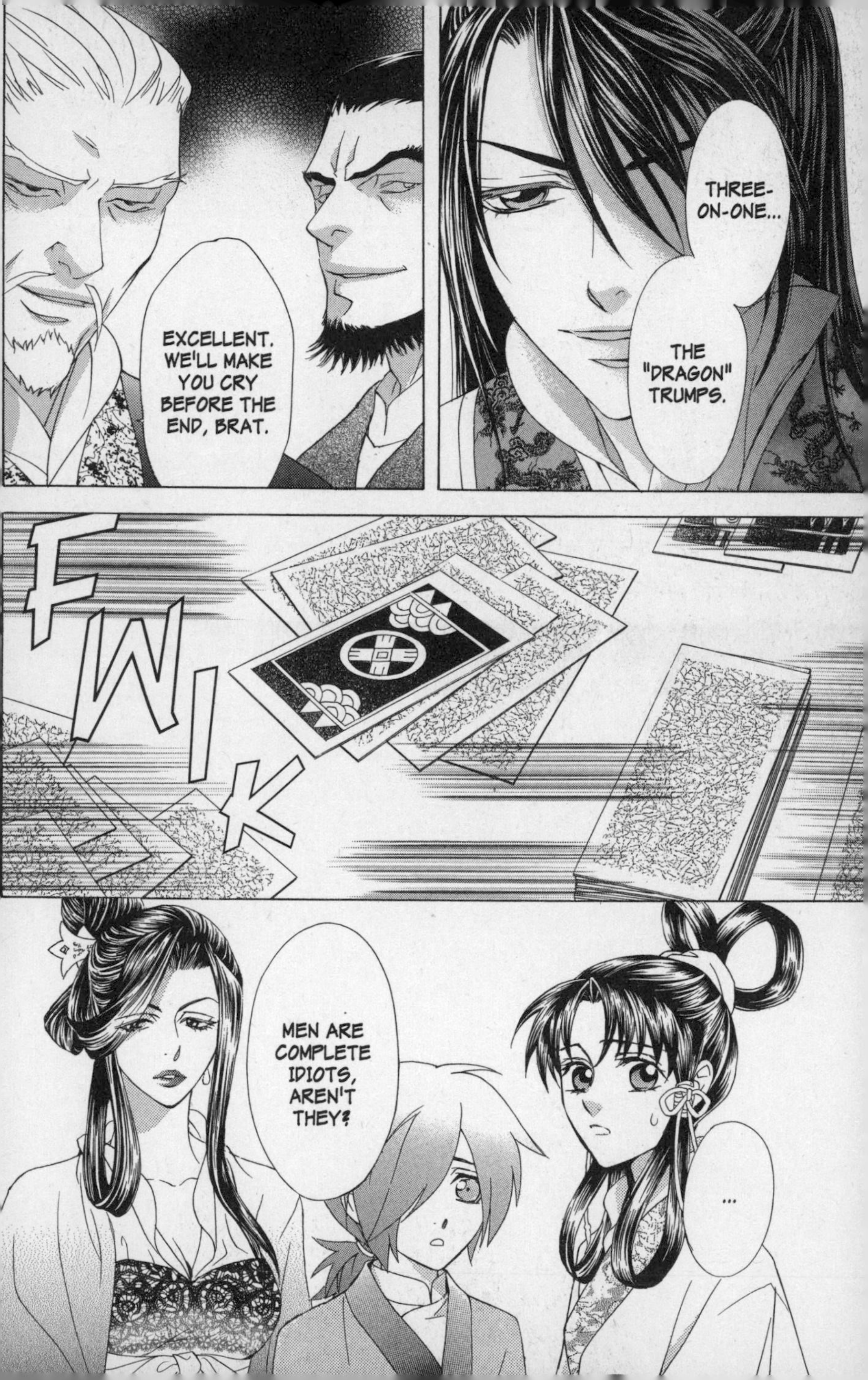
THREE-ON-ONE...
THE "DRAGON" TRUMPS.
EXCELLENT. WE'LL MAKE YOU CRY BEFORE THE END, BRAT.
FWIK
MEN ARE COMPLETE IDIOTS, AREN'T THEY?
...

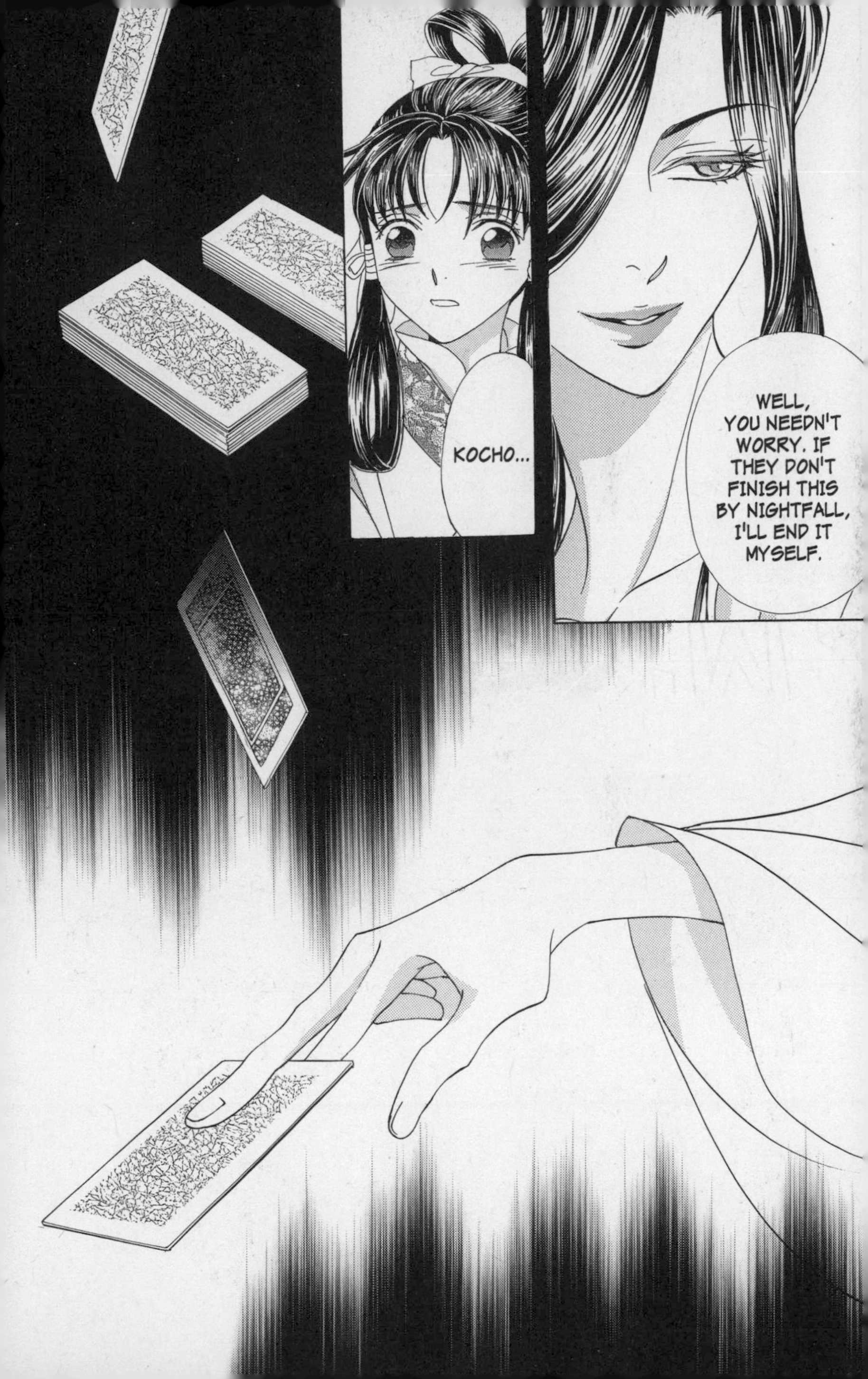
WELL, YOU NEEDN'T WORRY. IF THEY DON'T FINISH THIS BY NIGHTFALL, I'LL END IT MYSELF.
KOCHO...

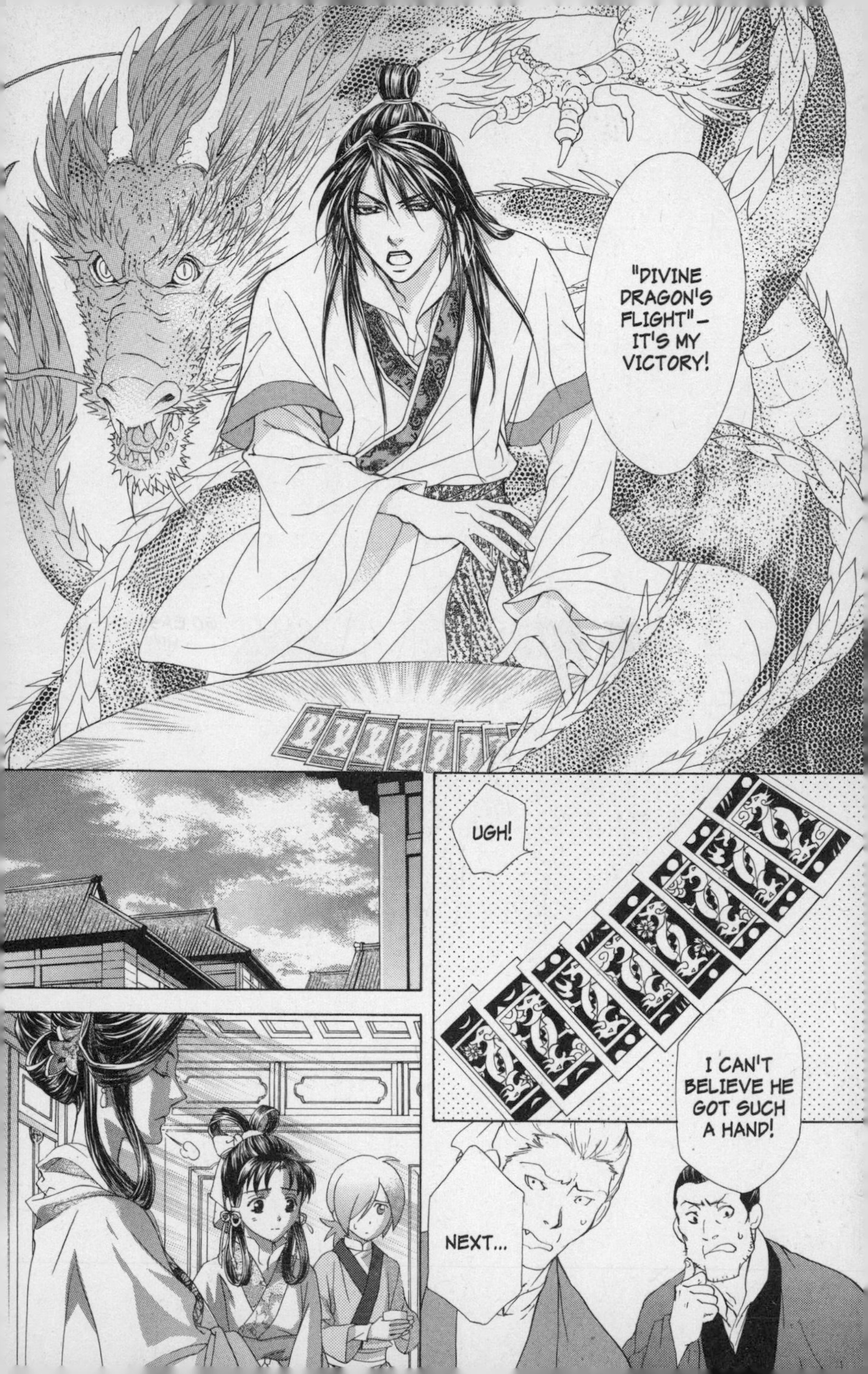
"DIVINE DRAGON'S FLIGHT"—IT'S MY VICTORY!
UGH!
I CAN'T BELIEVE HE GOT SUCH A HAND!
NEXT...

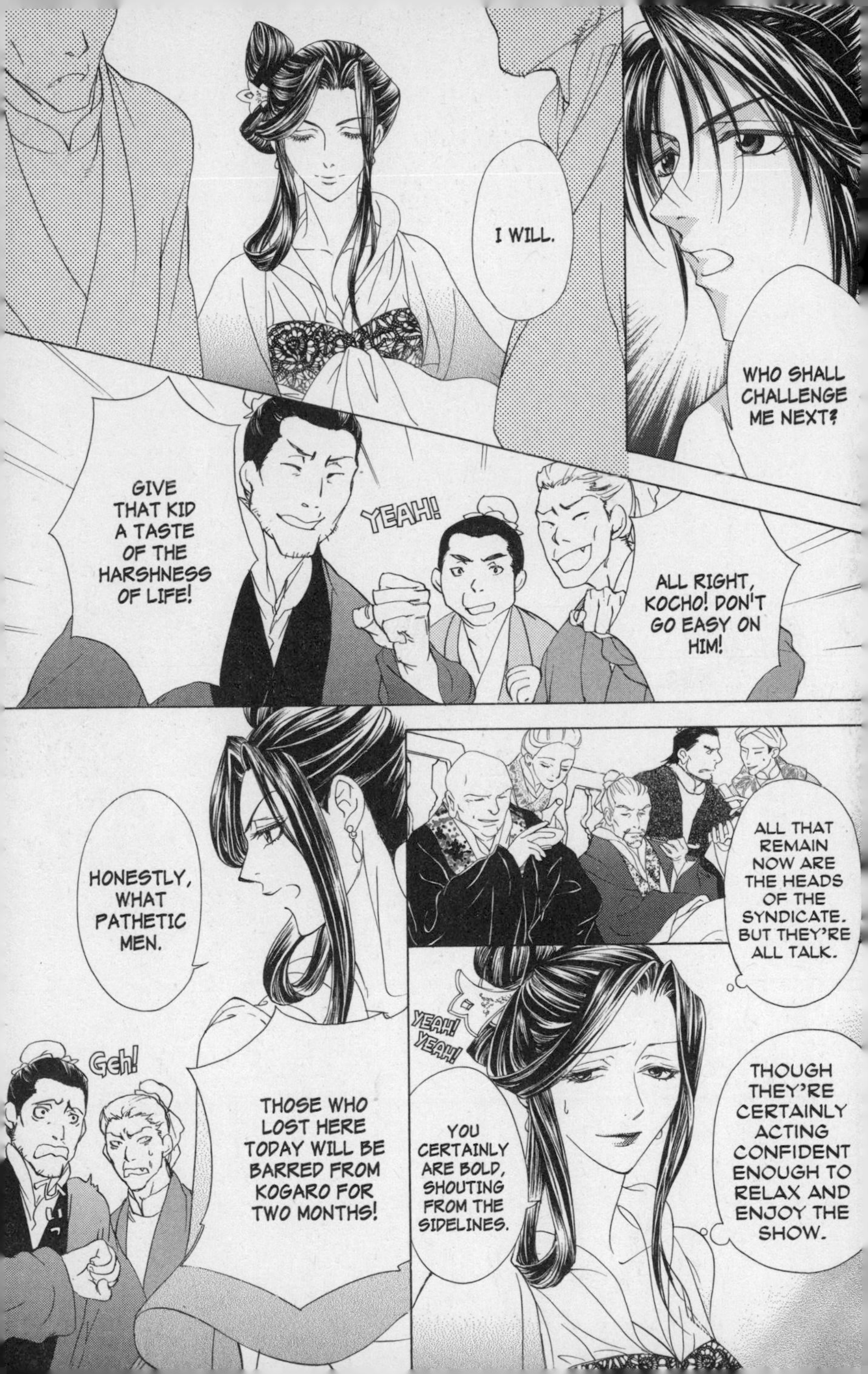
WHO SHALL CHALLENGE ME NEXT?
I WILL.
ALL RIGHT, KOCHO! DON'T GO EASY ON HIM!
YEAH!
GIVE THAT KID A TASTE OF THE HARSHNESS OF LIFE!
ALL THAT REMAIN NOW ARE THE HEADS OF THE SYNDICATE. BUT THEY'RE ALL TALK.
THOUGH THEY'RE CERTAINLY ACTING CONFIDENT ENOUGH TO RELAX AND ENJOY THE SHOW.
YEAH! YEAH!
YOU CERTAINLY ARE BOLD, SHOUTING FROM THE SIDELINES.
HONESTLY, WHAT PATHETIC MEN.
THOSE WHO LOST HERE TODAY WILL BE BARRED FROM KOGARO FOR TWO MONTHS!
Geh!

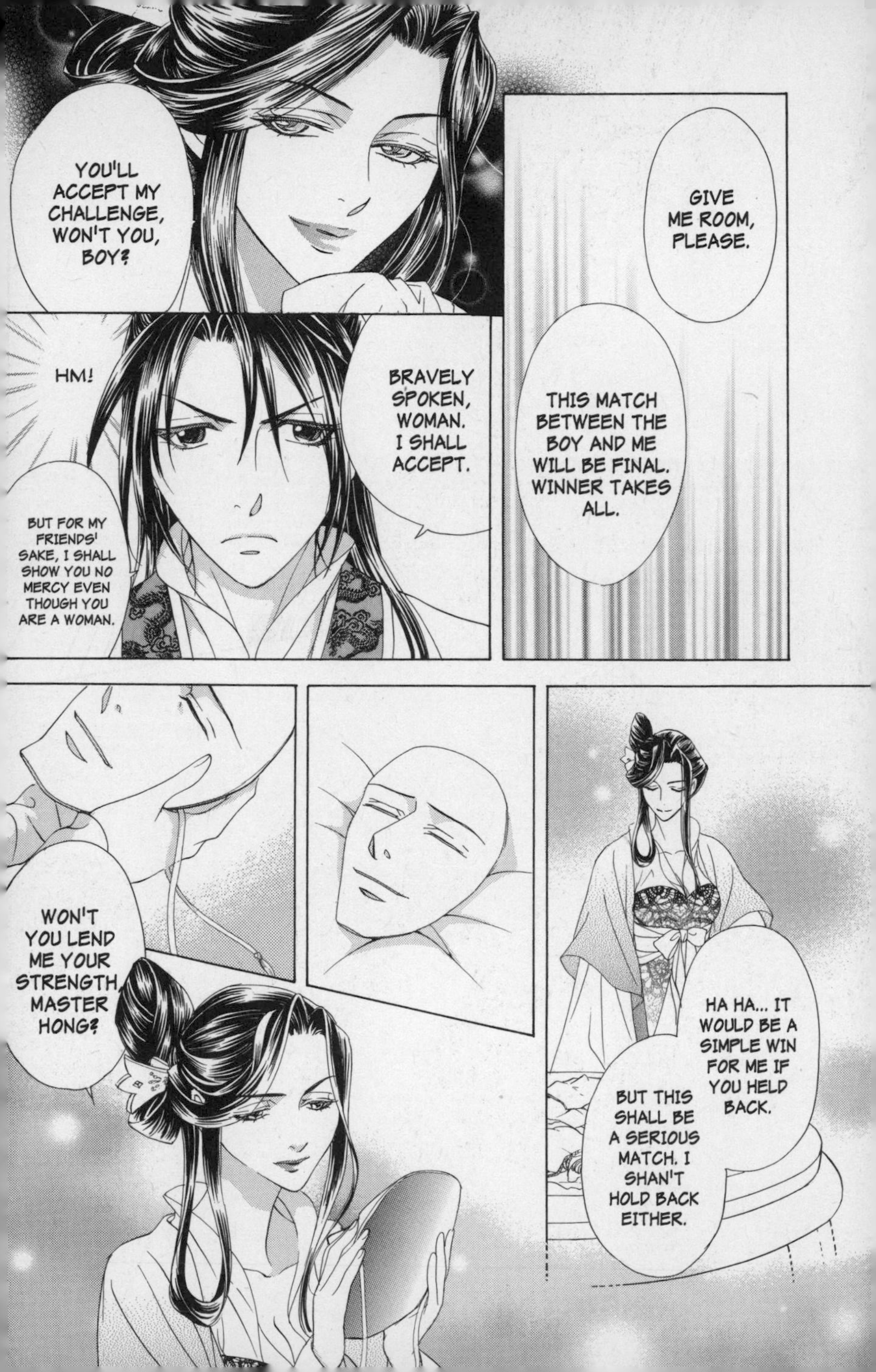
GIVE ME ROOM, PLEASE.
THIS MATCH BETWEEN THE BOY AND ME WILL BE FINAL. WINNER TAKES ALL.
YOU'LL ACCEPT MY CHALLENGE, WON'T YOU, BOY?
HM!
BRAVELY SPOKEN, WOMAN. I SHALL ACCEPT.
BUT FOR MY FRIENDS' SAKE, I SHALL SHOW YOU NO MERCY EVEN THOUGH YOU ARE A WOMAN.
HA HA... IT WOULD BE A SIMPLE WIN FOR ME IF YOU HELD BACK.
BUT THIS SHALL BE A SERIOUS MATCH. I SHAN'T HOLD BACK EITHER.
WON'T YOU LEND ME YOUR STRENGTH, MASTER HONG?

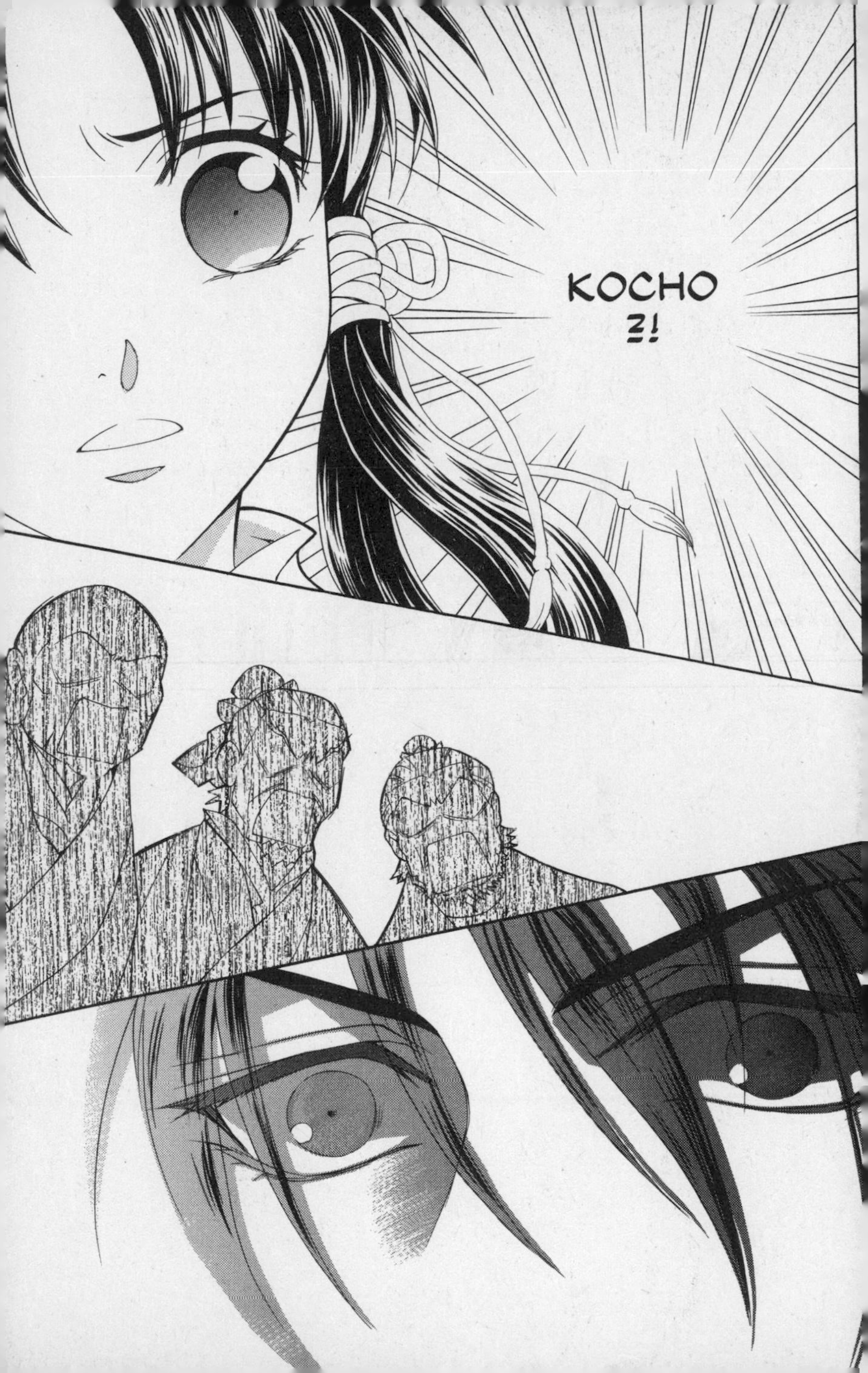
KOCHO ?!

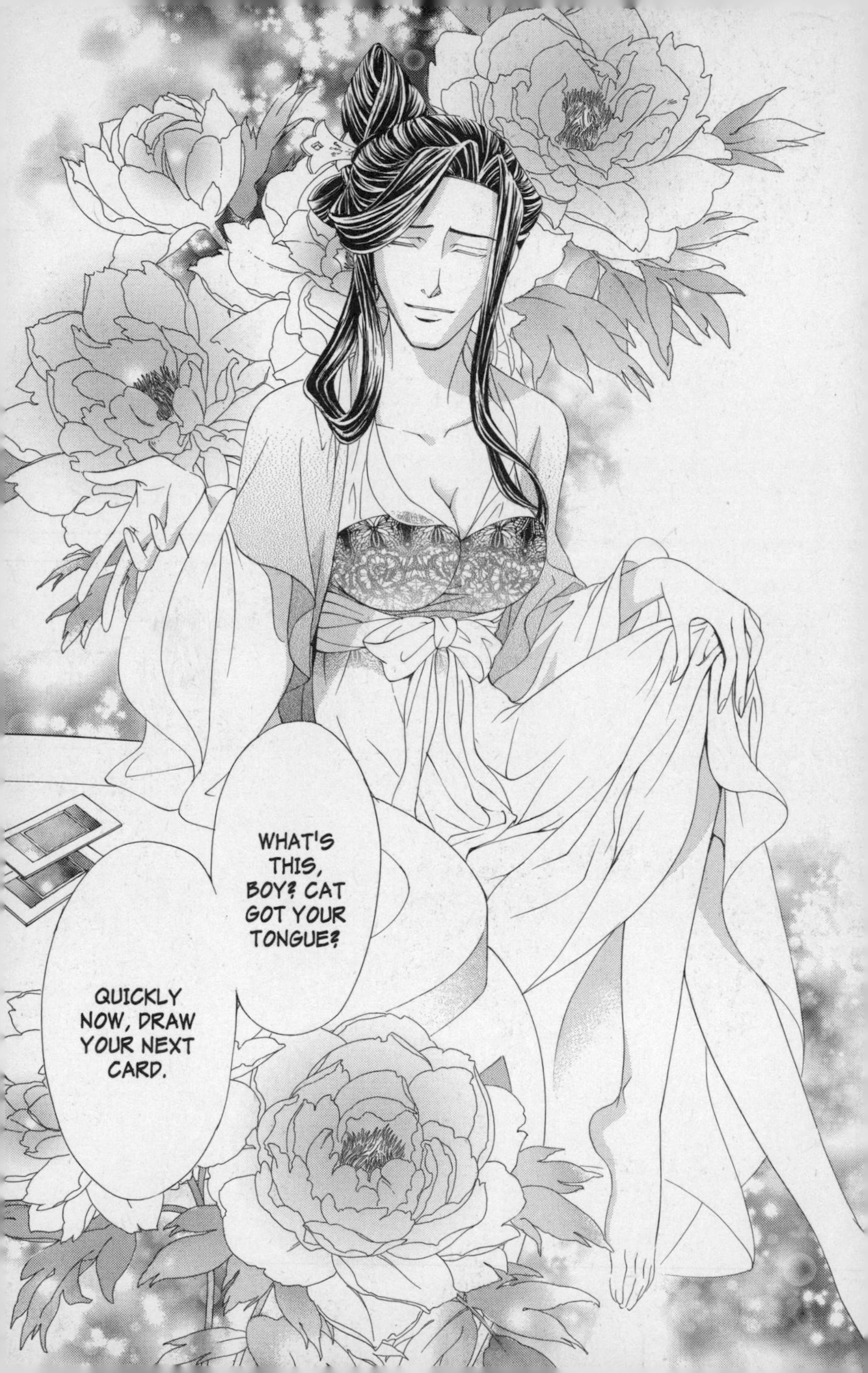
WHAT'S THIS, BOY? CAT GOT YOUR TONGUE?
QUICKLY NOW, DRAW YOUR NEXT CARD.

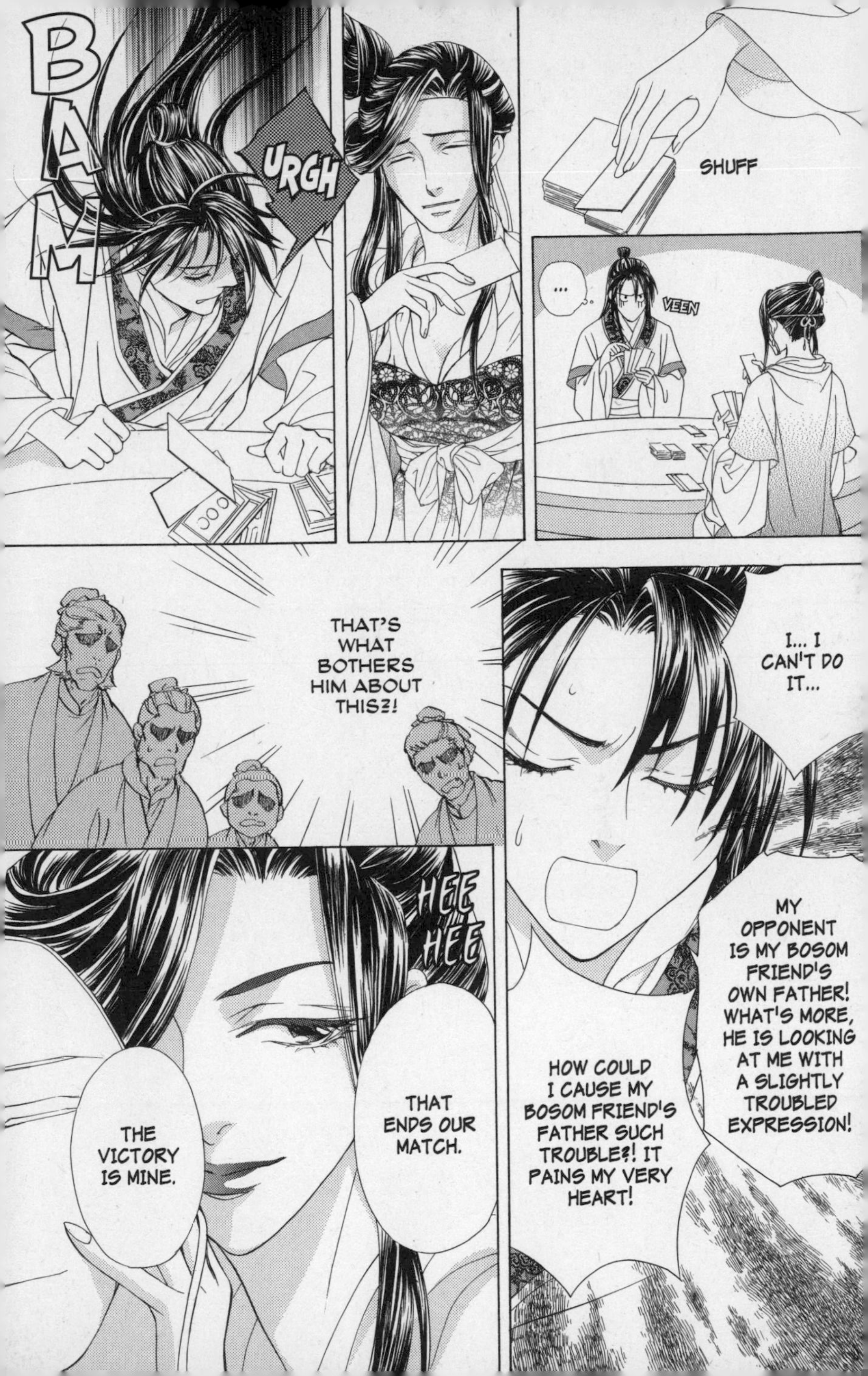
SHUFF
...
VEEN
BAM
URGH
I... I CAN'T DO IT...
MY OPPONENT IS MY BOSOM FRIEND'S OWN FATHER! WHAT'S MORE, HE IS LOOKING AT ME WITH A SLIGHTLY TROUBLED EXPRESSION!
HOW COULD I CAUSE MY BOSOM FRIEND'S FATHER SUCH TROUBLE?! IT PAINS MY VERY HEART!
THAT'S WHAT BOTHERS HIM ABOUT THIS?!
HEE HEE
THAT ENDS OUR MATCH.
THE VICTORY IS MINE.

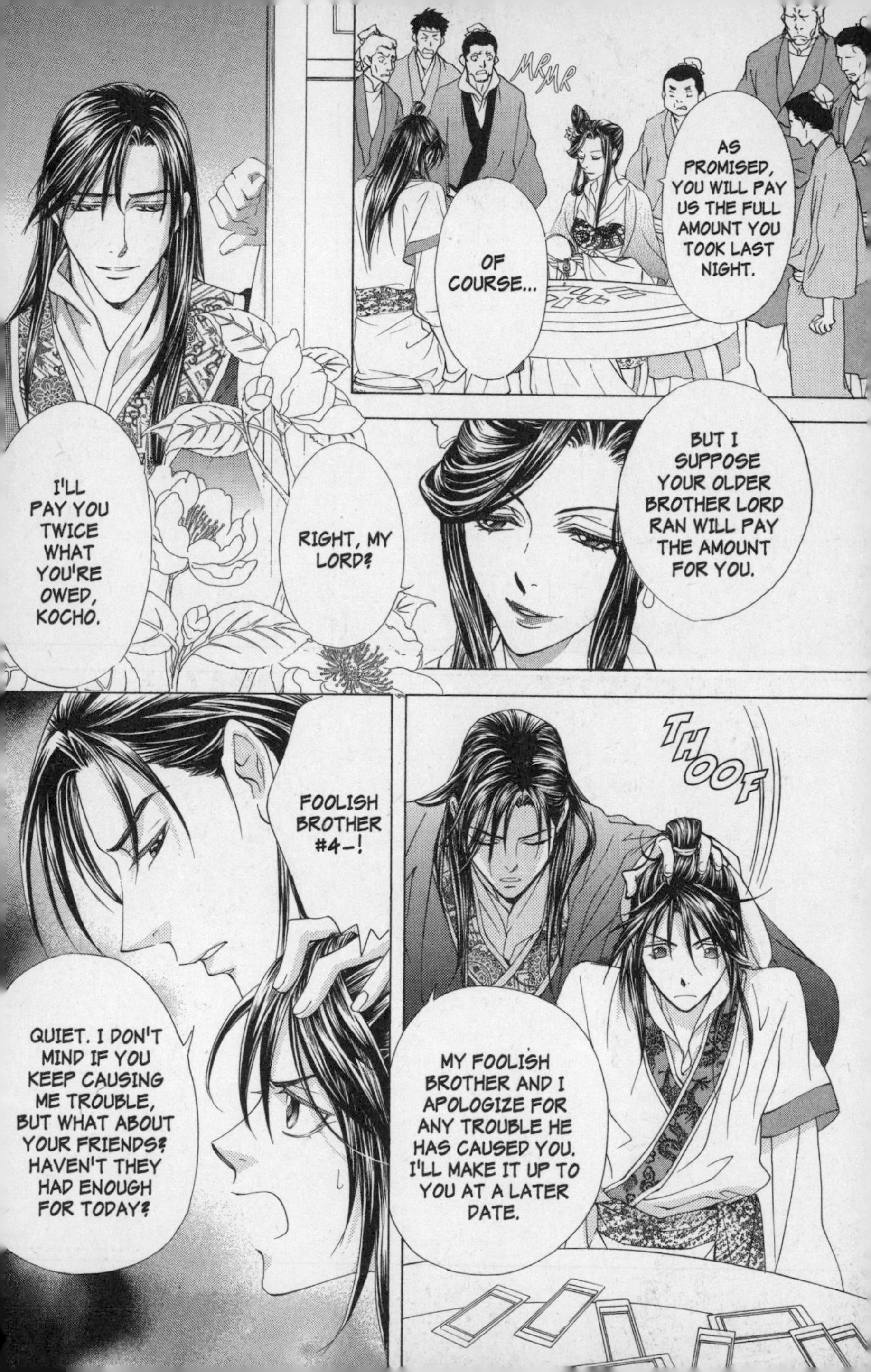
MR MR
AS PROMISED, YOU WILL PAY US THE FULL AMOUNT YOU TOOK LAST NIGHT.
OF COURSE...
BUT I SUPPOSE YOUR OLDER BROTHER LORD RAN WILL PAY THE AMOUNT FOR YOU.
RIGHT, MY LORD?
I'LL PAY YOU TWICE WHAT YOU'RE OWED, KOCHO.
THOOF
MY FOOLISH BROTHER AND I APOLOGIZE FOR ANY TROUBLE HE HAS CAUSED YOU. I'LL MAKE IT UP TO YOU AT A LATER DATE.
FOOLISH BROTHER #4–!
QUIET. I DON'T MIND IF YOU KEEP CAUSING ME TROUBLE, BUT WHAT ABOUT YOUR FRIENDS? HAVEN'T THEY HAD ENOUGH FOR TODAY?

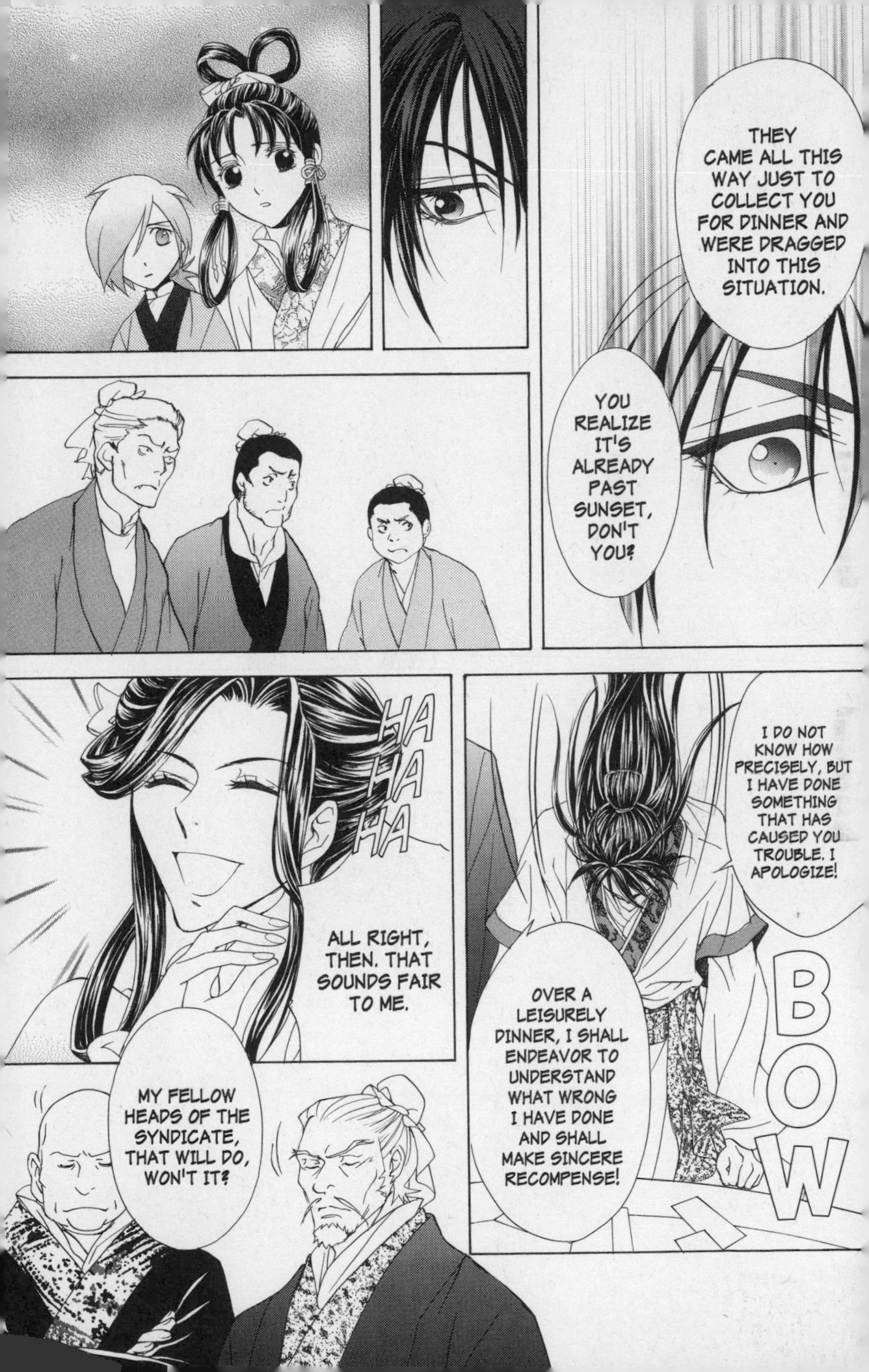
THEY CAME ALL THIS WAY JUST TO COLLECT YOU FOR DINNER AND WERE DRAGGED INTO THIS SITUATION.
YOU REALIZE IT'S ALREADY PAST SUNSET, DON'T YOU?
I DO NOT KNOW HOW PRECISELY, BUT I HAVE DONE SOMETHING THAT HAS CAUSED YOU TROUBLE. I APOLOGIZE!
BOW
OVER A LEISURELY DINNER, I SHALL ENDEAVOR TO UNDERSTAND WHAT WRONG I HAVE DONE AND SHALL MAKE SINCERE RECOMPENSE!
HA HA HA HA
ALL RIGHT, THEN. THAT SOUNDS FAIR TO ME.
MY FELLOW HEADS OF THE SYNDICATE, THAT WILL DO, WON'T IT?

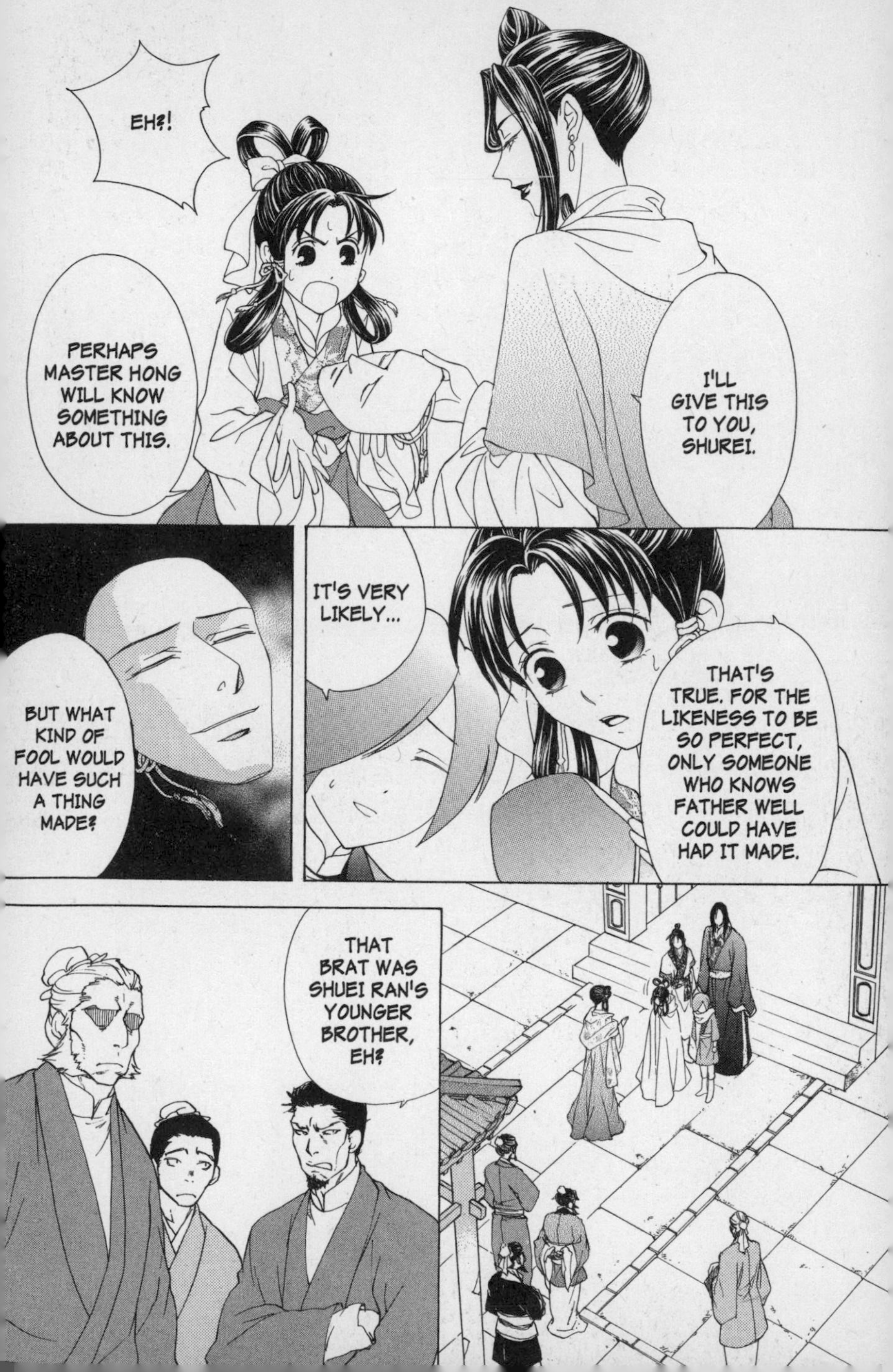
I'LL GIVE THIS TO YOU, SHUREI.
EH?!
PERHAPS MASTER HONG WILL KNOW SOMETHING ABOUT THIS.
IT'S VERY LIKELY...
THAT'S TRUE. FOR THE LIKENESS TO BE SO PERFECT, ONLY SOMEONE WHO KNOWS FATHER WELL COULD HAVE HAD IT MADE.
BUT WHAT KIND OF FOOL WOULD HAVE SUCH A THING MADE?
THAT BRAT WAS SHUEI RAN'S YOUNGER BROTHER, EH?

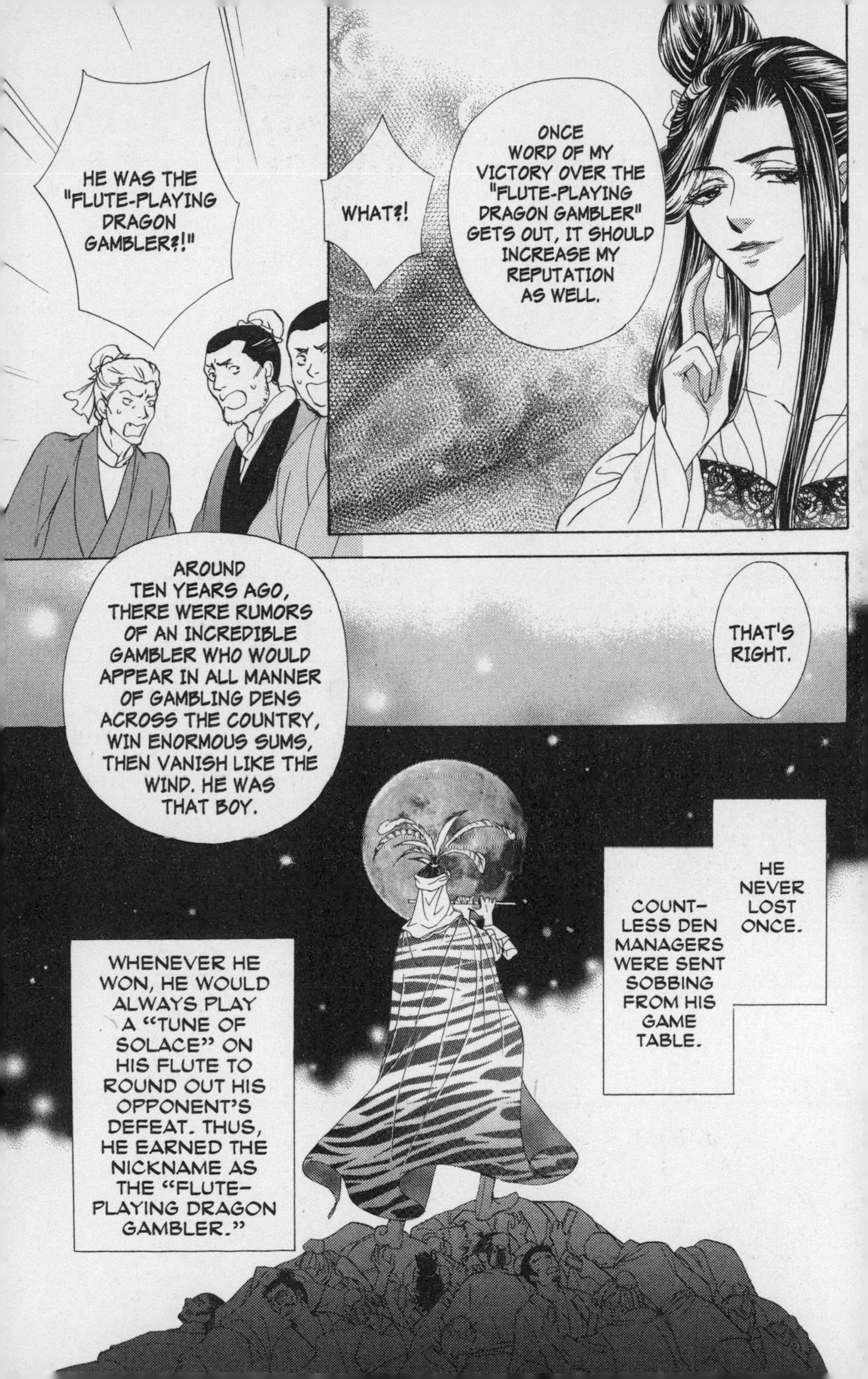
ONCE WORD OF MY VICTORY OVER THE "FLUTE-PLAYING DRAGON GAMBLER" GETS OUT, IT SHOULD INCREASE MY REPUTATION AS WELL.
WHAT?!
HE WAS THE "FLUTE-PLAYING DRAGON GAMBLER?!"
THAT'S RIGHT.
AROUND TEN YEARS AGO, THERE WERE RUMORS OF AN INCREDIBLE GAMBLER WHO WOULD APPEAR IN ALL MANNER OF GAMBLING DENS ACROSS THE COUNTRY, WIN ENORMOUS SUMS, THEN VANISH LIKE THE WIND. HE WAS THAT BOY.
HE NEVER LOST ONCE.
COUNT-LESS DEN MANAGERS WERE SENT SOBBING FROM HIS GAME TABLE.
WHENEVER HE WON, HE WOULD ALWAYS PLAY A "TUNE OF SOLACE" ON HIS FLUTE TO ROUND OUT HIS OPPONENT'S DEFEAT. THUS, HE EARNED THE NICKNAME AS THE "FLUTE-PLAYING DRAGON GAMBLER."

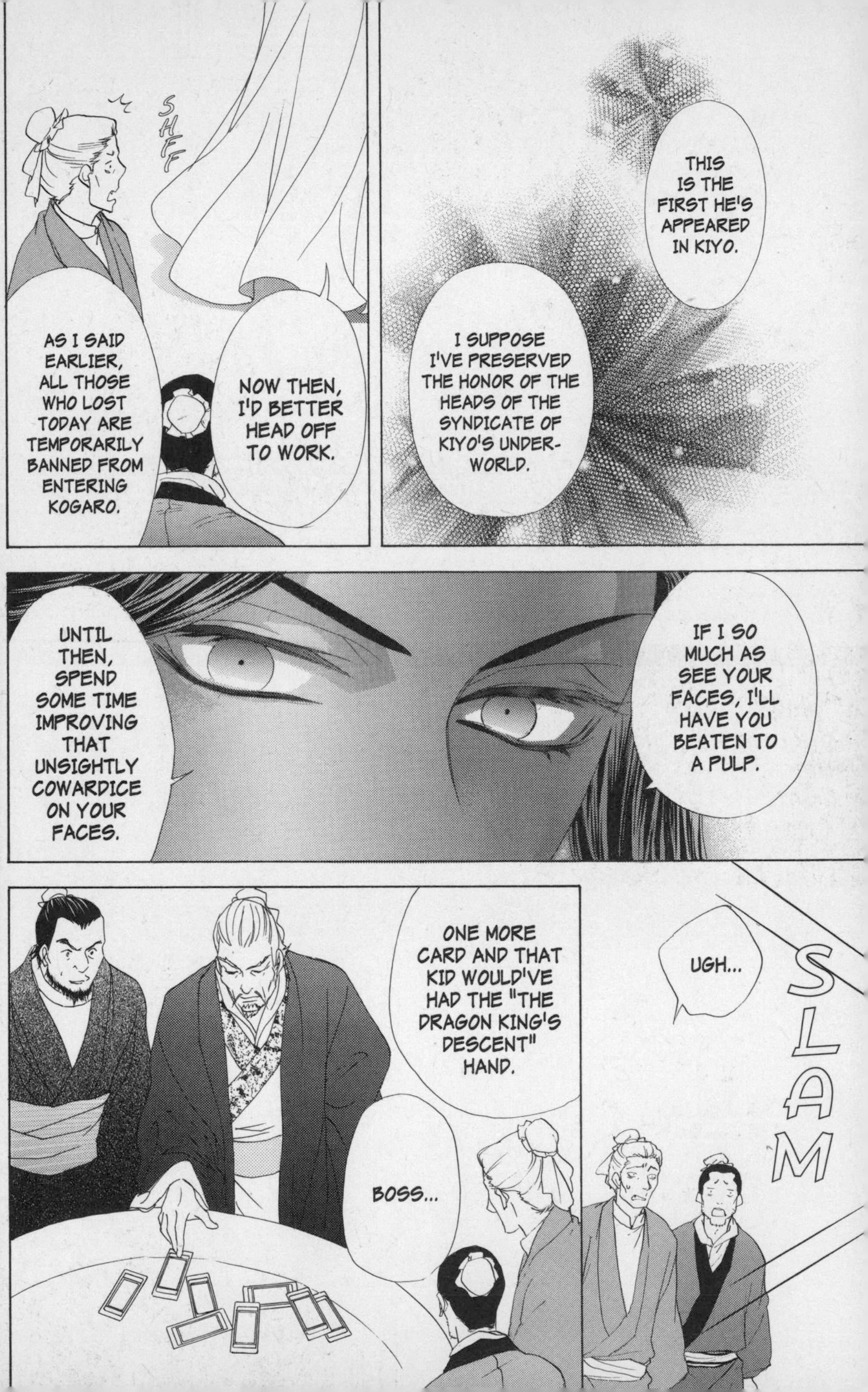
THIS IS THE FIRST HE'S APPEARED IN KIYO.
I SUPPOSE I'VE PRESERVED THE HONOR OF THE HEADS OF THE SYNDICATE OF KIYO'S UNDER-WORLD.
SHFF
NOW THEN, I'D BETTER HEAD OFF TO WORK.
AS I SAID EARLIER, ALL THOSE WHO LOST TODAY ARE TEMPORARILY BANNED FROM ENTERING KOGARO.
IF I SO MUCH AS SEE YOUR FACES, I'LL HAVE YOU BEATEN TO A PULP.
UNTIL THEN, SPEND SOME TIME IMPROVING THAT UNSIGHTLY COWARDICE ON YOUR FACES.
SLAM
UGH...
ONE MORE CARD AND THAT KID WOULD'VE HAD THE "THE DRAGON KING'S DESCENT" HAND.
BOSS...

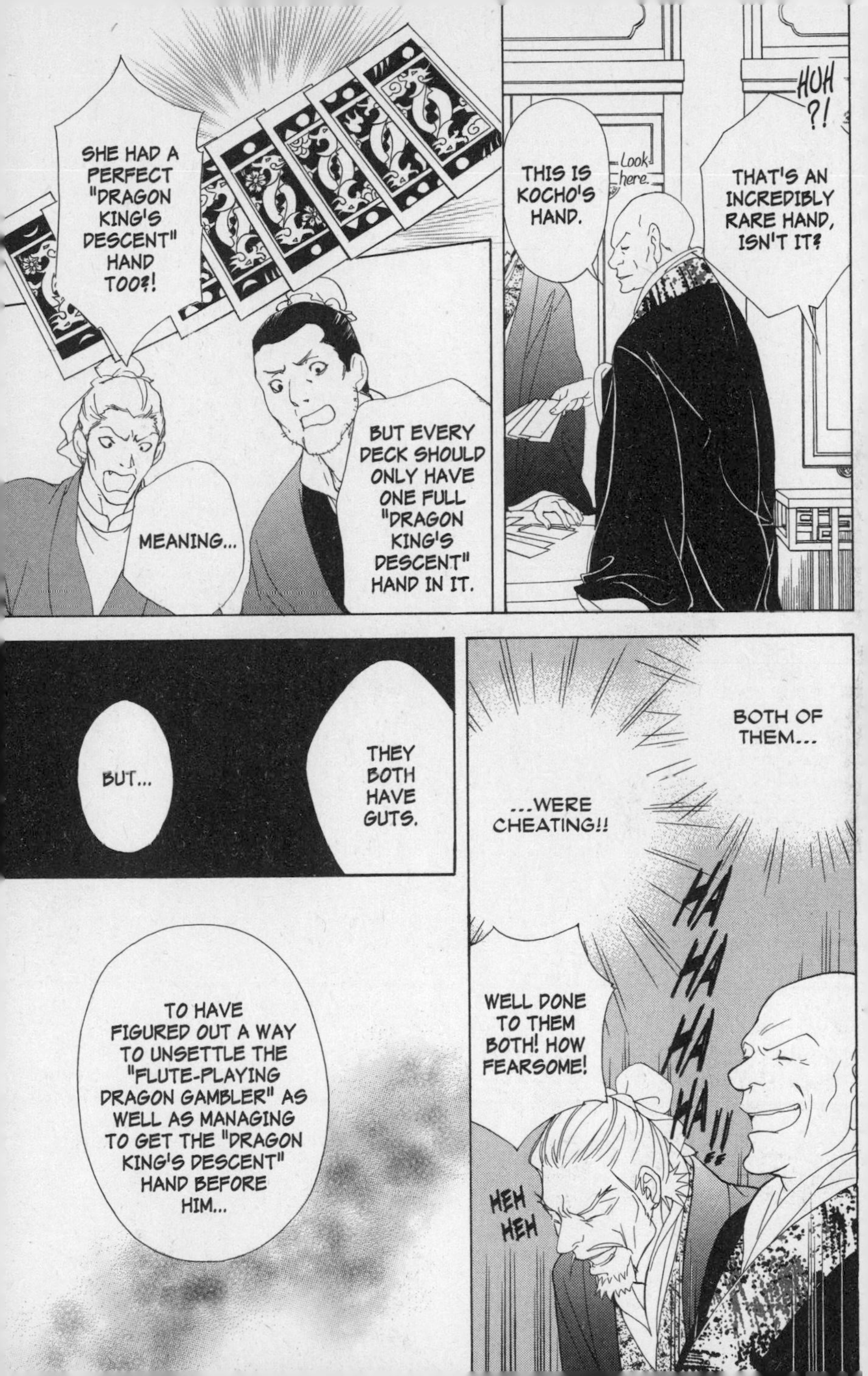
HUH?!
THAT'S AN INCREDIBLY RARE HAND, ISN'T IT?
Look here.
THIS IS KOCHO'S HAND.
SHE HAD A PERFECT "DRAGON KING'S DESCENT" HAND TOO?!
BUT EVERY DECK SHOULD ONLY HAVE ONE FULL "DRAGON KING'S DESCENT" HAND IN IT.
MEANING...
BOTH OF THEM...
...WERE CHEATING!!
HA HA HA HA!!
WELL DONE TO THEM BOTH! HOW FEARSOME!
HEH HEH
THEY BOTH HAVE GUTS.
BUT...
TO HAVE FIGURED OUT A WAY TO UNSETTLE THE "FLUTE-PLAYING DRAGON GAMBLER" AS WELL AS MANAGING TO GET THE "DRAGON KING'S DESCENT" HAND BEFORE HIM...

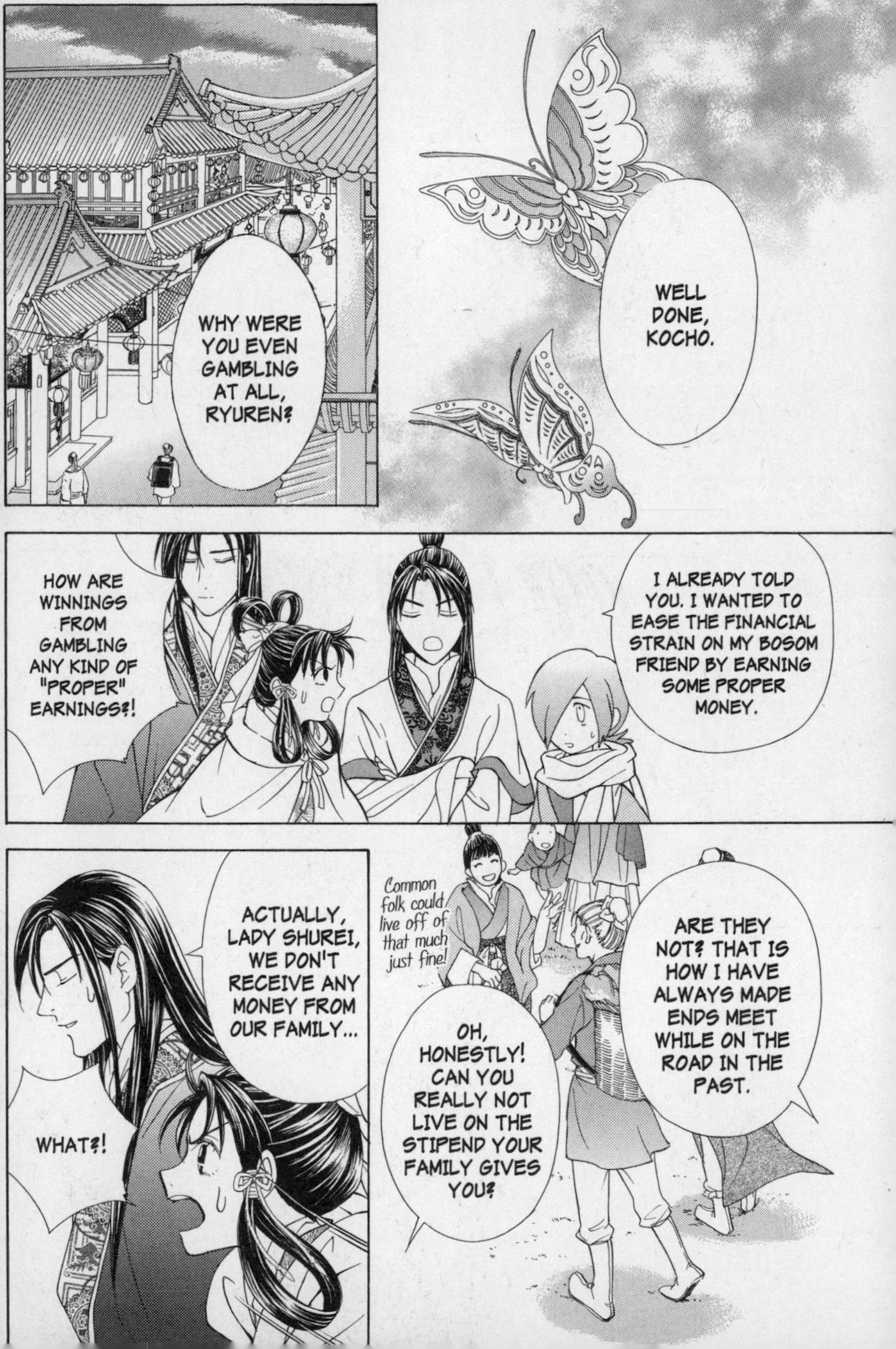
WELL DONE, KOCHO.
WHY WERE YOU EVEN GAMBLING AT ALL, RYUREN?
I ALREADY TOLD YOU. I WANTED TO EASE THE FINANCIAL STRAIN ON MY BOSOM FRIEND BY EARNING SOME PROPER MONEY.
HOW ARE WINNINGS FROM GAMBLING ANY KIND OF "PROPER" EARNINGS?!
ARE THEY NOT? THAT IS HOW I HAVE ALWAYS MADE ENDS MEET WHILE ON THE ROAD IN THE PAST.
Common folk could live off of that much just fine!
OH, HONESTLY! CAN YOU REALLY NOT LIVE ON THE STIPEND YOUR FAMILY GIVES YOU?
ACTUALLY, LADY SHUREI, WE DON'T RECEIVE ANY MONEY FROM OUR FAMILY...
WHAT?!

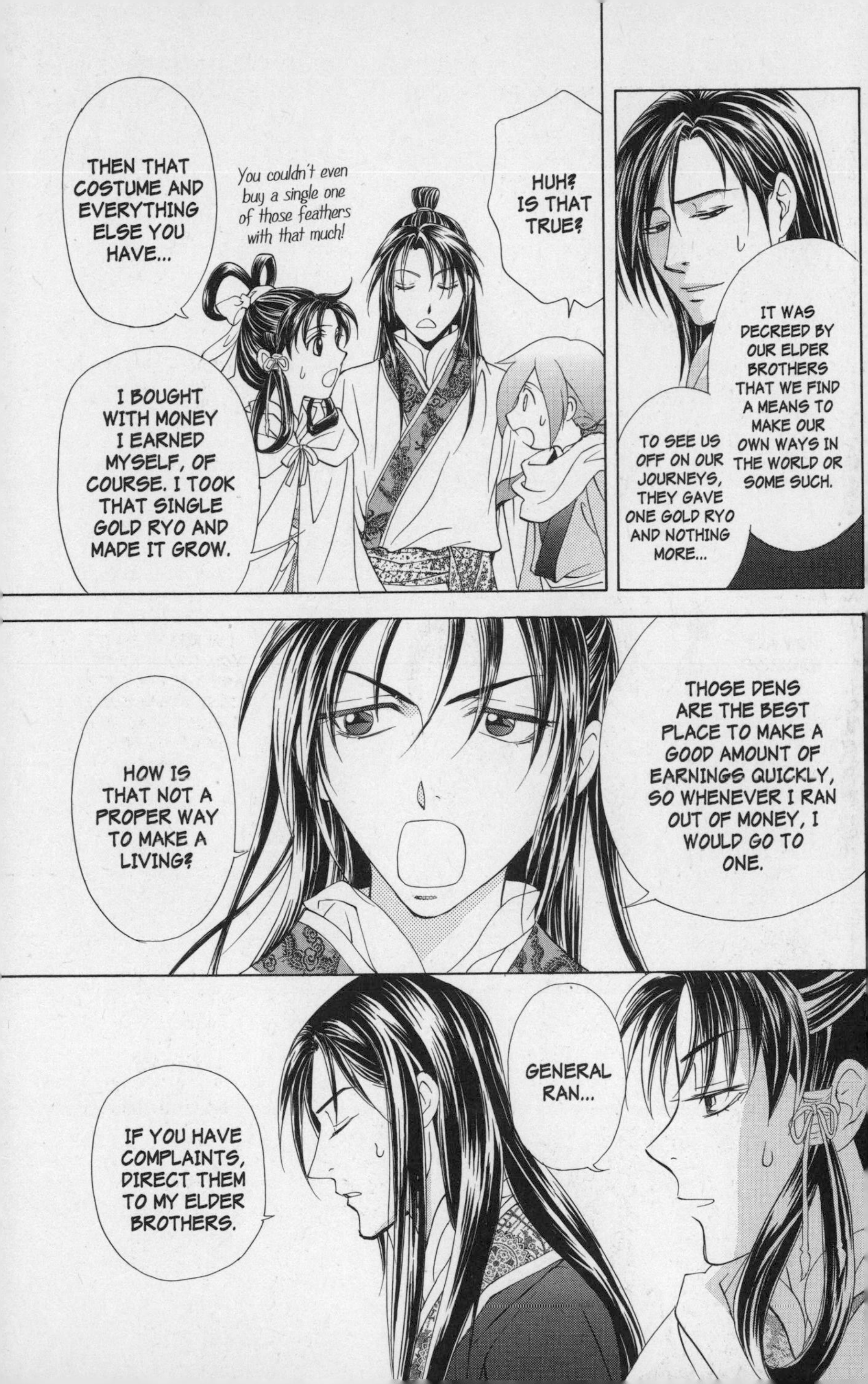
IT WAS DECREED BY OUR ELDER BROTHERS THAT WE FIND A MEANS TO MAKE OUR OWN WAYS IN THE WORLD OR SOME SUCH.
TO SEE US OFF ON OUR JOURNEYS, THEY GAVE ONE GOLD RYO AND NOTHING MORE...
HUH? IS THAT TRUE?
You couldn't even buy a single one of those feathers with that much!
THEN THAT COSTUME AND EVERYTHING ELSE YOU HAVE...
I BOUGHT WITH MONEY I EARNED MYSELF, OF COURSE. I TOOK THAT SINGLE GOLD RYO AND MADE IT GROW.
THOSE DENS ARE THE BEST PLACE TO MAKE A GOOD AMOUNT OF EARNINGS QUICKLY, SO WHENEVER I RAN OUT OF MONEY, I WOULD GO TO ONE.
HOW IS THAT NOT A PROPER WAY TO MAKE A LIVING?
GENERAL RAN...
IF YOU HAVE COMPLAINTS, DIRECT THEM TO MY ELDER BROTHERS.

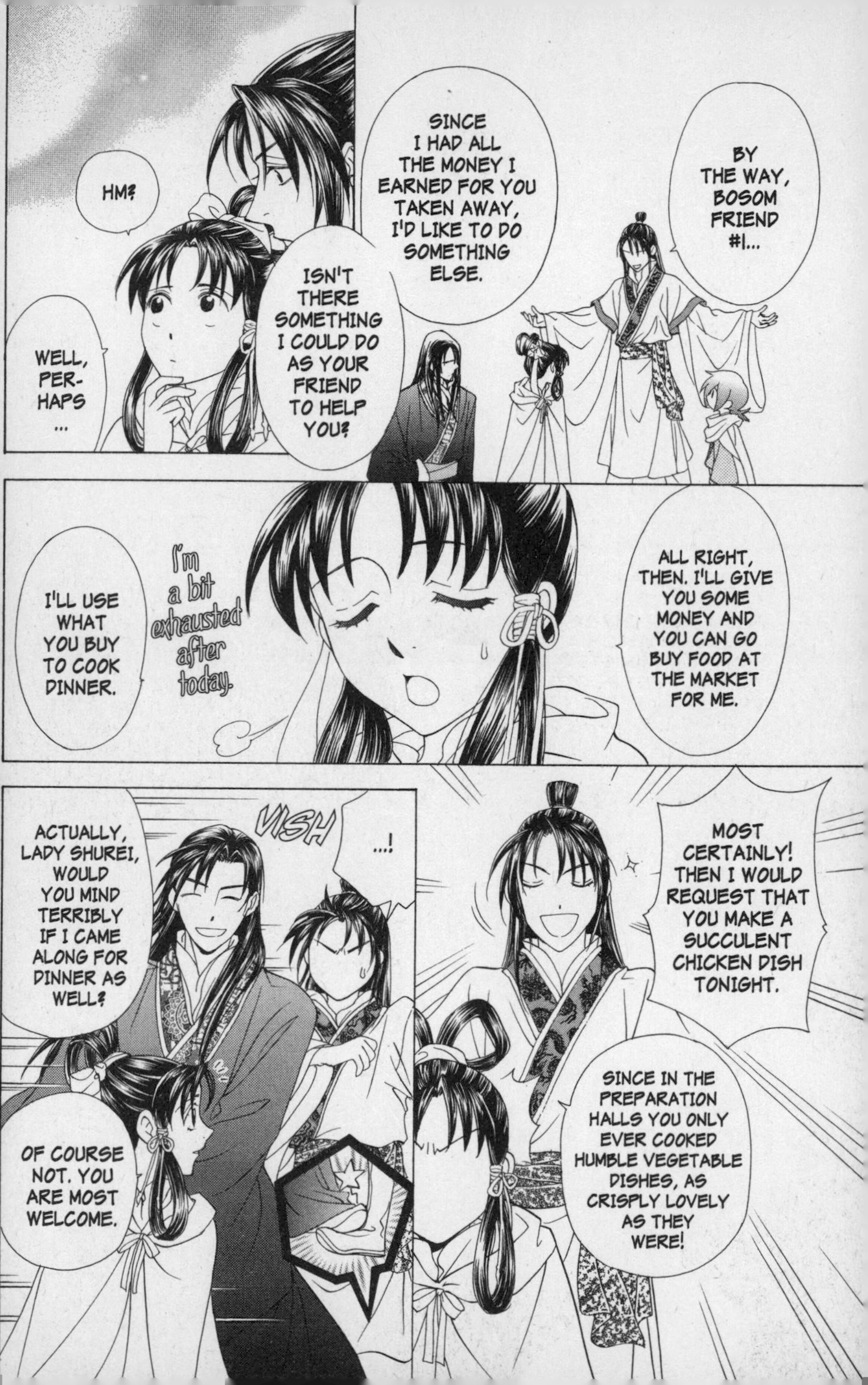
BY THE WAY, BOSOM FRIEND #1...
SINCE I HAD ALL THE MONEY I EARNED FOR YOU TAKEN AWAY, I'D LIKE TO DO SOMETHING ELSE.
ISN'T THERE SOMETHING I COULD DO AS YOUR FRIEND TO HELP YOU?
HM?
WELL, PER-HAPS ...
ALL RIGHT, THEN. I'LL GIVE YOU SOME MONEY AND YOU CAN GO BUY FOOD AT THE MARKET FOR ME.
I'm a bit exhausted after today.
I'LL USE WHAT YOU BUY TO COOK DINNER.
MOST CERTAINLY! THEN I WOULD REQUEST THAT YOU MAKE A SUCCULENT CHICKEN DISH TONIGHT.
SINCE IN THE PREPARATION HALLS YOU ONLY EVER COOKED HUMBLE VEGETABLE DISHES, AS CRISPLY LOVELY AS THEY WERE!
VISH
...!
ACTUALLY, LADY SHUREI, WOULD YOU MIND TERRIBLY IF I CAME ALONG FOR DINNER AS WELL?
OF COURSE NOT. YOU ARE MOST WELCOME.

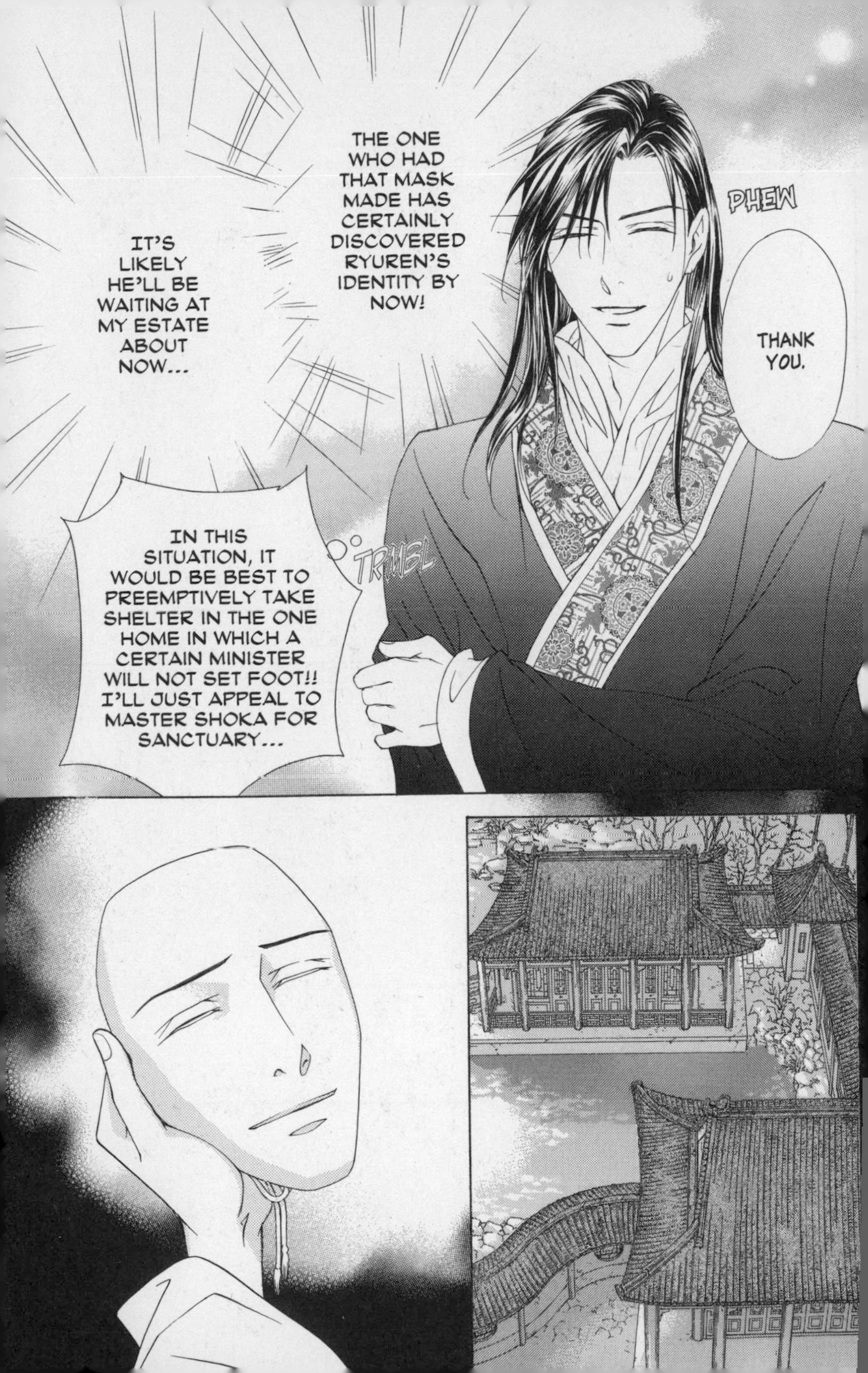
PHEW
THANK YOU.
THE ONE WHO HAD THAT MASK MADE HAS CERTAINLY DISCOVERED RYUREN'S IDENTITY BY NOW!
IT'S LIKELY HE'LL BE WAITING AT MY ESTATE ABOUT NOW...
TRMBL
IN THIS SITUATION, IT WOULD BE BEST TO PREEMPTIVELY TAKE SHELTER IN THE ONE HOME IN WHICH A CERTAIN MINISTER WILL NOT SET FOOT!! I'LL JUST APPEAL TO MASTER SHOKA FOR SANCTUARY...

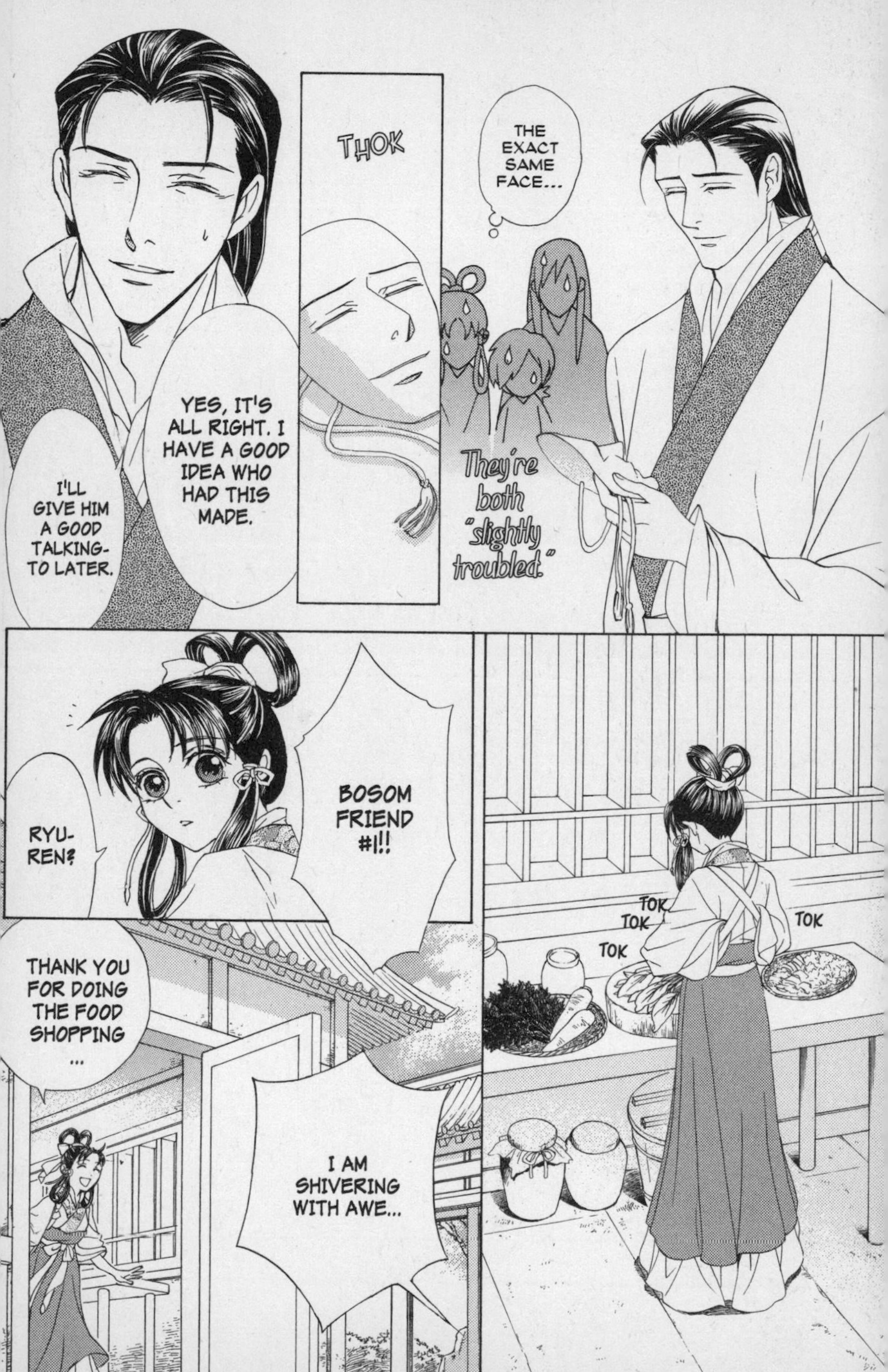
THE EXACT SAME FACE...
They're both "slightly troubled."
THOK
YES, IT'S ALL RIGHT. I HAVE A GOOD IDEA WHO HAD THIS MADE.
I'LL GIVE HIM A GOOD TALKING-TO LATER.
TOK
TOK
TOK
TOK
BOSOM FRIEND #1!!
RYU-REN?
THANK YOU FOR DOING THE FOOD SHOPPING ...
I AM SHIVERING WITH AWE...

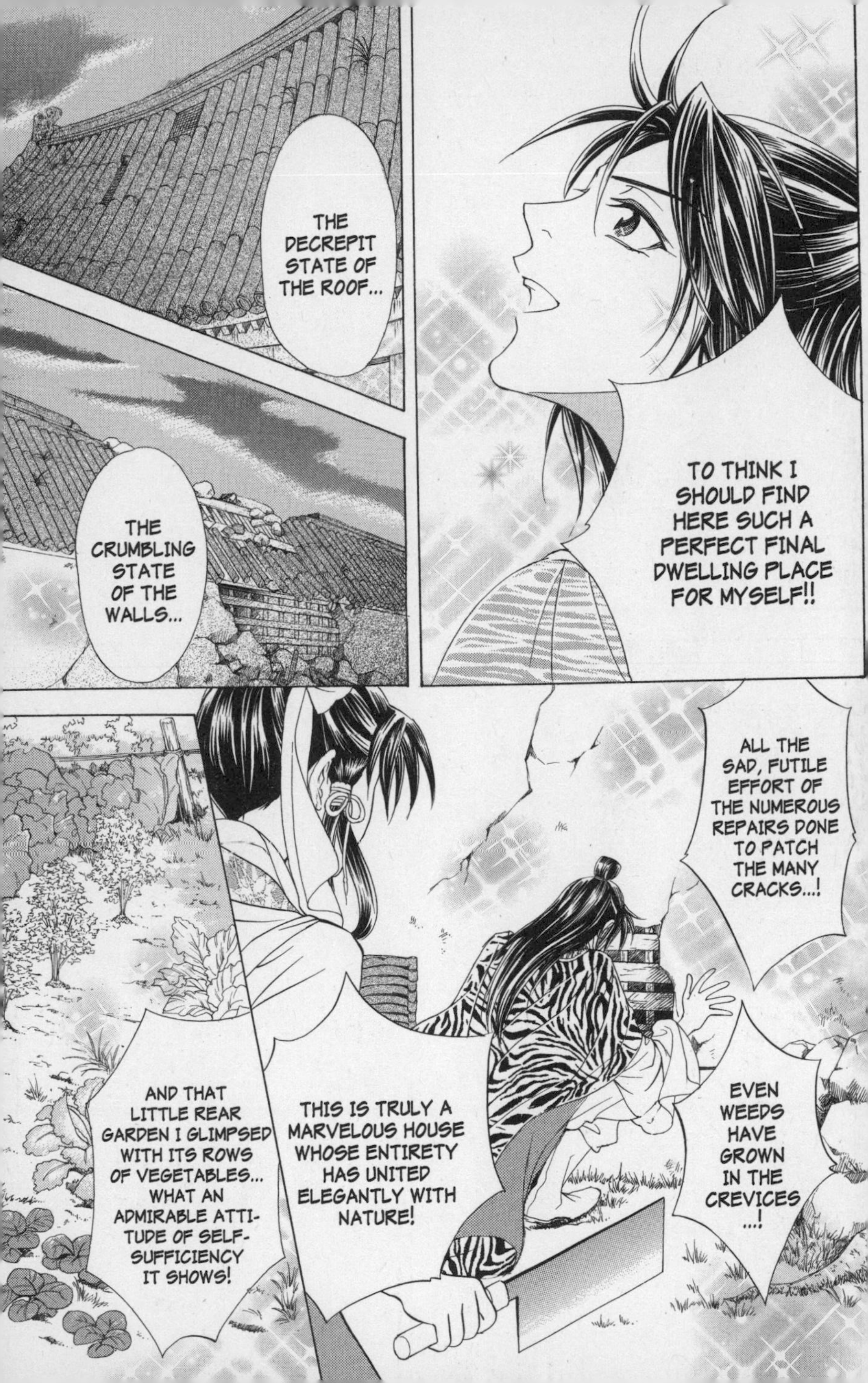
TO THINK I SHOULD FIND HERE SUCH A PERFECT FINAL DWELLING PLACE FOR MYSELF!!
THE DECREPIT STATE OF THE ROOF...
THE CRUMBLING STATE OF THE WALLS...
ALL THE SAD, FUTILE EFFORT OF THE NUMEROUS REPAIRS DONE TO PATCH THE MANY CRACKS...!
EVEN WEEDS HAVE GROWN IN THE CREVICES ...!
THIS IS TRULY A MARVELOUS HOUSE WHOSE ENTIRETY HAS UNITED ELEGANTLY WITH NATURE!
AND THAT LITTLE REAR GARDEN I GLIMPSED WITH ITS ROWS OF VEGETABLES... WHAT AN ADMIRABLE ATTI-TUDE OF SELF-SUFFICIENCY IT SHOWS!

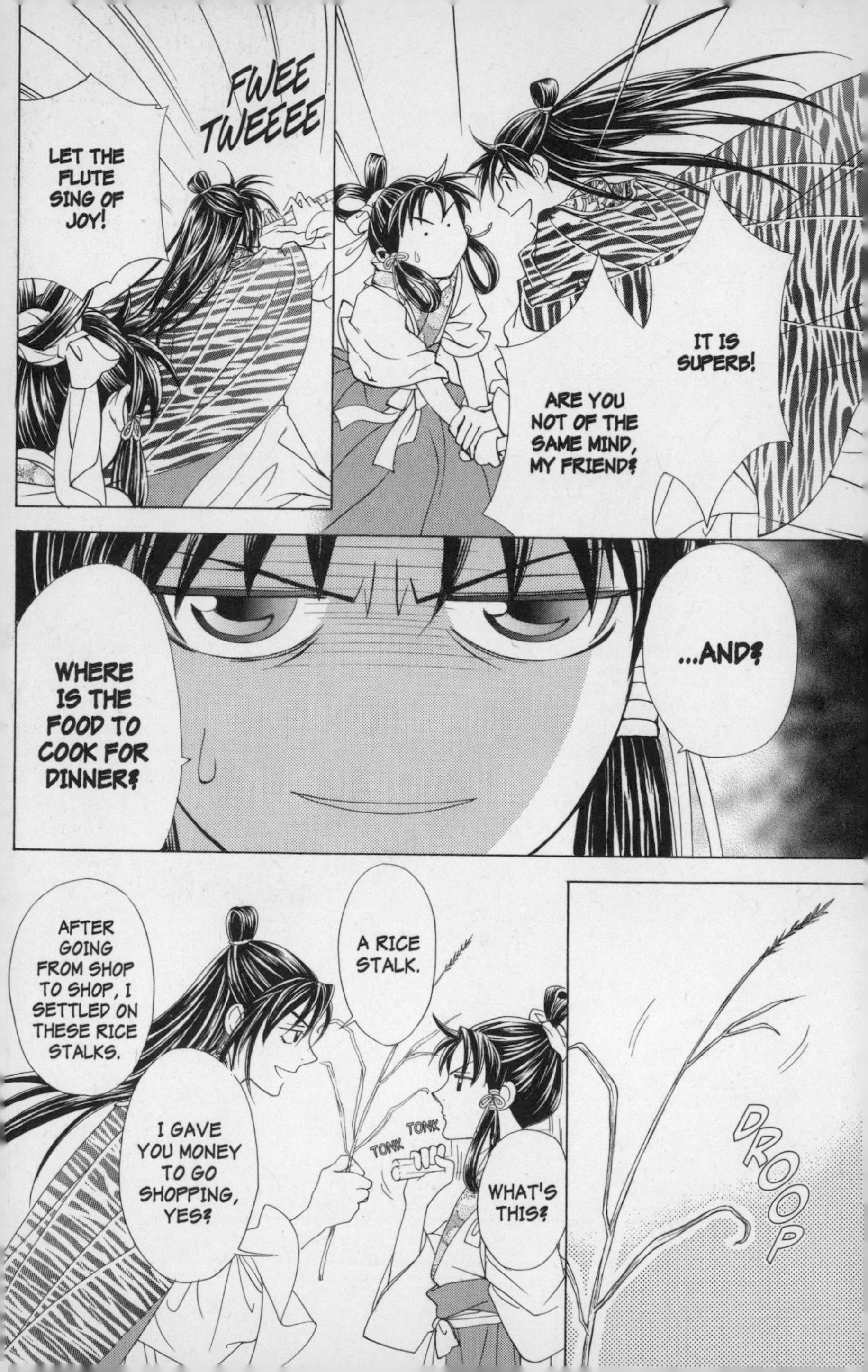
IT IS SUPERB!
ARE YOU NOT OF THE SAME MIND, MY FRIEND?
FWEE TWEEEE
LET THE FLUTE SING OF JOY!
...AND?
WHERE IS THE FOOD TO COOK FOR DINNER?
DROOP
A RICE STALK.
AFTER GOING FROM SHOP TO SHOP, I SETTLED ON THESE RICE STALKS.
TONK TONK
WHAT'S THIS?
I GAVE YOU MONEY TO GO SHOPPING, YES?

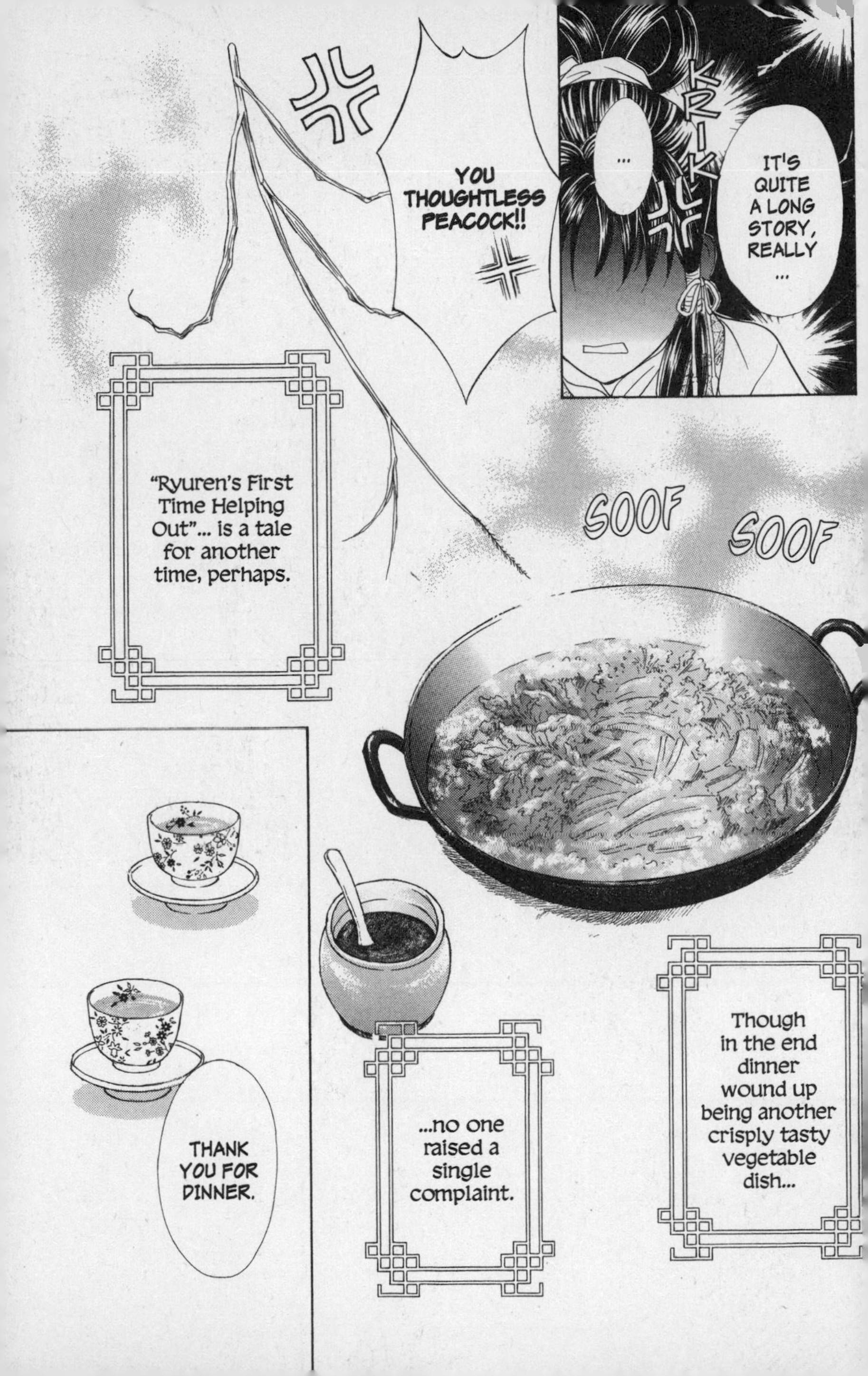
IT'S QUITE A LONG STORY, REALLY ...
...
KRIK
YOU THOUGHTLESS PEACOCK!!
"Ryuren's First Time Helping Out"... is a tale for another time, perhaps.
SOOF
SOOF
Though in the end dinner wound up being another crisply tasty vegetable dish...
...no one raised a single complaint.
THANK YOU FOR DINNER.

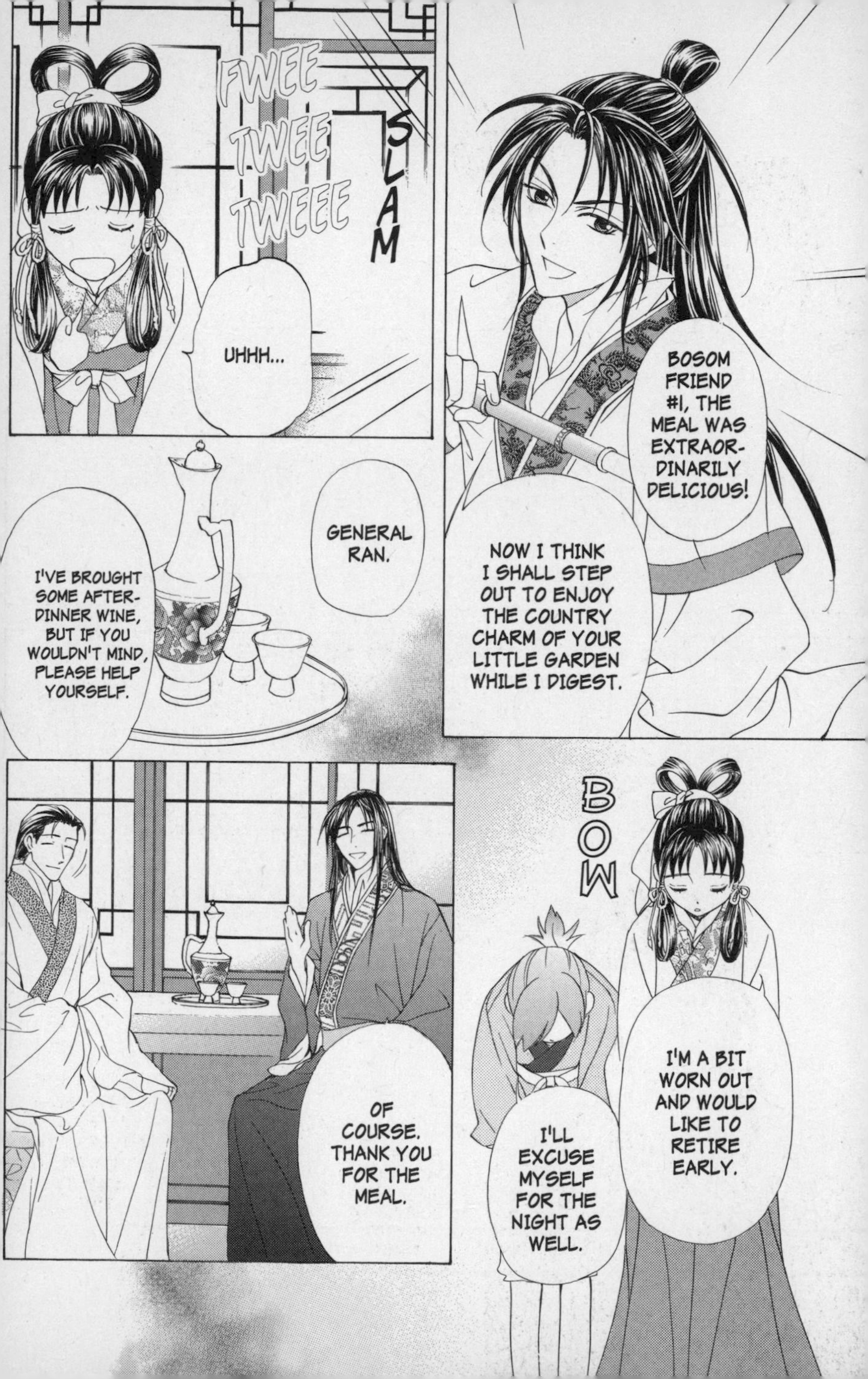
BOSOM FRIEND #1, THE MEAL WAS EXTRAOR-DINARILY DELICIOUS!
NOW I THINK I SHALL STEP OUT TO ENJOY THE COUNTRY CHARM OF YOUR LITTLE GARDEN WHILE I DIGEST.
SLAM
FWEE TWEE TWEEE
UHHH...
GENERAL RAN.
I'VE BROUGHT SOME AFTER-DINNER WINE, BUT IF YOU WOULDN'T MIND, PLEASE HELP YOURSELF.
BOW
I'M A BIT WORN OUT AND WOULD LIKE TO RETIRE EARLY.
I'LL EXCUSE MYSELF FOR THE NIGHT AS WELL.
OF COURSE. THANK YOU FOR THE MEAL.

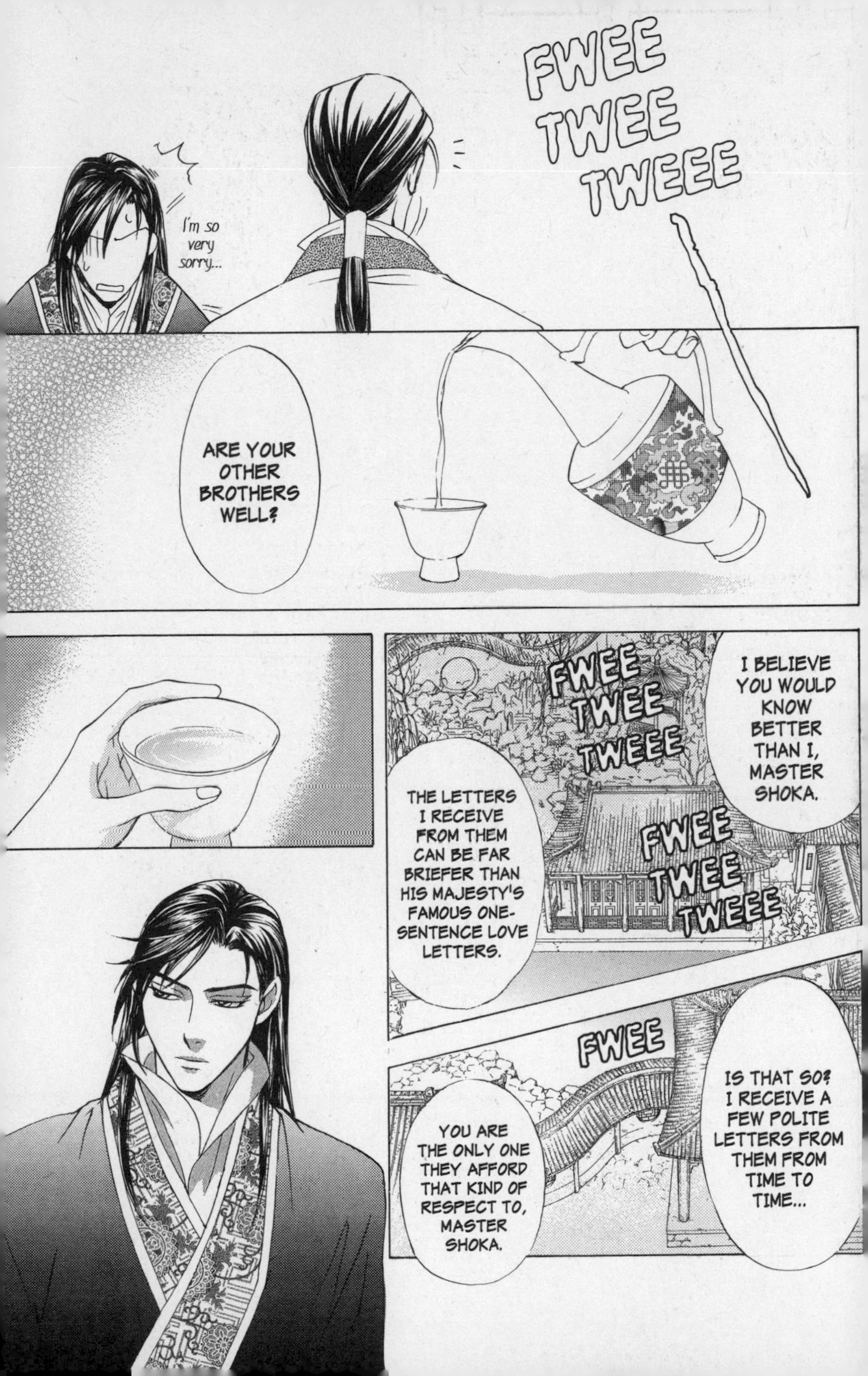

FWEE TWEE TWEEE
I'm so very sorry...
ARE YOUR OTHER BROTHERS WELL?
I BELIEVE YOU WOULD KNOW BETTER THAN I, MASTER SHOKA.
FWEE TWEE TWEEE
THE LETTERS I RECEIVE FROM THEM CAN BE FAR BRIEFER THAN HIS MAJESTY'S FAMOUS ONE-SENTENCE LOVE LETTERS.
FWEE TWEE TWEEE
FWEE
IS THAT SO? I RECEIVE A FEW POLITE LETTERS FROM THEM FROM TIME TO TIME...
YOU ARE THE ONLY ONE THEY AFFORD THAT KIND OF RESPECT TO, MASTER SHOKA.

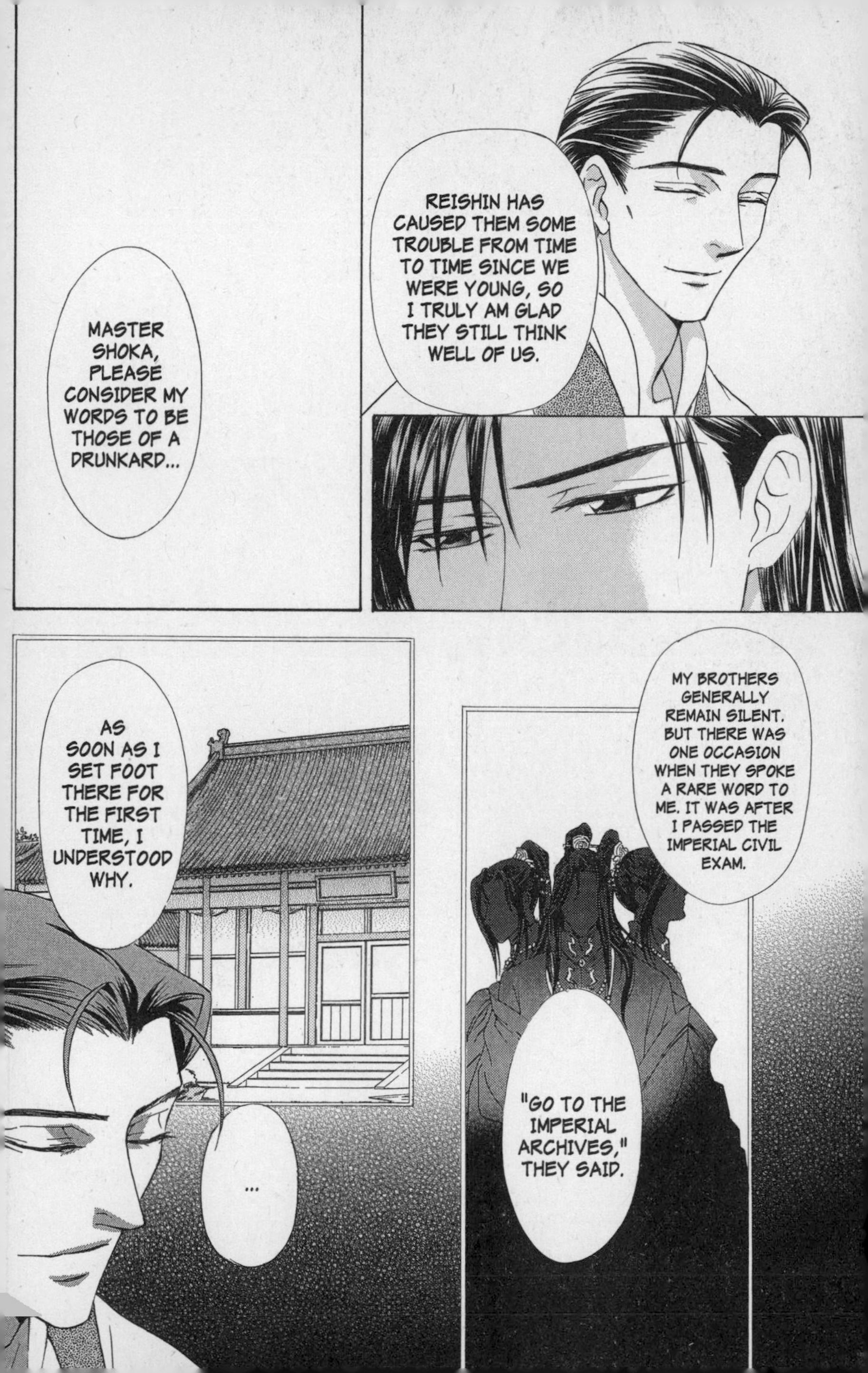
REISHIN HAS CAUSED THEM SOME TROUBLE FROM TIME TO TIME SINCE WE WERE YOUNG, SO I TRULY AM GLAD THEY STILL THINK WELL OF US.
MASTER SHOKA, PLEASE CONSIDER MY WORDS TO BE THOSE OF A DRUNKARD...
MY BROTHERS GENERALLY REMAIN SILENT. BUT THERE WAS ONE OCCASION WHEN THEY SPOKE A RARE WORD TO ME. IT WAS AFTER I PASSED THE IMPERIAL CIVIL EXAM.
"GO TO THE IMPERIAL ARCHIVES," THEY SAID.
AS SOON AS I SET FOOT THERE FOR THE FIRST TIME, I UNDERSTOOD WHY.
...

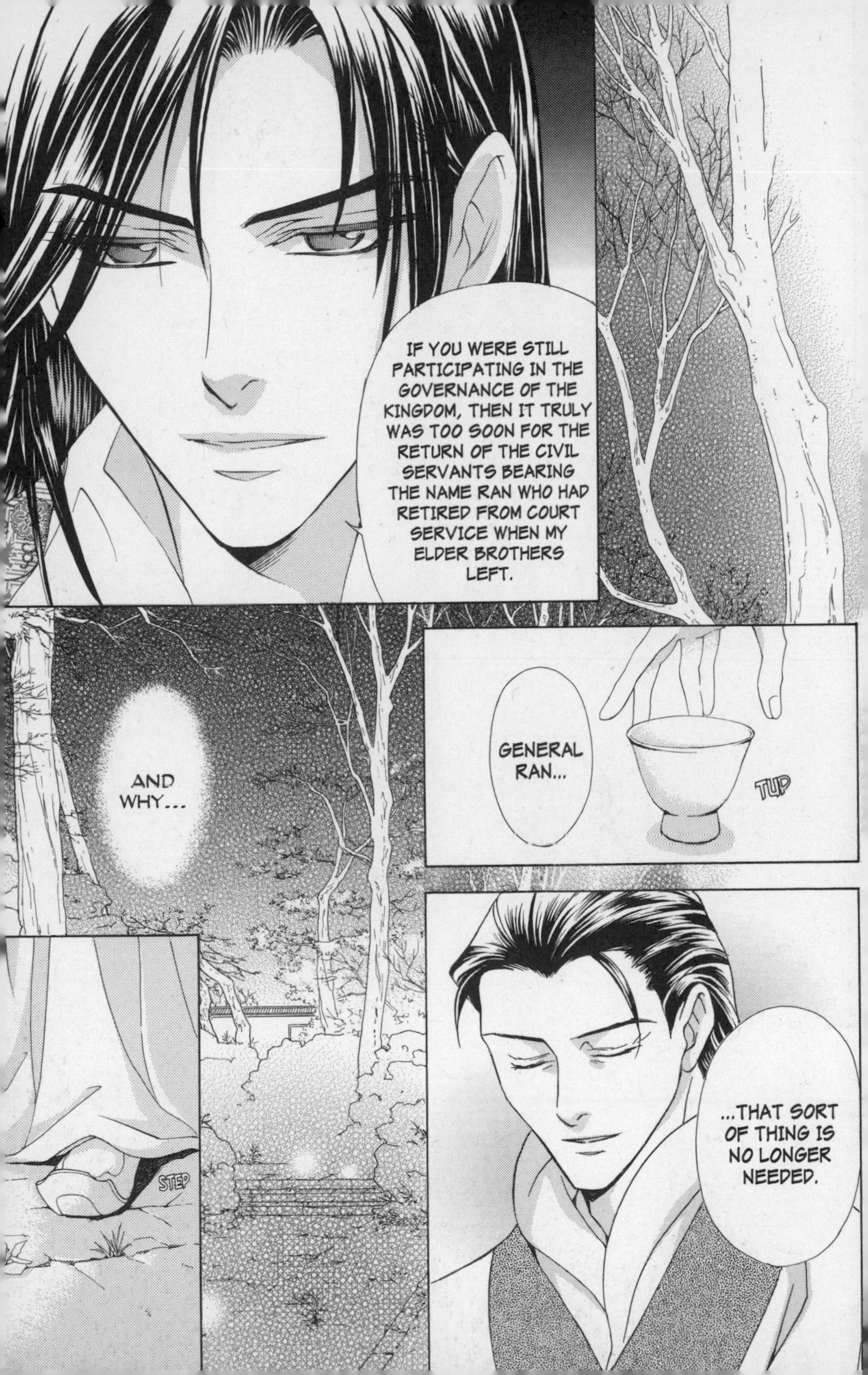
IF YOU WERE STILL PARTICIPATING IN THE GOVERNANCE OF THE KINGDOM, THEN IT TRULY WAS TOO SOON FOR THE RETURN OF THE CIVIL SERVANTS BEARING THE NAME RAN WHO HAD RETIRED FROM COURT SERVICE WHEN MY ELDER BROTHERS LEFT.
GENERAL RAN...
TUP
...THAT SORT OF THING IS NO LONGER NEEDED.
AND WHY...
STEP

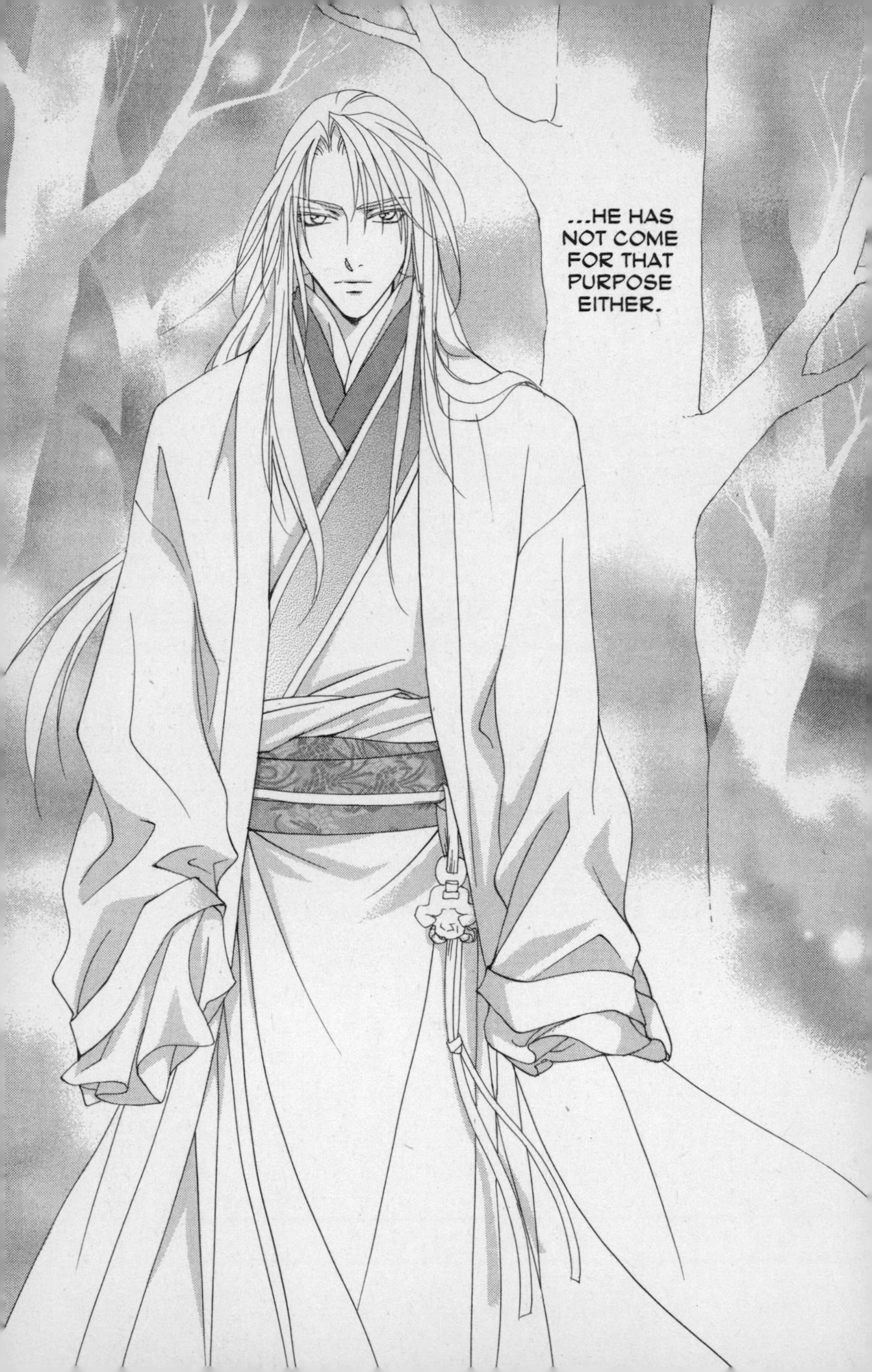
...HE HAS NOT COME FOR THAT PURPOSE EITHER.

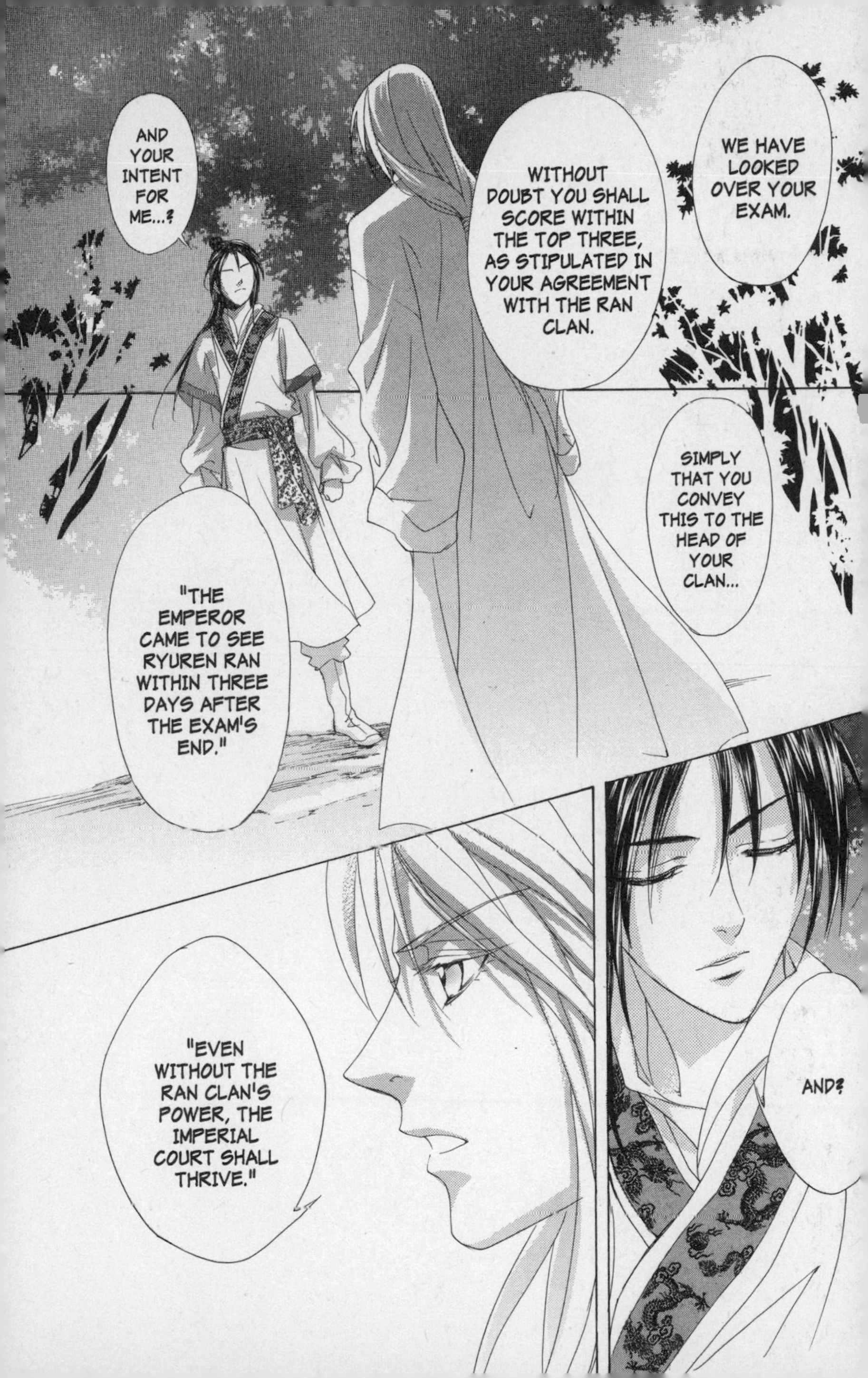
WE HAVE LOOKED OVER YOUR EXAM.
WITHOUT DOUBT YOU SHALL SCORE WITHIN THE TOP THREE, AS STIPULATED IN YOUR AGREEMENT WITH THE RAN CLAN.
AND YOUR INTENT FOR ME...?
SIMPLY THAT YOU CONVEY THIS TO THE HEAD OF YOUR CLAN...
"THE EMPEROR CAME TO SEE RYUREN RAN WITHIN THREE DAYS AFTER THE EXAM'S END."
AND?
"EVEN WITHOUT THE RAN CLAN'S POWER, THE IMPERIAL COURT SHALL THRIVE."

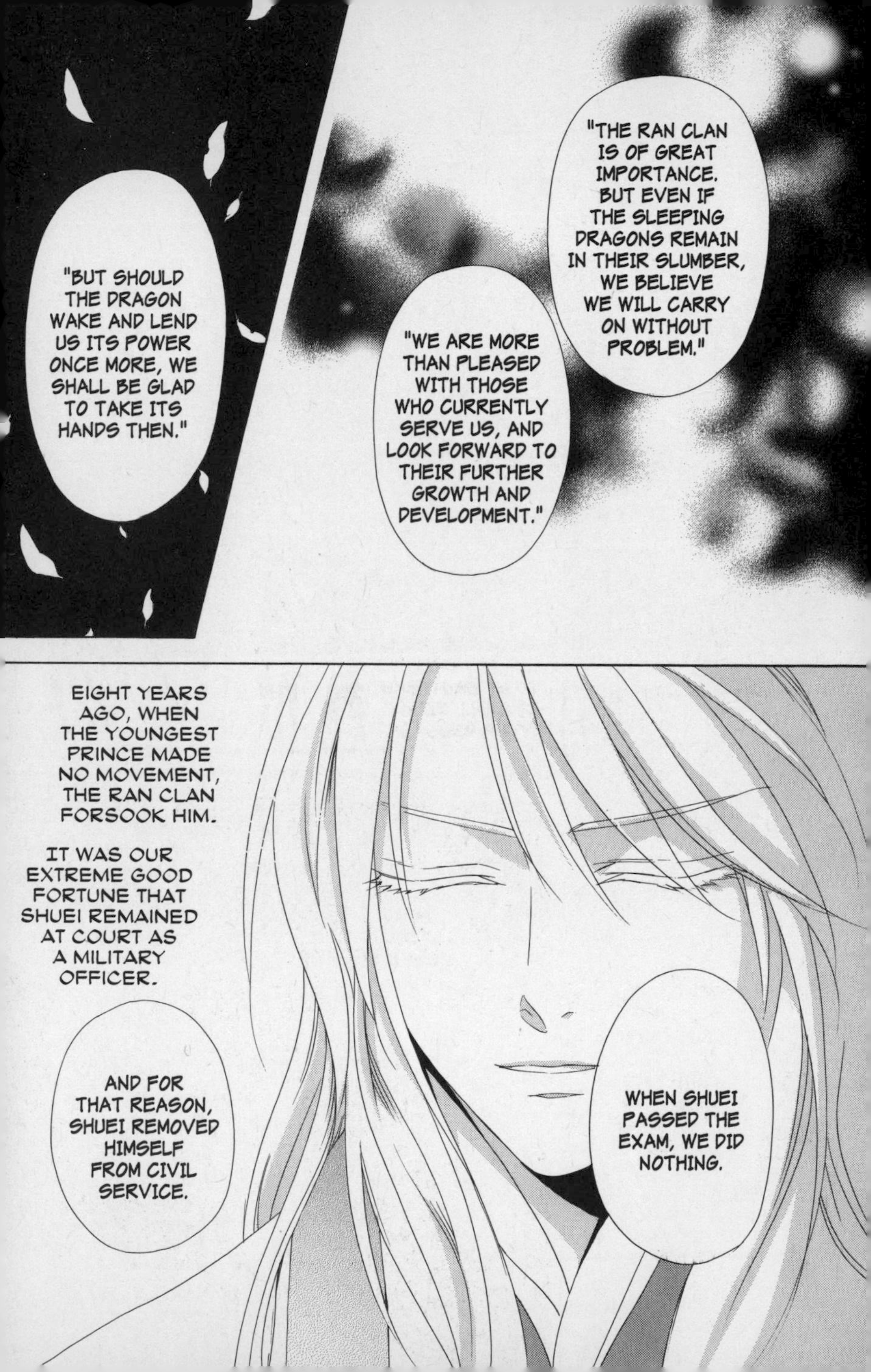
"THE RAN CLAN IS OF GREAT IMPORTANCE. BUT EVEN IF THE SLEEPING DRAGONS REMAIN IN THEIR SLUMBER, WE BELIEVE WE WILL CARRY ON WITHOUT PROBLEM."
"WE ARE MORE THAN PLEASED WITH THOSE WHO CURRENTLY SERVE US, AND LOOK FORWARD TO THEIR FURTHER GROWTH AND DEVELOPMENT."
"BUT SHOULD THE DRAGON WAKE AND LEND US ITS POWER ONCE MORE, WE SHALL BE GLAD TO TAKE ITS HANDS THEN."
EIGHT YEARS AGO, WHEN THE YOUNGEST PRINCE MADE NO MOVEMENT, THE RAN CLAN FORSOOK HIM.
IT WAS OUR EXTREME GOOD FORTUNE THAT SHUEI REMAINED AT COURT AS A MILITARY OFFICER.
WHEN SHUEI PASSED THE EXAM, WE DID NOTHING.
AND FOR THAT REASON, SHUEI REMOVED HIMSELF FROM CIVIL SERVICE.

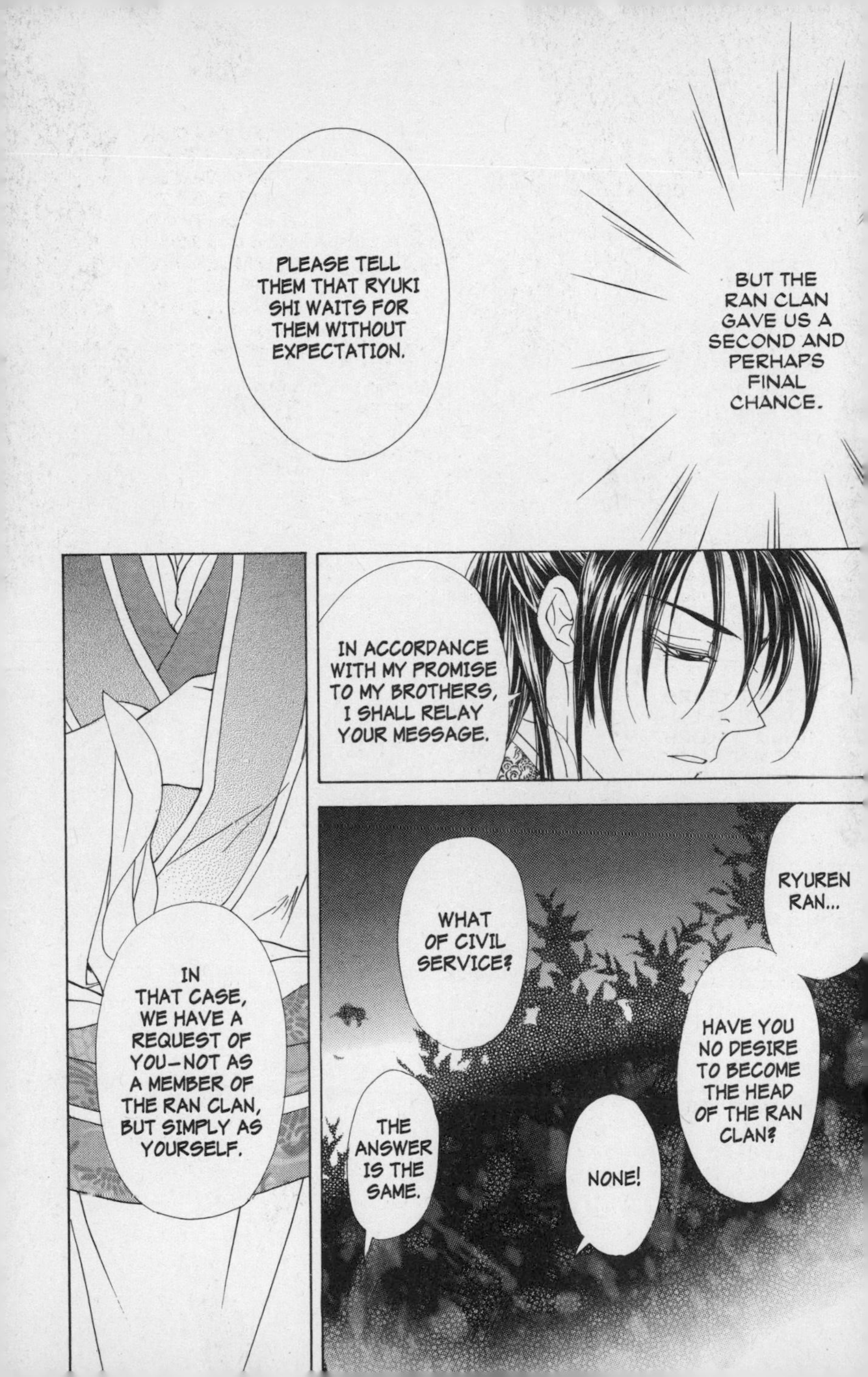
BUT THE RAN CLAN GAVE US A SECOND AND PERHAPS FINAL CHANCE.
PLEASE TELL THEM THAT RYUKI SHI WAITS FOR THEM WITHOUT EXPECTATION.
IN ACCORDANCE WITH MY PROMISE TO MY BROTHERS, I SHALL RELAY YOUR MESSAGE.
RYUREN RAN...
HAVE YOU NO DESIRE TO BECOME THE HEAD OF THE RAN CLAN?
NONE!
WHAT OF CIVIL SERVICE?
THE ANSWER IS THE SAME.
IN THAT CASE, WE HAVE A REQUEST OF YOU—NOT AS A MEMBER OF THE RAN CLAN, BUT SIMPLY AS YOURSELF.

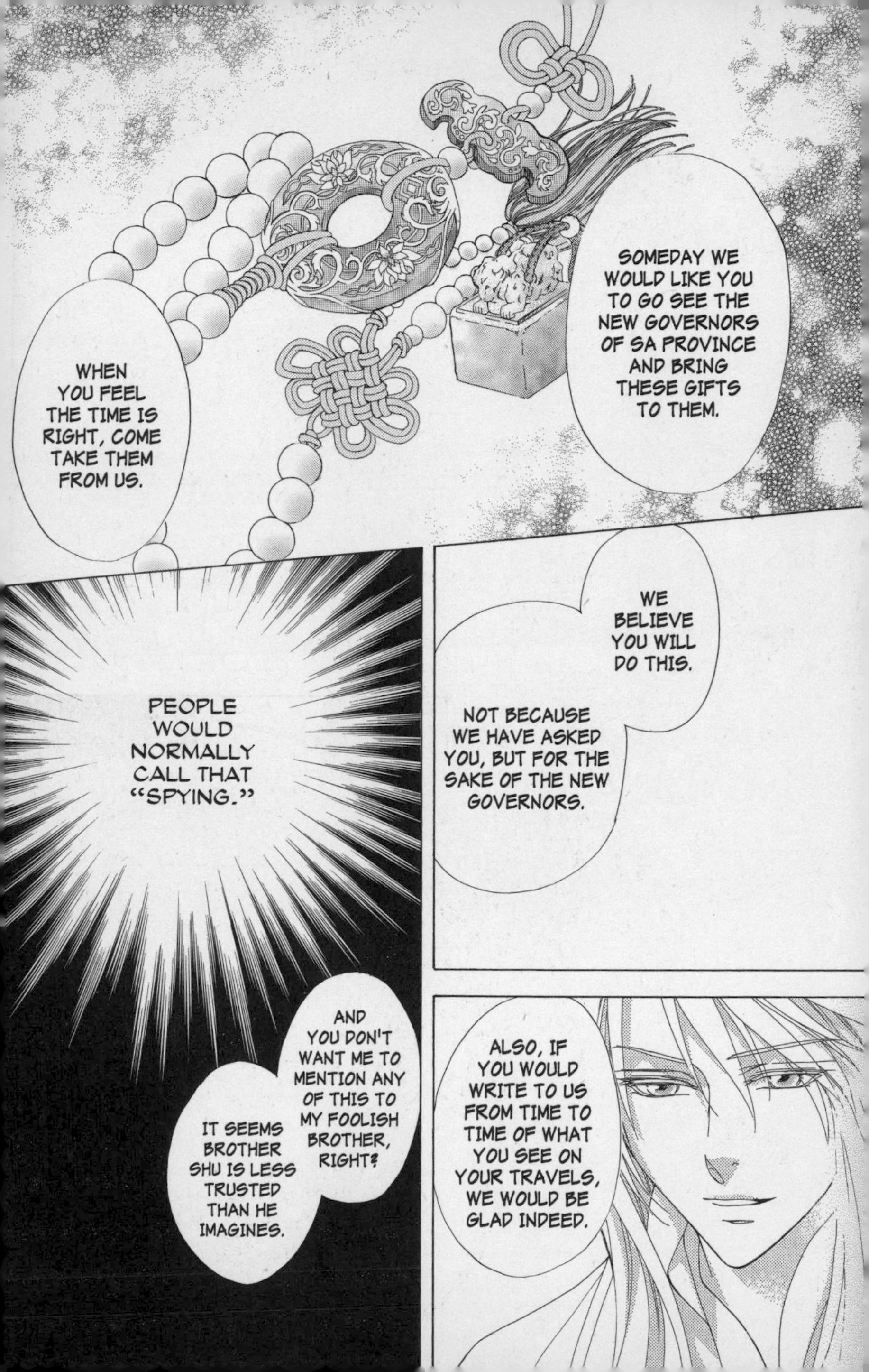
SOMEDAY WE WOULD LIKE YOU TO GO SEE THE NEW GOVERNORS OF SA PROVINCE AND BRING THESE GIFTS TO THEM.
WHEN YOU FEEL THE TIME IS RIGHT, COME TAKE THEM FROM US.
WE BELIEVE YOU WILL DO THIS.
NOT BECAUSE WE HAVE ASKED YOU, BUT FOR THE SAKE OF THE NEW GOVERNORS.
ALSO, IF YOU WOULD WRITE TO US FROM TIME TO TIME OF WHAT YOU SEE ON YOUR TRAVELS, WE WOULD BE GLAD INDEED.
PEOPLE WOULD NORMALLY CALL THAT "SPYING."
AND YOU DON'T WANT ME TO MENTION ANY OF THIS TO MY FOOLISH BROTHER, RIGHT?
IT SEEMS BROTHER SHU IS LESS TRUSTED THAN HE IMAGINES.

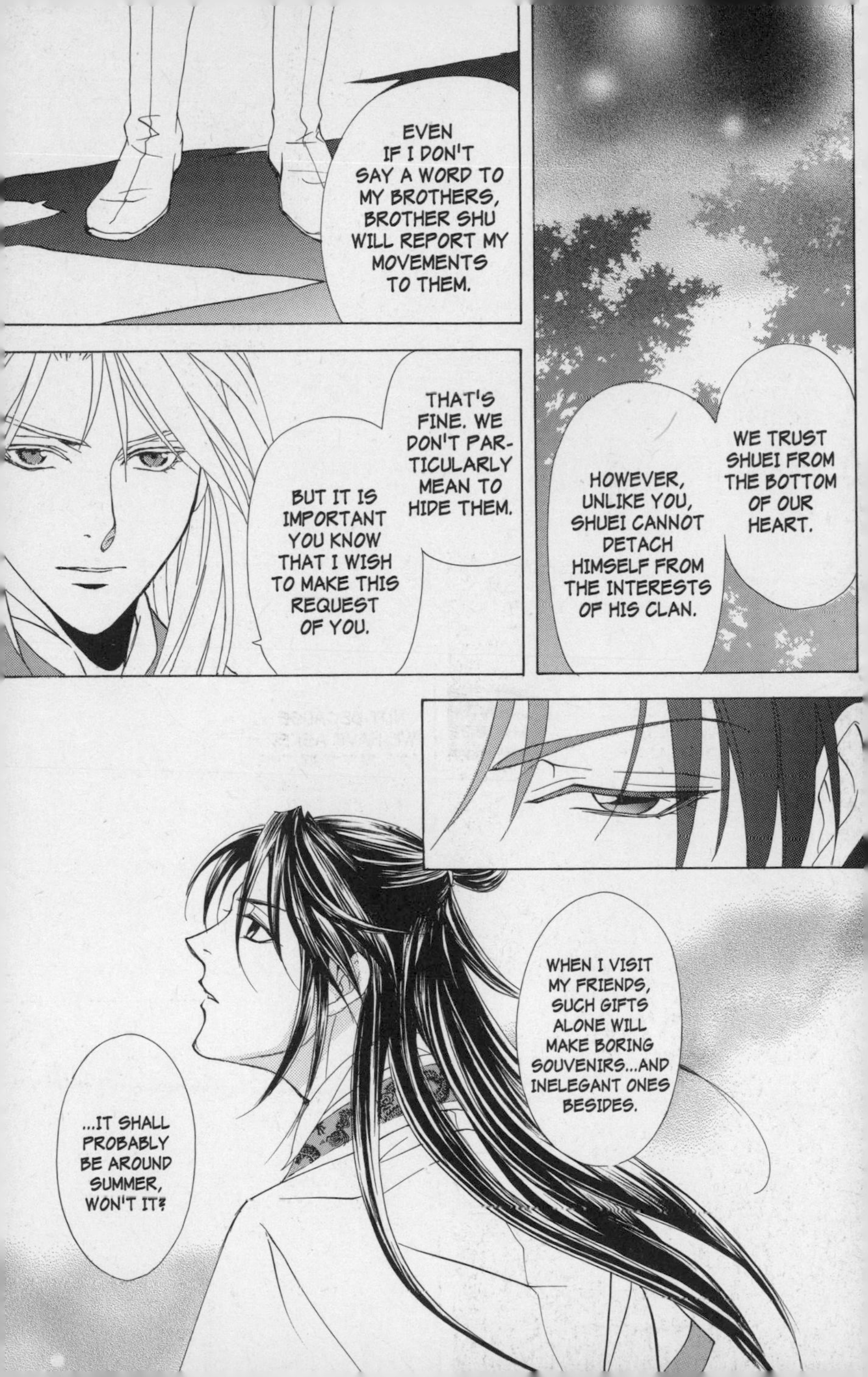
WE TRUST SHUEI FROM THE BOTTOM OF OUR HEART.
HOWEVER, UNLIKE YOU, SHUEI CANNOT DETACH HIMSELF FROM THE INTERESTS OF HIS CLAN.
EVEN IF I DON'T SAY A WORD TO MY BROTHERS, BROTHER SHU WILL REPORT MY MOVEMENTS TO THEM.
THAT'S FINE. WE DON'T PAR-TICULARLY MEAN TO HIDE THEM.
BUT IT IS IMPORTANT YOU KNOW THAT I WISH TO MAKE THIS REQUEST OF YOU.
WHEN I VISIT MY FRIENDS, SUCH GIFTS ALONE WILL MAKE BORING SOUVENIRS...AND INELEGANT ONES BESIDES.
...IT SHALL PROBABLY BE AROUND SUMMER, WON'T IT?

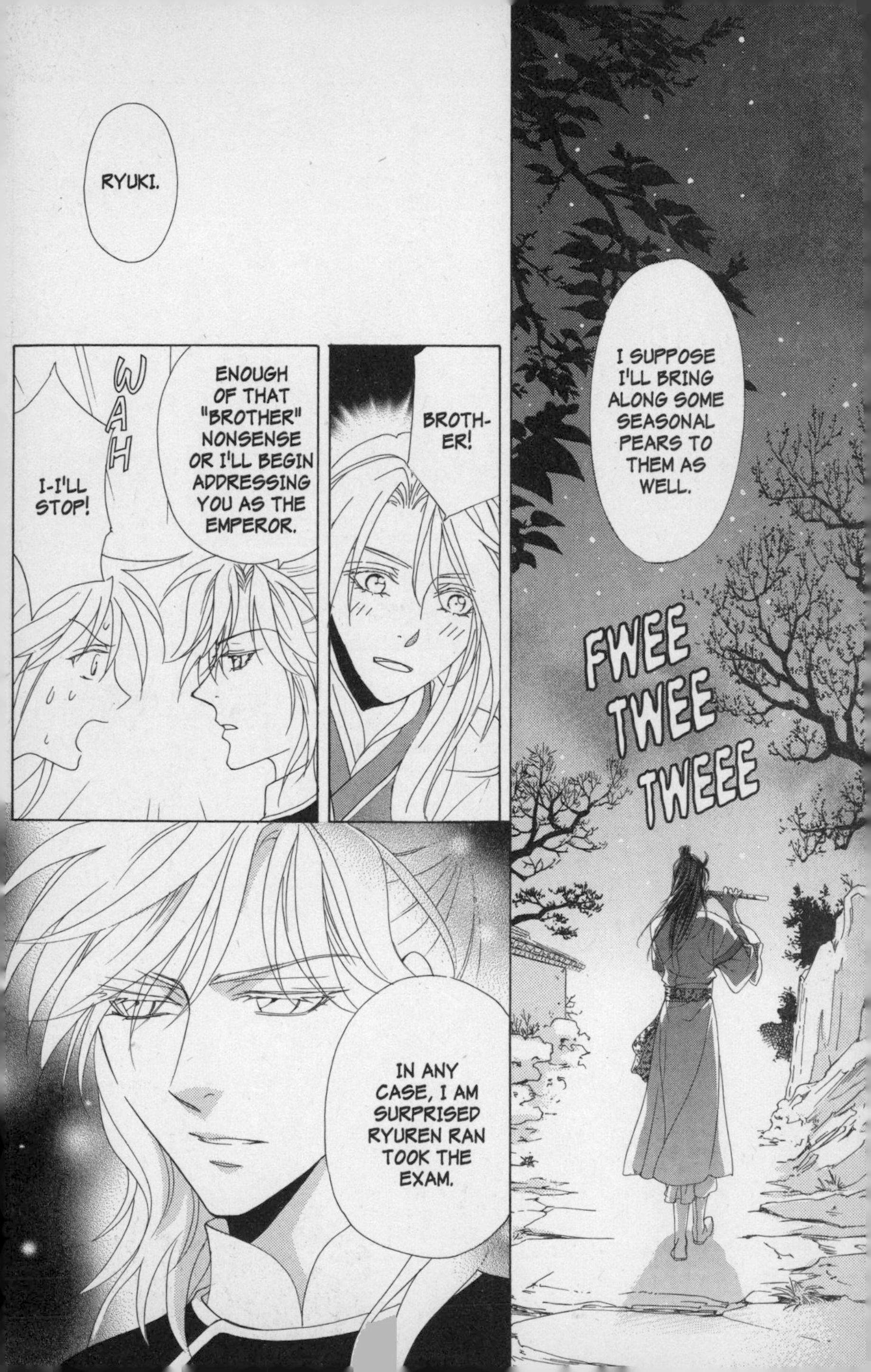
I SUPPOSE I'LL BRING ALONG SOME SEASONAL PEARS TO THEM AS WELL.
FWEE TWEE TWEEE
RYUKI.
BROTH-ER!
ENOUGH OF THAT "BROTHER" NONSENSE OR I'LL BEGIN ADDRESSING YOU AS THE EMPEROR.
WAH
I-I'LL STOP!
IN ANY CASE, I AM SURPRISED RYUREN RAN TOOK THE EXAM.

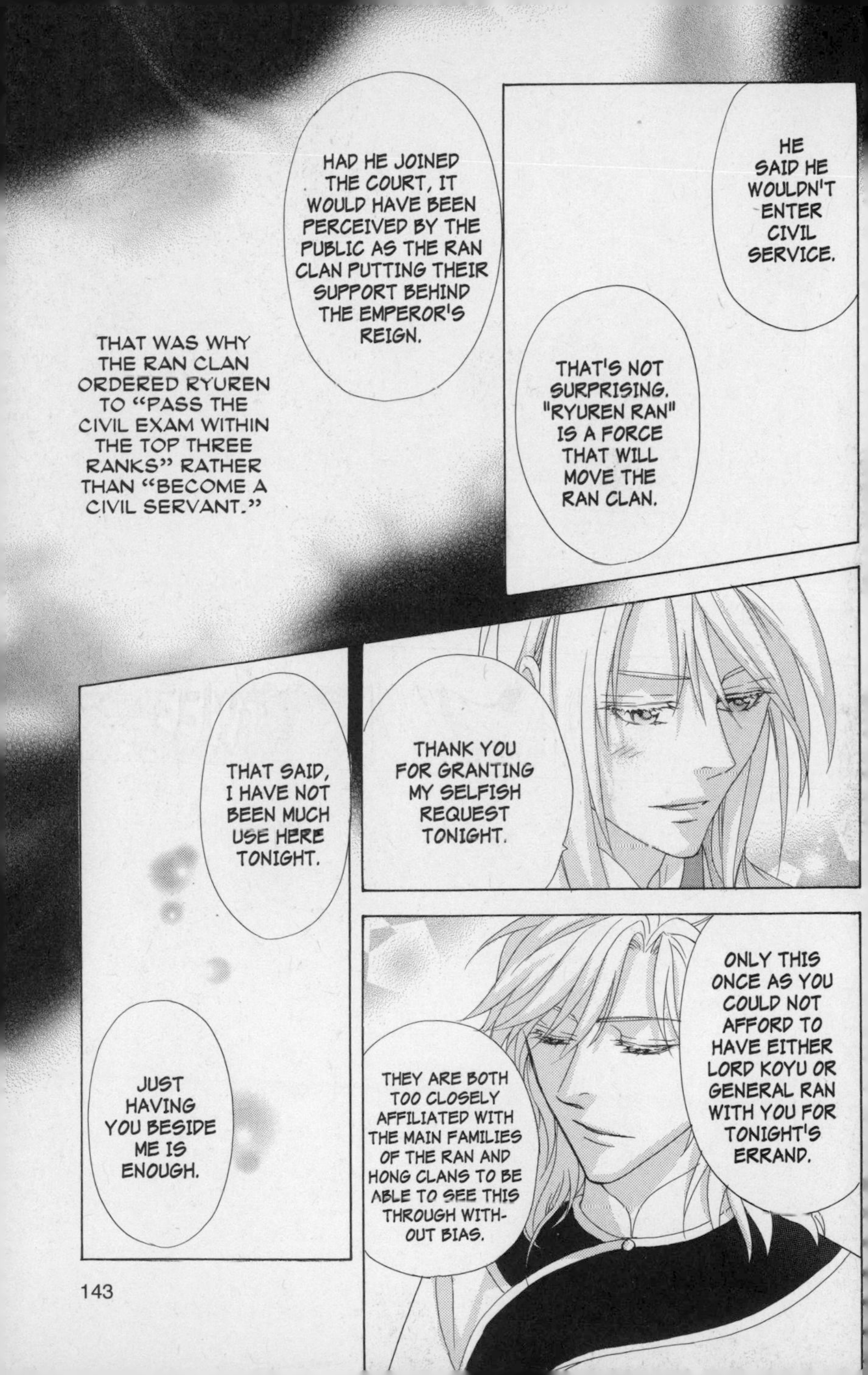
HE SAID HE WOULDN'T ENTER CIVIL SERVICE.
THAT'S NOT SURPRISING. "RYUREN RAN" IS A FORCE THAT WILL MOVE THE RAN CLAN.
HAD HE JOINED THE COURT, IT WOULD HAVE BEEN PERCEIVED BY THE PUBLIC AS THE RAN CLAN PUTTING THEIR SUPPORT BEHIND THE EMPEROR'S REIGN.
THAT WAS WHY THE RAN CLAN ORDERED RYUREN TO "PASS THE CIVIL EXAM WITHIN THE TOP THREE RANKS" RATHER THAN "BECOME A CIVIL SERVANT."
THANK YOU FOR GRANTING MY SELFISH REQUEST TONIGHT.
THAT SAID, I HAVE NOT BEEN MUCH USE HERE TONIGHT.
ONLY THIS ONCE AS YOU COULD NOT AFFORD TO HAVE EITHER LORD KOYU OR GENERAL RAN WITH YOU FOR TONIGHT'S ERRAND.
THEY ARE BOTH TOO CLOSELY AFFILIATED WITH THE MAIN FAMILIES OF THE RAN AND HONG CLANS TO BE ABLE TO SEE THIS THROUGH WITH-OUT BIAS.
JUST HAVING YOU BESIDE ME IS ENOUGH.

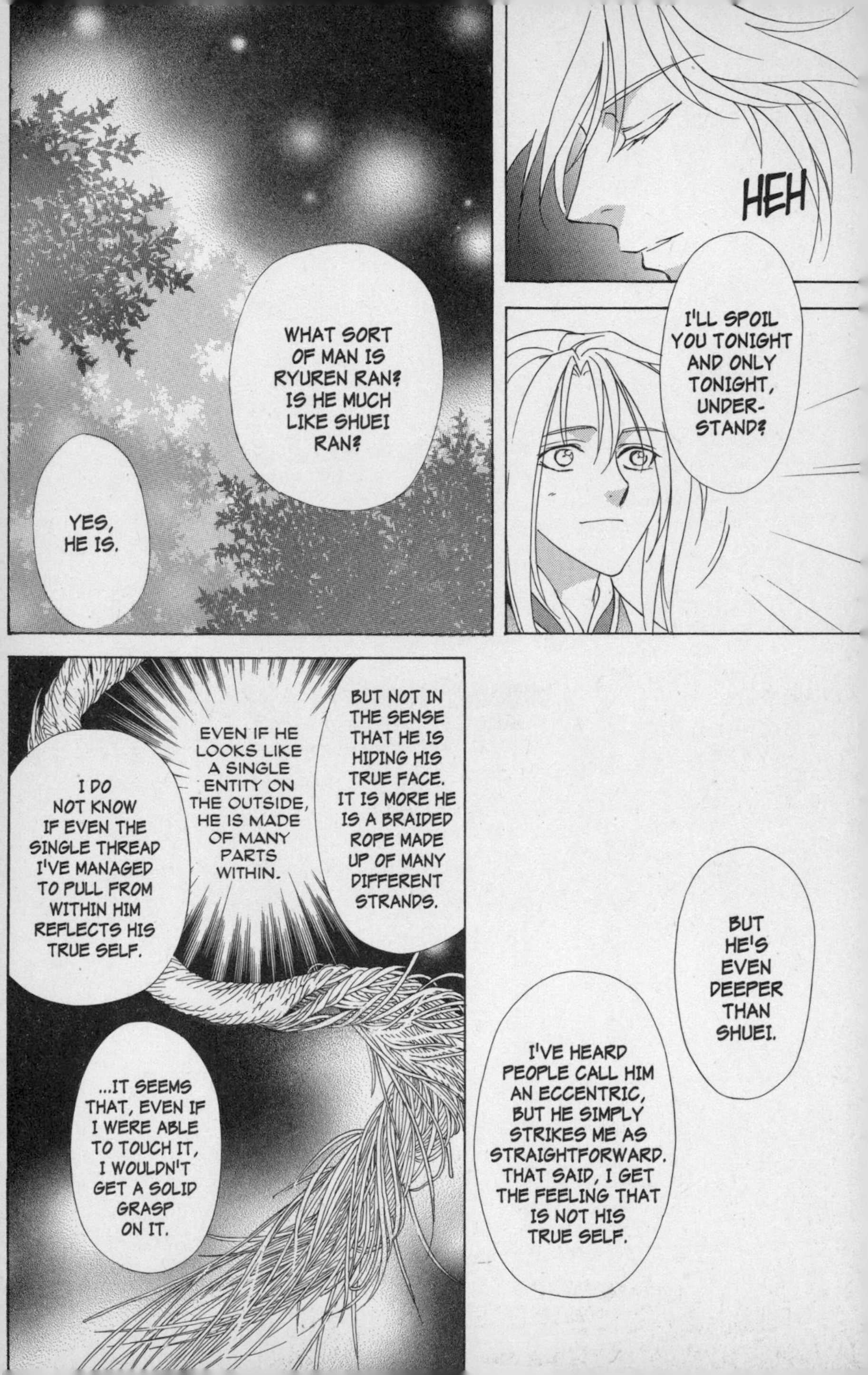
HEH
I'LL SPOIL YOU TONIGHT AND ONLY TONIGHT, UNDER-STAND?
WHAT SORT OF MAN IS RYUREN RAN? IS HE MUCH LIKE SHUEI RAN?
YES, HE IS.
BUT HE'S EVEN DEEPER THAN SHUEI.
I'VE HEARD PEOPLE CALL HIM AN ECCENTRIC, BUT HE SIMPLY STRIKES ME AS STRAIGHTFORWARD. THAT SAID, I GET THE FEELING THAT IS NOT HIS TRUE SELF.
BUT NOT IN THE SENSE THAT HE IS HIDING HIS TRUE FACE. IT IS MORE HE IS A BRAIDED ROPE MADE UP OF MANY DIFFERENT STRANDS.
EVEN IF HE LOOKS LIKE A SINGLE ENTITY ON THE OUTSIDE, HE IS MADE OF MANY PARTS WITHIN.
I DO NOT KNOW IF EVEN THE SINGLE THREAD I'VE MANAGED TO PULL FROM WITHIN HIM REFLECTS HIS TRUE SELF.
...IT SEEMS THAT, EVEN IF I WERE ABLE TO TOUCH IT, I WOULDN'T GET A SOLID GRASP ON IT.

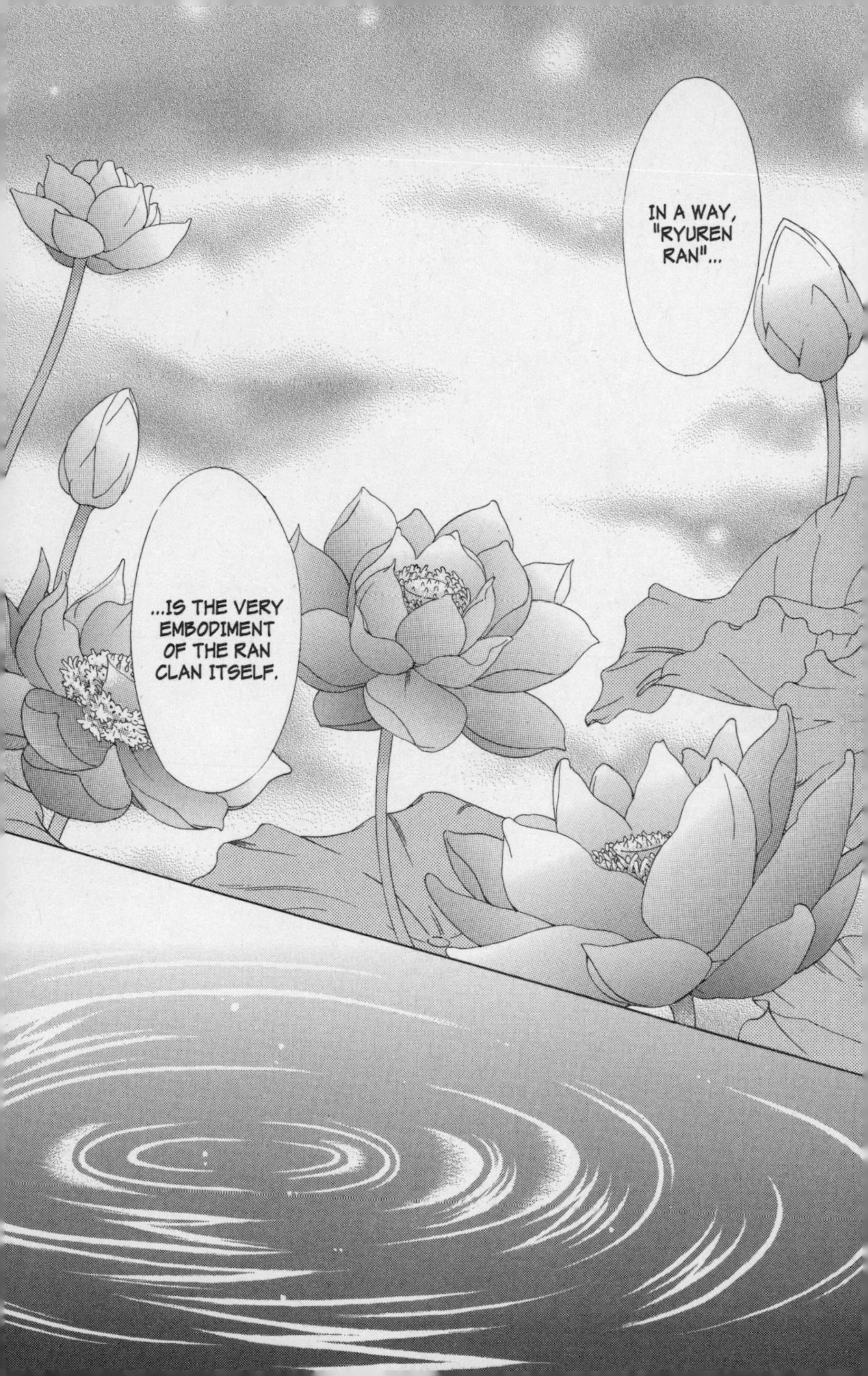
IN A WAY, "RYUREN RAN"...
...IS THE VERY EMBODIMENT OF THE RAN CLAN ITSELF.

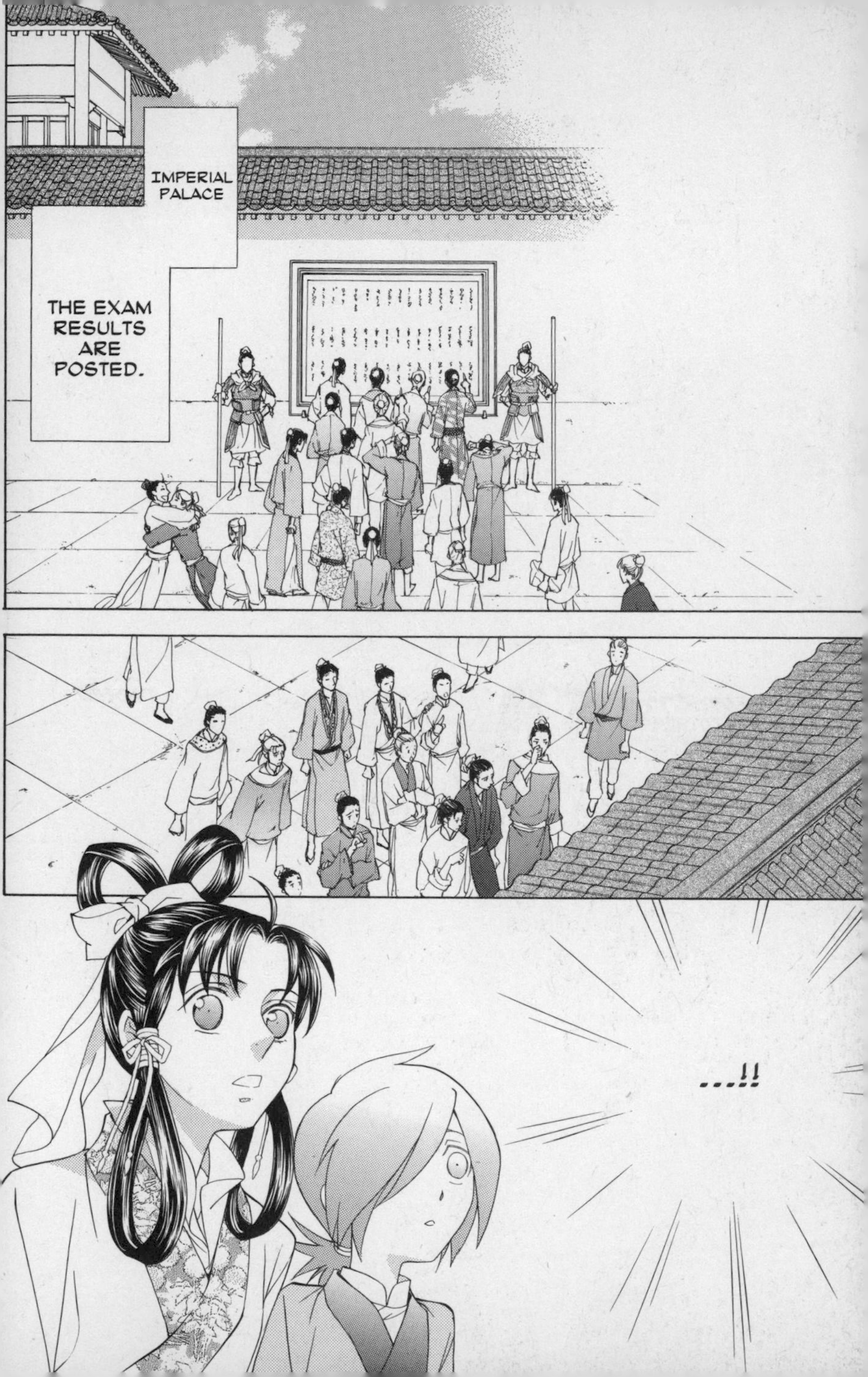
IMPERIAL PALACE
THE EXAM RESULTS ARE POSTED.
...!!

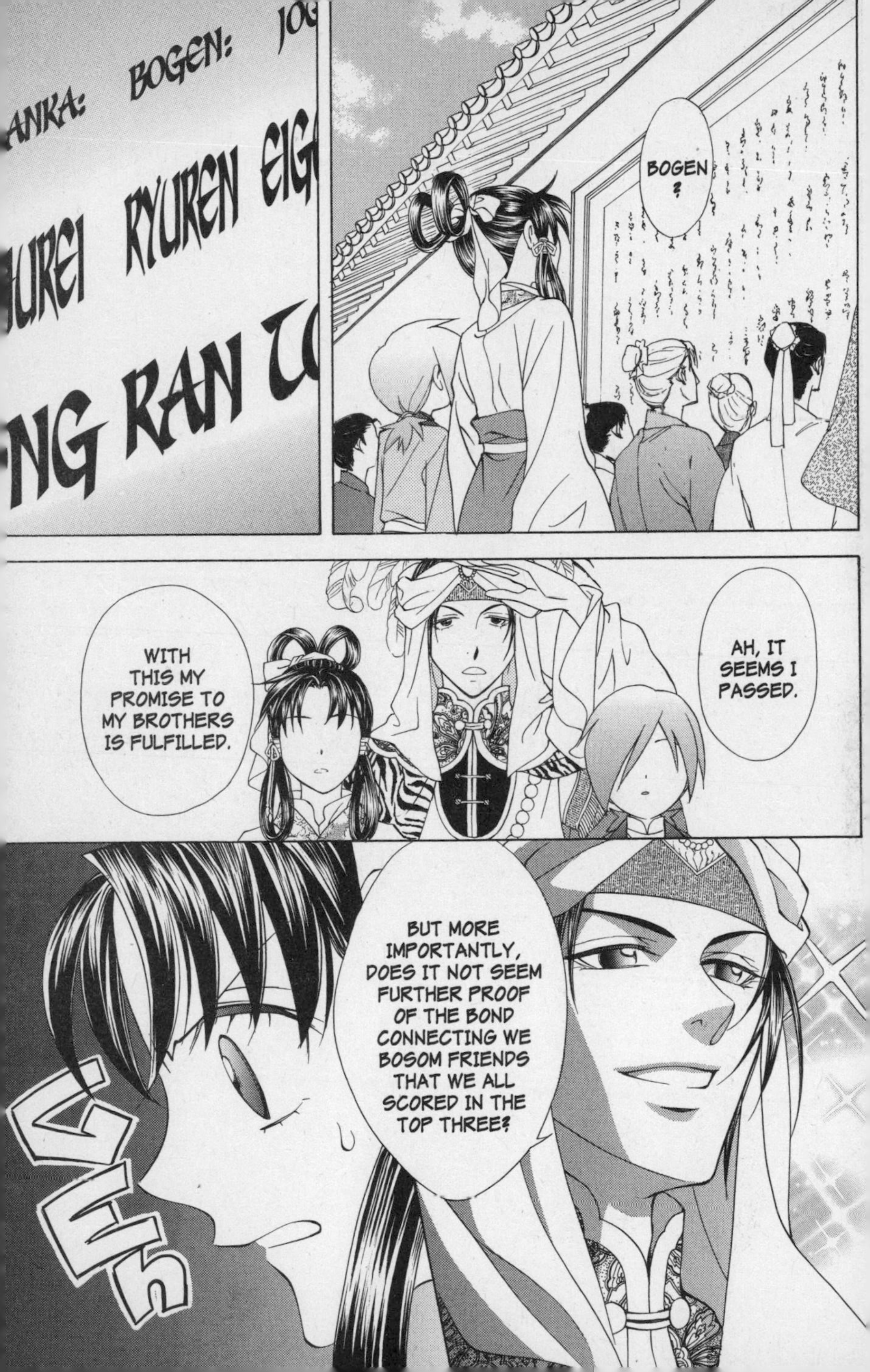
BOGEN?
ANKA: BOGEN: JOG
HUREI RYUREN EIG
NG RAN TO
AH, IT SEEMS I PASSED.
WITH THIS MY PROMISE TO MY BROTHERS IS FULFILLED.
BUT MORE IMPORTANTLY, DOES IT NOT SEEM FURTHER PROOF OF THE BOND CONNECTING WE BOSOM FRIENDS THAT WE ALL SCORED IN THE TOP THREE?

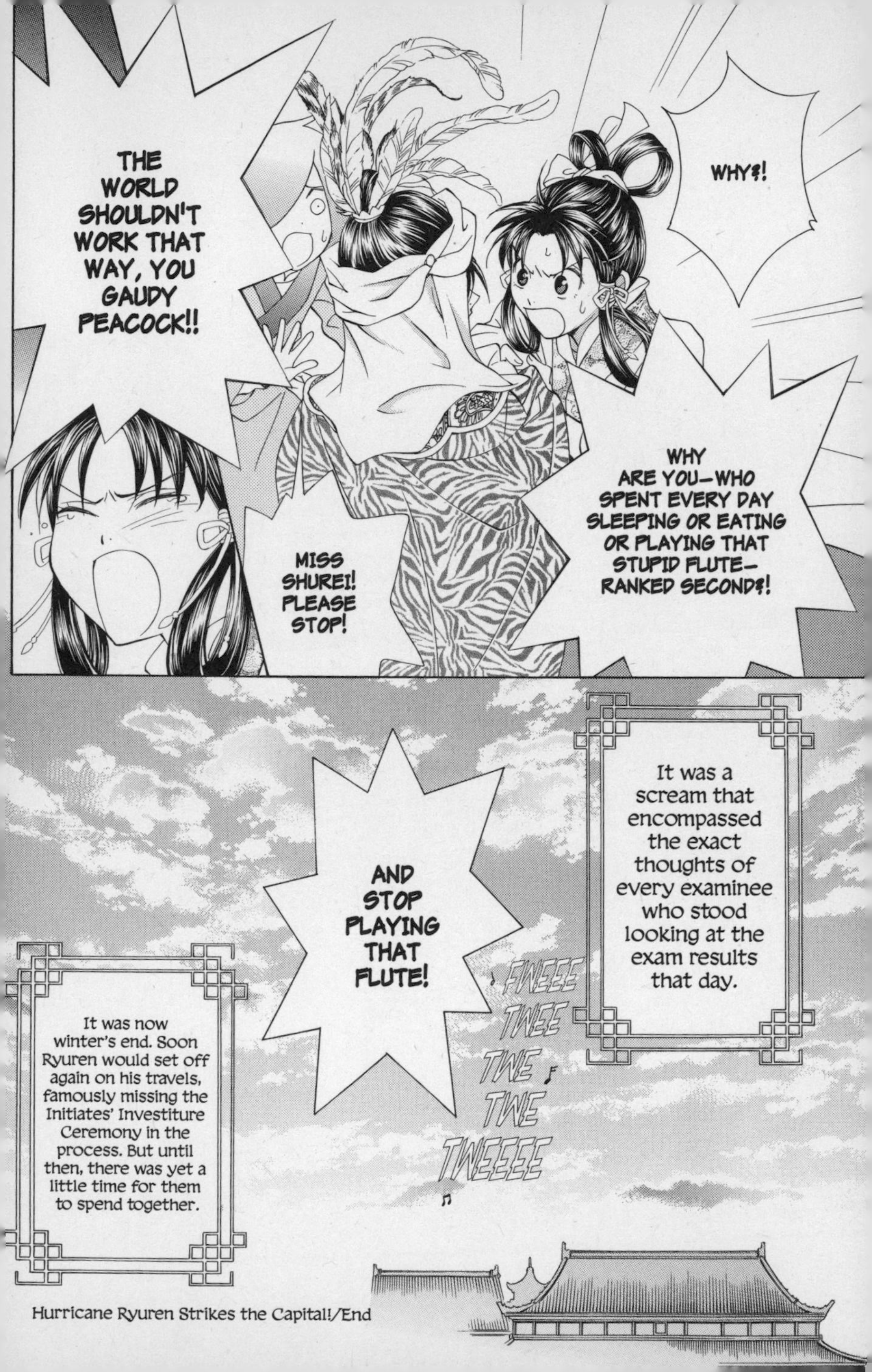
WHY?!
WHY ARE YOU—WHO SPENT EVERY DAY SLEEPING OR EATING OR PLAYING THAT STUPID FLUTE—RANKED SECOND?!
MISS SHUREI! PLEASE STOP!
THE WORLD SHOULDN'T WORK THAT WAY, YOU GAUDY PEACOCK!!
It was a scream that encompassed the exact thoughts of every examinee who stood looking at the exam results that day.
AND STOP PLAYING THAT FLUTE!
FWEEE TWEE TWE TWE TWEEEEE
It was now winter's end. Soon Ryuren would set off again on his travels, famously missing the Initiates' Investiture Ceremony in the process. But until then, there was yet a little time for them to spend together.
Hurricane Ryuren Strikes the Capital!/End

The Story of
SAIUNKOKU

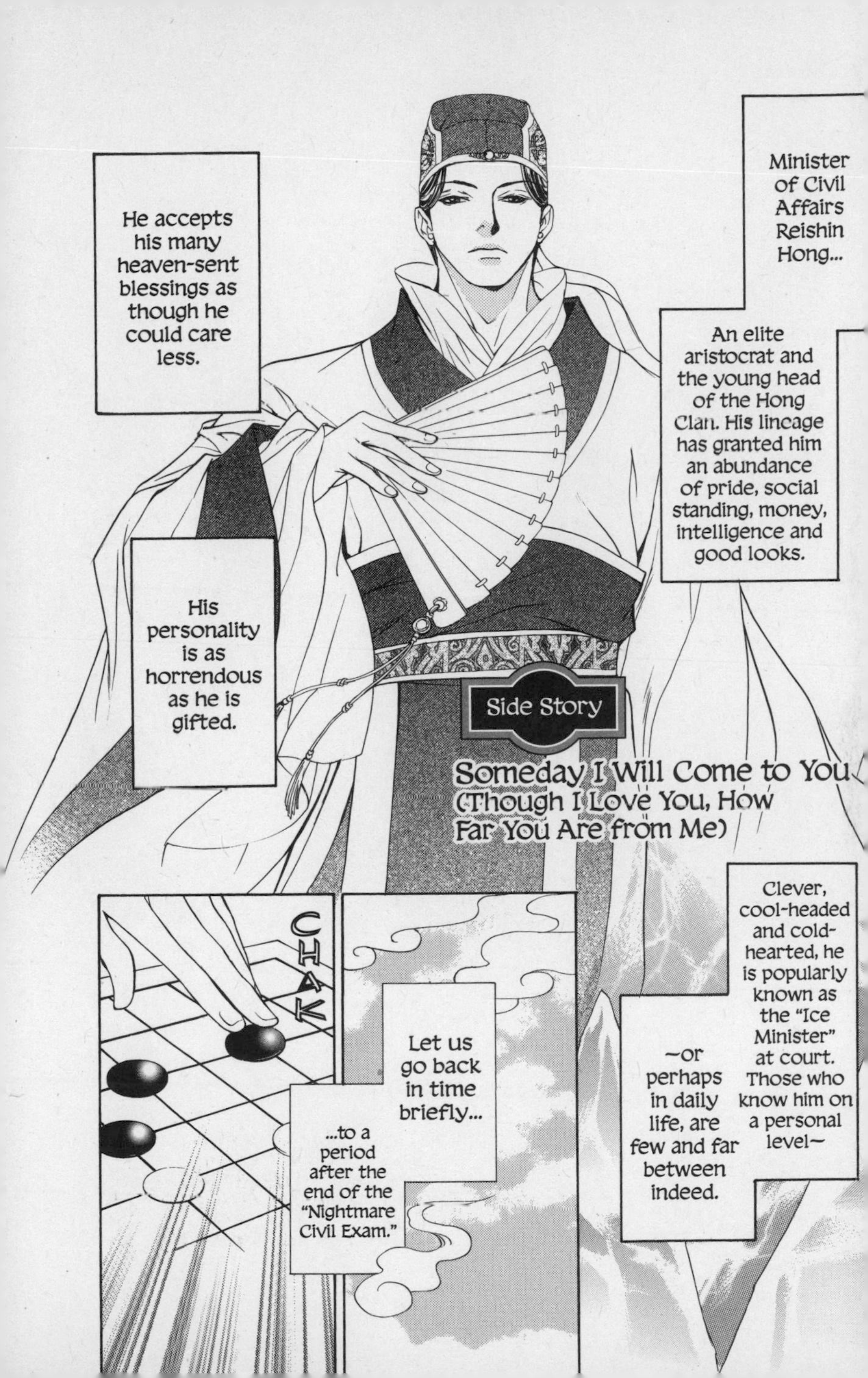
Minister of Civil Affairs Reishin Hong...
An elite aristocrat and the young head of the Hong Clan. His lineage has granted him an abundance of pride, social standing, money, intelligence and good looks.
He accepts his many heaven-sent blessings as though he could care less.
His personality is as horrendous as he is gifted.
Side Story
Someday I Will Come to You (Though I Love You, How Far You Are from Me)
Clever, cool-headed and cold-hearted, he is popularly known as the "Ice Minister" at court. Those who know him on a personal level—
—or perhaps in daily life, are few and far between indeed.
Let us go back in time briefly...
...to a period after the end of the "Nightmare Civil Exam."
CHAK

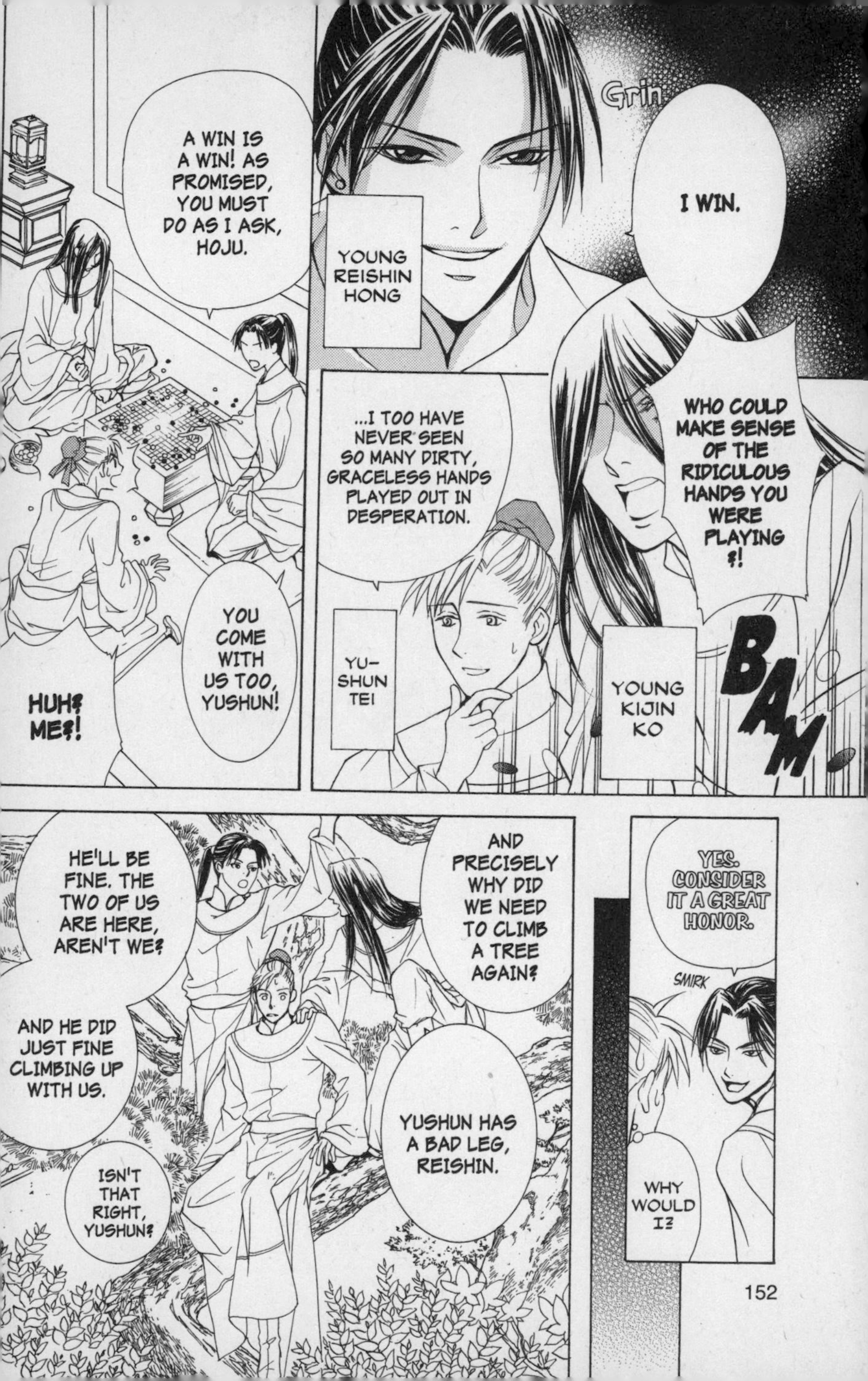
Grin
I WIN.
YOUNG REISHIN HONG
WHO COULD MAKE SENSE OF THE RIDICULOUS HANDS YOU WERE PLAYING?!
BAM
YOUNG KIJIN KO
...I TOO HAVE NEVER SEEN SO MANY DIRTY, GRACELESS HANDS PLAYED OUT IN DESPERATION.
YU-SHUN TEI
A WIN IS A WIN! AS PROMISED, YOU MUST DO AS I ASK, HOJU.
YOU COME WITH US TOO, YUSHUN!
HUH? ME?!
YES. CONSIDER IT A GREAT HONOR.
SMIRK
WHY WOULD I?
AND PRECISELY WHY DID WE NEED TO CLIMB A TREE AGAIN?
YUSHUN HAS A BAD LEG, REISHIN.
HE'LL BE FINE. THE TWO OF US ARE HERE, AREN'T WE?
AND HE DID JUST FINE CLIMBING UP WITH US.
ISN'T THAT RIGHT, YUSHUN?

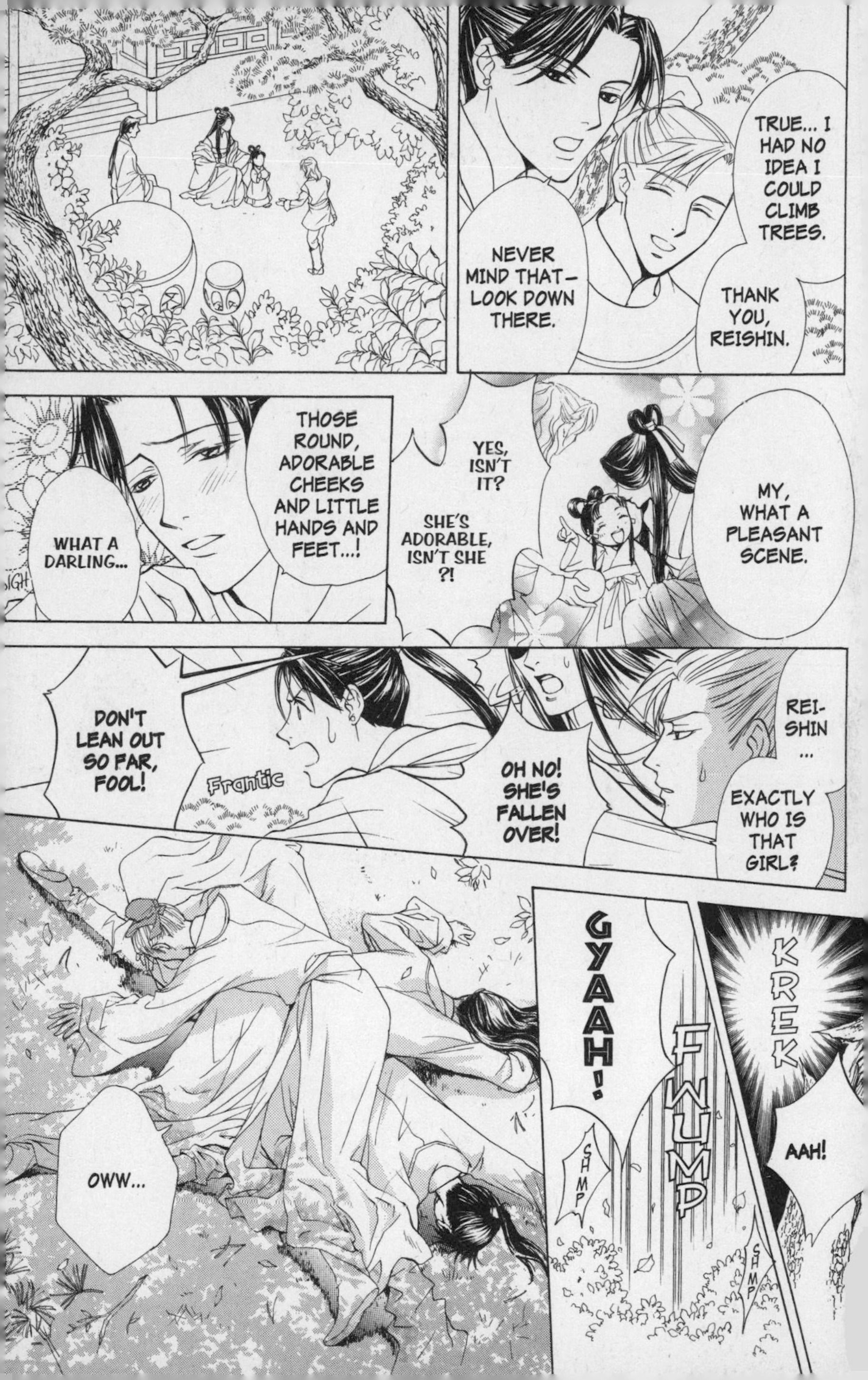
TRUE... I HAD NO IDEA I COULD CLIMB TREES.
THANK YOU, REISHIN.
NEVER MIND THAT— LOOK DOWN THERE.
MY, WHAT A PLEASANT SCENE.
YES, ISN'T IT?
SHE'S ADORABLE, ISN'T SHE ?!
THOSE ROUND, ADORABLE CHEEKS AND LITTLE HANDS AND FEET...!
WHAT A DARLING...
REI-SHIN ...
EXACTLY WHO IS THAT GIRL?
OH NO! SHE'S FALLEN OVER!
DON'T LEAN OUT SO FAR, FOOL!
Frantic
KREK
AAH!
GYAAH!
FWUMP
SHMP
SHMP
OWW...

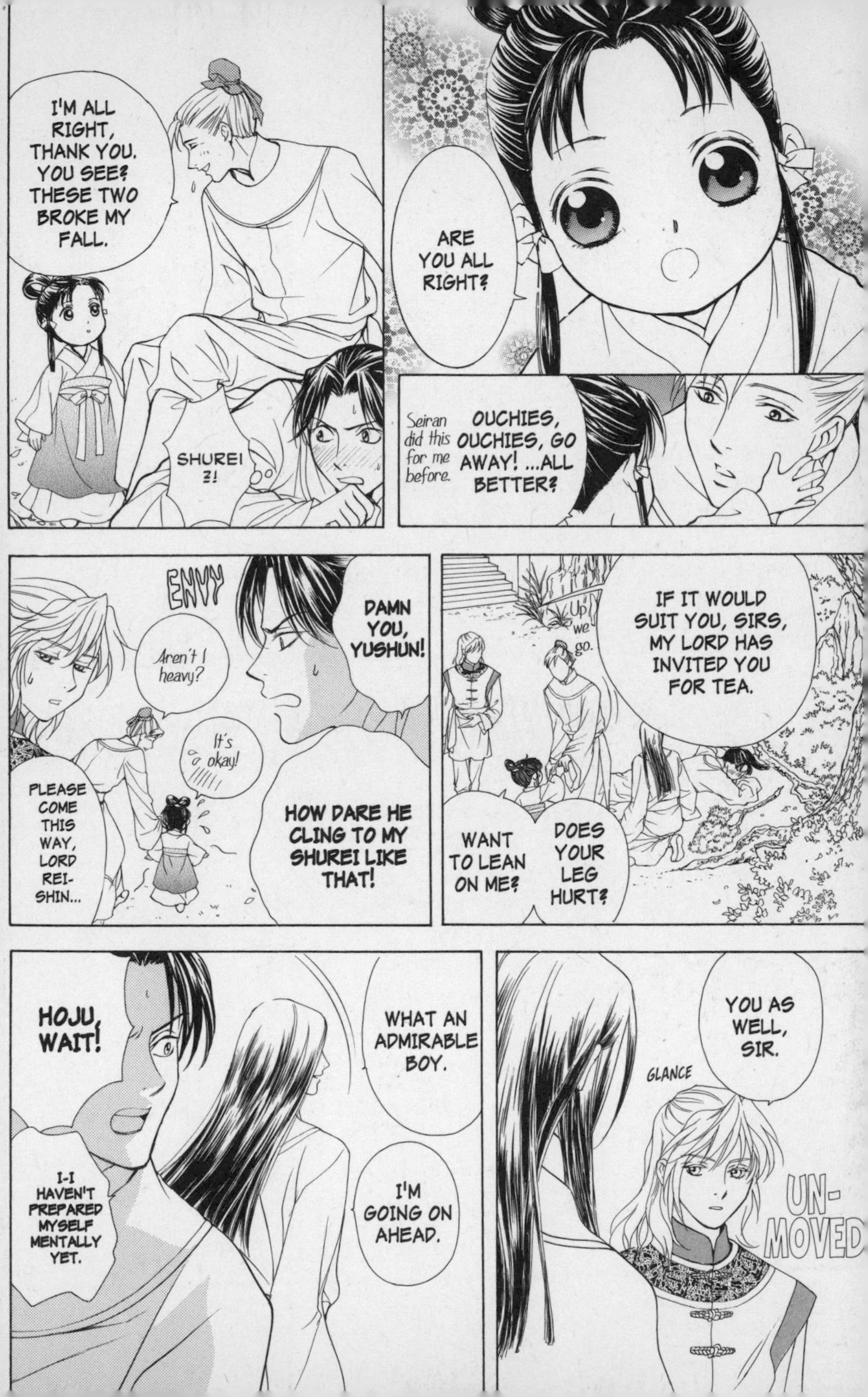
ARE YOU ALL RIGHT?
OUCHIES, OUCHIES, GO AWAY! ...ALL BETTER?
Seiran did this for me before.
I'M ALL RIGHT, THANK YOU. YOU SEE? THESE TWO BROKE MY FALL.
SHUREI?!
IF IT WOULD SUIT YOU, SIRS, MY LORD HAS INVITED YOU FOR TEA.
Up we go.
DOES YOUR LEG HURT?
WANT TO LEAN ON ME?
DAMN YOU, YUSHUN!
ENVY
Aren't I heavy?
It's okay!
HOW DARE HE CLING TO MY SHUREI LIKE THAT!
PLEASE COME THIS WAY, LORD REI-SHIN...
YOU AS WELL, SIR.
GLANCE
UN-MOVED
WHAT AN ADMIRABLE BOY.
I'M GOING ON AHEAD.
HOJU, WAIT!
I-I HAVEN'T PREPARED MYSELF MENTALLY YET.

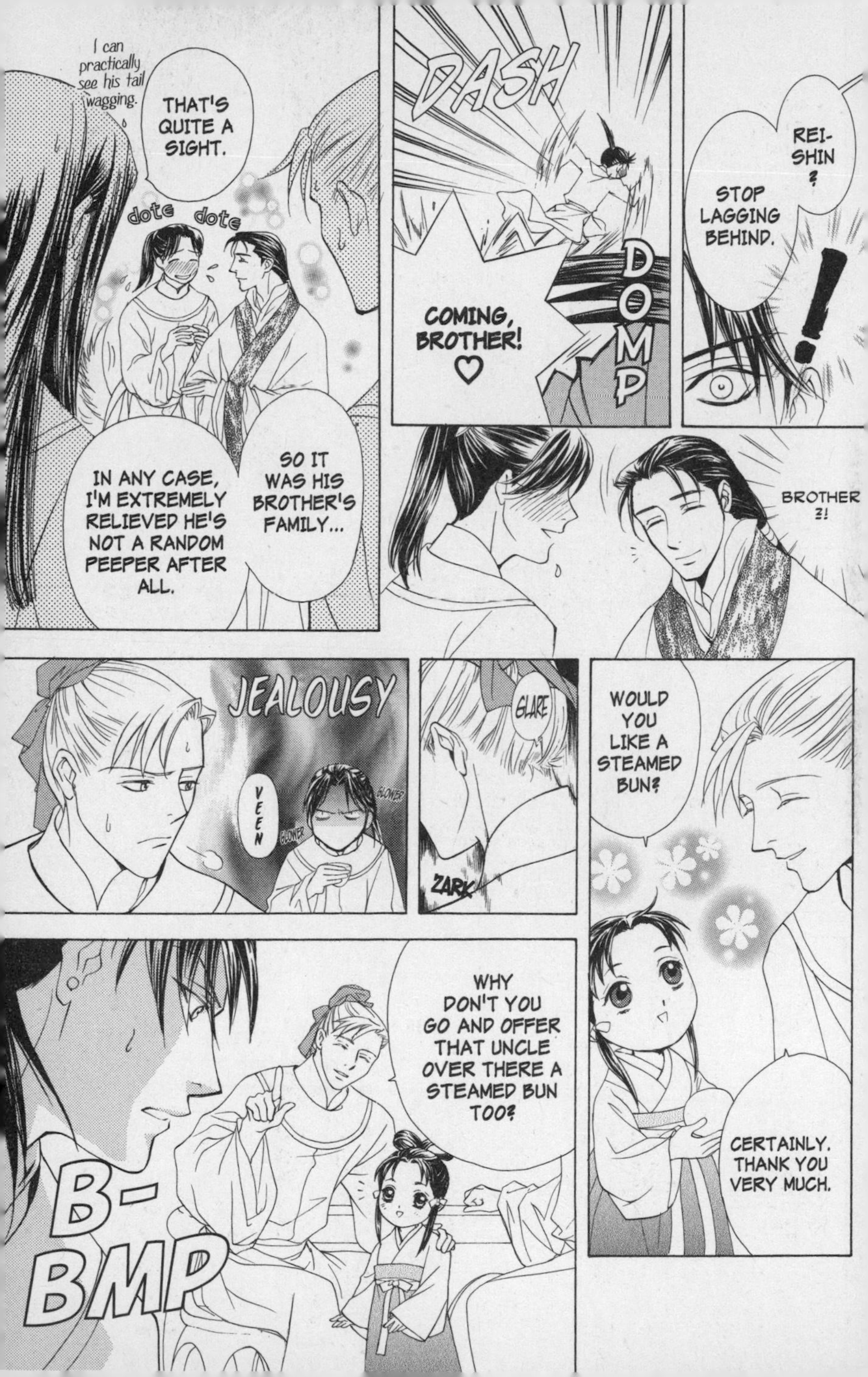
REI-SHIN?
STOP LAGGING BEHIND.
!
DASH
DOMP
COMING, BROTHER! ♡
BROTHER?!
I can practically see his tail wagging.
THAT'S QUITE A SIGHT.
dote dote
SO IT WAS HIS BROTHER'S FAMILY...
IN ANY CASE, I'M EXTREMELY RELIEVED HE'S NOT A RANDOM PEEPER AFTER ALL.
WOULD YOU LIKE A STEAMED BUN?
CERTAINLY. THANK YOU VERY MUCH.
GLARE
ZARK
JEALOUSY
VEEN
GLOWER
GLOWER
WHY DON'T YOU GO AND OFFER THAT UNCLE OVER THERE A STEAMED BUN TOO?
B-BMP

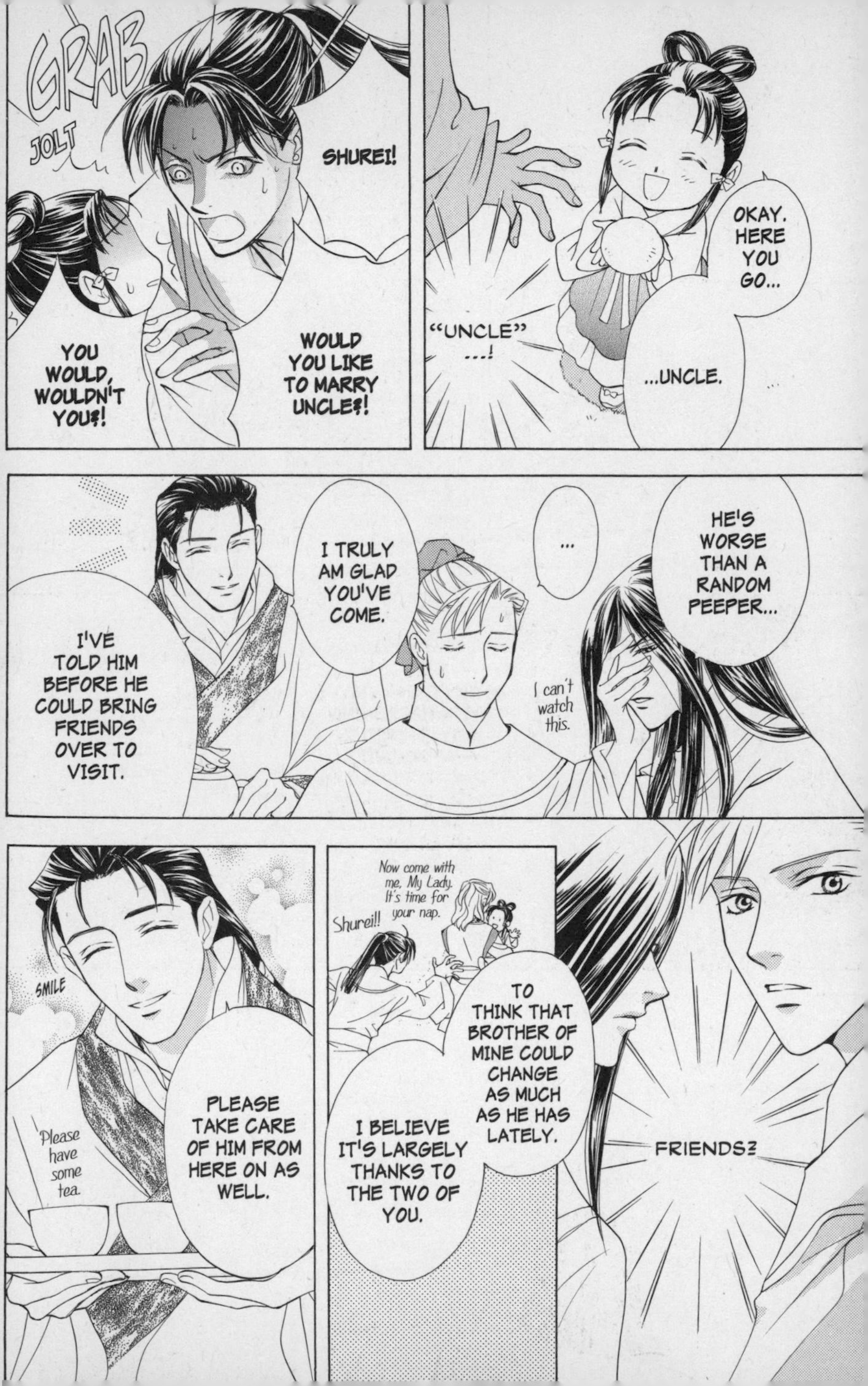
OKAY. HERE YOU GO...
...UNCLE.
“UNCLE” ...!
GRAB
JOLT
SHUREI!
WOULD YOU LIKE TO MARRY UNCLE?!
YOU WOULD, WOULDN'T YOU?!
HE'S WORSE THAN A RANDOM PEEPER...
I can't watch this.
...
I TRULY AM GLAD YOU'VE COME.
I'VE TOLD HIM BEFORE HE COULD BRING FRIENDS OVER TO VISIT.
FRIENDS?
Now come with me, My Lady. It's time for your nap.
Shurei!!
TO THINK THAT BROTHER OF MINE COULD CHANGE AS MUCH AS HE HAS LATELY.
I BELIEVE IT'S LARGELY THANKS TO THE TWO OF YOU.
SMILE
PLEASE TAKE CARE OF HIM FROM HERE ON AS WELL.
Please have some tea.

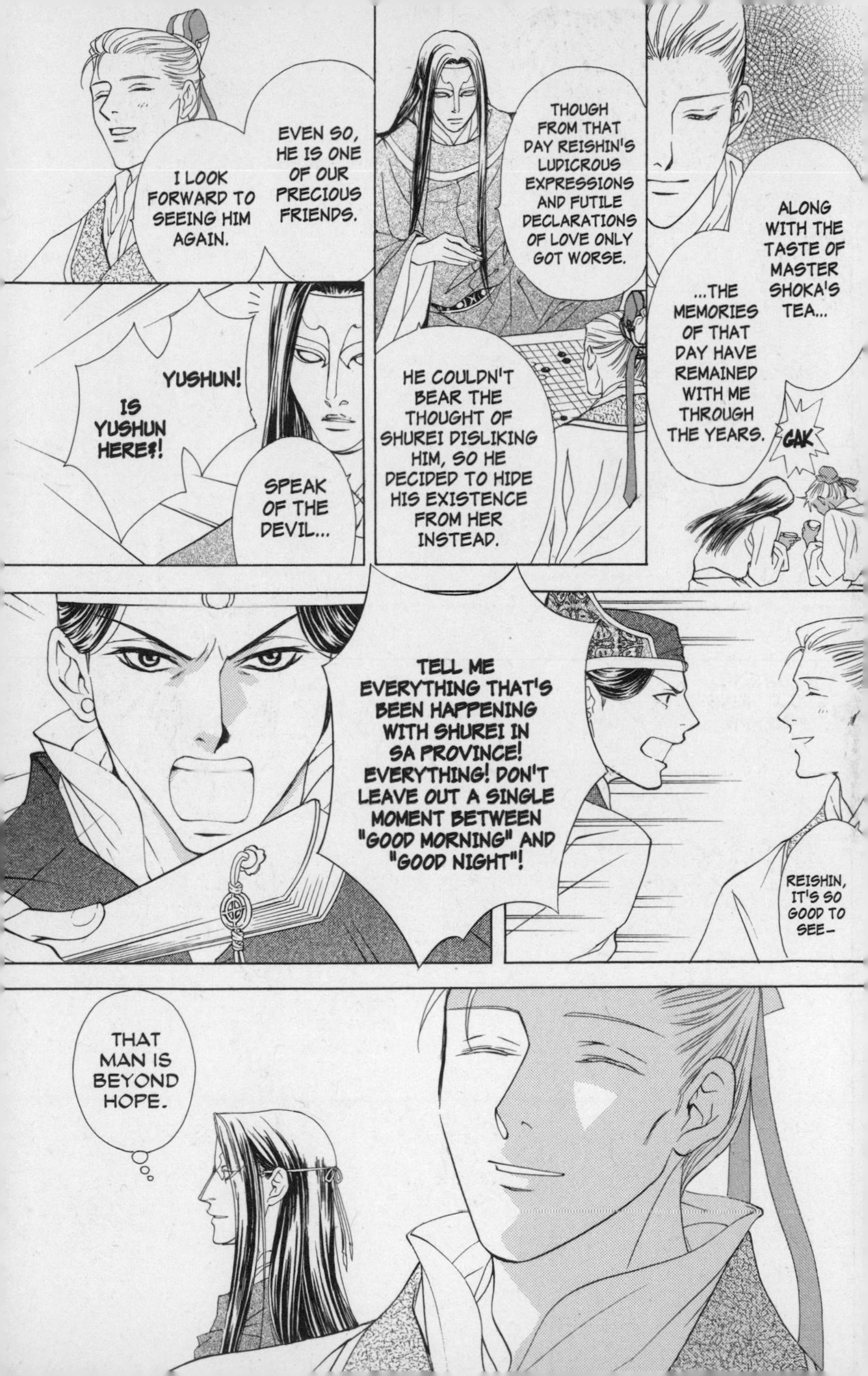
ALONG WITH THE TASTE OF MASTER SHOKA'S TEA...
...THE MEMORIES OF THAT DAY HAVE REMAINED WITH ME THROUGH THE YEARS.
THOUGH FROM THAT DAY REISHIN'S LUDICROUS EXPRESSIONS AND FUTILE DECLARATIONS OF LOVE ONLY GOT WORSE.
HE COULDN'T BEAR THE THOUGHT OF SHUREI DISLIKING HIM, SO HE DECIDED TO HIDE HIS EXISTENCE FROM HER INSTEAD.
GAK
EVEN SO, HE IS ONE OF OUR PRECIOUS FRIENDS.
I LOOK FORWARD TO SEEING HIM AGAIN.
YUSHUN!
IS YUSHUN HERE?!
SPEAK OF THE DEVIL...
REISHIN, IT'S SO GOOD TO SEE-
TELL ME EVERYTHING THAT'S BEEN HAPPENING WITH SHUREI IN SA PROVINCE! EVERYTHING! DON'T LEAVE OUT A SINGLE MOMENT BETWEEN "GOOD MORNING" AND "GOOD NIGHT"!
THAT MAN IS BEYOND HOPE.

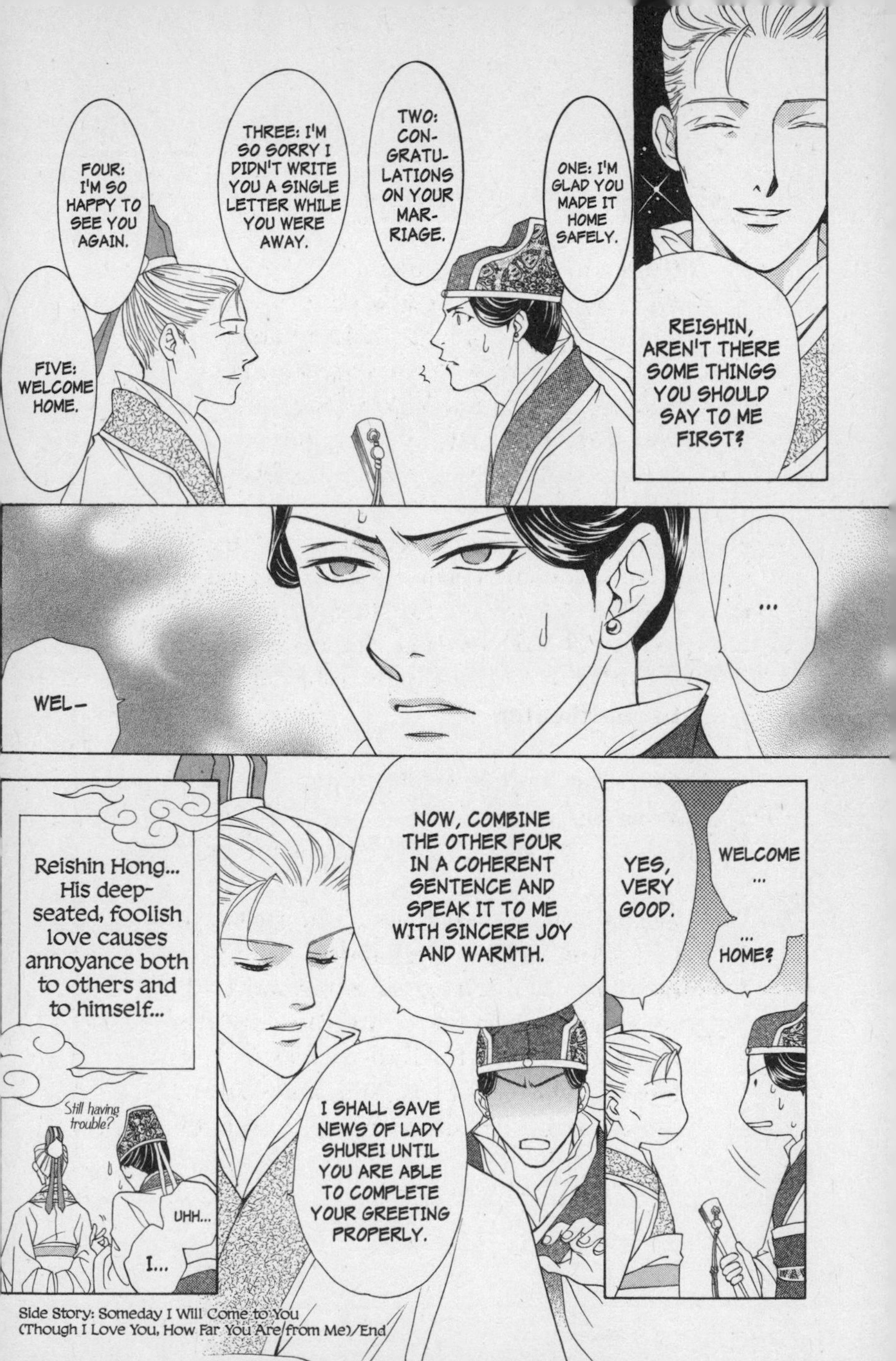
REISHIN, AREN'T THERE SOME THINGS YOU SHOULD SAY TO ME FIRST?
ONE: I'M GLAD YOU MADE IT HOME SAFELY.
TWO: CONGRATULATIONS ON YOUR MARRIAGE.
THREE: I'M SO SORRY I DIDN'T WRITE YOU A SINGLE LETTER WHILE YOU WERE AWAY.
FOUR: I'M SO HAPPY TO SEE YOU AGAIN.
FIVE: WELCOME HOME.
...
WEL-
WELCOME ... ... HOME?
YES, VERY GOOD.
NOW, COMBINE THE OTHER FOUR IN A COHERENT SENTENCE AND SPEAK IT TO ME WITH SINCERE JOY AND WARMTH.
I SHALL SAVE NEWS OF LADY SHUREI UNTIL YOU ARE ABLE TO COMPLETE YOUR GREETING PROPERLY.
Reishin Hong... His deep-seated, foolish love causes annoyance both to others and to himself...
Still having trouble?
UHH...
I...

Side Story: Someday I Will Come to You (Though I Love You, How Far You Are from Me)/End

If this manga adaptation of *The Story of Saiunkoku* has added to your enjoyment of the original novels, it has been my pleasure to draw it for you. To all my readers and to Sai Yukino Sensei, thank you from the bottom of my heart.

—Kairi Yura

Kairi Yura was born on January 16. She is the illustrator of both the manga and the YA novels for *The Story of Saiunkoku.* She is also the creator of the *Angelique* series. Yura's hobby is going to the theater.

Congrats on a great job done, Yura Sensei!

—Sai Yukino

Sai Yukino was born on January 26. She is author of both the manga and the YA novels for *The Story of Saiunkoku.* She received an honorable mention and the Readers' Award for Kadokawa's Beans Novel Taisho Awards. When she's not busy writing, Yukino enjoys massages.

THE STORY OF SAIUNKOKU
Volume 9

Shojo Beat Edition

ART
KAIRI YURA
STORY
SAI YUKINO

Translation & English Adaptation/Su Mon Han
Touch-up Art & Lettering/Deron Bennett
Design/Shawn Carrico
Editor/Nancy Thistlethwaite

Saiunkoku Monogatari Volume 9
© Kairi YURA 2012
© Sai YUKINO 2012
First published in Japan in 2012 by KADOKAWA SHOTEN Co., Ltd., Tokyo.
English translation rights arranged with KADOKAWA SHOTEN Co., Ltd., Tokyo.

Printed in Canada

Published by VIZ Media, LLC
P.O. Box 77010
San Francisco, CA 94107

10 9 8 7 6 5 4 3 2 1
First printing, April 2013

www.viz.com

www.shojobeat.com

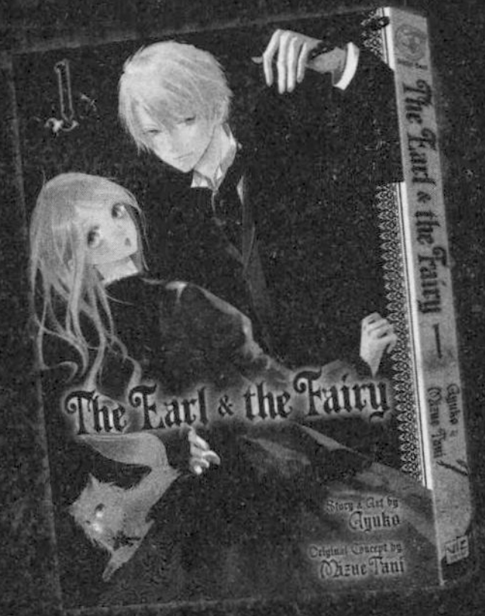
The Earl & the Fairy
1
Story & Art by Ayuko
Original Concept by Mizue Tani
viz

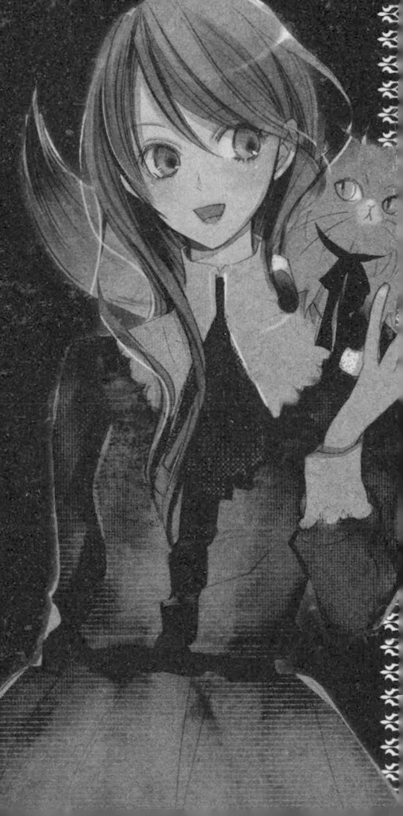

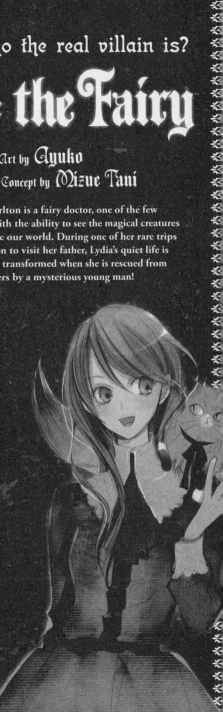

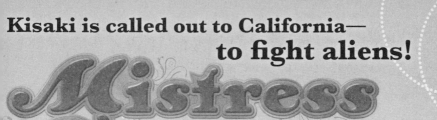